Enterprise CORBA

Dirk Slama

Jason Garbis

Perry Russell

Editorial/Production Supervision: *MetroVoice Publishing Services*
Acquisitions Editor: *Mary Franz*
Editorial Assistant: *Noreen Regina*
Cover Design Director: *Jerry Votta*
Cover Designer: *Design Source*
Cover Production Artist: *Talar Agasyan*
Manufacturing Manager: *Alexis R. Heydt*
Marketing Manager: *Lisa Konvelmann*
Total Concept Coordinator: *Anne Trowbridge*

Published by Prentice-Hall PTR
Prentice-Hall, Inc.
Upper Saddle River, NJ 07458

First Indian reprint, 1999

ISBN 981-4035-65-3

**This edition is manufactured in India and is authorized for sales only in
India, Bangladesh, Pakistan, Nepal, Sri Lanka, and Maldives**

Printed and bound at Replika Press Pvt. Ltd., 100% EOU,
Delhi 110 040, India

To Karen, who put up with me—P.R.
To Amy, for her patience—J.G.
To Olli, who always wanted to write a book—D.S.

Contents

Foreword

Sean Baker
Co-founder, IONA Technologies

Let's assume you are driven by the need to write an application in a complex software and hardware environment, or you are driven by the need to integrate a set of components/applications into a flexible enterprise-wide system. We'll also go on the assumption that you have a strong need to get your application running or your system integrated—and you are not interested in re-inventing the wheel. You therefore want as much help as you can get, both in terms of *enabling software* that you can buy-in, and *techniques* that you can adopt.

Perhaps the complexity arises because your application/enterprise must run on a distributed hardware system and hence you need to cater for the boundary that the network presents. Perhaps you have to deal with other boundaries such as the one that arises because different components are written in different languages; or perhaps they run on different operating systems. Or perhaps you are (the world's only architect or manager) dealing with a completely homogeneous environment, but your applications/components have to be accessed across the boundary between different departments or companies.

If any of these are the case, then you are likely to be using an Object Request Broker to help you to bridge those boundaries—and in fact the broker that you use is likely to adhere to the CORBA standard. The motivation for using CORBA is that the components of your system can communicate with each other across these boundaries without you having to write a software layer that provides the required bridges. CORBA addresses not just the basic communication needs, but it adds a great deal of richness. As well as point to point communication, CORBA can offer variations such as many-to-many communication and store-and-forward. Objects can be made secure; objects can be stored in databases; databases can be accessed across boundaries; multiple databases can be atomically updated in a single transaction; systems can be monitored and managed at different levels; objects can be found by name, or by properties if you wish.

So where does this book come in? Distributed systems research started around 1980 or a little earlier, giving us nearly two decades of improved understanding. This has been practically focused around areas such as interface definition, security, entity naming, transactions, communication alternatives, two and three-tier architectures, database integration, fault tolerance, system management, and so on. If you can acquire a good understanding of the aspects that are important to your system, then you can implement it faster and better. This book relates all of these areas, and more, to the CORBA environment, giving you practical advise on what approaches work well.

Dirk, Jason and Perry have a strong understanding of these areas. They have studied the research results, and they have acted as consultants on many projects that face these issues. Their contribution is that they have written about the aspects of this that are relevant to modern systems, and they have related each aspect in turn to the CORBA framework. CORBA is easy to use to bridge the boundaries in your system; this book describes the techniques that you may wish to use at the application level to make the best use of CORBA and to implement your system as easily as possible.

Where is CORBA going? In the early days (up to the mid 1990s), the aim was to provide a framework for bridging boundaries. The next phase (up to 1998) has added a great deal of richness to this (security, transactions, rich communication, database integration, and so on), and has also integrated many other technologies into CORBA. Therefore, CORBA works well in environments that also use COM; it has adopted Java as a first class language and added facilities that allow it to be used across an enterprise; and CORBA can be used safely across fire-walls. What are the targets for the next few years?

First, the integration with other technologies will continue. EJB is important here—or more specifically the continued adding of facilities to the Java environment to allow the writing of feature-rich clients and servers. Integration of CORBA with standard business applications will also be offered as off-the-shelf facilities, rather than having to be written for each application.

Second, CORBA will become easier and easier to use, as evidenced by the emerging programmer productivity tools. One of the key areas here is the script-based generation of clients and servers, or at least parts of them. C++ and Java code will be produced in this way, reducing the amount of application-specific code that you will have to write. Other ease of use tools will be aimed at system managers, with an increase in the monitoring and control available to them.

Third, the notion of a *component* will become more and more important. A component is an object that only has business-level code within it, and no code relating to aspects such as security, transactions, naming, and so on. A component can therefore be given different security properties without changing the object's code. In a sense, it can be "dropped" into different security environments without changing its code, even if these security environments are implemented in different ways. Similarly, whether or not the component is transactional is decided not by the component itself, but what environment (or *container*) it is dropped into.

The separation of business-level code from infrastructure code is one of the key aspects to increasing productivity. One useful result of this is that software can be future-proofed against changes in the environment in which you would like it to execute. The same component might be dropped into a pure CORBA container, or it could be dropped into an EJB container, or a COM container. So if it is dropped into a COM container than it would be communicated with natively using COM, and from other environments using an automatic bridge. If it was dropped into a CORBA container, CORBA would be its native communications environment, and an automatic bridge would be required to access it from COM. The business level code shouldn't have to change when this occurs.

Each of these improvements is underway, and will reduce the task of writing software that has to bridge boundaries. No amount of automation will remove the need for experienced software engineers and architects to understand the underlying techniques for distributed computing, and how to get the best from each one in different circumstances. I am very grateful to the three co-authors of this book that they have taken the time and trouble to relate these techniques to CORBA and made many years of research and development results accessible to a wide audience. They have taken the brave route of relating these techniques to today's CORBA, with no vapour-ware, and yet they have pointed out future directions where these are relevant.

Preface

Welcome to *Enterprise CORBA!* The ambitious aim of this book is to provide you with a guideline for building truly large-scale, enterprise-class CORBA systems. Obviously, distributed system engineering is such a complex topic that it is hardly possible to provide you with a single, general-purpose pattern that solves all your problems at once. Often, there is no "best" solution, and your choice of a solution depends on many factors—technical and non-technical. This book is based on the experience that we, the authors, have gained in the last few years, training and consulting with many CORBA users all over the world, in industries as diverse as manufacturing, finance, telecommunication, and transportation. We hope that we have managed to cover most of the topics that are relevant to real-world projects, offering you guidelines and solutions that are not abstract or academic, but instead focus on the practical requirements of information system development.

There are two general problems with a project like this book, which attempts to cover such a huge problem complex from a real-world perspective. First, it is impossible for any single person (or even three people) to know each and every detail of this domain, combining academic insight with results-oriented real-world experience. Second, our industry moves so quickly that it is nearly impossible to write a book that stays up-to-date for very long.

Finally, this book is targeted at programmers and architects that have at least some minimal knowledge of using CORBA. Thus, you are likely to have your own experience with building CORBA systems, and your own perspective on things.

To give you a chance to share your opinion with us and other readers, we have built an *Enterprise CORBA* website: www.middlewarehouse.com. This site is in a well-structured bulletin-board format, designed to serve as a platform for further discussions on *Enterprise CORBA*. Hopefully, this home page also solves the two problems mentioned before: more detailed technical discussions of individual problems, and up-to-the-minute information. This web site will evolve, and become a general source of knowledge related to middleware and enterprise system development. Please meet the authors at:

www.middlewarehouse.com

How the Book is Organized

This book is broken up into five parts, each with a different focus:

- Part 1: Foundations
- Part 2: Core Services
- Part 3: Database Integration and Transaction Processing
- Part 4: Scalability Issues
- Part 5: Engineering CORBA Systems

The following gives a brief overview of each of these five parts.

Part 1: Foundations

This book assumes that readers already have a solid grasp of CORBA; we do not attempt to give yet another detailed introduction to the CORBA architecture. In *Part 1: Foundations*, we achieve two things. First, we provide a critical review of the core ORB specification and the higher-level CORBA Services, since this is the framework that provides the technical foundations for building enterprise CORBA systems (Chapter 2, "CORBA Revisited," and Chapter 3, "CORBA Services Revisited"). Second, we provide some information that is fundamental for understanding the book itself. In particular, we introduce the StockWatch system, which is used throughout the book to serve as an example system (Chapter 4, "Overview of a Simple Example"). Finally, we discuss the performance implications of IDL design, since this has fundamental impacts on most of the discussions in the reminder of the book (Chapter 5, "Performance Considerations").

Part 2: Core Services

Some of the CORBA Services are more essential then others to building enterprise CORBA systems. In *Part 2: Core Services*, we concentrate on some of these most essential services. In Chapter 6, "Object Location," we discuss how to locate objects and services in a CORBA system, using services like the CORBA Naming Service and the CORBA Trading Service. In Chapter 7, "Messaging," we have a general discussion on CORBA and messaging. This covers unicast and multicast based ORBs, as well as higher level services like the Event Service and the Notification Service. In Chapter 8, "Security," we discuss how to design and implement security policies in a CORBA system.

Part 3: Database Integration and Transaction Processing

Exporting information stored in databases is potentially the most common usage of CORBA.[1] *Part 3: Database Integration and Transaction Processing*, addresses this topic. First, we provide a

---

[1] Therefore, CORBA Services related to this problem complex are clearly *core services*. Since this is such an important and complex topic, however, we decided to have the discussion on database integration and transaction processing in a separate part, following the *core services*.

general overview of object persistence (Chapter 9, "Object Persistence"). Based on this CORBA-independent introduction to object persistence, we then focus on persistent CORBA objects (Chapter 10, "Database Integration"). No discussion on CORBA and database integration would be complete without a discussion on CORBA and transaction processing. After a general discussion on transactions in a CORBA environment (Chapter 11), we focus on distributed transaction processing (Chapter 12). This includes a discussion of the CORBA Object Transaction Service. We finish part 3 with a discussion on user sessions (Chapter 13). This chapter covers several advanced topics, including long-lived versus short-lived transactions, and optimistic versus pessimistic locking.

Part 4: Scalability Issues

The CORBA specification provides many features intended to allow the implementation of very large-scale distributed object systems. Chapter 14, "Managing Server Resources," explains how some of these features can be utilized to increase the scalability of CORBA servers. In particular, this chapter covers memory management strategies, connection management, and multithreading. *Part 4: Scalability Issues* also covers some important issues related to building large-scale CORBA systems which are not currently addressed by existing CORBA Service specifications. In particular, this includes load balancing (Chapter 15), and fault tolerance (Chapter 16). Finally, system management and maintenance (Chapter 17) are essential for large-scale systems.

Part 5: Engineering CORBA Systems

The last part of the book addresses system engineering aspects of CORBA based system development. We look back at the more technical discussion that we had in the previous parts of the book, and discuss the consequences for the engineering process (Chapter 18). An important conclusion is that traditional object-oriented analysis and design can not be mapped one-to-one to distributed object computing. We explain how the traditional OO development process can be adapted to reflect the specifics of distributed object computing. Another important topic related to system engineering is automation. This is covered in Chapter 19, "Automating the Engineering Process." This chapter includes a discussion on CORBA-related CASE tools, code generation, and process wizards.

CORBA Compliance

We have tried to make this book as CORBA-centric as possible, instead of focusing on particular ORB implementations. In many cases we think we have achieved this. However, this is intended to be a real-world book, focusing on technology that is available today. In some cases we provide discussions of vendor specific, non-CORBA compliant technologies or feature, usually because we felt that this discussion provides a value that outweighs pure CORBA compliance (and in many cases a CORBA specification covering this aspect is in progress). All three authors work for IONA Technologies' Professional Services department. Therefore, quite naturally, you will find some discussions that are related to IONA-specific solutions. However, we hope we have managed to keep these occasions to a minimum, and stay CORBA-compliant wherever possible.

Acknowledgments

This book would not have been possible without the help and support of a great number of people during this long and often arduous process. Thanks to IONA Technologies (in particular, Sean O'Sullivan, Fiona Hayes, and Sean Baker) for their immense support of our efforts. Special thanks to Aisling Mackey, who gave up a weekend in San Francisco to deliver the Security chapter for us. Other people we wish to thank include: Alan Crilly, who was brave enough to review our entire first draft, and help us restructure it. Jürgen Oheim and Alastair Green for their invaluable comments on the DTP chapter. Stefan Tai for lots of discussion on OOA/D. Stefan Havenstein for his repeated reviews of the fault tolerance material. Many thanks to our many chapter reviewers, all of whom spent a great deal of their own time thoughtfully reviewing and commenting on our chapter drafts: Alan Conway, Alan Slattery, Andreas Walsh, Andrew Lee, Aoife Kavanagh, Bernard Normier, Brendan Holmes, Brian Dillon, Brian Kelly, Ciaran McHale, David Hayes, Eamon Walshe, Eamonn Dwyer, Gregor Raab, Jeremy Birrell, Ken Knox, Laura O'Brien, Marcus Creavin, Martin Bergljung, Matt Hansbury, Matthew Mihic, Ned Micelli, Paul Taylor, Thomas Sandholm, and Vaidya Nathan. Thanks also to Peter Krupp, Declan O'Sullivan, and Liz Hughes for their support and help with management issues, and to Amanda Murphy for her administrative support.

We'd also like to thank Mary Franz and Noreen Regina from Prentice Hall for guiding us through this process. Finally, and most importantly, we need to thank our families and friends. Their patience and support during this project has made all the difference—we couldn't have done it without you.

PART 1

Foundations

Building and deploying software systems across the enterprise is a complex task. CORBA (Common Object Request Broker Architecture) provides a powerful framework for accomplishing this. With CORBA, we can much more easily develop heterogeneous distributed systems. However, it is still quite difficult to develop such systems well. The CORBA specification offers little guidance on the intricacies of developing real-world systems. This book is intended to help educate CORBA system developers about the design issues, approaches, and considerations necessary to develop large-scale CORBA systems.

In order to properly discuss these complex topics, however, we need a common vocabulary of terms and notation, a common understanding of the important aspects of object adapters, and a common sense of the performance characteristics of CORBA systems. This is the purpose of Part I of the book.

Chapter 1, "Introduction," defines some common terms and introduces a set of graphical notations used throughout the book.

Next, we examine the CORBA specification from an application programmer's perspective, in Chapter 2, "CORBA Revisited." Rather than discussing the minutiae of the specification, we instead focus on the two major generations of ORBs—those based on the Basic Object Adapter (BOA) and the Portable Object Adapter (POA). We introduce two important topics, the lifecycle of a CORBA invocation and the lifecycle of a CORBA object, and discussed them from the perspective of both BOA ORBs and POA ORBs.

Chapter 3, "CORBA Services Revisited," briefly introduces some of the services defined as part of the CORBA specification, many of which are covered later in the book.

The example system is described in Chapter 4. This provides the context for many of the discussions throughout the book. The example is simple enough to be easily understood, yet complex enough to be able to illustrate many of the facets of CORBA systems.

Finally, Chapter 5, "Performance Considerations," discusses the performance aspects of CORBA systems, with a particular focus on IDL (Interface Definition Language) design.

PART

Foundations

B

CHAPTER 1

Introduction

Corba has recently grown from an academic research topic to a mainstream technology. Organizations are building and deploying real-world CORBA systems, using CORBA technology to solve fundamental problems in industries ranging from finance to telecommunication, insurance to manufacturing, health care to petrochemicals.

CORBA combines two important trends in the computer industry: object-oriented software development and client/server computing. But CORBA is more than just an object-oriented Remote Procedure Call mechanism. The OMG's Object Management Architecture is a framework that defines different levels of abstraction. The core ORB provides an abstraction from the complexity of network programming. The CORBA services offer classic system-level functionality, in an object-oriented fashion. The CORBA facilities offer standardized approaches to solving domain-specific problems.

While programming with an object request broker has become a mainstream technique, applying the higher level CORBA services to build large-scale enterprise CORBA systems is still anything but trivial. CORBA and the CORBA services provide a certain level of abstraction, but the complexity that is inherent in such large problem domains like transaction processing, security, and messaging remains.

This book focuses on building enterprise CORBA systems using technology that is available *today*. The book reflects the experience that we, the authors, have collected as CORBA consultants, using CORBA in many different software projects. Now and then we might refer to some of the upcoming developments in the CORBA community, but the focus is really on technology that we have used in the real world, and that is available right now.

On the one hand, this means that we are focusing on the application of some of the core services that are available as commercial products and have been used in real-world systems. On the other hand, not all the CORBA services are commercially available today, and not all problems in large-scale enterprise systems are sufficiently covered by existing CORBA service specifications. In the case where no standard services are available, we try to describe patterns and techniques we have used, based on existing CORBA technology.

Overview

This book is broken up into five parts. Each of these parts addresses a different facet of CORBA systems. Part 1, *Foundations*, provides the common vocabulary which we use throughout the book. We define frequently used terms, and we also introduce a graphical notation for the diagrams we use in this book. We revisit the CORBA architecture and try to identify common elements of CORBA independently of the particular CORBA version. This is important, since many of the following chapters will rely on these elements, and we don't want to have to differentiate different CORBA versions all the time. We also revisit the CORBA services, discussing the current state and the applicability of the different services. This will form the foundation for the following parts of the book, which discuss the application of some of the core services in more detail. Also, the first part introduces the *StockWatch* example, which is referenced throughout the book. Finally, the first part discusses some fundamental performance implications of CORBA systems design.

Part 2, *Core Services*, covers CORBA support for essential aspects of many enterprise systems. We cover CORBA support for such basic requirements as object location, messaging, and security.

Part 3, *Database Integration and Transaction Processing*, addresses issues related to CORBA and persistence. First, we cover object persistence in general. The result of this discussion forms the basis for our discussion on CORBA and database integration. After a brief introduction to transactions with CORBA, we cover distributed transaction processing, and the CORBA object transaction service. Finally, we discuss approaches to handling long-lived transactions involving human users.

Part 4, *Scalability Issues*, covers topics that generally begin to be important as CORBA systems grow larger. Server resource management discusses approaches to handling connections, memory, and threads. The two somewhat related topics of load balancing and fault tolerance are covered, as is component testing, deployment, and management.

Part 5, *Engineering CORBA Systems*, draws the conclusion, examining the impacts of CORBA and distributed object computing on the classic object-oriented software engineering process. We also formalize extensions to the UML (Unified Modeling Language) notation, to help in modeling the CORBA specifics of our systems more precisely. Finally, we examine the extent to which current CASE systems, modeling tools, and code generation utilities can help in automating the CORBA-based software development process.

Short Glossary of Terms

We don't intend to give a comprehensive set of all the terms possibly related to CORBA and distributed object computing. The following lists only a few key terms and describes their use in this book:

- **CORBA object.** An *abstract* entity with an identity, an interface defined in IDL, and an implementation. We discuss why a CORBA object is *abstract* in more detail in Chapter 2, "CORBA Revisited," section "What is a CORBA Object, Really?."
- **Servant.** A concrete programming language entity that implements the functionality of a CORBA object.

- **Client, server.** We use the terms client and server as roles: clients invoke on CORBA objects that reside in servers. A server can also play the role of a client by invoking on an object in another server.
- **CORBA component.** A CORBA component is implemented by a set of CORBA objects, and provides a more complex service than a single object normally would. To make use of the service provided by a component, the user of the component interacts with the different objects implemented by the component. A more detailed discussion of components can be found in Chapter 18, "Consequences for the Engineering Process."
- **Component entry point.** A component will usually provide an entry point, that is, a dedicated object which is the first point of contact for the user of a component. Starting from this object, the user of the component can obtain references to other objects provided by the component. The entry point object is often chosen for registration with the naming service or trading service, to make the component's services publicly available.

Graphical Notation

Imagine the following situation: somebody draws two boxes on a whiteboard, adds a circle to the right box, and a line that goes from the left box to the circle in the right box. Most people who have ever discussed the design or implementation of a CORBA system will immediately agree that this is usually the start of a discussion of some CORBA related topic: a client makes an invocation on a remote object in a server. This ad hoc notation works out quite well for many whiteboard situations, since it allows us to describe a particular example schematically. But this is also the problem: it is only an example—that is, it is not very generic. It is like modeling on the object level, rather than on the class level: object diagrams are useful to discuss specific examples, but we use class diagrams to express a design in a generic way. To keep the models in this book as generic as possible, we are using class diagrams based on the Unified Modeling Language (UML).

Figure 1.1 is an overview of some standard UML elements. A class is represented as a box with the name of the class in bold face. An object is represented as a box with the name of the object

Figure 1.1   Important UML elements

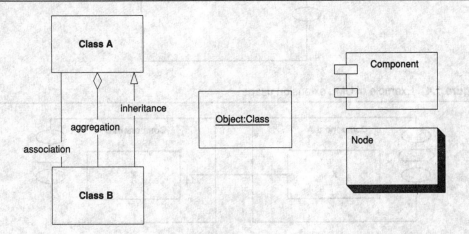

and the name of the class underlined, and separated by a colon. Important types of relationships include association, aggregation, and inheritance, as shown between classes A and B in the overview. A component is an executable software module with an identity and a well-defined interface. A node is a computational unit, that is, a piece of hardware.

To reflect CORBA-specific aspects, we are using some extensions to the standard UML. A detailed discussion of these extensions can be found in Chapter 18, "Consequences for the Engineering Process." We are using UML stereotypes to define these extensions. The first stereotype that we want to define is a <<CORBA interface>>, represented by the T-connector symbol, as shown in Figure 1.2. A class can be associated with a <<CORBA interface>>, meaning that instances of this class can be access by the normal means of CORBA remote invocations.

The second stereotype that we define is a <<CORBA component>>, as defined in the glossary above. A <<CORBA component>> is used throughout this book to group elements of a CORBA system. Elements of a <<CORBA component>> can only be accessed through CORBA IDL interfaces. The symbol for a <<CORBA component>> is a UML component with a stylized ORB symbol at the border, as shown in Figure 1.3.

Figure 1.4 shows a very simple example of using these extensions to UML. Component B implements a class Z, which exposes the CORBA interface Y. Component A implements a

Figure 1.2   <<CORBA Interface>> Stereotype

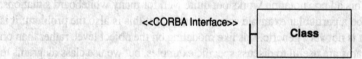

Figure 1.3   <<CORBA Component>> Stereotype

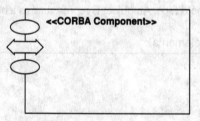

Figure 1.4   Example of UML extension usage

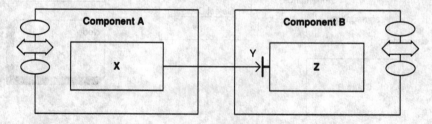

class X, which is accessing instances of class Z in component B via the CORBA interface Y. Class X itself does not expose a CORBA interface, thus the class is not accessible for elements outside component A.

Finally, we must admit that the "box and circle" notation makes sense for certain whiteboard-style discussions, so we will use a schematic notation from time to time. The basic elements that we use for the schematic description of CORBA systems are shown in Figure 1.5. A host is represented as a small computer symbol. Operating system processes are represented as square boxes, possibly referring to the host they are running on. CORBA objects are represented as shaded circles with a T-connector symbol to indicate the CORBA interface. Sometimes it makes sense to also show proxy objects in a diagram. In these cases, the proxy is shown as a small, shaded circle. CORBA messages are symbolized as little envelopes.

Figure 1.5 Schematic notation

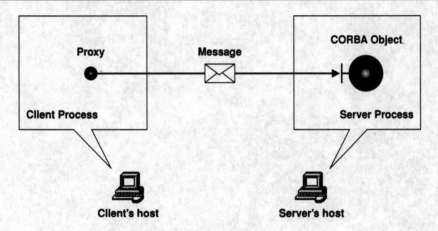

CHAPTER 2

CORBA Revisited

We do not intend to give yet another introduction to the CORBA architecture. It is assumed that the reader of this book has some basic understanding of the concepts of the CORBA architecture and ideally also some hands-on experience using an ORB. What we intend to do here is to revisit CORBA, and explore the gap between the abstract world of CORBA specifications and the real world of ORB implementations and applications based on these ORBs. This helps us to set a common ground for further discussions by identifying and defining key elements.

First, we want to revisit the CORBA architecture with respect to the lifecycles of CORBA invocations and CORBA objects. Processing a CORBA invocation can involve complex interactions between ORB and application, and we want to examine the different events that can occur during an invocation's lifecycle. Of course, the target of a CORBA invocation is always a CORBA object. This means that there is a close relationship between invocation and object lifecycles.

As we will see throughout the rest of this book, many design and implementation decisions are strongly influenced by the lifecycles of CORBA invocations and objects. Therefore, this chapter defines concepts that are the basis for many of the following discussions. To reflect the constant progress of the CORBA architecture, we look at the invocation and object lifecycles from an evolutionary perspective.

The Evolution of CORBA

We briefly need to discuss the evolution of the CORBA architecture. The problem is that there have been many minor and major revisions, and it can be sometimes quite confusing. We are not interested in investigating the differences between all the different minor revisions. Instead, this chapter intends to set the scope for discussing the CORBA architecture from an evolutionary perspective.

One of the first important documents published by the Object Management Group was the Object Management Architecture—OMA. The OMA defines the basic elements of a distributed object system. We all have seen these diagrams where the ORB as a software bus connects higher level components like common services, common facilities, and application level objects. So CORBA is really only one piece of the picture. But without an ORB, we cannot build the services, facilities, and application objects. Therefore, the initial focus was on the ORB architecture itself.

This made the term CORBA so popular that suddenly everything was CORBA: CORBA services, CORBA facilities, etc.

The first generation of the CORBA architecture mainly focused on defining an infrastructure for distributed object computing. A key element for making the infrastructure independent of technologies and programming languages was the definition of the Interface Definition Language—IDL. Initial mappings for IDL were defined for the C programming language. The first generation of CORBA was accompanied by some basic services like naming, events, and life cycle.

The second generation of the CORBA architecture added ORB interoperability, based on an ORB-independent protocol for interoperation: General Inter-ORB Protocol (GIOP), and its TCP/IP based specialization, the Internet Inter-ORB Protocol (IIOP). Additional language mappings were added, for instance, for C++, and a large number of additional services were defined, such as services for distributed transaction processing, security, object relationships, concurrency, query processing, service trading, and time. Many of these services add important value to the basic ORB, enabling developers to make use of higher level system functionality with an ORB out of the box. However, some of the services turned out to be problematic: some are very academic, and not very scalable in the real world; others are so complex that it is very hard to implement and use them. We discuss the quality of the different CORBA service specifications in Chapter 3, "CORBA Services Revisited."

BOA vs. POA Generation

As we said before, we are not interested in having a detailed discussion of the different major and minor versions of the CORBA architecture. To help us structure the discussion of the invocation and object lifecycles, we identify two different generations of CORBA, the BOA (Basic Object Adapter) and the POA (Portable Object Adapter) generations. This distinction will allow us to define two important milestones in the evolution of the core ORB architecture.

BOA Generation

The BOA generation of the CORBA architecture defines an object adapter as "the primary interface that the application uses to access ORB functions.... It includes ... interfaces for generating object references, registering implementations that consist of one or more programs [and] activating implementations."[1]

Notice that when talking about registering and activating implementations the BOA focuses on CORBA server implementations, rather than on CORBA object implementations. A major weakness of the BOA specification is its vagueness when it comes to things like this. This is also exemplified by the lack of naming conventions for the generated server-side skeletons, which makes it impossible to associate skeletons with object implementations in a CORBA-compliant manner.

In the following, we are using the IONA Technologies Orbix™ 2.x implementation of CORBA as a reference for the BOA generation of ORBs.

---

[1] Object Management Group Common Object Request Broker: Architecture and Specification, Revision 2.1, August 1997, p. 8-1.

POA Generation

The portable object adapter attempts to overcome the vagueness of the original BOA specification on the one hand, and to provide a set of advanced services for object lifecycle management on the other.

An in-depth discussion of the POA itself can be found in Schmidt and Vinoski, 1997, which also provides the following definition: "An Object Adapter is the CORBA component responsible for adapting CORBA's concept of objects to a programming language's concept of servants." This definition indicates that the emphasis for registration and activation of implementations shifts from the process level to the object level. We look at the difference between CORBA objects and CORBA object implementations later in this chapter, in the object lifecycle section.

Regarding the object lifecycle, the POA itself is not the only interesting change in the evolution of the CORBA architecture. Other interesting new features include interceptors, which allow the monitoring of the invocation lifecycle, and the *service context*. A service context supports sending additional information with a standard CORBA invocation. Although the last two features are not related to the concept of an object adapter, we are subsuming them in our definition of "POA generation." This means our view of the BOA and POA generations encapsulates CORBA's detailed version history, allowing us to focus on concepts.

The Invocation Lifecycle

At this point we describe the different steps in the lifecycle of a CORBA invocation. We define a catalog of different aspects which are of importance in the lifecycle of a invocation, and then use this catalogue to analyze the lifecycle of invocations for the BOA and POA generations of ORB implementations.

CORBA Request

The main purpose of the CORBA architecture is to define a framework that describes how clients can send requests to remote object implementations, and potentially get a reply back from the object. Object interfaces are described using the programming-language-neutral Interface Definition Language. There are basically two different ways that clients and object implementations can send and receive requests: static and dynamic. The static method requires that all IDL interfaces be known at compile time, so that an IDL compiler can generate stub and skeleton code, which must be linked to the implementation. The dynamic method enables us to implement applications that can handle any type of request, without having knowledge about the different IDL interfaces at compile time. The dynamic way of processing requests requires the use of the Dynamic Invocation Interface (DII) on the client side, and the Dynamic Skeleton Interface (DSI) on the server side. DII and DSI are often used for building generic system-level components like bridges.

For normal applications, the use of static stubs and skeletons is much more common. The benefit of the static approach is that it enables us to use CORBA objects as if they were normal elements of the programming language that we are using. On the client side, this is achieved using proxy objects. A proxy is the local representative of the remote target object. A proxy contains enough information to send requests to the remote target object, encapsulating details about network addresses, port numbers, etc. The proxy object also provides a means of accessing the target object in a type-safe manner, using the standard types of the client programming language. If a client wants to use an object that implements the Stock IDL interface, the stub code provides him with the equivalent of a Stock interface in the particular programming language, for example, a Stock class in C++. If the client wants to send a message to the remote Stock object implementation, he simply invokes a method on the local proxy. The stub code, that is, the generated proxy implementation, is responsible for marshalling the request arguments, so that the client's ORB runtime can send a message to the target server. The server's ORB runtime will read the message from the network, and pass the message on to the generated skeleton code to enable the skeleton code to unmarshal the request arguments so that it can pass them to the target object implementation. The generated skeleton delivers the request as a normal method call on the server side, allowing both client and server to treat a CORBA object as a normal programming language object. The reply to a request can be sent back to the client in a similar manner.

Since the static interfaces are more commonly used than the dynamic interfaces, we concentrate on the static interfaces. Figure 2.1 summarizes the principle of a CORBA remote invocation using the static interfaces.

The CORBA model of a request assumes that each request has a target, an operation, and a set of arguments. The target identifies the target object, the operation describes the name of the operation that was invoked, and the arguments are the arguments that need to be passed. A request must provide a kind of *invoke* functionality. The invoke functionality can have different semantics, for example, blocking vs. non-blocking calls, or oneway semantics. For the remainder of this chapter we assume that a reply is expected, and that the call is blocking (that is, a standard two-way CORBA remote invocation).

Figure 2.1 Principle of a CORBA remote invocation using the static interfaces

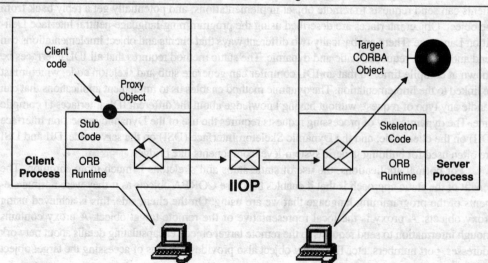

Figure 2.2 Model of a CORBA request

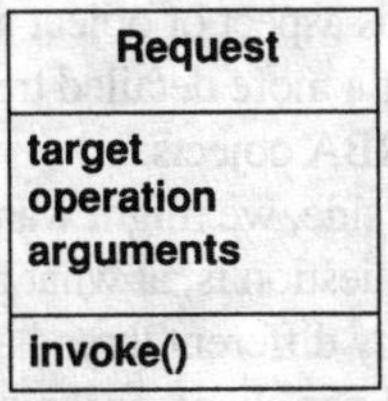

```
            Request

    target
    operation
    arguments

    invoke()
```

Invocation Lifecycle: Evaluation Criteria

In the following, we define a catalogue of evaluation criteria that are of interest when discussing the lifecycle of a CORBA invocation. These criteria should apply to BOA-generation ORBs as well as to POA-generation ORBs. We look at invocation monitoring, context information passing, object activation, thread allocation on the server side, collocation, and request redirection.

- **Invocation monitoring.** During the lifecycle of an invocation, there are many points where a service library or an application might want to intervene before allowing the ORB to continue processing the invocation or even asking the ORB to abort the invocation. In general, the points that we are interested in monitoring are outgoing requests and incoming replies on the client side, and incoming requests and outgoing replies on the server side. Invocations can be monitored on two different levels: *request object* and *message buffer*. The request object can give us access to the attributes of the request, for example, target, operation name, arguments. The message buffer contains the marshaled version of the request, that is, all request arguments are flattened. There are many different reasons to monitor invocations, for instance, logging, tracing, encryption, or access control. Also, monitoring points are sometimes used as hooks to trigger other important invocation lifecycle events such as server-side thread allocation.
- **Request context.** In many cases we want to transfer additional information with each request. For example, a transaction service might want to send information about a transaction along with requests, so that a transaction service can ensure on the server side that all data is updated on behalf of the particular transaction. Or a security service implementation might want to send a security token with each request, which is used by the receiver to implement access control logic. We want to provide such services in a generic fashion, that is, independent of the application's specific IDL. It would be a bad idea if applications had to add an extra argument to each IDL operation to pass a security token. The mechanism for sending an implicit request context is used to implement services like transactions and security in a manner that makes them independent from the IDL used on the application level.
- **Object activation.** When a request arrives on the server side, the server's ORB runtime tries to locate an object implementation that is capable of processing the request. If no such object can be found, the ORB usually raises an exception, to indicate to the client that the object does not exist on the server side. However, it is desirable for an ORB to provide a mechanism

that enables the server implementation to activate objects on demand. This means if the ORB can't locate the target object, it would ask the application to provide it with an object that can be used to process the request. This aspect of object activation is actually very closely related to the object lifecycle, so we defer a more detailed treatment of object activation to our later discussion of the lifecycle of CORBA objects.

- **Thread allocation.** On the server side, we might want to be able to process multiple requests concurrently, using threads. The question is, at what point in the lifecycle of the request can a thread be allocated. There are many different thread allocation policies one can think of, for instance, thread-per-object, thread-per-client, or thread-per-request. An important question is whether it is the ORB's or the application's responsibility to allocate threads and to implement a certain threading policy.
- **Collocation.** Collocation is the idea of linking client and server logic into the same executable, and having the client invoke on the local object implementation. For performance reasons, a collocated call should obviously not be sent over the network. An interesting question is whether or not a collocated call will also bypass the invocation monitoring points.
- **Customized proxies.** In many cases, it would make sense to extend the standard functionality of a proxy, that is, use a proxy for more than marshalling and unmarshalling requests. For example, a customized proxy could be used to implement a client-side load-balancing mechanism. Another example of a customized proxy would be a proxy that caches object attributes. Customized proxy implementations make sense in particular when an advanced code-generation tool is used. We will have a more detailed discussion on code generation in Chapter 19, "Automating the Engineering Process."
- **Client redirection.** Finally, we require the ability to redirect requests when an object is relocated. An important aspect here is client transparency—that is, will a client that invokes on a proxy be notified if a request must be resent due to a redirection, or not.

Invocation Lifecycle: Evaluating The BOA Generation

First, we examine the BOA generation of CORBA ORBs with respect to the different invocation lifecycle evaluation criteria, as described above. The problem is that the BOA specification is very vague and does not address most of these aspects. Therefore, we are using the 2.x generation of IONA Technologies Orbix as a reference implementation for the BOA generation. Since the BOA specification is so vague with respect to almost all of the aspects that we want to discuss, other ORBs are likely to provide other implementations of these aspects, or even no implementations at all. However, we do not intend to provide a discussion of how different ORB implementations deal with the vagueness of the BOA specification, but rather to show one example of how a BOA-generation ORB implements the invocation lifecycle.

Invocation Monitoring

The BOA specification does not address the problem of invocation monitoring. The Orbix ORB provides two hooks that can be used to monitor invocations:

- **Filters.** An application can implement a filter object, and register it with the ORB runtime. The ORB runtime will then invoke at certain points in the lifecycle of an invocation on the registered filter object, giving the filter a chance to react to the event in an application-specific manner. Orbix will pass a request object to the filter, representing the current request. However, the request arguments are not accessible.

• **Request transformer.** Similar to filters, an application can register a request transformer with the ORB runtime. The ORB will make outgoing and incoming message buffers available to the application for both requests and replies.

Request Context

Request contexts are not really tightly related to object adapters, but more to the GIOP/IIOP specification. As we will see in the discussion of the POA generation, this problem is indeed addressed at the protocol level in later versions of CORBA. The initial approach to this problem was to introduce the concept of an additional (or implicit) argument. If an IDL operations is defined to have arguments a_1 to a_n, then the context could be sent as an additional argument a_{n+1}. This was used, for example, in the CORBA OTS 1.0 specification.

The Orbix ORB allows applications to send implicit request contexts in a similar manner, using "piggy backing." Orbix filters, as described above, can be used to add additional arguments to, and extract them from, requests. The problem is that there is no way for an application to determine whether or not a request contains a context. Therefore, this approach requires a lot of discipline and coordination between the client and server programmers.

Object Activation

Although the BOA generation of CORBA makes a clear differentiation between object and server activation, it does not clearly define how late binding can be implemented, that is, how objects can be activated on demand.

The Orbix ORB provides the "loader" mechanism: an application can implement a loader, and register an instance with a server ORB runtime. If the ORB cannot locate a requested target object, it will invoke the `load()` method on the loader, giving the application a chance to create and return an object implementation which will then be used by the ORB to process the request.

Thread Allocation

Again, the BOA generation of the CORBA specification does not describe how a server-side ORB runtime should handle thread allocation.

The Orbix ORB allows an application to install a special kind of filter, called a thread filter. The implementation of such a thread filter can allocate a thread and tell the ORB to use that particular thread to continue processing the request. Since thread allocation is totally up to the implementation, any kind of threading policy can be implemented. We discuss different possible thread policies in Chapter 14, "Managing Server Resources."

Collocation

The CORBA architecture is designed to support remote and collocated invocations on CORBA objects in the most transparent way. For example, the memory management rules for the IDL-to-C++ mapping are designed in a way that makes the remote and the collocated case look alike, from a client's as well as from a server's point of view.

As we said in the introduction, the interesting question is the extent to which this transparency can be also ensured for other aspects of the invocation lifecycle, for instance, invocation monitoring. Again, the BOA specification is very weak here. Orbix deals with collocation by using a particular stub/skeleton hierarchy.

Figure 2.3 describes the Orbix C++ stub/skeleton hierarchy from the view of clients and servers. The client always sees the interface class, "X" in the figure, regardless of whether this is a proxy or the real implementation. This means that in the collocated case, the client is directly invoking on the object implementation. On the one hand, this is the most efficient implementation, since it means that a collocated call is a single virtual function call. On the other hand, this means that the ORB cannot intercept the invocation, and therefore nobody can call any monitoring points.

Now, how bad is this? For request transformers, this seems to makes sense, since they are usually used for things such as encryption, which we will not need for a collocated call. For request level filters, this might be a problem. Let's say an implementation of the Object Transaction Service uses filters to transparently propagate transaction context information from a client to a server (for a more detailed explanation of OTS see Chapter 12, "Distributed Transaction Processing").

Figure 2.3 Orbix stub/skeleton class hierarchy for interface X

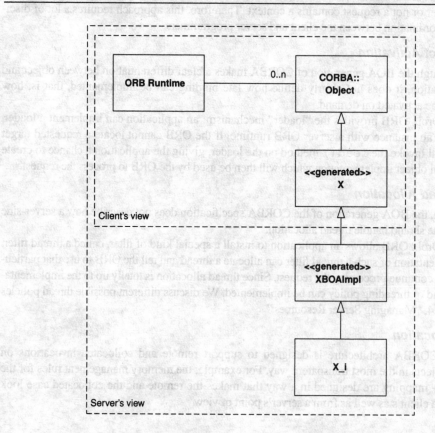

The client's thread is associated with the transaction context. So there seems to be no problem here, since the object uses the same thread to execute the call. Any initialization calls should have reached the DBMS beforehand. But what about a security service that uses server-side filters to implement an access control mechanism, possibly on a per-object basis? This access control mechanism would be bypassed in the collocated case. Depending on the security requirements, this might be acceptable. If not, then a special solution must be found for collocated calls.

Customized Proxies

When unmarshalling an object reference, the ORB creates a proxy object that enables the client to use the object reference. To support customized proxies, the ORB has to provide a hook that enables the application to provide the ORB with a customized proxy instance. The BOA generation of the CORBA specification does not define such a hook.

Many ORBs implement a proprietary mechanism to support customized proxies. For example, VisiBroker has the concept of *smart stubs;* Orbix calls them *smart proxies*. The Orbix ORB uses *proxy factories* to create proxies. The application can install specialized proxy factories, which can provide the ORB with customized proxies on demand.

Client Redirection

The BOA generation GIOP specification defines a special reply status type, called LOCATION_FORWARD. A location forward reply should contain a new object reference, which can then be used by the client to transparently re-send the request (and following requests) to the new target object. Unfortunately, the BOA generation GIOP specification does not define a public API, so the location forward mechanism can only be used by the ORB internally or via a proprietary API.

Summary

Figure 2.4 describes the invocation lifecycle in a BOA generation ORB, Orbix in this case. On the client side, the application invokes on a proxy. The outgoing request might be intercepted as a request object, using a client-side filter. Alternatively, the message buffer can be accessed using a request transformer. On the server side, the incoming message can be accessed again by a server-side request transformer. The first thing that Orbix does now is to try to locate the object in an internal table. If the target object cannot be located, Orbix will try the registered loaders. If the target object can be located, the next step is to allocate a thread, which will be used to continue processing the request. This can be either the default thread used by the ORB, or a thread that is provided by the application in a thread filter. Next, the ORB calls the in-request filter points, before calling the target object. Once the target object has finished processing the request, a reply is sent back to the client. During the lifecycle of a request, an exception might be thrown. In this case, the ORB will not continue processing the invocation. However, Orbix provides failure filter points, which will be called in the case of an exception.

Figure 2.4   Overview of the lifecycle of an Orbix invocation

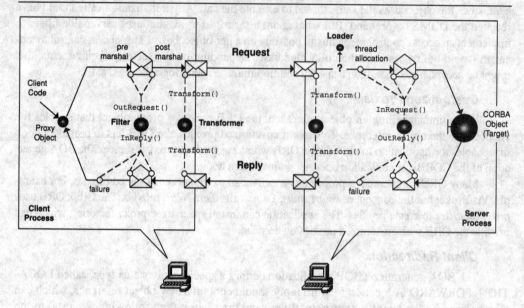

Invocation Lifecycle: Evaluating The POA Generation

Having discussed the invocation lifecycle from a BOA perspective, we now want to examine the same aspects from a POA viewpoint. The POA specification was introduced in CORBA 2.2. All other elements that we subsume under the general term "POA generation" were also introduced in one of the CORBA 2.x specifications. At the time of this writing, most ORB vendors had begun shipping POA-generation ORBs, or had announced plans to do so. Since portability is supposedly one of the main benefits of the POA, we are not concentrating on a particular implementation—the concepts discussed here should apply to all faithful implementations of the POA-generation CORBA specification.

Invocation Monitoring

The CORBA 2.2 specification introduces the concept of interceptors, which can be used as hooks into the invocation lifecycle. Interceptors can be used to monitor the invocation lifecycle on the client and the server side, allowing us to monitor requests and replies. On each side, multiple interceptors can be installed, which will be processed in turn. The specification defines two different kinds of interceptors:

- **Request-level interceptor.** The ORB will call the request interceptor and make the structured request available to it.
- **Message-level interceptor.** The ORB will call the message level interceptor, and make the target object and the unstructured message buffer available to it.

Note that some critical voices say that the current interceptor architecture is under-specified and too difficult to implement. The OMG's Request For Proposal on Portable Interceptors is beginning the process of addressing these issues.

Request Context

The CORBA 2.0 specification defines the concept of *service contexts*. These service contexts can be used to send, along with requests and replies, context information which might be needed by a CORBA service like a transaction or a security service. A service context has an ID and some data, in the form of a sequence of octets. Any number of service contexts can be sent along with requests and replies. Sender and receiver are de-coupled. The receiver can ignore contexts that it does not understand, and can also handle requests that do not contain all expected contexts.

Including service contexts as part of a CORBA request, and defining how these service contexts are to be marshaled into a message solves the problems with the piggybacking approach, described in our discussion of request contexts in the BOA generation. Additional data can now be sent in a standard and type-safe manner.

Object Activation

The POA specification does an extremely good job at specifying exactly how an ORB should deal with late binding. Several different approaches for object activation are possible with a POA. A POA-based server usually uses a set of different POA instances. Each of these POA instances is associated with a set of object implementations (that is, servants). POAs are associated with policies, which control their behavior. How a POA deals with object activation depends on the policies that are specified for the particular POA. For example, an application can provide a `ServantActivator`, which is invoked on by a POA in case of an object fault. There is a more detailed discussion of the POA architecture later in this chapter.

Thread Allocation

The POA specification defines two different policies that determine how a POA should deal with allocating threads to requests. The first policy indicates that the POA should use only a single thread, and the second policy determines that the ORB should control the thread allocation policy. Obviously, this is not specific enough, since applications often need to control the type of threading policy the ORB should use, as well as how the ORB handles things such as peak loads, thresholds, and thread reuse. Other questions that are unanswered include how the application can control the policy that is to be used by the ORB, and how an application can implement its own threading policy. We expect that future revisions of the POA specification will address these issues.

Collocation

The POA generation of CORBA requires an ORB to support request-level interception even in the collocated case. As mentioned earlier, this is not possible if the stub and skeleton hierarchy is designed in such a way that the client holds a pointer that points directly to the collocated implementation object. This is one of the reasons why the POA generation of CORBA allows an ORB implementation to have separate inheritance hierarchies for the client-side interface classes and server-side object implementations. This allows an ORB to easily implement a delegation mechanism, where a client thread invokes on a proxy, which in turn delegates the call to the real implementation object. This additional delegation step has the advantage that the ORB can now call interceptors before invoking on the target object. There is obviously also a small drawback: the additional delegation step (where we deal with an abstract request object) is more expensive than the single virtual function call used in the collocated case by most of the BOA-generation ORBs. The class hierarchy for POA-based ORBs is shown in Figure 2.5.

Customized Proxies

The POA generation of the CORBA specification does not address how an ORB can provide a hook for the application to control the creation of proxies. That means that there is currently no standard way for ORB vendors to implement this in a CORBA-compliant manner.

Client Redirection

As we discussed for the BOA generation of ORBs, the CORBA specification defines the special reply status type LOCATION_FORWARD, which is used for redirecting clients to the new object implementation. The POA specification defines a public API to this redirection feature using an exception called `ForwardRequest`, which has a single member of type `Object`. This exception can be raised by the application in a servant manager that uses the exception mechanism

Figure 2.5 POA stub/skeleton class hierarchy for interface X

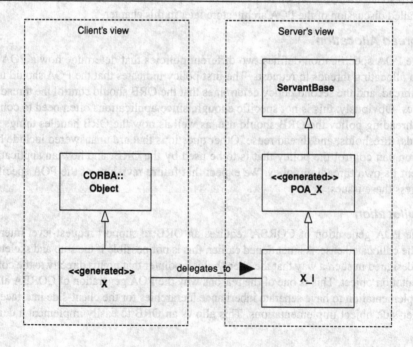

to redirect clients to a new object implementation, for instance, in a different server. The specification states that the ORB should from then on send all requests to the new object. A reference to the new object was returned as a result of the request being raised.

Figure 2.6 shows a collaboration diagram, describing an example of a client redirection. A client on host A attempts to send a request to an object, which is supposedly located in a server on host B. The object is not available in the server, so the request can't be processed. A servant manager in the server throws a `ForwardRequest` exception containing an object reference. This reference points to an implementation on host C. It is the client ORB's responsibility to transparently re-send the request to the new location. Also, all further requests must be sent to the object on host C. We explore the application of such mechanisms in much more detail in Chapters 15, "Load Balancing," and 16, "Fault Tolerance."

Summary

Figure 2.7 shows the invocation lifecycle with a POA-generation ORB, using a schema similar to the description of a BOA-generation ORB in Figure 2.4. Again, a client invokes on a proxy. The first interesting event during the invocation's lifecycle is the client-side request interceptor: the ORB calls `client_invoke()` on the first installed request interceptor. Notice that the call is blocking and only returns when the target has processed the request. The request interceptor continues the request's lifecycle using the DII function `invoke()` (not shown). If there is no other request-level interceptor, the ORB will continue by calling the first message interceptor using `send_message()`, passing the message (or a part of the message) to the interceptor. The inter-

Figure 2.6   Example for LOCATION_FORWARD

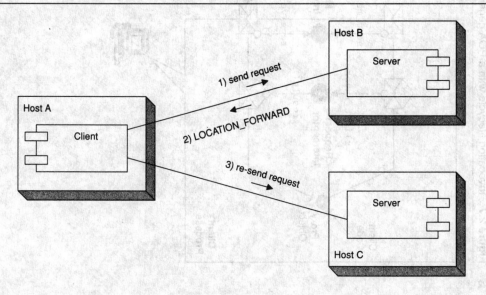

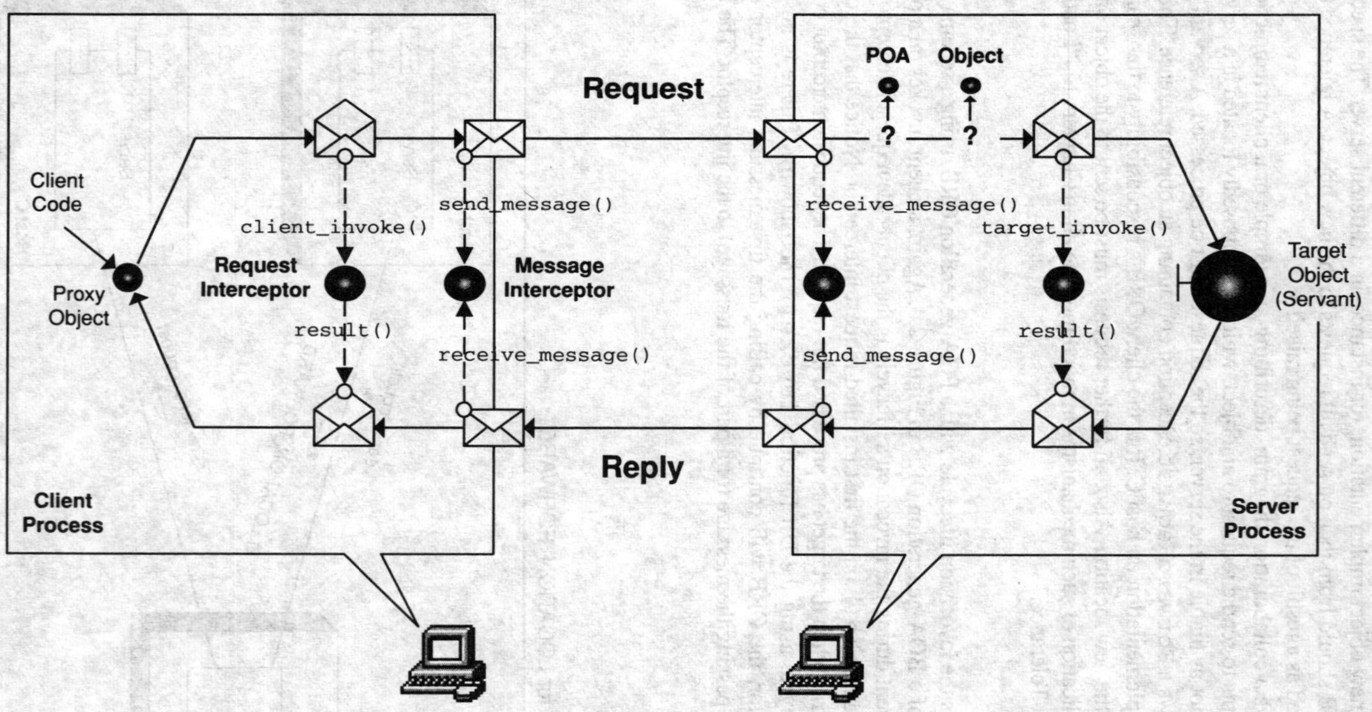

Figure 2.7 Invocation lifecycle with a POA generation ORB

ceptor continues the request's lifecycle by calling `send()` (not shown), which usually returns without completing the request. It is the ORB's responsibility to send the message to the target server.

On the server side, the server's ORB runtime reads the request from the network, and begins processing it by calling `receive_message()` on the first installed message interceptor. The object key used by the ORB to identify the target must contain the name of the POA (or POAs) through which the object can be reached. Having found the right POA, the next step is to look up the object itself. How this is done depends on the policies defined for the object's POA, and we will have a closer look at this later in this chapter. If the object could be located, the ORB continues processing the request by calling `target_invoke()` on the first installed request interceptor, which in turn continues processing the request using the DII function `invoke()`, as already discussed for the client side. Assuming that there is only one request interceptor installed, the request is finally dispatched to the implementation of the target object.

When the object has finished processing the request, the message interceptor's `invoke()` call returns, and the interceptor now has a chance to examine the result of the operation by invoking `result()` on the request object before returning to the ORB runtime. The last thing on the server side is the ORB's invocation of `send_message()` on the server's message interceptors. On the client side, the interceptors are processed in a similar manner: first the ORB calls the message interceptor's `receive_message()` methods, and then the request interceptor's blocking calls to `invoke()` return, again enabling them to examine the request's result. Finally, the method invoked by the client on the proxy returns, providing the result to the client.

A problem with the first version of the POA specification is that it is very hard to determine the exact order of lifecycle events, especially on the server side. For example, the specification does not exactly define at which point in time on the server side the allocation of a thread for a particular request should be done—many thread policies would require the information that is provided in the request object. Also, the specification is not crystal clear about the order of POA and object lookup in relationship to request interceptors, so the order in our diagram is based on their logical relationship.

The Object Lifecycle

In this section, we examine the lifecycle of CORBA objects and their implementations, looking at the object lifecycle in general, and then again examining the specifics of the BOA and POA ORB generations.

We look at the object lifecycle primarily from an application point of view rather than an ORB point of view, so we'll begin by looking at what an application usually requires to efficiently manage the lifecycle of CORBA objects.

What is a CORBA Object, Really?

First of all, let's examine the nature of a CORBA object: what is a CORBA object, really? Let's say we have a client application which is used to monitor the price of a stock by interacting with a stock object in an application server. The stock object implements an IDL interface `Stock`, and has an object key `"IONAY."` The CORBA server that contains the stock object is implemented in COBOL, running on an MVS mainframe. The stock implementation uses a VSAM database to store its state persistently.

Now, in a re-engineering effort, the provider of the financial information service decides to re-implement the application in C++ on a Unix system, using an RDBMS to store stock-related infor-mation. Over night, the mainframe is switched off, and replaced with the Unix system. The next morning, our stockbroker comes to work, and happily uses his stock price monitoring system. For him (and the client application that he uses), this whole change was completely transparent.

The new implementation of the stock object is offering the same interface and has the same identity, but the implementation and the structure of the persistent data schema have changed drastically. The new object implementation seems to have the same behavior, at least our stock broker can see no difference. The question is, is our stockbroker still accessing the same CORBA object?

CORBA Objects

The POA specification defines a CORBA object as an *abstract* entity with an identity, an interface, and an implementation. Our discussion above has shown why we say a CORBA object is abstract—it is not tied directly to the mechanism used to implement it.

From a client's perspective, an object is represented as an object reference, which encapsu-lates the object's interface type and identity, and also contains enough information to locate an implementation of the object. But what about the server's perspective?

Servants

The POA specification introduces the concept of a *servant*, to enable the clean separation of the *abstract* CORBA object and the *concrete* programming language entity that implements the object functionality. So from a server's perspective, a CORBA object is implemented as a servant. Recall that CORBA is a programming-language-independent architecture. Servants can be imple-mented as C++ or Java classes, as well as a set of COBOL paragraphs or C functions. The concept of servants also helps reflect this programming-language-independence.

So how does an ORB find the right servant for an incoming request? There must be some binding between CORBA object keys and servants. In the following, we examine this binding and discuss how an application can control it.

Object Adapters

The CORBA architecture defines the concepts of *object adapters*, to deal with the problem of how the application and the ORB interact to manage servant and CORBA object lifecycles. A very good definition of an object adapter is taken from Schmidt and Vinoski (1997):[2] "An object adapter is the CORBA component which is responsible for adapting CORBA's concepts of objects to a programming language's concept of servant." Having discussed that CORBA objects are *abstract*, and *servants* are concrete, this makes a lot of sense.

Object Lifecycle Events

For a CORBA object, the following two lifecycle events are of importance:

---

[2] Schmidt, D. C. and Vinoski, S., "Object Adapters: Concepts and Terminology," SIGS C++ Report, Vol 9, No 11, November/ December, 1997. Reprinted by permission of SIGS Publications.

- **Creation.** The lifecycle of a CORBA object begins with the *create* event. CORBA objects are usually created via factory objects, that is, objects that offer operations to create new objects. Recall that, on the IDL level, CORBA does not have the concept of static functions such as constructors.
- **Deletion.** The lifecycle of a CORBA object ends with the *delete* event. Usually, CORBA objects that can be deleted define some kind of `delete()` operation in their IDL interface. Sometimes, CORBA objects are deleted via other objects, for instance, the factory that created them.

Since we said CORBA objects are actually implemented by servants, we also need to look at the lifecycle of servants. We define the following two lifecycle events for servants:

- **Activation.** The activation event makes the servant available to process requests that come in for a particular CORBA object.[3] This implies that a binding between the abstract CORBA object and the concrete servant is created via the object ID. Often, but not necessarily, the activation event also comprises the instantiation of a servant.
- **Deactivation.** The deactivation event results in unbinding the servant from the CORBA object. Often, but not necessarily, the deactivation event also comprises the destruction of the servant.

Notice that there is a fundamental difference between the creation and deletion of CORBA objects, and their activation and deactivation. For many types of CORBA objects, the lifecycle of the CORBA object will include multiple servant activations and deactivations, as described in Figure 2.8.

Figure 2.8   Lifecycle of a CORBA object

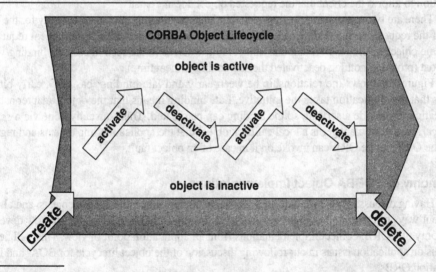

---

[3] Notice that the POA specification differentiates between object *activation* and object *incarnation*. We feel that this differentiation is too fine for our level of discussion. An excellent discussion of the POA can be found in "Object Adapters: Concepts and Terminology," Schmidt and Vinoski, 1997.

Early vs. Late Binding

In the definition of the servant lifecycle events, we said that servants are bound to CORBA objects via the CORBA object's ID. We will discuss the concept of a CORBA object ID separately for the BOA and POA generation of ORBs. Nevertheless, the idea of a binding between servant and CORBA object makes sense. The object adapter must provide the necessary interfaces that enable us to execute this binding. The question is, what triggers the actual binding: some standard application logic, or an incoming request? We will refer to the first case as *early binding*, and to the second case as *late binding*, or *binding on demand*.

Early Binding

Early binding usually describes the case where some standard application logic executes the binding via the object adapter. For example, a factory object might offer an operation for creating new objects. The implementation of this operation could create a new CORBA object and also activate a servant for it, before returning a reference to the newly created object. Since the CORBA object is now active—that is, a binding to a servant exists—the client can now use the reference and make invocations on the newly created CORBA object.

Late Binding

Late binding implies that the binding is only created on demand, that is, in the case of an object fault. An object fault occurs if there exists no binding in the target server's ORB runtime between the requested target object and a servant, that is, the ORB can't find an implementation for the target object.

In the case of such an object fault, the ORB can ask the application to provide a servant so it can be bound to the target object. If the application can't fulfill this request, the ORB will raise an exception to inform the client that the requested object doesn't exist.

There are two options for creating a late binding: the binding can be created only for the duration of the request, or the binding can outlive the request. In the first case, a subsequent request for the same object would result in another object fault, whereas in the second case the binding would still exist (provided nothing deactivated the servant in the meantime).

Figure 2.9 shows the relationship between early and late binding: basically, early binding means that the application takes the initiative. Late binding means that the object adapter asks the application to provide a servant, so the binding can be created. This is usually done via a *servant manager*. A servant manager is a local callback object that the application implements and registers with the ORB, so the ORB can invoke on it in case of an object fault.

Taxonomy of CORBA Object Implementations

Having discussed the different lifecycle events for servants and CORBA objects, and also the different ways of creating bindings between servants and CORBA objects, we can now develop a taxonomy of CORBA object implementations from an application point of view. This will help us to focus on application issues in our following discussion of the object lifecycle for BOA- and POA-generation ORBs.

Figure 2.9   Early binding vs. late binding

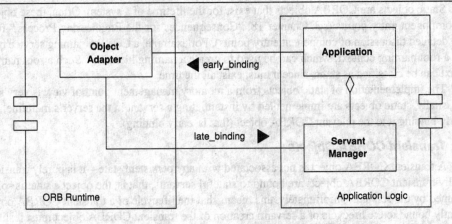

Servants and State

Our first classification is related to the state of servants. Basically, we can identify two distinct classes of servants: stateless servants and stateful servants. We briefly introduce them here, since we will need the distinction for the following discussion. A more in-depth discussion of state management can be found in Chapter 10, "Database Integration."

Stateless Servants

A stateless servant is not associated with any application-specific state in memory. This does not imply that the CORBA object, which is implemented by the servant, is necessarily stateless. For example, the CORBA object's state might reside in a database, which is accessed by the servant to execute the request. In this case, the servant is like a transient capsule, which delegates all incoming CORBA requests to a database server by executing SQL statements.

Stateful Servants

A stateful servant is associated with some application-specific state, which is accessed by the IDL operations implemented by the servant.

CORBA Object Implementations and Memory Management

Having classified servants with respect to their state, we can now define a classification of CORBA objects based on memory management aspects. Obviously, this discussion is closely related to the lifecycle of servants. At this point, we are focusing on the classification, so we discuss memory management issues only briefly, and introduce a general management pattern in the following. Refer to Chapter 14, "Managing Server Resources," for a refinement of the pattern and a more detailed discussion of memory management strategies.

Static CORBA Objects

Static objects are CORBA objects that exist for the lifetime of a system. Often, these objects are component entry points (see Chapter 18, "Consequences for the Engineering Process," for a more detailed discussion of component entry points). For example, a CORBA naming service must offer a root naming context, which can be used to create a naming hierarchy. Such a root naming context can be classified as static, since it must exist all the time.

The implementation of static objects from a memory management point of view is very simple. Usually, static objects are implemented by instantiating a servant in the server's mainline, and directly binding it to the relevant CORBA object (that is, early binding).

Transient CORBA Objects

A transient CORBA object is not associated with any persistent state—it is purely transient. Usually transient CORBA objects are bound to stateful servants, that is, the object's state is solely contained by the servant. Unfortunately, this means that the lifecycle of a transient CORBA object is tightly bound to the lifecycle of a servant: creation of the transient CORBA object must result in immediate activation of a servant to implement the object. The other way around, destruction of the servant will immediately result in the deletion of the related CORBA object, since all the state is gone with the servant.

A good example of a transient object is an iterator, which enables us to iterate over the result set of a query (see the StockPrice Iterator example in Chapter 14, "Managing Server Resources"). The iterator object is not bound to any persistent state, since a query result is usually transient. Finding a good memory management strategy for transient CORBA objects can be very difficult. We discuss this topic also in Chapter 14, "Managing Server Resources."

Persistent CORBA Objects

Finally, persistent CORBA objects are associated with some persistent state, maintained by a data management system. This enables us to employ very flexible memory management strategies for the implementations of these objects, since we can dynamically activate and deactivate servants, using late binding.

The Servant Pool Pattern

Our taxonomy of CORBA object implementations has shown that different objects have different requirements from a memory management point of view. The servant pool pattern defines a general framework for servant management. The basic idea is to have a pool manager, which manages the pool of active servants. Each servant is associated with an eviction policy, which describes when the servant should be evicted. The pool manager has two roles, *keeper* and *evictor*. The keeper ensures that objects are kept while needed. For example, a transient object can't be recreated, so it must be kept until the client is finished with it. The evictor must ensure that servants are frequently evicted, to avoid unnecessary resource consumption. A detailed description of the servant pool pattern can be found in Chapter 14, "Managing Server Resources."

Object Lifecycle: Evaluation Criteria

So far, we have examined the CORBA object lifecycle in general, including lifecycle events, a discussion of early and late binding, and a general taxonomy of CORBA object implementations. Obviously, we expect an ORB to provide applications with support for an efficient implementation of all these different aspects of the CORBA object lifecycle. The ORB provides this support via the object adapter (OA). The following defines a set of evaluation criteria under which an object adapter should be analyzed with respect to efficient support of the CORBA object lifecycle. We then take these different evaluation criteria and apply them to the BOA and POA generations of object adapters.

- **Adapter architecture.** The first important aspect is the general architecture of the adapter.
- **Object identity.** Object identity in a CORBA system is non-trivial, and we must carefully examine how a particular ORB generation supports the concept of object identity for CORBA objects.
- **Early binding.** We need to examine the ways in which the different ORB generations support early binding. Of particular interest here is how much binding and servant creation are related to each other.
- **Late binding.** The mechanism provided by the different ORBs for late binding must be examined, particularly with respect to usefulness for applications that need to support persistent objects.
- **Stateless servants.** We want to examine the support that the ORB generation provides for implementing stateless servants. The idea is that for stateless servants, we don't really need a servant instance per CORBA object—a single servant object could act as the transient capsule for multiple CORBA objects, assuming the identity of a particular CORBA object on a per request basis.
- **Stateful servants.** As we discussed earlier, for stateful servants it is often important to ensure that we don't have to reactivate them for every request and still ensure that a certain threshold of active servants is not exceeded.

Object Lifecycle: Evaluating The BOA Generation

In the following we want to examine the basic object adapter under each of the object-lifecycle-related evaluation criteria that we defined above. The section after this will do the same for the portable object adapter.

BOA Architecture

As mentioned before, the BOA architecture is extremely vague on many points. A lot of the features that are required by an application to efficiently manage the object lifecycle are under-specified. The BOA defines some functions for activation of CORBA servers and CORBA object implementations. Unfortunately, the BOA focuses on server activation, and not on important issues such as late binding and dynamic object activation. The BOA also defines some functions for the generation and interpretation of object references. The BOA implies a one-to-one relationship between servant and CORBA object, that is, a dedicated servant instance is required for each CORBA object supported by a particular loader server.

Because the BOA specification is so vague, we are using IONA Technologies Orbix 2.x ORB as a reference implementation. Again, our intention is not to give a comprehensive comparison of different BOA generation ORBs, but to discuss general concepts using one ORB as an example.

Object Identity

The BOA generation of ORBs associates an object reference with *reference data* on creation. The reference data is a sequence of octets, and it is under ORB control. This makes it difficult to provide application-defined object IDs in a CORBA-compliant manner.

The Orbix ORB offers the `_marker()` API to specify application-defined reference data for CORBA objects. The marker is a string that can be provided by the application and that is stored by the ORB as part of the reference data.

Early Binding

Most of the BOA-generation ORBs provide a very tight coupling between the client-side stub class hierarchy, and the server-side skeleton class hierarchy, as discussed earlier. The result of this is that servant creation usually implicitly results in object activation, because servants inherit a constructor that will implicitly create a binding between the servant and the ORB runtime. This implies that if we want to return an object reference to a client, we also have to create and activate a servant instance, that is, using early binding.

Late Binding

The BOA architecture does not define how ORB and an application can interact to support late binding, or object activation on demand. Therefore, we look to the Orbix ORB as an example of how a BOA ORB addresses the problem.

The Orbix ORB supports late binding using a *loader* mechanism as shown in Figure 2.10. The loader plays a role of a servant manager, as introduced earlier. The basic idea is that the application registers loader instances with the ORB runtime, which in turn invokes the `load()` method on the loaders in case of an object fault. This gives the loaders a chance to activate the requested object, so that the ORB can dispatch to it.

It is up to the application to decide whether the servant should serve only the particular request or stay active for subsequent requests. The Orbix loader feature can be used by the applica-

Figure 2.10   Orbix loader mechanism

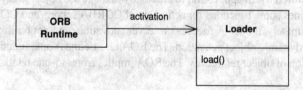

tion to implement the servant pool pattern for objects that can be activated on demand, that is, persistent objects.

Stateless Servants

The BOA generation of ORB implementations does not provide special support for stateless servants. Basically, the one-to-one relationship between CORBA objects and servants implies that we must activate a servant for each CORBA object. Depending on the cost for instantiating and activating a stateless servant, we should decide whether or not it is worth implementing the pool pattern to reduce the frequency of object activation/deactivation. This includes investigating the overhead for servant activation/deactivation that is imposed by the ORB, as well as application-related costs. The question is whether it is more expensive from a performance point of view to activate servants on a per-request basis, or to maintain an object pool.

Stateful Servants

As discussed above, for stateful servants it will often turn out that servant activation/deactivation is quite costly, especially if it involves a database lookup. In this case, it makes sense to combine late binding with an object pool. Since the BOA specification is not very precise here, we have to rely on proprietary ORB support, like the Orbix loader, for late binding.

Object Lifecycle: Evaluating The POA Generation

We now apply each of our evaluation criteria to the portable object adapter.

POA Architecture

The POA architecture can be quite overwhelming in the beginning, since it provides a lot of advanced features for managing the lifecycle of servants and CORBA objects. Fortunately, it is possible to use the POA initially in a very simple manner. However, the different requirements for different types of objects really do require the sophisticated support mechanisms of the POA.

Figure 2.11 gives an overview of the top level elements of the POA architecture. The ORB manages servants via POAs. Each ORB is associated with a root POA. A POA can be used to create

Figure 2.11   POA Overview

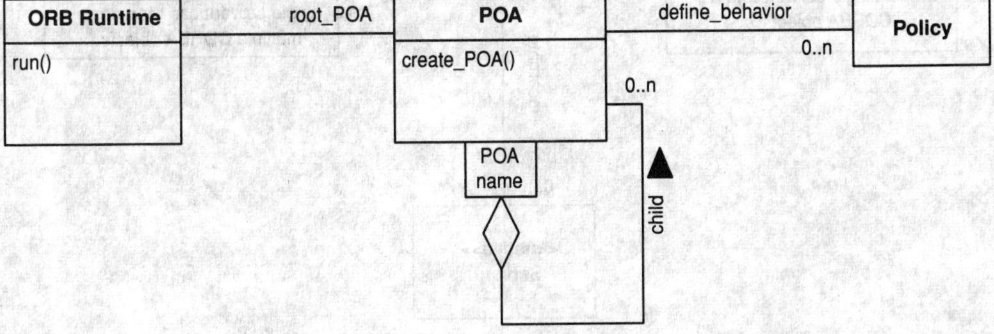

nested POAs by calling `create_POA()` on the POA, passing the name of the new POA. This is the only way to create new POAs, which means the application cannot provide its own implementation of a POA. Instead, the application defines the specific behavior of a new POA by associating it with a set of policies. These policies define a POA's behavior with respect to things such as servant activation, servant lifespan, ID management, and thread allocation.

Figure 2.12 gives an overview of the relationship between POAs and servants. The POA specification coins the term *incarnation* to indicate the association of a servant with a CORBA Object. In the class diagram we can see the incarnation relationship, which is qualified by an object ID, that is, the POA can locate a servant via the associated object ID. Obviously, each POA can be associated with many servants. What's more surprising is that a single servant can represent multiple CORBA objects! In fact, it is not only possible to register a servant for multiple objects, it is even possible to register a default servant, which will get all requests for objects that are not explicitly associated with a servant via an ID. We discuss the usefulness of this feature below. The POA specification also introduces the term *etherealize*, which is the opposite of incarnation. This is the act of disassociating a servant from a CORBA object.

Object Identity

The POA generation of CORBA makes a distinction between the terms *object key* and *object ID*. The object key identifies an object at the communication endpoint. For example, the object key

Figure 2.12   POA and servants.

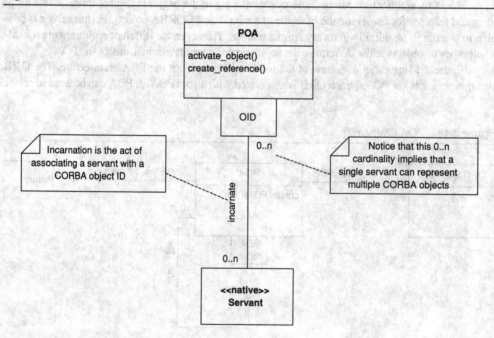

should contain the name of the POA through which the target object implementation can be reached. In addition, the object key should also contain an object ID. The object ID identifies the object relative to a specific POA. Depending on the particular POA's policies, the object ID for a newly created object can be defined by the POA or by the application.

Early Binding

To use early binding with the POA, we use a policy called *servant retention* with explicit activation (using `activate_object()`, or `activate_object_with_id()`).

Notice that the POA specification separates the activation of a servant and the creation of an object reference. Returning an object reference to a client now does not necessarily mean that the server must also activate the object; that is, we can return object references without executing an early binding. This means we can use late binding more often than before. This can be a benefit when using stateless servers in combination with a single servant that represents all stateless servants; in this case, we only ever have to instantiate a single servant and register it as the default servant. The default servant will handle the incoming requests for all objects that we made available by simply creating and exporting references for them.

Late Binding

The POA supports the concept of servant managers as the basic mechanism for late binding, as described in Figure 2.13. In case of an object fault, the POA will invoke on the registered servant managers, in an attempt to get an incarnation of the requested object. This can mean either that the binding between servant and CORBA object is created only for the particular request (when using a *servant locator*), or that the binding will last longer than the request duration (when using a *servant activator*).

Figure 2.13 Late binding support from POA

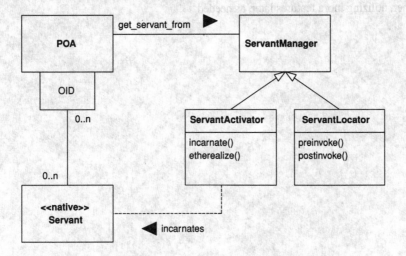

Stateless Servants

The POA specification provides support for stateless servants in two different ways. First of all, an application can register a default servant, which can process all incoming request for the objects that are accessible via the particular POA. Second of all, the servant locator can be used: the servant locator will make a servant available to a POA only for the duration of a request. This means that a servant takes on a particular ID for the duration of a request. The POA provides an API that enables the servant to find out about its current identity while executing the request.

Stateful Servants

As discussed before, for stateful servants we usually want to maintain a pool of active servants to reduce the frequency of activation, which can be quite costly. We discuss the servant pool pattern in Chapter 14, "Managing Server Resources." One important question is who actually maintains the mapping from CORBA object to servant. In Figure 2.12 we indicated that a servant is associated with a POA via its ID. However, this is not always the case. With the servant locator mechanism, we can create the object/servant association on a per-request basis.

Notice that the servant locator will often manage its own object ID/servant mapping, outside of the ORB's control. This is the easiest way to implement an efficient eviction mechanism.

Summary

In this chapter we have discussed the lifecycle of remote CORBA invocations, and the lifecycle of CORBA objects. Many of the concepts that we have introduced here are important foundations for the topics covered in the remainder of the book. We examined invocation and object lifecycle events for the BOA and the POA generation of ORB implementations. As we could see, the BOA specification is often very vague, and does not address many of the features which are required to efficiently manage the lifecycle of remote invocations and CORBA objects. The POA specification might seem overwhelmingly complex initially. But on the other hand, the POA specification covers many features that BOA-generation ORBs implement in a proprietary way because these features are not covered by the BOA specification. And finally, a developer can start using the POA in a simple manner, utilizing more features later, as needed.

CORBA Services Revisited

OMA, the Object Management Architecture, defines a set of services, which are intended to provide higher system-level services on top of the basic ORB functionality. These services deal with core system-level functionality such as persistence and transactions, security, messaging, and directory services. These services form the framework for building higher level facilities and business functionality. The specifications deal mainly with defining IDL interfaces for the services, and informally describing the semantics of these interfaces. Only very few service specifications deal with quality of service issues. This means most of the specifications don't describe what quality of service an implementation has to provide, or how an application could control the quality of service through standardized interfaces.

As in the previous section, we focus on the gap between the abstract world of OMG specifications and the real world of service implementations, and on applications that use these implementations. We look from a very high level at the usability and importance of the different services, discussing some of their strengths and weaknesses; at quality-of-service and scalability issues; and at some of the current developments in the OMG. This discussion identifies the core services needed for enterprise CORBA. It also sets the scope for the remainder of the book, that is, the discussion on how we can use existing services to build enterprise CORBA systems, and how we can overcome limitations in the real world.

Core Services

First, we look at the different directory services that are defined by the OMG. The most prominent directory service is the *CORBA naming service*, which provides a relatively static mapping between structured names and object references. Servers publish name/reference mappings with the naming service, and clients can look up references by name. This is a very fundamental service, and is frequently used in the real world. The structure of the service is very simple. However, there are a lot of issues to be discussed, for instance, selecting objects to be published, managing large numbers of entries, and structuring name spaces. We examine these topics in Chapter 6, "Object Location." Another important directory service specified by the OMG is the *CORBA object trading service*, which provides a flexible way of exporting and locating object services by associating them with a set of properties. These properties support sophisticated methods of describing the services provided by an object. One main difference is that a client only needs to know the kind of object being looked for, not the precise name of one particular object. As with the naming service, there are a lot of issues, for instance, the structure of the service offer space, quality of implementation, and the underlying persistence mechanism.

The basic CORBA model of request processing is inherently synchronous and tightly coupled. Many applications require a more asynchronous and loosely coupled messaging paradigm, since this is a model which many business situations require. The CORBA event service addresses this problem by defining an architecture which is based on the synchronous, tightly coupled CORBA request model, but provides asynchronous and loosely coupled messaging by introducing the concept of an intermediate event channel. The event service specification really only defines common roles like event supplier, consumer, and channel, and the interfaces between them. The specification does not define the quality of service that an event channel has to implement, for instance, guaranteed delivery versus best effort. An extension to the event service, the *CORBA notification service*, addresses this issue by defining a set of interfaces that enable the user to define the required quality of service, for instance, on a per channel and a per event basis. In addition, the notification service also introduces a sophisticated mechanism for event filtering, which will be of particular importance to large-scale applications. These services will be discussed and compared in Chapter 7, "Messaging," especially from a scalability point of view.

An important aspect of enterprise systems that designers often tend to treat like an unwanted stepchild is security. Today's businesses depend on their IT systems, and protecting their business is vital. Security in a distributed system comprises not only encryption, but also concepts like authentication, authorization, and non-repudiation. The CORBA specification defines several levels of security, and follows recent development like the standardization of the Secure Socket Layer protocol, by integrating them into the CORBA standard. In Chapter 8, "Security," we will discuss the different aspects of security and how they can be addressed in CORBA systems.

Database Integration and Transaction Processing

Persistence, database integration, and transaction processing are complex problems, and are addressed by several OMG standards.

The initial *persistent object service* (POS) was flawed. It was based on a two-level storage model and was extremely complex. In addition, it was not integrated with other services that deal with persistence-related topics like transactions and concurrency. For all these reasons, the OMG decided to completely revise the persistence specification, which is now called the *persistent state service 2.0* (PSS). The new PSS 2.0 will be more closely integrated with services like the object transaction service (OTS), objects-by-value (ObV), and the portable object adapter (POA), and will prove useful in practice.

Closely related to persistence is the *CORBA object transaction service* (OTS). The OTS enables distributed transaction processing in a CORBA environment by providing essential features like transaction management, transaction propagation, and two-phase commit-based transaction resolution. Traditionally, transaction processing systems have an image of being relatively heavyweight, based on complicated TP monitor technology. In particular, the high cost of two-phase commit transaction resolution has added to the image of being a heavyweight technology. In Chapter 12, "Distributed Transaction Processing," we discuss how the OTS makes distributed transaction processing more easily accessible for people without a TP monitor background. In Chapter 13, "User Sessions," we discuss how the OTS can be useful even in single database environments, helping with the difficult task of keeping data consistent in a three-tier environment, without the burden of real two-phase commit processing.

Dealing with relationships is traditionally a domain of database management systems. RDBMSs deal with relationships in the first tier, by processing them directly in the database server, for instance, performing complex joins that set rows into relationship. ODBMSs enable us to navigate highly complex objects graphs in an extremely efficient manner. Usually the navigation logic is implemented in the second tier, that is, in some database client. Most ODBMSs also provide a mechanism to send queries directly to the database server, so they can be evaluated most efficiently in the first tier. The *CORBA relationship service* makes relationships accessible to the third tier: relationships between CORBA objects are represented themselves as CORBA objects. This is theoretically a very good idea, since it enables us to express and navigate relationships using standard CORBA mechanisms. Practically, navigating relationships in the third tier is severely limited for simple performance reasons: each step from one object to another object involves multiple remote invocations. Other than an ODBMS client, a CORBA client has no standard way of caching object and relationship information locally. Therefore care must be taken when designing a system that accesses relationships in the third tier using an implementation of the relationship service. Use of the relationship service tends to be restricted to scenarios where performance is not the most critical issue, and the number of relationships that need to be navigated is relatively small. We discuss this in more detail in Chapter 10, "Database Integration."

An interesting aspect of the relationship service is the tight integration with the *CORBA lifecycle service*, providing lifecycle management for compound objects. The lifecycle service addresses the problem of object lifecycle management on the IDL level, using higher-level concepts like factories and factory finders. Notice that this is a fundamentally different approach from the object-adapter-based lifecycle management for servants and CORBA objects that we discussed in Chapter 2, "CORBA Revisited." Combining lifecycle service and relationship service to address the lifecycle management for compound objects seems compelling, but again we have to carefully look at the performance issues discussed previously.

The definition of the *CORBA query service* is not only driven by the need to execute queries as closely to the data as possible, but by the general need to deal with collections of objects which allow selection, insertion, update, and deletion of members. The CORBA query service tries to avoid re-inventing the wheel by integrating standards like SQL 92 and OQL 93. However, lack of commercially available implementations makes it difficult to make a statement on the quality of the specification.

Another important topic with respect to persistence and transactions is concurrency control. Again, concurrency control is another traditional DBMS domain. Concurrency control on the database level is a very complex topic, and standards like SQL 92 are very vague about concurrency issues. Again, the *CORBA concurrency services* deals with concurrency on the IDL level, defining interfaces to perform tasks such as acquiring and releasing locks. In most cases, we have found that applications deal with concurrency on the database level, rather than using a higher-level abstraction like the CORBA Concurrency Service—particularly because most implementations of the concurrency service do not provide a tight integration with commercial database management systems.

There are some cases where a higher-level concurrency mechanism is required—for example, in some kind of workflow management system with specific policies for managing people working in parallel. We discuss concurrency control issues at several different places: in Chapter 12, "Distributed Transaction Processing," and Chapter 13, "User Sessions."

Scalability Issues

As CORBA systems grow in size, complexity, and functionality, they become much more important to the enterprise in which they are deployed. Large-scale CORBA systems must address the difficult topics of load balancing and fault tolerance. Unfortunately, there are currently no CORBA standards available that address load balancing and fault tolerance directly. We address these topics in Chapter 15, "Load Balancing," and Chapter 16, "Fault Tolerance."

Finally, CORBA system developers must address testing, deployment, and system management. Testing is an area that hasn't been addressed by the OMG at all. Similarly, deployment is still an issue that each ORB vendor addresses with proprietary solutions. System management is an area that the OMG has started to work on, but no concrete standard was available at the time of writing. We cover these three topics in Chapter 17, "Testing, Deploying, and Managing Components."

Summary

Many of the CORBA services are critical to building large-scale CORBA systems. In the second part of this book, *Core Services*, we cover some of these key CORBA services, concentrating on object location, messaging, and security. The third part of the book addresses the issues of persistence, database integration, and transaction processing. This part is separate from the core services part, since there is currently no integrated solution, as the original *persistent object service* is being replaced by the emerging *persistent state service* specification. Also, we have seen that it does not always make sense to use CORBA services in this area, for example, in the case where native database concurrency control mechanisms make more sense than the concurrency service. The fourth part of the book addresses important scalability issues like resource management, fault tolerance, and load balancing, that are currently not covered by CORBA specifications.

There are many other CORBA services such as the licensing service, time service, and property service, and specifications that address topics such as compound document management. Time will tell how these services will be implemented and used to build real-world CORBA applications.

CHAPTER 4

Overview of a Simple Example

When reading about the technical features of CORBA, it's often difficult to relate them to real-world problems. This chapter introduces an example which demonstrates some of the business requirements that would drive us to develop a CORBA system, and shows how we can fulfil those requirements using CORBA components. Throughout the book, we return to this example to illustrate particular aspects of CORBA design and development. Topics introduced here are explored in further detail in later chapters.

Introduction

Investment banks like Goldman Sachs, Lehman Brothers, and Merrill Lynch are shifting around billions of dollars every day. To succeed in their business, they need to closely monitor the trends in the world economy. Reading the *Wall Street Journal* with breakfast is every portfolio manager's duty. But from where do the traders get statistical information about past and current financial events, which they need to identify their investment strategies? Companies like Bloomberg, Reuters, and Quotetron deal with financial information, selling this vital asset to all the J.P. Morgans and Merril Lynches of the world. But if these financial information providers are selling the same information to all the investment banks, how can the banks differentiate their business? Most investment banks these days rely heavily on the services provided by their own IT departments, which provide systems that can be used by the brokers and traders to succeed in their business. Making financial information accessible in a variety of different ways is an important part of the game.

The first systems offered by financial information providers were often bundled with a front end. For example, an information provider would not only offer a physical link to access the information, but also a terminal that provided a stock ticker service, or some such. Obviously, investment banks were interested in feeding the information into their own systems to gain the competitive edge they need to succeed in business. The first systems that enabled the bank's IT departments to access the information services directly often simply provided a physical link, such as a leased line, which could be used to access the services via a low-level network protocol like TCP/IP. The financial information provider also offered specifications of the message and data formats that were to be used to interact with the information service. These specifications were long, complicated documents, for example, using something like a BNF grammar to describe the different formats. Every time the functionality of the information service was changed, the format specifications had to be changed, and the customers had to change the implementation of their systems to adopt to the new formats. Because of the limitations of this "raw sockets" approach, some information providers started to offer their customers program libraries, encapsulating the network message formats, that made it easier to access the information services. Although this was an important step forward, it didn't really solve the problems. The libraries use vendor-proprietary APIs, they are difficult to use, and they have to be customized for new programming languages and compiler versions, and operating systems.

Figure 4.1 shows, at a very high level, the interaction between consumers of financial information and an information provider. These consumers potentially include many types of organizations, such as traders, portfolio managers, financial analysts, or news agencies, each using the information in different ways. An organizational boundary exists between the information provider and the end users of the information. Because of this, the information provider does not know in advance how customers will use its service. That means the information provider has to define interfaces that are flexible enough to satisfy all different kinds of customer demands. In traditional systems, there is a trade-off between this flexibility and the difficulty of developing client applications. A financial information provider usually provides historical data, which is accessed using a *pull* style communication, and continuous information updates which are provided using *push* style communication. This is illustrated in Figure 4.1, where clients pull historical data [1], and the server pushes stock price updates [2].

Given that this is a CORBA book, you will not be surprised if we tell you that CORBA provides an obvious way to solve all these problems. Using a CORBA-based approach, the provider defines the interface to its information in IDL. The provider then gives customers the IDL definitions and access to the server. Customers can take advantage of CORBA's standard, object-oriented programming approach to create client applications that meet their requirements. These applications can access the financial information service using standard TCP/IP connections, for instance over a dial-up line, or over the Internet.

Figure 4.1   Financial information provider

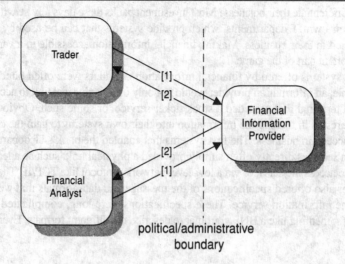

Exporting the services supplied by the financial information provider via CORBA IDL offers some major benefits. CORBA IDL is an accepted standard for defining interfaces, so programmers don't have to learn system-specific data and message formats and access mechanisms for each new system. CORBA leverages the strengths of object-orientation at the enterprise level. This means programmers can concentrate on creating functionally rich applications, without worrying about network-level programming. CORBA IDL compilers automatically generate the code that is required to make the interfaces accessible to clients, and also the code that is required for integrating the server-side implementation into the system. CORBA IDL compilers are available for a large variety of programming languages and operating systems. All this means that the service provider does not have to maintain, port, and distribute proprietary class libraries, but can rely on CORBA as a standard way of defining and accessing remote services.

The remainder of this chapter introduces an example in the domain of financial information services and stock trading. The example comprises two components. The first component offers a simple financial information service by providing information about stock prices. The second component is a portfolio management system, which uses the financial information service to offer services like calculating the current value of a specific portfolio. While the first component is likely to be offered by a financial information provider, the second component could be implemented by an investment bank for internal use, or even by a retail broker, possibly offering portfolio management over the Internet.

The StockWatch Component

Our first demonstration component, which we call the *StockWatch* example, initially provides access only to historical stock data. The service assumes that clients want to select a particular stock and then access the history of the stock price. Although the StockWatch service can be used by any kind of CORBA client, the financial information provider offers a simple client implementation for demonstration purposes. The demonstration client implements a simple GUI, which displays the available stock symbols and displays a stock's price history upon selection of a particular symbol. Figure 4.2 is an overview of the simple GUI client.

Figure 4.2 StockWatch GUI

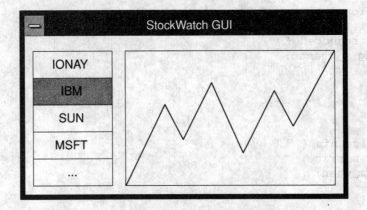

Figure 4.3   StockWatch Overview

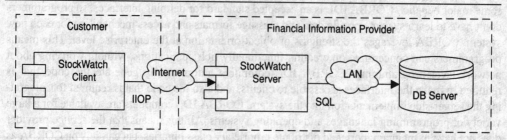

The GUI client communicates with the financial information server, which in turn accesses a database to obtain stock information. The server implements two types of CORBA objects: a StockWatch object, which allows clients to select a particular stock, and Stock objects, which provide access to information about particular stocks. When using the GUI client, our initial system has a simple three-tier architecture as shown in Figure 4.3.

StockWatch Interfaces

The IDL for the StockWatch and Stock objects is shown below:

```
// IDL : StockWatch Example

//
// Basic type definitions
//
typedef string Date;
typedef float Money;
typedef string Symbol;
typedef sequence<Symbol> SymbolSeq;


//
// Exceptions
//
exception rejected {
    string m_reason;
};


//
// Structs
//
struct PriceInfo {
    Money m_price;
    Date m_when;
};
```

```
typedef sequence<PriceInfo> PriceInfoSeq;


//
// Interfaces
//
interface Stock {
    Symbol getSymbol();
    string getDescription () raises (rejected);
    Money getCurrentPrice () raises (rejected);
    PriceInfoSeq getRecentPrices () raises (rejected);
    };

interface StockWatch {
    SymbolSeq getSymbols () raises (rejected);
    Stock getStockBySymbol (in Symbol aSymbol)
      raises (rejected);
};
```

A client first contacts the financial information server by obtaining a reference to a Stock-Watch object. The StockWatch interface includes two operations:

- getSymbols() returns a list of all known stock symbols.
- getStockBySymbol() returns the stock object associated with a particular symbol.

The StockWatch object acts as an entry point to the financial information service, allowing a client to obtain a reference to the Stock object associated with a specified stock.

Once a client obtains a reference to a Stock object, it can query the object for information about the corresponding stock:

- getCurrentPrice() returns the current price of the stock.
- getRecentPrices() returns a history of the recent prices of the stock.
- getDescription() returns a text description of the stock.

Database Schema

To obtain information about stock prices, the server interacts with a relational database management system, using embedded SQL. The following shows the database tables used to store stocks and stock prices:

Table STOCK	
string SYMBOL	string DESCRIPTION

Table STOCK_PRICE		
string SYMBOL	number PRICE	date DATE

The STOCK table uses a stock symbol as primary key. The STOCK_PRICE table uses a combination of stock symbol and date. In the STOCK_PRICE table, the SYMBOL column is also a foreign key that relates a stock price to an entry in the STOCK table.

The data volume for such a database is potentially very large, due to the large number of stocks and the fact that historical data must be stored. Also, the content of the table is likely to change very frequently. Stock prices change many times during each day and these changes must be captured over a long period of time.

Extending the StockWatch's System Architecture

Obviously, a financial information server like that described here must be able to cope with massive volumes of data and network communications. A real-world system is likely to have large numbers of clients, demanding high performance and even real-time information updates. Storing and transmitting such a large amount of data under these constraints could be extremely difficult. However, in this section we describe how CORBA makes it possible to scale applications to real-world levels.

Increasing Scalability using Load Balancing

Our financial information service is likely to be accessed by a large number of clients. If we want to make the application truly scalable, we cannot rely on a single server process to deliver information simultaneously to them all. To maintain acceptable levels of performance, we should balance the processing load across several server processes.

In our case study, we want to use a naming service-based load-balancing mechanism, which we describe in more detail in Chapter 15, "Load Balancing." The basic idea is that this load-balancing-enabled naming service allows multiple objects to be registered under the same name, so that a single name represents a group of objects that offer the same interface and functionality. If a client resolves a name, the naming service has to select one of the objects, for example, using a simple random selection strategy. We refer to this simple load-balancing mechanism as the *object group* pattern.

Figure 4.4 shows the StockWatch system with load balancing based on object groups. Each client connects to the financial service provider's naming service. The client then invokes the resolve() operation on the root naming context, passing the name of the StockWatch object it wants to contact. The load-balancing-enabled naming service returns a reference to one of the objects in the corresponding object group. In this example, a client uses a single server process during the client's entire lifetime. We can easily imagine other scenarios—for example, one in which clients obtain Stock objects from a pool of server processes. We explore load balancing in greater depth in Chapter 15, "Load Balancing."

Publishing Stock Price Updates using Event Notification

In our StockWatch example, consider the case in which the financial information provider would like to provide live stock price updates to customers. Our server must be able to deliver updates to any number of consumers without being closely coupled to the customers' applications. To achieve this, we use the CORBA event service.

Figure 4.4 Load-balanced version of StockWatch

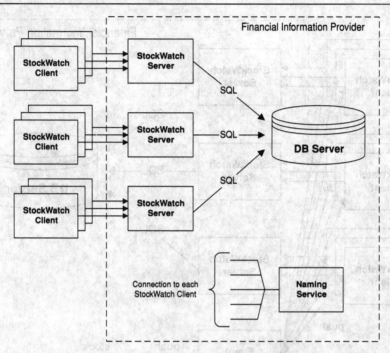

The event service allows us to de-couple communications between clients and servers using event channels, as described in Chapter 7, "Messaging." In our example, it makes sense to have one event channel per stock. Consumers subscribe to the event channels for all the stocks in which they are interested. Servers send price updates to the clients using the appropriate event channels. This architecture is illustrated in Figure 4.5.

To implement this architecture, we add an operation to the Stock interface described above. This operation, named getFeed(), allows a client to obtain a reference to the event channel associated with a Stock object. The IDL definition for this operation is shown below:

```
// IDL
interface Stock {
    // Operations as before.
    // ...

    // Operation to obtain the event channel
    // administration object, for event consumers.
    CosEventChannelAdmin::ConsumerAdmin getFeed();
};
```

The mechanism that is responsible for managing stock price updates will feed each price update into the channel that is associated with the particular stock. The event service pushes the price updates to all consumers, which are registered with the particular channel.

Figure 4.5   StockWatch with event notification

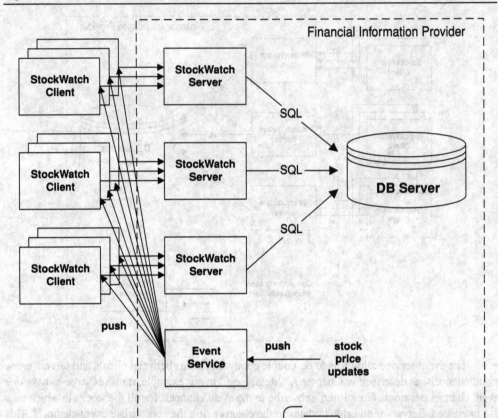

The Portfolio Manager Component

Throughout this book, we refer to the StockWatch application when describing CORBA design and development issues. For some of these descriptions, we must extend the example to allow for more advanced design discussions. Here, we describe a suitable client application, known as the *Portfolio Manager* component.

Imagine a stockbroker firm wants to provide its clients with an Internet-based portfolio management system. The firm provides its clients with a simple GUI which communicates with a back-end portfolio manager. The GUI is implemented as a Java applet, using a Java ORB. The portfolio manager is a CORBA server which implements several distributed objects.

Figure 4.6   Portfolio Manager class diagram

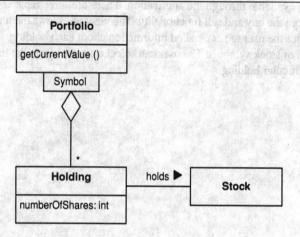

Figure 4.7   Portfolio Manager GUI

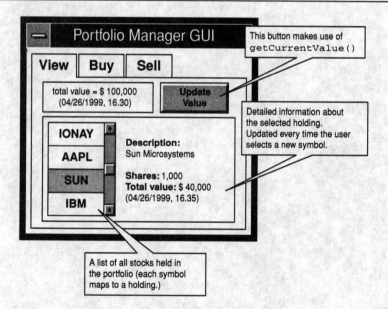

Figure 4.6 shows the class diagram for the portfolio manager. In UML terminology, a portfolio aggregates a set of holdings. A holding indicates the number of shares a customer holds in a given stock. We can retrieve a specific holding from a portfolio by specifying the symbol of the corresponding stock. Finally, a portfolio provides a method to get the portfolio's current value, which is the sum of the current values of all holdings.

The Portfolio Manager GUI is shown in Figure 4.7. This simple GUI allows clients to access all the functionality available through the application. There are three tabs: *view*, *buy*, and *sell*. In this section, we ignore the buy and sell functionality. The view tab shows the total value of the portfolio, and also enables the user to get detailed information about each holding. Current holdings are represented by a list of stock symbols. The user can select a symbol from the list to get more information about the particular holding.

Performance Considerations

 $\mathbf{Y}$ ou might be surprised to find a chapter on performance in the foundations part of this book. However, we feel that performance is such a fundamental topic for enterprise CORBA that we decided this is the right place to discuss it. This chapter provides foundations that are required for our discussions in the following parts of the book.

We occasionally hear the myth that CORBA performs poorly. The problem is that developers often forget about the complexity of the underlying network and distribution infrastructure that CORBA allows us to abstract from; this complexity is not going away. CORBA provides a powerful abstraction mechanism, which is extremely important and helpful, but it doesn't mean that building large-scale, high-performance, distributed systems becomes a trivial task. Abstraction is one of the main benefits of CORBA, since it allows the developer to concentrate on business functionality and not on system-level functionality. However, abstraction does not mean that we can totally ignore that underneath the abstraction layer we are dealing with complex, distributed systems. Naive CORBA IDL can lead to poor performance and poor scalability. The first part of this chapter looks at the performance implications of IDL interface design. The second part looks at performance engineering in a CORBA environment from a more general perspective.

Performance Implications of IDL Design

Designing interfaces for distributed objects requires more sensitivity to performance issues than designing interfaces for objects that reside in a single address space. Obviously, a simple in-memory method invocation outperforms a CORBA remote method invocation by orders of magnitude—this is not very surprising. From a CORBA point of view, the following factors have a strong influence on the performance of a distributed system:

- The number of remote method invocations that are made within the system.
- The amount of data that is transferred with each remote method invocation.
- The marshalling costs of the different IDL data types used by the system.

In the following sections, we explore how these different factors affect the performance of a distributed CORBA system. For example, in a standard LAN environment, the number of remote invocations will often have the greatest impact. In a high-speed network with low latency, the mar-shalling costs might become more pronounced. This section does not give precise performance fig-ures, since these will be different for each individual configuration of hardware, network, operating system, programming language, and object request broker. Rather, this section attempts to help you understand the extent to which particular IDL designs influence the performance of a CORBA sys-tem. Therefore, the performance graphs and charts in this section do not show concrete figures, but rather performance characteristics.

Access Patterns

CORBA IDL interface design differs from designing interfaces for traditional, monolithic object models, where all objects reside in a single process space. In a distributed environment, we must carefully consider the anticipated object access patterns. Each remote method invoca-tion adds a constant performance overhead. An IDL design that ignores this fact can lead to very poor performance. Because of the overhead of each remote method invocation, we must try to keep the number of remote method invocations to a level that ensures we get the performance we need.

In the following, we use an example to illustrate the problems. Recall our description of the Port-folio Manager component in Chapter 4. We want to design IDL interfaces that export the Portfolio Manager's object model as described in Figure 4.6. A client application will access the Portfolio Man-ager component enabling the customers to access their portfolios via a GUI.

First Version of Portfolio Manager IDL

Ignoring access patterns and distribution aspects, a straightforward interface design for port-folios and holdings might be as follows:

```
// CORBA IDL (first version of portfolio example):

#include <StockWatch.idl>

interface Holding;
typedef sequence<Holding> HoldingSeq;

interface Portfolio {
    Money getCurrentValue ();
    HoldingSeq getHoldings ();
};

interface Holding {
    unsigned long getNumberOfShares ();
    Stock getStock ();
};
```

Our Portfolio Manager GUI displays a list of all stocks that are held by the actual portfolio. The function that displays the list of symbols must get a list of all holdings, and then the symbol for each holding's stock. Let's assume that our GUI is implemented in Java, using a Java ORB to access the remote objects. The function that retrieves and displays all symbols could be implemented like the following:

```
// First version of Java code for Portfolio Manager GUI

public void displaySymbols (_PortfolioRef thePortfolio)
{
    HoldingSeq holdings = thePortfolio.getHoldings ();
    for (int idx=0; idx<holdings.length; idx++) {
      String symbol =
      holdings.buffer[idx].getStock().getSymbol(); // (1)
      holdingList.add (symbol);
    }
}
```

It is important to notice that each time the `for` loop executes **(1)**, we are making two remote invocations: `getStock()` and `getSymbol()`. This is shown in Figure 5.1. The problem with this

Figure 5.1 Access pattern of first `displaySymbols()` version

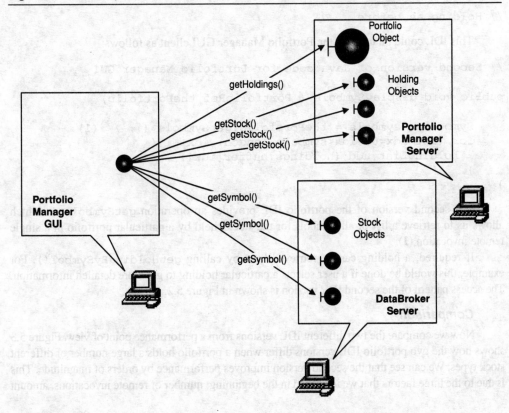

approach is that for a portfolio holding N stocks, we have 1 + 2*N remote method invocations. Recall that each remote invocation adds a considerable overhead. If we expect our portfolios to hold only a few stocks each, this is not a problem. But if portfolios hold large numbers of different stock types, a system with the above design will suffer from poor response time.

Second Version of Portfolio Manager IDL

The following change in the Portfolio interface drastically changes the access pattern of our portfolio manager client:

```
// CORBA IDL (second version of portfolio example):

#include <StockWatch.idl>

interface Holding;

interface Portfolio {
    Money getCurrentValue ();
    SymbolSeq getSymbols ();
    Holding getHoldingBySymbol (in Symbol aSymbol);
};

// Holding as before ...
```

This IDL could be used by the Portfolio Manager GUI client as follows:

```
// Second version of Java code for Portfolio Manager GUI

public void displaySymbols (_PortfolioRef thePortfolio)
{
    SymbolSeq symbols = thePortfolio.getSymbols (); // (1)
    for (int idx=0; idx<symbols.length; idx++) {
      holdingList.add (holdings.buffer[idx]);
    }
}
```

The second version of the portfolio IDL provides an operation getSymbols(), which allows us to retrieve a list of all symbols for the stocks held by a particular portfolio in a single remote invocation (1).

If required, a holding can be retrieved later by calling getHoldingBySymbol(). For example, this would be done if a user selects a particular holding to get more detailed information. The access pattern of the second IDL version is shown in Figure 5.2.

Comparison

Now we compare the two different IDL versions from a performance point of view. Figure 5.3 shows how the two portfolio IDL versions differ when a portfolio holds a large number of different stock types. We can see that the second version improves performance by orders of magnitude. This is due to the three factors that we identified in the beginning: number of remote invocations, amount

Figure 5.2   Access pattern of second `displaySymbols()` version

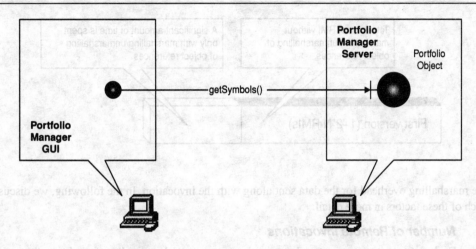

Figure 5.3   Comparing the two versions of `displaySymbols()`

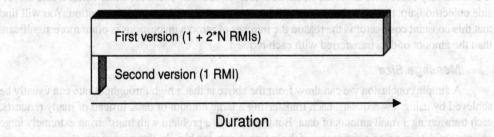

Duration

of data transferred with each remote invocation, and the data types of the request arguments. We have already noted that the first version issues 1+2*N remote invocations per `displaySym-bols()`, compared to one remote invocation in the second version. What about the amount of data? In both versions, we transfer the same number of symbols (`string`), but in the first version we also transfer 2*N object references (`Holding`, `Stock`). Not only are we transferring a larger amount of data, we are also transferring a data type which has a higher cost for marshalling: the marshalling costs for object references are significantly higher than for simple data types. Figure 5.4 shows a breakdown of the costs for the first version of `displaySymbols()`. Later, we will discuss the marshalling overhead for different IDL data types in more detail.

Critical Factors that Impact Performance

The three factors that have the most impact on the performance of a CORBA application are the number of remote invocations, the amount of data transferred with each remote invocation, and

Figure 5.4   Breakdown of costs for first version of `displaySymbols()`

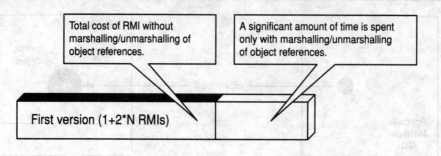

the marshalling overhead for the data sent along with the invocation. In the following, we discuss each of these factors in more detail.

Number of Remote Invocations

Each request sent over a network connection imposes a delay, usually referred to as "network latency." This delay adds a considerable amount of time for the processing of each CORBA remote invocation, especially in TCP/IP networks. The network latency imposed by each request and reply is not the only cost factor involved in each remote invocation. There are other factors, like server-side object-lookup, that contribute to a constant cost factor for each remote invocation. You will find that this constant cost factor is the reason the number of remote invocations is often more significant than the amount of data transferred with each request.

Message Size

A simple conclusion we can draw from the above is that a high throughput rate can usually be achieved by using few requests, each transferring a large amount of data, instead of many requests, each transferring a small amount of data. But there is also a problem with transferring extremely large amounts of data in a single message—if the message gets too big, the throughput rate decreases again. Reasons for this decrease in throughput include TCP buffering issues and growing process sizes.

Figure 5.5 shows the dependency between the average message size of a system and the average throughput of a system. This diagram looks different from network to network, especially when comparing WANs and LANs, low-speed and high-speed networks. Other factors also play an important role—for example, the configuration of IP buffer sizes.[1] As a general abstraction, however, in most networks the throughput curve has three characteristic sections:

Section	Message Size	Throughput
I	Small	Low
II	Relatively large	High
III	Extremely high	Low

---

[1] A number of excellent papers on CORBA performance can be found at Douglas Schmidt's homepage at the Department of Computer Science of the Washington University in St. Louis (http://www.cs.wustl.edu)

Figure 5.5   Dependency between data throughput and message size

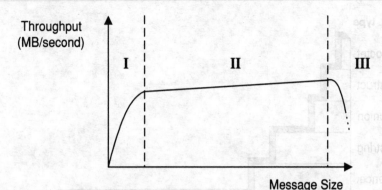

Marshalling Overhead for Different IDL Data Types

Figure 5.6 compares the relative costs for marshalling and unmarshalling several different CORBA data types (for the remainder of this section, we subsume marshalling and unmarshalling costs under the term "marshalling overhead"). The relative costs shown in this figure will be different for different ORBs, programming languages, operating systems, hardware platforms, and network types. The diagram is intended only to help you understand the order of magnitude of the relative costs for marshalling different IDL data types. The following briefly discusses each data type:

- **Octet.** An octet is the simplest data type CORBA IDL provides. The marshalling overhead for an octet is very small. An ORB is not even responsible for the byte ordering of an octet.
- **Struct.** A struct is also very simple, therefore the marshalling overhead is quite small. Obviously, the marshalling overhead of a struct is determined by the types of the struct's members. The diagram indicates the overhead for the struct itself, not for any data contained in the struct.
- **Union.** Unions are slightly more complex than structs, since they can store different types of values. Therefore, the marshalling overhead is usually slightly greater than for a struct. The cost for marshalling a union depends on the type of the data contained in the union. This diagram indicates only the overhead for the union itself.
- **String.** A string is a variable-length data type. The problem with variable-length data types is that they usually involve costly memory management operations. For example, when copying a sequence of strings, the ORB can not pre-allocate the memory for all the strings at once, but must allocate memory individually for each string. In general, you will find that variable-length data types are more expensive than constant-length data types.
- **Sequence.** A sequence is not only a variable-length data type, it can also store complex IDL types. Again, the marshalling overhead for a sequence depends on the type of the sequence's elements.

Figure 5.6   Relative costs for marshalling/unmarshalling different IDL data types

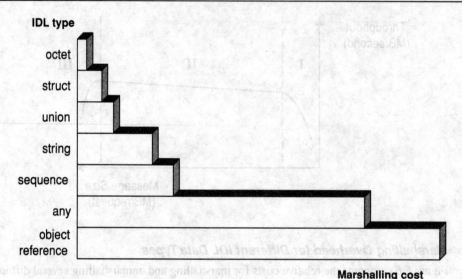

- **Any.** The type any is the most complex basic data type provided by IDL, since it is essentially a dynamic type and has to handle dynamic type codes during marshalling and unmarshalling. The marshaling cost for type any depends heavily on the programming language (some languages are better suited to supporting dynamic types than others) and the ORB implementation. In general, an any is significantly more expensive than other basic data types.
- **Object reference.** Object references provide a powerful abstraction mechanism. They encapsulate information such as host addresses and object identifiers, and mappings to active network connections. The price of this abstraction is the relatively high marshalling overhead for object references. Often, the unmarshalling of object references on the receiver side is especially costly because it involves the creation of proxy objects.

As we can see, the choice of IDL data types significantly influences the performance behavior of a system. Highly structured data results in increased marshalling and unmarshalling costs. Not only does the time for marshalling increase; the size of the message that represents the data increases as well. The marshalling routines need to add information about the structure of the data, so that the unmarshalling routines can recreate the original structure from the flat message.

Design Examples

In the following we apply these performance considerations to some examples. The first explains the concept of secondary OIDs, and the second discusses recursive data structures.

Using Secondary Object Identifiers

If our IDL interface provides an operation which returns, for example, a sequence of object references, we must understand the consequences. If we anticipate that an operation will usually return a small or moderate number of object references, there is no problem. But if the operation returns a large number of object references, this will most likely result in poor performance. First, the marshalling overhead for object references is considerable. Second and even worse, the transfer of a large number of object references is often followed by a large number of remote method invocations, since the receiver of the object references may use each of them in turn.

Instead of returning large numbers of object references, it is often a better idea to use a combination of secondary object identifiers (OIDs) and data structures. A secondary object identifier is some IDL data type that uniquely identifies a CORBA object, *often relative to another CORBA object*. For example, in our StockWatch IDL, we use stock symbols as secondary OIDs which identify holdings relative to a portfolio. Instead of returning a large number of object references, we return the secondary OIDs and provide a method such as getStockBySymbol () to allow a client to obtain a CORBA object reference in exchange for a secondary OID.

But this alone does not solve the problem. Often, an operation which returns a large number of object references is used by a client for some sort of selection process. For example, the displaySymbols() function displays symbols to a user who then selects some of these symbols to get more details. To prevent the client from making invocations on all possible objects, we need to provide the client with enough information so that it can execute the selection process locally and continue processing with the few selected objects. It is often a good idea to return a data structure with enough information for the selection process, plus a secondary OID to identify the real object. Let's say we want to implement a system to manage employees. An employee is represented as a first-class CORBA object (that is, an object with an IDL interface). We need an administrator interface to select specific employees. Initially, this selection should be done using the employee's name, in combination with wildcards. Since names are not unique, and wildcards might match different names, the query result will most likely contain many employees. From this initial query result, a specific employee is selected, using title, first name, and last name.

```
// IDL
typedef unsigned long EmployeeID;
interface Employee;

struct EmployeeData {
    string m_title;
    string m_firstName;
    string m_lastName;
    EmployeeID m_id;
};
typedef sequence<EmployeeData> EmployeeDataSeq;
```

```
interface EmployeeAdmin
{
    EmployeeDataSeq queryUsingWildcard (in string name);
    Employee getEmployeeByID (in EmployeeID id);
};
```

The `EmployeeAdmin` interface allows the administrator to obtain data for a set of employees using wildcards, and then select a particular employee from the result set to continue processing with one particular employee object.

The first query result is represented as a sequence of data structures. Each data structure contains a secondary OID (`EmployeeID`), plus some additional information. The additional information is used for the selection process. This is very important: the query result contains sufficient information to execute the selection on the client side, so that no interaction with the server is required. Only when a particular employee is selected will the client retrieve the real employee object using `getEmployeeByID()`.

Recursive Data Structures

This example is based on shapes and diagrams; a diagram contains a collection of shapes. There are different types of shapes: a line has a start and end point; a compound shape is a collection of shapes. This is illustrated with the object model shown in Figure 5.7.

Figure 5.7   Recursive Class Hierarchy

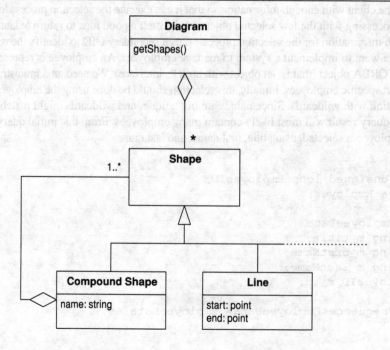

We have a simple inheritance hierarchy with a recursive aggregation: CompoundShape inherits from Shape on the one hand, and aggregates a set of Shape objects on the other.

Our task is to map this simple object model to IDL in a way that allows shapes to be transferred by value, that is, as data, not as object references. This means we should use IDL data types such as struct, union, or sequence. The IDL type interface cannot be used for shapes. The only interface in the example should be Diagram, which provides an operation getShapes(). This operation can be used by a client to obtain a sequence of shape values.

Mapping an object model to IDL data types rather than IDL interfaces is often a non-trivial task. The problem is that the following restrictions apply to IDL data types:

• IDL data types don't support inheritance
• IDL data types can't be used to describe recursive data structures[2]

We next explore workarounds for these problems. However, such workarounds can result in IDL that is not very clear or readable.

One approach to mapping an object model to IDL data types is to map the object model's classes to IDL structs. Using this approach, aggregation relationships can be mapped easily to IDL sequences. Mapping inheritance is more difficult. In general, inheritance in the object model can be mapped to aggregation on the IDL level. Often, this is done using the IDL type union. A base class is mapped to a struct with a member of type union, which can be used to store the attributes of any subclass. If the base class does not have any attributes, the base class can be directly mapped to a union. The second restriction is recursive type declarations. In the following example, we ignore this restriction resulting in invalid IDL:

```
// IDL : invalid version of shape example
struct CompoundShape {
    string           m_name;
    sequence<Shape>        m_shapes;                   // (1) Error!
};

struct Line {
    point m_start;
    point m_end;
};

union Shape switch (short) {
    case 1: Line          m_Line;
    case 2: CompoundShapem_CompoundShape;
};
```

The problem is that in (1) we use the type Shape, which hasn't been declared at this point in the IDL file. However, if we move the declaration for Shape to the top of the IDL, we would have a

---

[2] There is one exception to these recursive type declaration rules—it is possible to have a recursive type declaration in the new type itself—for example, if the new type is used as a sequence member. The following is an example for such a valid recursive type declaration: struct A { sequence<A> m_aSeq; };

similar problem, since Shape refers to the types Line and CompoundShape. We cannot use recursive type declarations in IDL, because IDL does not allow forward declarations of IDL data types. Forward declarations can only be used for IDL interfaces.

So how do we handle recursive data types? One approach would be to combine IDL data types and IDL interfaces. This would mean that some of our data would be transferred by value, whereas other data would only be accessible remotely. Often, this is not what we really want. Another approach is to use the generic IDL type any, which can represent any IDL type. The following example uses type any to solve the problem of recursive type declarations:

```
// CORBA IDL (first version of Shape example)
struct Shape {
    any m_details;                          // (2)
};

struct CompoundShape {
    string m_name;
    sequence<Shape> m_shapes;               // (3)
};

struct Line {
    point m_start;
    point m_end;
};
```

In (2) we add a field m_details of type any to the Shape struct. This field should always contain either a CompoundShape, or a Line. Since Shape is now a valid type, we can use it in the declaration of CompoundShape (3).

However, using the type any to solve the problem of recursive type declarations can have a significant impact on system performance; any is one of the most complex types, and therefore usually one of the most inefficient ones.

What can we do to optimize the efficiency of our IDL? The problem is not the number of type declarations in our IDL that use the type any. The problem is the number of anys that are transferred at runtime. In our example, let's assume that 90% of shapes are actually lines, and only 10% of the shapes are compound shapes. If we could find a way to map our object model to IDL so that only the compound shapes are mapped to type any, this would significantly increase the performance of our application. The following example shows how this could be done:

```
// IDL
struct Line {                               // (4)
    point start;
    point end;
};

union Shape switch (short) {                // (5)
    case 1: Line m_line;
    case 2: any m_CompoundShape;            // (6)
};
```

```
struct CompoundShape {
    string m_name;
    sequence<Shape> m_shapes;          // (7)
};
```

We start by declaring the data types which are leaf classes in our object model, but do not recursively refer back to the base class. In our example, this is only one class: Line (4). Next, we map the base class to an IDL union (5). This union has one member for each leaf class. Only those classes which refer back to the base class are mapped to type any (6). Finally, we can define these classes as normal structs, adding references back to the base class without problems (7).

The benefit of this solution is that we can now transfer shapes as sequences of unions, which contain normal structs in 90% of the cases. Only 10% of the sequence elements will contain an any. This will not necessarily increase performance by 90%, but it should help improve performance significantly.

All objects are equal, but some are more equal than others

Remember your first book on object orientation? Remember a discussion on how to find candidates for classes and methods? Remember instructions like *Write down your problem description. Underline nouns and verbs. Determine whether the nouns are good candidates for classes. Similarly, investigate the extent to which the verbs can be used as methods for your class candidates.* Over the years, you probably found out that there is no general-purpose solution to the problem of designing an object model, but that the process requires a lot of abstraction, intuition, and redrawing of existing class diagrams. With CORBA, the question arises as to which objects should become first-class CORBA citizens, and which ones not. This decision should be heavily influenced by the impact of IDL design on the performance of a system.

Remember your first program in an object-oriented language: a shape has a draw() method. A line and a circle inherit from a shape. We can iterate over a sequence of shapes, and invoke draw() on each shape. Soon, our screen starts to be filled with lines and circles. After our discussion of the impact of IDL design on a system's performance, it is obvious that mapping a fine-grained design, such as the one in this example, directly to CORBA interfaces would likely result in an implementation with very poor performance. That means that in the CORBA world we often have to change our old design strategies, and find new strategies for finding good CORBA objects. A Smalltalk programmer might wrinkle his nose, but it is a fact that in a CORBA world not each and every entity can become an object, at least not as long as the *object-by-value* specification is not commonly available (discussed later in this chapter). Even then, the question remains: which objects should be invoked remotely and which objects should be transferred by value?

That means the CORBA designer has to find a balance between good object-oriented design and performance requirements. You will find that in a CORBA world objects often have more of a "service" character; that is, they will often not provide fine-grained business objects, but rather an interface to manipulate them on the server side. Also, you will often find a combination of service objects and more fine-grained business objects: the service objects can be used to manipulate and select specific business objects, and once a particular object is selected, the client can proceed by working with the selected object directly. This means the service object provides services that can affect large numbers of finer-grained objects (for instance, queries) on the server side, to avoid having too many remote interactions. Therefore, try to find a compromise between the extremely fine-grained Smalltalk design approach and the extremely large-grained procedural approach. Often, you will find that IDL design is a tradeoff between semantic richness and performance.

The distributed nature of CORBA objects and the performance implications of IDL design have a significant impact on the object-oriented software development process. Throughout this book we identify other aspects that are also important from this perspective, and we describe the consequences for the object-oriented software development process in Chapter 18, "Consequences for the Engineering Process."

Transferring Large Amounts of Data

In our discussion on CORBA-related performance issues so far, we have seen that an ORB is not designed to act as a File Transfer Program (FTP)—that is, an ORB is not designed to transfer arbitrarily large amounts of data. However, we could easily use an ORB to build an FTP. In the following we look at aspects related to the transfer of large amounts of data using an ORB.

Iterators

When transferring large amounts of data, iterators are a relatively common technique to ensure optimal throughput (that is, ensure that a system operates in section II of the throughput graph described in Figure 5.5). An iterator allows you to iterate over a large set of data in chunks, instead of transferring the whole set of data in one chunk. Let's assume we want to add an operation queryPrices() to our StockWatch interface, which supports a query for historical stock prices. The result of this operation can potentially be very large. Instead of returning this data directly as a sequence of stock prices, we use an iterator. An example is shown in the following IDL.

```
// CORBA IDL (stock price iterator)

interface StockWatch {
    StockPriceIterator queryPrices(in QueryExpression aQuery);

    // Other operations as before…
};

interface StockPriceIterator {
    void getNextChunk (out StockPriceSeq nextChunk,
                       out boolean hasMore);
};
```

There are several benefits to this approach. First of all, we can optimize the average size of requests, ensuring that we get optimal throughput. Furthermore, iterators give clients control over when to receive data—for instance, the client can control the timing, potentially giving faster response to the end user. Note that the implementation of CORBA iterator objects is non-trivial, as we discuss in Chapter 14, "Managing Server Resources," in the Memory Management section.

Passing Objects by Value

Standard IDL data types have many restrictions that can make it difficult to handle complex data structures. Currently, the OMG is working on an extension to the CORBA specification to enable the passing of objects by value. This extension will introduce a new IDL type value, which provides a bridge from ordinary CORBA structs to CORBA interfaces. The new value type allows the representation of a complex state (that is, arbitrary graphs of objects, including recursion and cycles). Of course, a value type is always transferred by value. Values have no identity—their value is their identity. All valid CORBA types can be used as the types for the members of a value, and the members can be public or private. Single inheritance is provided for value types. A value type can also support a set of interfaces by inheriting from CORBA interface types. This means value types support single inheritance of value and multiple inheritance of interfaces. Values can be abstract.

Since a CORBA server cannot make any assumptions about the implementation language of a client (and vice versa), only the data part of a value object is transferred, not the implementation. The specification defines a policy for locating a compatible implementation within the receiving process. However, only structural compatibility is specified, no semantic guarantees are given. Operations defined in the value type, or inherited from a base value, are always executed locally. Operations inherited from an interface, or from an interface supported by a base value, are always executed remotely, that is on an object in the sending process. To ensure that values can be implemented efficiently, a value is not necessarily registered with the ORB. A value must be registered with the ORB only if it supports an interface. If an interface operation is invoked on a value and the value is not registered with the ORB, an OBJ_NOT_EXIST exception will be raised.

On one hand, the new object-by-value specification provides a standard solution to a problem that has been addressed up to now by proprietary streaming solutions, as described in the next section. However, the object-by-value approach violates the fundamental CORBA concept of encapsulation. Normally, an object's implementation is fully hidden from its clients. To transfer an object by value, however, the receiver of the object must be able to provide an implementation of the object. This breaks the object's encapsulation, which is one of the strengths of the CORBA architecture. For simple reasons like performance, it seems unlikely that any architecture for distributed object computing will ever be able to provide full location transparency, unless we are able to eliminate network latency. Objects-by-value could be a chance to increase location transparency—for example, by addressing performance issues like local vs. remote access. However, there is the danger that objects-by-value will complicate things for ORB vendors, IDL designers, server programmers, and even client programmers. It may even turn out that the decreased location transparency is counterproductive. But it remains to be seen what will happen when the first enterprise type of applications based on objects-by-value are built and deployed in the real world.

Proprietary Streaming Solutions

In addition to the CORBA objects-by-value specification, some proprietary solutions for passing objects by value exist. These implementations have been around for a while, they can be considered predecessors to the CORBA Objects-by-Value specification. Most of these proprietary streaming solutions are based on non-CORBA-compliant ORB features, like IONA Technologies' opaque datatype: if a type is declared as opaque, nothing about the type is known at the IDL level. Marshalling and unmarshalling routines for the opaque argument are not provided by the ORB, but must be provided by the proprietary streaming library or the application. The opaque type can be used to implement specialized marshalling and unmarshalling methods, for example to pass objects by value. There are some commercial implementations available for passing objects by value using the Orbix opaque extension. Two examples are Streaming<Toolkit> from Object Space (http://www.objectspace.com), and Tools.h++ from RogueWave (http://www.roguewave.com).

Audio/Video Streams

In our discussion of transferring data or objects by value, we use the term "streaming," meaning that we stream an object from the sender to the receiver. However, the term "stream" is also often used for continuous data streams, which are fundamentally different from the simple object-by-value transfer discussed before. The CORBA 3.0 specification will contain a specification for the control and management of streams. Although any kind of data could be streamed between two points, this specification focuses on audio and video streams, and related quality-of-service issues. The specification defines a stream as a continuous flow of data in a specific direction—that is, from a data source to a data sink.

The emphasis of the specification is not on defining new protocols for the actual data stream transfer. Rather, the specification focuses on providing an administrative framework for dealing with streams. The specification defines interfaces for streams and flows, operations to set up, modify, and release streams, and functions for dealing with quality of service. The intention is to have a generic framework for stream management that can be used with a variety of lower-level network protocols.

Summary

In this chapter we have looked at the three factors that have the strongest impact on the performance of a CORBA system: the frequency of remote invocations, the amount of data that passed, and the overhead of the different IDL data types. We also looked at the impact of different access patterns in a distributed system, and how IDL can be designed to result in access patterns for optimal performance.

We made some general quantitative statements about performance, using diagrams to set things into relationship. Obviously, it is difficult to make specific performance statements, because too many factors influence the performance behavior of a CORBA system, ranging from network and hardware infrastructure to programming language and quality of the ORB implementation.

Finally, we looked at ways of transferring large amounts of data in a CORBA environment, ranging from the new CORBA object-by-value specification to proprietary streaming solutions.

Core Services

This part of the book focuses on several important aspects of distributed object systems. These core services are central to many CORBA systems.

Chapter 6, "Object Location," explores how clients obtain objects. Every CORBA system must make objects available to clients, so an understanding of this topic is essential. Basically, servers publish object references to an object directory, and clients later look up objects in the directory. We discuss the different mechanisms that systems can use to accomplish this, and the strengths and weaknesses of each approach.

Chapter 7, "Messaging," discusses support for asynchronous, decoupled communication with CORBA. Normal CORBA invocations cause the client to block until a reply is received from the target object. Clients and servers are also tightly coupled, with a direct network connection between them. Sometimes, our systems require different behavior. We explore current and forthcoming support for such messaging features in CORBA.

Chapter 8, "Security," provides a working definition of security in a distributed system, and the many different levels that can be applied. After exploring the CORBA standards for security, we discuss practical applications of security with existing products.

Object Location

Every CORBA system must, somehow, answer the same question: how do client components obtain object references? There are many possible ways to answer this question, and each approach has its own set of strengths and weaknesses. Solutions can be simple to use but less flexible and scalable, or more powerful but more complex. Likewise, solutions can be proprietary to a specific ORB implementation or CORBA-compliant. The ideal approach would allow a client to easily obtain a reference to an arbitrary object on an arbitrary host, be CORBA-compliant, and be flexible enough to scale up to large CORBA systems.

In this chapter, we first introduce a model of how clients obtain references to objects in servers. Then, we discuss the CORBA-compliant approaches to obtaining object references, as well as touching on some ORB-specific mechanisms. Each of these mechanisms has its own set of strengths and weaknesses, and is best applied in different situations.

A Model for Locating Objects

There are three steps involved in making objects available to clients, as shown in Figure 6.1. This abstract model sets the stage for our discussion on the practical mechanisms that can be used to locate objects.

Figure 6.1   Exporting and locating objects

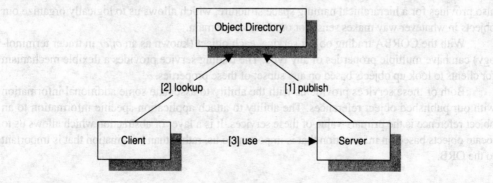

This model is made up of several pieces. *Server* and *client* are our familiar application components, which implement and use our business objects, respectively. The third component is the *object directory*. This piece is responsible for storing object references, along with some descriptive data that can optionally be associated with the reference. For example, the CORBA naming service is an object directory which stores object references, associating them with a name. Likewise, the CORBA trading object service is an object directory which stores object references, associating them with a set of properties. Even something as simple as an object reference string stored in a configuration file follows this model.

To locate objects, our systems perform the following steps. First, the server publishes a number of objects to the directory, providing some attributes that identify the object in a meaningful way. Next, clients look up objects in the directory. Clients provide a set of desired attributes to the directory so that it can return a set of matching objects. Once a client has obtained one or more objects from the directory, it can begin using them.

The details of how a server publishes objects, and how clients look up objects is, of course, specific to a particular object directory. Likewise, the number and type of the attributes associated with an object is specific to each concrete object directory implementation.

What is an Object Reference?

What exactly is it that these directories are storing? Our servers are not actually publishing objects to the directory, rather they are publishing *object references*. A reference contains the IDL type of the object, as well as enough information for an ORB to be able to find the target object in its server process on its host. When a client obtains an object reference from the directory, the ORB turns this into a local programming language object—a proxy—which the client application code uses to make invocations on the remote target object.

CORBA Object Location Services

The CORBA specification introduces several instances of object directories. The CORBA naming service and the CORBA trading object service are the most commonly used, and provide different levels of flexibility and complexity for object publication and lookup.

The CORBA naming service stores a name with each object reference. The naming service also provides for a hierarchical naming space structure, which allows us to logically organize our objects in whatever way makes sense for our business domain.

With the CORBA trading object service, each object (known as an *offer* in trader terminology) can have multiple properties of any type. The trading service provides a flexible mechanism for clients to look up objects based on any subset of these properties.

Both of these services provide us with the ability to associate some additional information with our published object references. The ability to attach application-specific information to an object reference is the primary value of these services. It is a layer of abstraction which allows us to locate objects based on information that is important to us, rather than information that is important to the ORB.

The CORBA Naming Service

The CORBA naming service is a simple example of an object directory. It stores objects references in a hierarchical structure much like a Unix-style file system, so many of the concepts are familiar to us. Each object reference has a *name* associated with it. A name consists of two string fields, *id* and *kind*. Conceptually, these correspond to a file-system filename and extension. The hierarchy is made up of *naming contexts*, which can contain object references as well as other naming contexts. In this sense, they correspond to directories in a file system. A naming context can store multiple object references, which must be differentiated by either the id or kind fields of the name structure. A simple naming service hierarchy is shown in Figure 6.2.

Our root naming context object contains two elements, both of which are naming contexts. Each of these elements has a name associated with it; one is "StockWatch," and the other is "PortfolioManager." (In this example, we only use the id part of the name, and don't use the kind field). The "StockWatch" naming context contains two elements, "NASDAQ" and "NYSE," both of which are application object references that our server has published.

Notice that the naming contexts shown in Figure 6.2 have the T-bar notation, which indicates that they are CORBA objects. This is, in fact, how our application components use the naming service—they make invocations on naming context objects. Naming contexts support a number of operations, only two of which are important for this discussion. Pictorially, this is shown in Figure 6.3. The IDL for these methods is shown below. (For a full introduction to the naming service IDL, see the CORBA specification, or your naming service programmer's guide).

Figure 6.2 Sample Naming Service Hierarchy

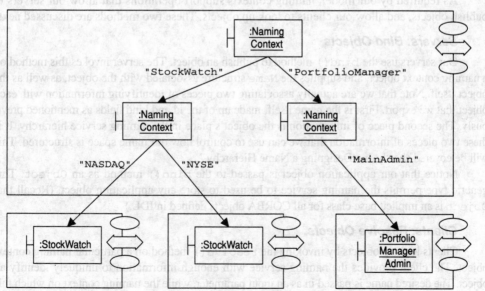

Figure 6.3 Naming Service Class Diagram

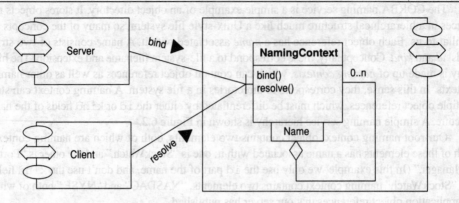

```
// IDL Fragment : CORBA Naming Service
// Simplified IDL : exceptions and typedefs omitted
interface NamingContext
{
     void bind(in Name n, in Object obj);

     Object resolve (in Name n);

// other methods not shown...
}
```

As required by our model, naming contexts support operations that allow our servers to publish objects, and allow our clients to look up objects. These two methods are discussed next.

Servers: Bind Objects

Our servers use the `bind()` method to publish an object. The server invokes this method on a naming context object, and supplies the `Name` structure associated with the object, as well as the object itself. Note that we are actually associating two pieces of identifying information with each object that we export. First is the name itself, made up of the id and kind fields as mentioned previously. The second piece of information is the object's place in the naming service hierarchy. It is these two pieces of information that we can use to control how our name space is structured. This will be covered shortly, in "Designing a Name Hierarchy."

Notice that our application object is passed to the `bind()` method as an `Object`. This generic type permits the naming service to be used to store any application object. (Recall that `Object` is an implicit base class for all CORBA objects defined in IDL.)

Clients: Resolve Objects

Clients look up objects by invoking the `resolve()` method on a particular naming context object. The client provides the naming service with enough information to uniquely identify an object. The desired name is passed in as an input parameter, while the naming context on which this method is invoked determines the place in the hierarchy from which the service will perform the lookup. If a matching object is found, it is returned as a generic `Object`. The client application simply narrows this to the appropriate application object, then uses it.

Designing a Name Hierarchy

In making use of the naming service, the first thing to focus on is the structure of the hierarchy itself. We can make it as deep or wide as necessary, depending on our business requirements. We can also choose how to use the `id` and `kind` fields of our entries in the naming service. Applying these two aspects lets us arrange our hierarchy in any number of ways. Generally, we will use the hierarchical structure to separate logically distinct objects, while related objects will be grouped together and distinguished by their unique names.

Let's briefly explore an example. Imagine that each StockWatch server application implements two interfaces. One is our familiar `StockWatch` interface, which implements our business logic. The other is `ServerManager`, which is a management and instrumentation interface. This is used by a system administration application to observe and control the server processes as they are running.

One possible structure for our name hierarchy is shown in Figure 6.4. In order to simplify our name hierarchy diagrams, we will avoid using the formal notation. Instead, we'll use the simpler format shown below. Each context and object is simply denoted by its name, in an `id.kind` string format. The leaf nodes of the hierarchy are the object references.

Here, we have chosen to have a flat hierarchy, with two object references with `id` *NASDAQ* in the *StockWatch* naming context. These references are differentiated by their `kind` field. Likewise, there are two *NYSE* references in the naming context, one reference for each of the interfaces supported by our server process.

Alternatively, we could have chosen not to use the `kind` field at all. In this case, we would have a deeper name hierarchy, with a naming context for each of the stock exchanges. Each of these contexts would contain the two exported objects. This is shown in Figure 6.5.

Figure 6.4 Flat Name Hierarchy

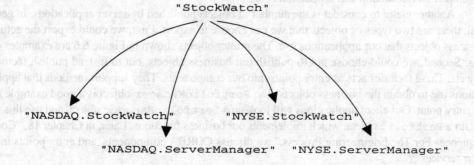

Figure 6.5 Deep name hierarchy

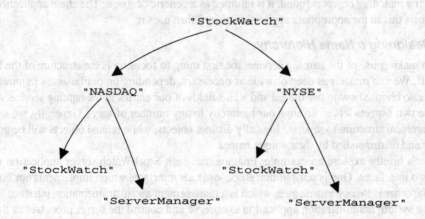

When designing a name hierarchy, there are a number of factors to be considered. First, consider the complexity of your applications, and the domain that this name hierarchy will cover. Obviously, a hierarchy for a single departmental application can be much simpler than one for a collection of applications spanning the enterprise. Also think about the intended usage of the hierarchy. Is the structure of the hierarchy going to be exposed to end users through an application? Or, will the hierarchy only be accessed by the application program and administrators? This factor will often determine whether a hierarchy is made up of many contexts with descriptive names, or fewer contexts with names in a standard format.

For instance, two potential hierarchies are shown in Figures 6.6 and 6.7. The first is well-suited for browsing by end users. We could easily imagine an application that browses the hierarchy and lets users choose the printer they wish to use. Compare this to the second hierarchy, which is much more compact. This structure is better used for applications that hide the structure from end users. The application may be configured once by an administrator to use a particular printer, so that these names are not visible to end users. The structure in Figure 6.7 is simpler, so that it can be used by simpler administration and application code.

Another factor to consider is the number of objects published by server applications. In general, there are two types of objects that we can choose to export. First, we could export the actual business objects that our applications use. The printer objects shown in Figure 6.6 are examples of this. Second, we could choose not to publish our business objects, but to instead publish factory objects. These factories acts as entry points into our components. They support methods that applications use to obtain the business objects. The `PortfolioManager` object is a good example of an entry point. Our client applications will look up a `PortfolioManager` object, and use this to obtain a `Portfolio` object, which implements our business functions. Later, in Chapter 18, "Consequences For The Engineering Process," we discuss CORBA components, and entry points into their services.

Figure 6.6   Descriptive naming hierarchy

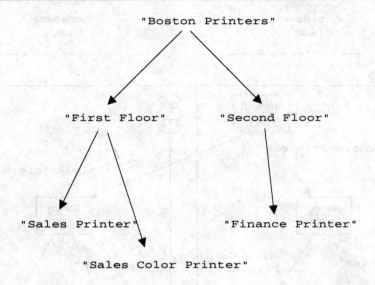

Figure 6.7   Compact naming hierarchy

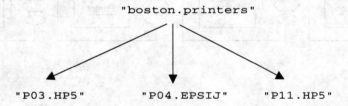

One additional factor to be considered is the quality of service required by a naming structure. This is especially important if you intend to use the structure to store large numbers of objects, or very complex hierarchies. Once you have designed your hierarchy, evaluate the capabilities of your naming service. Consider the persistent storage mechanisms supported—does it use a file-based system, or is it connected to an industrial-strength database? Evaluate its performance with the intended numbers of contexts and objects. Does it meet your performance requirements? Consider its robustness—does it support replication of its data store, for instance? Make sure that the product you choose meets your needs.

When designing a name hierarchy, also consider the naming service's ability to federate (that is, link) name hierarchies together. Recall that naming contexts are simply objects, implemented in a particular CORBA server. When you insert a naming context into a hierarchy, you actually supply

Figure 6.8   Federated name hierarchies

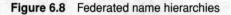

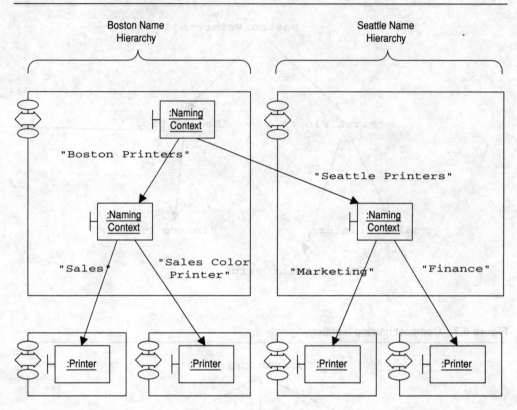

a reference to the new naming context. Typically, this new context is implemented in the same server as the containing context. However, because these are simply CORBA object references, the naming context can in fact be implemented in another naming service process. An example of federation is shown in Figure 6.8.

   This example shows our Boston naming hierarchy linked to another hierarchy in our Seattle office. These hierarchies are stored by two separate naming service implementations, running on separate hosts. By federating them, we can provide transparent access to multiple hierarchies. In this example, our Boston-based end users can easily use a printer in the Seattle office, by simply navigating to the naming context named "Seattle Printers."

   Federating naming hierarchies allows us to provide global access to objects, while still maintaining local control of these objects. As long as these two offices agree on the structure and format of the namespace, we'll be able to easily and transparently share services across the organization.

The CORBA Trading Object Service

The CORBA trading object service provides us with a powerful, flexible means of publishing and looking up our objects. When our servers publish objects, they associate any number of properties of any type with the object. When clients perform a lookup, they specify a set of desired properties. The trader evaluates this lookup query, and returns a set of matching objects.

Unlike a name hierarchy, the trader's object directory is not structured in any formal way. Instead, the trading service is based on the concept of a *service type*. A service type contains an IDL interface identifier, as well as some additional data defining the attributes that can be associated with this type. Before our servers can actually publish any objects, we must properly define the number and type of attributes that can be associated with objects of this type. Once we have defined a service type, our servers publish objects of this type. In trader terminology, this is known as *exporting a service offer*. Servers export an object reference, along with attributes that identify this particular service offer. These offers must follow the format described by a previously defined service type. The collection of offers exported by servers to a trader makes up its *trading space*.

Clients look up objects in the trading space by performing a *query*. Clients specify a service type, as well as a set of desired properties and constraints. The trading service evaluates the supplied criteria and returns an ordered set of matching objects.

The trading object service IDL is complex, and we do not fully explain it here. Instead, we will work with an abstraction of the IDL, which is simpler to explain and conceptually provides the same set of operations. For a fully detailed explanation, see the CORBA specification or your trading object service programming guide.

Figure 6.9 illustrates our application components' use of the trading service. The simplified IDL shown below contains the essential arguments for each of the methods implemented by the trader.

Figure 6.9 Trading Object Service Diagram

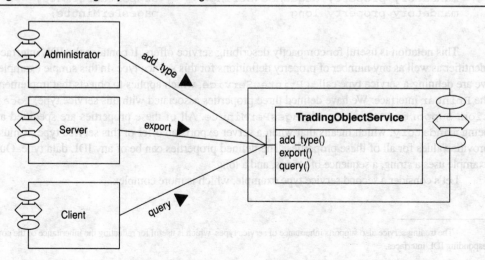

```
// pseudo-IDL
interface TradingService
{
    // define a new service type
    serviceTypeID add_type(in string serviceTypeName,
                       in string IDLInterfaceIdentifier,
                       in propertyDefinitionSeq definedProperties);
    // publish an offer to the trader
    offerId export(in Object reference,
                   in string serviceTypeName,
                   in propertySeq properties);

    // look up one or more matching offers
    void query (in string serviceTypeName,
              in string constraint,
              in specifiedProperties propertiesToReturn,
              out offerSeq offers);
};
```

Administrator: Define Service Types

When using the trading service, the first step is to define the service types that will be supported. Each service type corresponds to a single IDL interface[1] and defines the set of attributes that can be used to describe this service offer. Let's examine a simple example. This uses the simple service type notation from the OMG CORBA trading object service specification. (Note that this is not IDL, but is just a convenient notation for specifying service types.)

```
service PrinterService {
    interface Printer;
    mandatory property string              location;
    mandatory property sequence<string>    supportedFormats;
    mandatory property long                pagesPerMinute;
};
```

This notation is useful for compactly describing service offers. It contains the IDL interface identifier as well as any number of property definitions for this service type. In this simple example, we are defining a service type called PrinterService, which applies to objects that implement the Printer interface. We have defined three properties associated with this service type, location, supportedFormats, and pagesPerMinute. All of these properties are specified as being mandatory, which means that when a server exports an offer of this service type, it must provide values for all of these properties. The defined properties can be of any IDL data type. Our example uses a string, a sequence of strings, and a long.

Let's consider a second service type example, which is more complex.

---

[1] The trading service also supports inheritance of service types, which is useful for reflecting the inheritance of the corresponding IDL interfaces.

```
service CompanyResearchService {
    interface Company;
    mandatory property string                companyName;
    mandatory property sequence<string>         sectors;
            property float                currentStockPrice;
};
```

Here, we have defined a service type called CompanyResearchService. This service type is used to describe objects that implement the IDL interface Company. This service type has defined a number of properties, of varying IDL types. One of these properties is not defined as mandatory, which means that offers exported by servers are not required to provide a value for this property. So far, all the properties we have mentioned are *static properties*. A static property has a value provided for it at the time the server exports its offer. For instance, when our server exports a PrinterService offer, it will provide values for the location and supportedFormats properties.

The trading service also supports *dynamic properties*. Rather than supplying a value when the offer is exported, our server instead supplies a callback object. Only when a client performs a query will the trader obtain a value for this property. It does so by making an invocation on this callback object. The server that exported this offer must determine the property's value current value, and return it.

Dynamic properties are very useful when we have attributes that we decide are important for our clients to be able to query on, but happen to frequently change in value. In this example, the currentStockPrice property is a dynamic property. Our client application needs to be able to find companies based on their stock price. Since a company's stock price changes frequently, dynamic properties allow us to perform this query, in a standard, efficient manner.[2]

Servers: Export Offers

Once our administrator has defined the service types that will be used by our applications, our servers can export their objects to the trading service. Servers accomplish this by invoking the export() method on an object in the trading service, supplying an object, a string identifying the service type, and a sequence of properties.

The object is, of course, an object that implements a particular IDL interface. In particular, it must implement the interface associated with the specified service type.[3] The server also provides a sequence of properties, which are name-value structures. Each property name must match a property name defined in the specified service type. The server must also supply a value for each of the properties. This value is either a concrete value (for static properties), or a callback object (for dynamic properties).

The trader, of course, imposes some consistency checks on offers. In particular, it verifies that the exported object is of an appropriate type, and that values have been supplied for all the mandatory properties.

---

[2] Interestingly, dynamic properties are not specified as such at the time of service type definition. Instead, this is specified when each offer is exported by a server. Any property can be a dynamic property if the exporting server chooses to implement it as such. Therefore, a single property could have a static value supplied for it in one offer, and support dynamic evaluation in another offer.

[3] The exported object can also be of a type that inherits from the service type's interface.

Clients: Query for Matching Offers

This final step is to have our clients look up objects in the trading service. Clients of the trader invoke a `query()` method on an object in the trader, supplying a number of parameters. First, the client specifies the desired service type. This must match a service type previously defined by the administrator. Recall that a service type defines a set of property names and data types. When servers export offers, they supply values for some (or all) of these properties. Our clients query this set of exported offers by supplying a set of constraints. The trading service evaluates this query and finds a set of offers that match the specified constraints. These offers are returned to the client.

Unlike the name service (which can only return a single object reference as the result of a lookup), the trading service is designed to return multiple offers from a single query. These offers contain not just the object reference, but also some (or all) of the offer's properties. Rather than having the trader automatically returning all of an offer's (potentially many) properties, clients have complete control over the set of properties that are returned with the matching offers.

Let's examine the parameters to `query()` in more detail. The constraint string specified by the client is conceptually similar to a SQL WHERE clause. It specifies the required values for properties against which all offers of a particular service type are to be filtered. This string follows a format specified by the OMG, as part of the trading object service specification. Let's take a look at an sample constraint string, from a case where our client is querying for a `PrinterService` offer:

```
(location == 'first floor') and (pagesPerMinute > 10)
```

This constraint string searches for offers that are on the first floor, and can print more than 10 pages per minute.

Here's another sample constraint string, where our client is querying on the `CompanyResearchService` offers:

```
('airline' in sectors) and (currentStockPrice < 100.00)
```

This query searches for companies in the airline sector, with a current stock price of less than 100.00.

This constraint language provides a flexible mechanism that allows our clients to specify an arbitrarily complex set of criteria for the trader to use to filter the offers.

The client also specifies a list of properties which should be returned by the trader. Recall that the trader returns a sequence of matching offers to the client. This allows the client to further qualify the matching offers before it begins using one. For example, information about the matching offers could be presented to a user, who would then choose the appropriate target. Or, the application could look at the returned values and perform some additional processing on them before determining which offer to use. Rather than having the trader automatically return the values for all of an offer's properties, the client supplies a `specifiedProperties` type. This union contains an enumerated type indicating whether the client wants all of an offer's properties, none of the properties, or some of the properties. If the client wants some of the properties, it specifies which ones by passing in a sequence of property name strings.

The trader returns a sequence of offers to the client. Each offer contains the object reference, as well as a (possibly empty) sequence of name-value pairs, for the requested properties.

Designing a Trading Space

Designing a trading space is primarily a matter of defining service types. Evaluate the ways in which your client applications need to be able to find objects, and define service types made up of those properties. Then, your servers simply export offers, and your clients query the trading service for matches. The trading service does the heavy lifting.

One factor to consider is, of course, the logical and geographical separation of your components. Applications may best be serviced by traders that are close to them, logically or physically. However, a single trader can only return matches from the set of offers that have been directly exported to that trader instance. To overcome this limitation, the trading service supports *linked traders*. When traders are linked together, they can forward client queries to other traders, to find additional matching offers. This *link follow behavior* is determined by both the trader's configuration and some additional options supplied by the client when it performs a query. By linking traders together (also known as *federating*), we form a graph of linked traders. By federating traders across domains, we can provide a wide variety of services to our clients.

Federation depends, of course, on a standardized set of service types. All the linked traders must agree on the precise naming conventions for service types, IDL interfaces, and property names. Today, such an agreement is only likely within a particular organization. However, as the commercial acceptance of CORBA becomes even more widespread, we envision standardized trading spaces defined for entire industry domains.

Other Ways to Locate Objects

In addition to using CORBA services to locate objects, there are other ways to accomplish this as well. We first mention using object reference strings, which is a CORBA-compliant approach that fits into our object location model. Then, we discuss factory pattern. Factories are simply objects that return other objects. This pattern is commonly used throughout CORBA, and is very effective. Next, we cover ORB-specific approaches. These proprietary mechanisms are useful, but are often limited in ways that the CORBA services are not. Finally, we discuss the issue of bootstrapping, which is a CORBA-compliant way for an object to obtain a reference to one of the CORBA services.

Using Object Reference Strings

Another CORBA-compliant way of obtaining object references is to use object reference strings. The CORBA specification requires that ORBs support the COBRA::ORB::object_to_string() method. This method *stringifies* the supplied object reference, converting it into a standard string format. A client application invokes the CORBA::ORB::string_to_object() method, and the ORB converts this string back into an object reference.

This approach follows our model for locating objects, although the object directory in this case is not a service, but rather just a container chosen by the application designer. Our server publishes its objects by stringifying them, and writing the string to some output location. Logically, these stringified object references are stored in an object directory. In practice, these tend to be stored in client-side configuration files or shell scripts. Client applications look up objects by retrieving the string from its storage location and converting it back into an object reference.

Of course, our client and server programmers must agree on how these object reference strings are managed. When a server writes an object reference to a file, for instance, client developers must know what this file is called, and what object is denoted by the reference contained in it. They must then transfer this string to the client application, which must use it appropriately. This administrative coordination is comparable to that required when using the naming or trading services. In both those instances, client and server developers must agree on the structure and names of entities as well.

Using Factory Objects

A commonly used pattern in CORBA systems is that of the factory object. A factory is any object that returns a reference to another object as the result of a method invocation. We've already seen an example of a factory object—the PortfolioManager object in our Portfolio Manager. It's important to note that factory objects are not just used for creating new CORBA objects, but can also be used to return references to existing CORBA objects. This is demonstrated in the PortfolioManager IDL, part of which is shown below.

```
// IDL fragment from PortfolioManager
interface PortfolioManager
{
    // This method creates and returns a new Portfolio
    // object
    Portfolio newPortfolio(in string id,
                           in string password);

    // This method returns a reference to an
    // existing Portfolio object
    Portfolio login(in string id,
                    in string password);
}
```

Factory objects are extremely useful, especially when there are a large number of objects that clients can use. Rather than publishing references to all the servant objects, the server can publish just a few factory objects, which the client then uses to obtain references to the remaining objects that it needs. Note that factories are also useful for reducing the number of objects that have to be active in a server process at one time. Rather than eagerly instantiating all possible objects, factories allow the server programmer to defer the instantiation of an object until clients explicitly request it. Both of these benefits make factories important for most large-scale CORBA systems.

In the IDL shown above, the factory returns an object of a specific type, a Portfolio. A common alternative to this is to have the factory return an object of the generic type Object. This is the approach taken, for example, by the naming service IDL. It allows a factory to return object references of arbitrary types, at the cost of requiring the caller to perform a _narrow() on the returned reference.

ORB-Specific Approaches

In addition to supporting the compliant methods specified by CORBA, commercial ORBs will typically also support a proprietary mechanism for locating objects. These mechanisms tend to be very simple to use, and are appealing from that perspective.

For instance, ORBs from both IONA Technologies and Inprise implement proprietary _bind() methods, which are generated by the IDL compiler for each interface. The details of these two mechanisms are quite different, but they both suffer from the same limitation—a lack of abstraction.

In both cases, client programmers must provide information that uniquely identifies the target object within an ORB domain. In particular, this information is closely tied to the object instance and system configuration. For example, the client may have to specify information such as the host on which the servant object is running, or the ORB's internal identifier for the object. There is no facility for associating any higher-level information about an object. Clients can only look up objects using this low-level information.

Nonetheless, these proprietary approaches have achieved widespread use. In many cases, this is due to their simplicity. They are very easy to use, and this tended to make them the first choice of object location mechanisms. Over time, we expect that use of these mechanisms will diminish. New applications will make use of the more flexible approaches discussed here, and ORB vendors will deprecate these proprietary methods.

Bootstrapping

The naming and trading services are implemented, naturally, by servant objects that provide a particular interface. Our components (both clients and servers) act as clients when communicating with these services. Just like any CORBA client, however, we need to obtain a reference to these objects before we can begin using them. So, how can we get these references? The recommended way to obtain a reference is to use the naming or trading service. Clearly, we need some other way to bootstrap our programs so that they can obtain an initial reference to an object in one of these services.

One CORBA-compliant way to bootstrap is through the CORBA::ORB::resolve_initial_references() method. This call takes as input a single string parameter, and returns an object reference. This string identifies the service from which the caller wants an object reference. Legal values for this string include "NameService" and "TradingService." These strings are specified by the OMG, and all ORBs must return an object reference for the corresponding service.

Another approach would be to obtain an object reference for the desired service, in string form. This stringified object reference could either be output by the service itself or generated by an IOR creation tool. Once our clients have obtained this string (read in from a configuration file, for instance), they can call CORBA::ORB::string_to_object() to create a reference for the object.

No matter which bootstrapping mechanism we use, once our applications obtain an initial reference to the repository, they can simply begin using it to publish or lookup application objects.

Selecting An Object Location Mechanism

Choosing which object location mechanism to use is an important decision. Selecting an inappropriate tool can result in an inflexible, difficult-to-maintain system. Although the object location mechanisms differ in their complexity, none of them are truly difficult to use. Once the administrative infrastructure has been defined, all the approaches are straightforward to use (perhaps aided by some client-side wrapper classes customized for your particular environment).

Our primary consideration should be the complexity of our environment. How many objects are going to be published to the object directory? How complex are the criteria that our clients will be using to look up objects? What qualities of service do we require? It's important to make certain that we have a good understanding of how our clients will be looking up objects.

In general, we recommend avoiding the use of ORB-specific mechanisms, for the reasons mentioned earlier. They rely on proprietary mechanisms, have no facility for associating higher-level information with an object, and cannot interoperate with other ORBs.

For very simple, static environments, the use of object reference strings is appropriate. This approach does not rely on the availability of any additional service. Clients just use the object reference string and connect to the appropriate server. Often, clients will retrieve a single object reference string from a configuration file, then use this object as a factory to gain access to the business objects needed.

Of course, if the servant objects are ever moved, our clients will have to be reconfigured with a new object reference string. With large numbers of clients, or geographically distributed clients, this can be difficult and expensive. If this limitation is acceptable, then we can use object reference strings effectively.

Comparing the Naming and Trading Services

For more complex environments, the naming or trading services are more appropriate. They do require some forethought, but provide us with a great deal more functionality than the other approaches. The naming and trading services are most beneficial in slightly differing situations.

The trading space differs from a name hierarchy in that it is multidimensional. Every service type can have any number of properties, and each property defined within a service type is orthogonal to all the others. In addition, new properties can be added to a service type without affecting existing offers. Compare this to the name hierarchy, which is really just two-dimensional. Each object that our servers bind to a name hierarchy only has two pieces of information associated with it—its name and its place in the hierarchy.

Consider our printer objects. As we expressed in the PrinterService service type, our clients need to be able to locate printers based on their physical location as well as their print speed. In some cases, end users will want to print to the closest printer, while in other cases they want to find the fastest printer. As we have already seen, supporting these different types of lookup operations is straightforward when using the trader. Trying to duplicate this functionality with the name service, however, is difficult. We would end up with two parallel hierarchies, or a deeply nested hierarchy.

Now, consider what happens if we decide to add a third attribute on which clients can look up objects. Adding this to our service type in the trader is trivial. However, adding this to the name hierarchy requires a complete reworking of the hierarchy. In cases such as this, it quickly becomes apparent that the naming service is not a good choice.

In general, if our clients are only looking up objects based on a fixed set of criteria, then the naming service can usually model this well. If, on the other hand, our clients use varying sets of criteria to look up objects, then the trading service is often a better choice.

Selecting Objects For Publication

How should we decide which of our servant objects should be published to the object directory? The answer, of course, depends on how our system is architected, and how the clients will be using the servant objects. Some systems contain a relatively small, fixed set of servant objects that all clients utilize. In cases such as this, it often makes sense to publish all of these objects. Other systems contain a relatively small number of factory objects, which are used to create short-lived, transient objects that clients will use temporarily. In these cases, we should just publish the factory objects. The transient objects are returned to clients by a factory, and are typically dedicated to one client, containing client-specific state. Because of this, we don't want them to be generally available, so there's no reason to publish them. Also, since these objects don't exist until requested by clients, publishing and looking them up would simply be unnecessary overhead.

Now, let's consider a system with a large number of objects—our Portfolio Manager system, with thousands of `Portfolio` objects in our database. We need to decide how to structure our naming service hierarchy. One approach would be to create an entry for each Portfolio object, named by its unique account number. Alternatively, we could simply export our `PortfolioManager` object, and have clients use that to obtain a reference to a specific `Portfolio` object. This is the preferred approach, for a number of reasons. First, it saves us the trouble of having to instantiate each `Portfolio` object, and bind it to the naming service. Second, adding many entries to the naming service will increase the size of its database, and slow down its processing. Third, by just exporting the `PortfolioManager` factory, it is much easier to relocate our server, or to provide a group of objects for load balancing. We can temporarily (or permanently) relocate our server by simply replacing one entry in the naming service, rather than having to enumerate through thousands of objects.

When our system contains a large number of objects within a single server process, it is often better to export a small number of factory objects from that process, rather than exporting all the servant objects. If our system, however, has objects distributed among many server processes, then it can make sense to export all the servant objects.

Messaging

I n this book we discuss CORBA systems primarily from a specific perspective on the remote method invocations made by clients. In particular, we assume that our client and server components are linked by a TCP/IP connection, and that our servers are actively listening for incoming requests from clients. When one is received, the server processes the request and returns the results to the client which made the request. The client, which is blocked while awaiting the response, can continue processing only once the reply has been received. That is, our invocations are assumed to be synchronous and tightly coupled. More formally, the implied CORBA model for remote method invocations is characterized as follows:

- **Synchronous method invocations.** Standard CORBA remote method invocations are executed synchronously—that is, clients block while waiting for a reply to an invocation.
- **Tightly coupled components.** A client invokes on a specific object in a specific server in a specific host. Client-side proxies refer to one (and only one) target object. If the target host or server cannot be contacted, or the target object does not exist, the client will receive an exception.

In many cases, this synchronous and tightly coupled behavior is precisely what we are looking for. Our logic often dictates that our clients block until the results of a request are received, and only then continue processing. Why make a request in the first place, unless the results are needed right away? Many times a tight coupling between clients and servers is required.

CORBA and Messaging

In some cases, however, our applications would benefit from a different communication model. Many systems have a fundamentally asynchronous character, and often require a more decoupled style of interaction. For instance, the stock price update part of our StockWatch case study is an example of such a system.

This type of communication is known as *messaging*. For our purposes, we loosely define messaging as decoupled, asynchronous communication between application components. These components are decoupled in that there is no direct link between them. Their communication may occur using a connectionless multicast network protocol, or via an intermediate component. Their communication is asynchronous in that callers remain unblocked after sending a message to recipients. They can continue their processing without waiting for the recipient to fully process the message. Messaging is also characterized by the potential for one-to-many and many-to-many communication.

As we have defined it, our CORBA systems are not using messaging to communicate. But it is possible to achieve asynchronous, decoupled communication with CORBA. Next, we explore the support for this offered by ORBs. Later in the chapter, we discuss the relevant CORBA services.

ORB Support for Messaging

The CORBA specification addresses some of the support needed for messaging. ORBs are required to support some degree of asynchronous communications, through the use of the IDL keyword oneway, as well as through deferred synchronous invocations when using the dynamic invocation interface.

Asynchronous Oneway Invocations

A synchronous remote method invocation on an object implies that the calling application blocks until the method is processed by the server and the results are returned. The truth is slightly more complex: A CORBA method invocation will cause the calling thread to block until the results are returned except where the call is defined as oneway in IDL. Recall that IDL supports the concept of one-way operations, which are sent by the client asynchronously. That is, the client sends off a one-way request, then continues processing without waiting for the server to handle the request.[1] One-way requests must abide by certain restrictions (no return values or out parameters), but can be quite useful. We will discuss one-way requests below, but first we discuss why synchronous invocations are sometimes undesirable.

Consider a single-threaded client that makes a blocking invocation. The client is, by definition, blocked until the server replies to the invocation. This means that our client program cannot do anything else while it is awaiting a reply. If this program does not interact with a user, this is often not a problem. However, if a user is waiting for this reply to return and it takes a while, it can appear to the user that the program has hung. In general, it is preferable to provide some sort of feedback during potentially long-running requests, possibly giving the user a chance to cancel the operation.[2]

Consider also a single-threaded server that, at times, acts as a client. While this server is busy processing requests for a client, it is unavailable to perform work for any other client. We expect and accept this behavior (we only have one application thread, so this is unavoidable). However, when

---

[1] This is a true statement, although not sufficiently precise to indicate the real behavior. Since most ORBs use TCP as their underlying transport, even our supposedly non-blocking call is, in fact, a blocking call at the TCP level, since TCP is a reliable protocol. Our client program may not wait for the server application to receive and begin processing the request, but the client's TCP/IP stack does wait until the request buffer has been successfully received (and acknowledged) by the server's TCP/IP stack.

[2] Note that in many commercially available ORBs it is not possible to cancel a request already in progress. However, it is certainly possible to cancel things at an application level, so that when the reply is received it is simply ignored.

this server acts as a client and makes a request, it is blocked awaiting a reply. During this time, it is not performing any useful work, but cannot process any incoming requests either. This situation is undesirable. It can reduce the throughput of our system and can even lead to deadlock if our servers create a cyclic call graph. One way to avoid these problems is, of course, to make our components multithreaded rather than single-threaded. However, sometimes we cannot (or choose not to) do so. Let's examine some ways in which we can use CORBA to improve the throughput of our system, without multithreading.

One approach to solving this problem is to break up our standard blocking call into a pair of one-way operations. That is, rather than having our clients make a request and block until the results are returned, our clients make their invocations, then continue processing. Later, when the server has finished processing the request, it "returns" the results to the client by making a corresponding one-way invocation back on the client, sending the results. Let's briefly examine some IDL demonstrating this.

```
// *** Original IDL ***
interface Stock
{
    PriceInfoSeq getHistoricalPrices(in Date startDate,
    in Date endDate);}

// *** Modified IDL ***
interface PriceInfoCallback
{
    oneway void historicalPriceResults(in PriceInfoSeq);};

interface Stock
{
    oneway void getHistoricalPrices(in Date startDate,
    in Date endDate,
    in PriceInfoCallback
    callbackObject);
};
```

Our client program implements the `PriceInfoCallback` class and passes an object reference to the server, as part of the `Stock::getHistoricalPrices` invocation. Our server processes the request and, when the results are ready, passes them to the client by making the `historicalPriceResults` invocation on this callback object. In this way, the calling application is not blocked during the time the server is busy looking up and tabulating the historical stock prices. The client is free to handle input from the user for the potentially long duration of the call. Interaction diagrams for the two approaches are shown in Figures 7.1 and 7.2. A similar approach can be applied when our servers act as clients here the benefit is even clearer—our server is now free to handle incoming requests from other clients during this time. This can help our system achieve improved throughput even without multithreading. Note, however, that there is a price to be paid for this improvement: increased server complexity. Specifically, this requires the ability to break up application logic so that it can handle disconnected processing. In a single-threaded application, the ability to make a one-way request, put the current work aside for a while, then

Figure 7.1 Synchronous invocation example

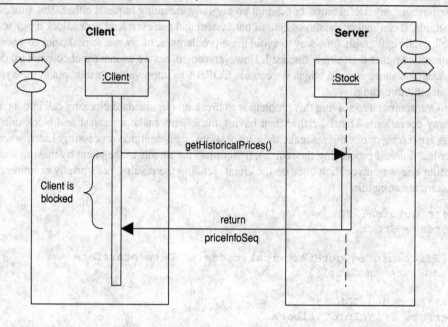

Figure 7.2 Asynchronous invocation example

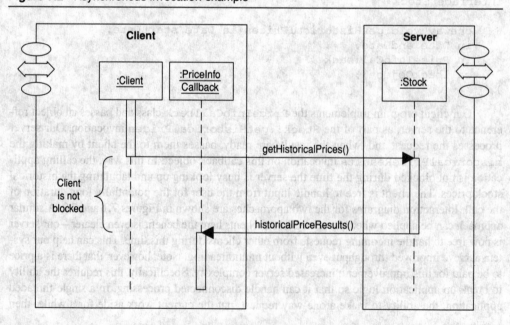

resume the work when the corresponding one-way request containing the results is received, is essential. Depending on how our application is structured, this may be difficult to achieve.

Deferred Synchronous Invocations

CORBA supports one additional approach to making non-blocking calls, through the use of the dynamic invocation interface (DII). Recall that the DII can be used to make invocations on interfaces about which client programs are unaware of at compile time. Compare this to the normal, static invocation interface (SII), in which our client programmers simply make a method invocation on a proxy object. This proxy object class, which was generated by the IDL compiler, is responsible for marshalling the arguments, making the remote invocation, and unmarshalling the results. With DII, our client programmer must perform this work. Clearly, this is a much more complex approach, but for certain classes of applications (such as gateways, or browsers) it is important to be independent of any particular IDL.

DII also supports the concept of a *deferred synchronous* invocation. This is a means of making a non-blocking remote invocation without any of the IDL restrictions imposed by one-way methods. That is, our clients can make non-blocking invocations even if the method invocation returns some data (clients are responsible for checking results at some point in time after the request has been sent). This can be very beneficial. The downside is that this approach is only available when using the DII approach and is therefore not very practical for many applications. One point to note is that like with a pair of one-way requests, when using deferred synchronous invocation, our clients must be able to break up their logic into discrete steps to be handled at different points in time. Also, client-side use of deferred synchronous invocation is transparent to our servers.

Have We Achieved Messaging?

The functionality supported by ORBs is a step toward messaging. Using oneway requests or deferred synchronous invocation provides us some level of asynchronous communication. However, there are a number of areas in which current ORB support falls short. Our components are still tightly coupled together: there must be a direct communication link between clients and servers, and these components must be explicitly aware of one another. Other messaging features that we may want in a system include persistent storage of messages (so that clients and servers do not have to be running simultaneously), one-to-many communications (so that a message can be propagated to many recipients with one invocation), or transactional message delivery.

In order to get an idea of the spectrum of functionality that comprises messaging, we briefly explore commercially available message-oriented middleware products next. These widely accepted systems provide a rich set of features and a variety of qualities-of-service (capabilities of their message-delivery mechanisms), which are needed to solve real-world business problems. Later, we will see how CORBA services offer a similar set of features.

The Need for Message-Oriented Middleware

Often, business requirements demand that applications be able to communicate in an asynchronous and decoupled manner. This is commonly achieved through software generally classified as *message-oriented middleware*. These are products that permit applications to send messages without blocking, without a direct communication link between sender and receiver, and with certain delivery characteristics.

Existing Message-Oriented Middleware Products

Today's commercially available message-oriented middleware products include MQSeries from IBM, Microsoft Message Queue Server, ETX from TICBO Inc., and PIPES from PeerLogic, Inc. These products generally offer asynchronous message queuing and persistent message storage, along with various support services, such as transactional interfaces to the queues.

Asynchronous messaging permits applications to enqueue messages without blocking. Persistent message storage provides a way for messages to be delivered even if sender and receiver applications are not running at the same time. There may also be transactional access to the message queue. This facility provides applications with the guarantee that a message will be delivered, and that it will be delivered only once.

Related CORBA Services

The designers of the CORBA specification recognized the need for these various features and qualities of service, and defined a number of services to address this. By using these features within a CORBA framework, we can build functionally rich systems in a standard manner. Next, we examine some of the current and forthcoming CORBA standards.

The CORBA Event Service

The CORBA event service, which was briefly introduced earlier, provides a generic model for push- and pull-based message passing (also known as *event notification*). This CORBA service defines a framework for transmitting messages between decoupled components, without specifying any quality of service aspects (this is left to the implementing vendor to decide). In fact, communication is often based on standard CORBA remote method invocations. Although CORBA invocations are synchronous and tightly coupled, the overall architecture of the CORBA event service is decoupled and asynchronous. This is accomplished through the use of logical event channels, as shown in Figure 7.3. An event channel, as defined in the CORBA event service, is an object that performs the work of delivering events from producers to all interested consumers.

Component interaction occurs through normal, synchronous invocations, but the event channel decouples the StockWatch server from the StockWatch clients. Consider what happens when the StockWatch server pushes a stock price update for IBM. Pushing a stock price update blocks the StockWatch server, but only temporarily. The event channel returns control almost immediately, so the StockWatch server can continue its work. It is only after this that the event channel will begin pushing the stock price out to all StockWatch clients (consumers) interested in receiving updated IBM prices. In this way, the event service provides asynchronous behavior, even while utilizing synchronous calls.

The key to using the event service is the choice of event channels. Each channel transmits events from all suppliers to all consumers. Applications register themselves as suppliers or consumers of a particular channel, based on their interest. It is important to select channels carefully. All events sent to a particular channel are forwarded by the event service to all consumers who have

Figure 7.3 Event channels

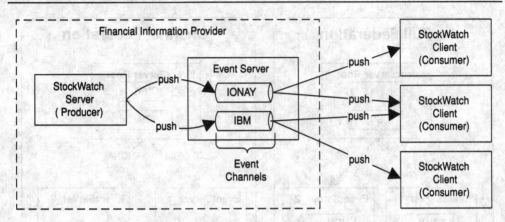

subscribed to that channel. Each channel should carry events for a logically related set of occurrences. In the example above, there is one event channel per stock symbol. This permits clients to receive updates on only those stocks they are interested in.

One alternative configuration would be to have just one event channel, through which price updates for all stocks would be sent. Clearly, this would be a poor design. The StockWatch clients are likely to be interested in only a small fraction of the stocks at any one time. This is an extreme example, but it illustrates an important point. Event channels should be fine-grained enough that subscribers will be interested in all or most of the events sent through that channel.

Events channels are implemented as CORBA objects, which consume resources in the event server process. If a design calls for large numbers of event channels, ensure that the event service implementation can support this.

Federating Event Services

Assume that our StockWatch system can be accessed by potentially thousands of clients. In this case, a single event server process would clearly be unable to service all these consumers from a performance, resource usage, and fault tolerance perspective. Fortunately, the event service can easily be scaled up by using a technique called *event channel federation*. Event channels can be federated by registering one event channel as the consumer of another event channel, which acts as producer. In this way, we can form a tree of federated event channels, distributed over many event server processes.

The CORBA event service is very flexible and event channels can be used in many ways. Once we have decided how our event channels are to be used, we must decide how to best structure our event channel federation. Figure 7.4 shows two possible approaches. In the first approach, called *full federation*, each event server process contains instances of all the event channels. Each channel in the root event server is attached to the corresponding channel in each of the child event server processes. In the second approach, termed *channel federation*, each root event channel is forwarded

Figure 7.4   Event channel federation

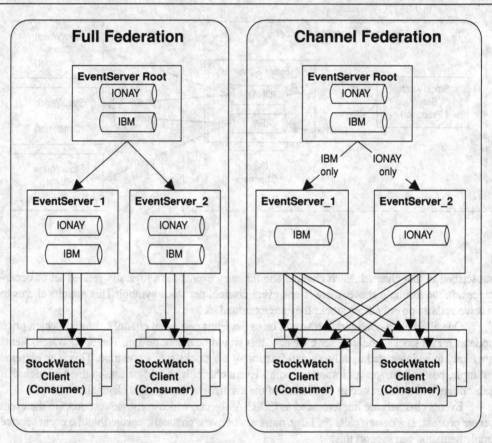

into a single event server process. This results in as many child event server processes as there are channels. Each of these child event servers contains a single event channel.

Full federation is usually preferable, primarily because each client interacts with only a single event server. Also, the event channels are replicated across all event servers, which provides better load balancing. Channel federation, on the other hand, can result in clients with connections to multiple event servers, which does little to eliminate problems that motivated us to federate in the first place. This approach does, however, work well when our clients are only ever interested in one event channel.

Finding Event Channels

An interesting topic is that of how consumers find event channels. Because an event channel is implemented as a normal CORBA object, we can use any of the solutions discussed previously—for instance, the trading service or the naming service. We can easily imagine using a name hierarchy to contain our event channels. From a system designer's perspective, however, we want to be careful how we structure our hierarchy, so that we follow the rules implicit in our federation diagram. For instance, if we are using full federation, then we want to ensure that our StockWatch clients connect only to a single event server, for all its event channels. If a client mistakenly obtained references to event channels in multiple event servers, then the goals we hoped to accomplish via full federation would be lost.

Thus, we need some way of ensuring that clients will always connect to a single event server. One way to accomplish this is to expose each event server as a unique object in a name hierarchy. Each client will be configured to use (or will choose at random) a single event server, for its entire lifetime. This is a simple approach, but suffers from being static, in that it cannot react to changing conditions at run time. A more transparent approach, which is more flexible and better lends itself to dynamically managing the system, is to have clients obtain a reference to an event channel through an invocation on some other object. For instance, we could have the client application invoke a method on a `Stock` object, which would return a reference to the associated event channel. The application server would internally keep track of which clients use which event servers, to ensure that clients are given references to channels in the same event server process each time they ask.

Such an approach will also allow our application server to use only as many event servers as are necessary to handle the current load. If many more clients suddenly want to subscribe to stock price updates, the server could then launch new event servers, adding to a dynamically growing pool. A more in-depth discussion of these areas be found in the chapters on load balancing and fault tolerance.

Limitations of the CORBA Event Service

The CORBA event service provides our applications with a means to communicate in a decoupled, asynchronous way. Commercial implementations of the event service typically use IIOP as their network protocol, so that integrating this service into a CORBA system is straightforward. However, this service also suffers from a number of limitations.

First, there are no qualities of service specified by the event service. For example, the specification does not address persistent storage of events, guaranteed delivery of events, or delivery within a specified time period. Each event service implementation is left to support its own set of features. Ideally, each implementation would support the same qualities of service, in a standard manner.

Second, the only means of distinguishing events is on the event channel level. We, as application designers, decide on the number and type of events that will be sent along a particular event channel. However, this does not provide for fine-grained distinction of events. The channel delivers all events to all consumers, whether they are truly interested in them or not. For example, our stock price client may be interested in monitoring IBM for price changes. However, our client application is not interested in all the small price updates. At an application level, we are only interested if the stock price changes significantly (say, more than 2%). With the event service, this type of filtering can only occur in the client application, which leads to increased network and client utilization.

Third, the service does not maintain any higher-level data about an event channel. For instance, event suppliers may want to know if there are any consumers interested in a particular type of event. If there are currently no subscribers, the supplier can avoid wasting network resources by sending unwanted events. Likewise, consumers of events may want to find out what types of events are available from suppliers. The CORBA notification service was developed to address these limitations.

The CORBA Notification Service

The CORBA notification service provides a standard means of filtering events, maintaining higher-level information about event channels, and specifying qualities of service. It is also a natural extension to the event service. Each interface defined in the notification service inherits from its counterpart in the event service, providing backward compatibility with applications that use the event service.

With the notification service, each consumer can associate a list of constraints with an event channel. A constraint is a boolean expression, in an OMG-specified constraint language. If a consumer is registered with an event channel and has specified one or more constraints, the event channel will apply the constraints to each incoming event, allowing the event channel to decide whether the event should be forwarded to each consumer. This will prevent the transmission of events that the listener application would just discard, if they were received.

Another feature of the notification service is its capability to manage aspects of quality of service. Quality of service can be specified on different levels of granularity: per event, per consumer/producer, or per event channel. Examples of quality of service are delivery guarantees, timeouts, and priorities. Delivery guarantee can range from no guarantee at all, to the guarantee that an event will not be discarded from a channel until it has been successfully delivered to all registered consumers. Timeouts specify how much time should be allowed until an event is discarded, regardless of whether it was successfully delivered to all consumers, or not. Priorities specify the relative priority of an event with regard to other events. The notification service also provides transactional interfaces to the event channel, so that event producers and consumers can rely on events being delivered exactly once. Finally, the notification service provides for the management of the qualities of service. Applications can apply quality of service requirements to elements of the service, such as event channels, proxies, and even individual events.

We anticipate that commercial implementations of the notification service will become widely accepted. The compatibility with the event service provides an easy migration path, while the additional features provide a large incentive for organizations to migrate to the notification service.

Forthcoming CORBA Services

At the time of this writing, the OMG was in the process of developing a CORBA messaging specification. This standard addresses the need for messaging by extending the support for asynchronous communication in the core ORB. Features such as asynchronous method invocation (AMI), time independent invocation (TII), and messaging qualities of service are covered.

The AMI provides two standard ways of making asynchronous invocations that return values. Clients can either pass in a callback object (which the server makes an invocation on when the request has completed), or ask for a polling object (on which the client can poll for the results). This callback approach is similar to oneway callback approach that we discussed earlier in this chapter.

The TII provides a standard mechanism by which clients and servers do not have to be running at the same time. It provides a standard store-and-forward mechanism to accomplish this.

Messaging qualities of service (which apply to both synchronous and asynchronous messages) provide standardized support for the degree of synchronization with the target ORB, as well as control of server-side message processing. We anticipate that when these features are supported by commercial ORBs, developers will quickly begin using their features.

Multicast Messaging

So far, the communication between our clients and servers has used IIOP. This protocol runs on top of TCP/IP, which provides us with a reliable, connection-oriented communication link between our components. However, there are other network protocols available, which can be usefully applied in CORBA environments. In this section, we focus on using IP multicast. After explaining the network terminology, we examine the OrbixTalk product from IONA Technologies, which uses multicast to provide efficient, connectionless communication between our components.

Network Terms

Networks today generally use the TCP/IP set of protocols for communications. A basic view of the network protocols is shown in Figure 7.5. Each of these protocols is introduced below.

Internet Protocol

The Internet Protocol (IP) is the basis of the Internet as we know it today. It is used to send packets from one host to another. IP is a connectionless protocol and does not provide reliability. This means the sender has no guarantee that any given packet is received by the destination host. Although *most* IP packets will reach their destination, there is always the chance that some will not. Therefore, most protocols built on top of IP provide higher-level features that *do* guarantee delivery of all messages.

Every host on a network has a unique IP address (for instance 192.190.230.2). The IP address of the destination host is contained in every IP packet. When a packet is sent, this address is examined at each of the routing points, and forwarded either directly to the destination host, or to another routing point which will be able to forward this packet to a point closer to its destination. Different classes of IP addresses have been defined and determine whether the packet is intended for one, some, or all hosts in a given network segment:

- **Unicast,** sent to a single host
- **Multicast,** sent to a group of hosts, called a *multicast group*
- **Broadcast,** sent to all hosts in a network segment

The physics of Ethernet dictate that only one message can be sent at any one point in time on a given network segment. Clearly, this has an impact as our systems begin to grow. If we wish to send a

Figure 7.5   Basic network protocols

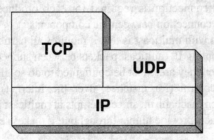

message to multiple hosts, unicast requires that we must repeatedly send the same message, once to each destination host. This is the behavior that we see in our IIOP-based systems. If, however, we are utilizing multicast, we can simply send the message once, and rely on the multicast feature of IP to deliver the message to each host. If we are sending many messages to many hosts, a multicast approach will certainly provide much better performance than unicast could. We'll return to multicast after a brief discussion of TCP/IP and UDP.

Transmission Control Protocol

Transmission control protocol (TCP) is a reliable, connection-oriented protocol based on IP. A logical connection is established between two processes (possibly on distinct hosts), enabling these processes to send and receive streams of data in a reliable manner. Since it is based on the unreliable IP protocol, TCP must provide its own reliable guarantee of message delivery. It accomplishes this through a combination of packet numbering, acknowledgments, and timeouts.

User Datagram Protocol

Since TCP/IP is connection-oriented, it only supports communication between two dedicated processes (unicast). To use broadcast or multicast communication, a connectionless protocol such as user datagram protocol (UDP) is required. UDP provides a much simpler service to the application layer than TCP/IP and is, in fact, unreliable, like the underlying IP protocol. It does not, therefore, provide any guarantee that the message packets reach their intended destination.

Multicast requests are sent to all members of a multicast group at the same time. Like Ethernet messages, every packet is received by every network card on the subnet. For unicast messages, however, only the destination host's network software actually processes the message. All other hosts examine the packet, and discard it because it is not intended for them. Using multicast, however, we can enable multiple hosts to receive and process the same network packet. This is implemented by having processes join a so-called *multicast group*. This informs the network software that it should listen for packets directed to certain multicast addresses, in addition to the host's unicast IP address. Membership in these multicast groups is dynamic, as processes join and leave the group. Thus, multicast is a powerful and interesting mechanism for large-scale systems.

Unicast vs. Multicast

How does unicast communication of IIOP-based event services compare with IP multicast-based products? The major benefits of multicast-based products are high throughput and high scalability. With the unicast-based event services, the event channel has to send a separate message to each event receiver. This can significantly slow down event delivery for large numbers of event consumers. In addition, a TCP connection is required for each producer and consumer of events, although there is not a direct connection between the components.

One potential problem with multicast is that it requires all participants to be connected by a network that is capable of routing IP multicast packets between subnets. Not all routers are physically capable of this, and when they are, must be configured to do so. If we are communicating outside of domains that we control (for instance, over the Internet), it makes sense to use a TCP/IP-based communication mechanism, since attempts at multicast may fail to reach their destination. Since multicast products provide higher throughput, it makes sense to use it for event distribution in a controlled environment such as an intranet, where routing policies can be applied to entire the network.

Multicast Case Study: The OrbixTalk Product

So far, we have discussed messaging solutions based on IIOP, which is of course based in turn on the TCP/IP protocol. TCP/IP is a connection-oriented network protocol, and is used for unicast communication, where messages are sent directly from a single client process to a single server process (and from the single server to the single client). This has significant consequences for messaging based on IIOP, since it requires a direct TCP connection between clients and servers (this is the *tightly coupled* attribute of our previous discussion).

In the following section, we examine a real-world product that uses IP multicast to provide truly decoupled communication between CORBA components: OrbixTalk from IONA Technologies. We explain how this product overcomes the limitations of multicast through the use of a reliable protocol built on top of the unreliable UDP.

The OrbixTalk Reliable Multicast Protocol

The multicast capability of UDP makes it interesting and useful as a protocol for building higher-level messaging solutions. One of the drawbacks of UDP and multicast, of course, is that it is an unreliable protocol. To solve this problem, IONA Technologies has developed the reliable multicast protocol (RMP), which is layered on top of UDP, and is employed in the OrbixTalk product.

How does RMP work? An important part of the TCP/IP implementation of reliable transport is that of positive acknowledgements. At the TCP level, the receiver responds to each message by sending an acknowledgement to the sender, indicating that the message was received properly. Using acknowledgements in conjunction with multicast is a bad idea, for obvious reasons: If there are N recipients of a message, this would result in N acknowledgements sent back to the sender, and would quickly eliminate much of the benefit of using multicast. Instead, IONA's reliable multicast protocol uses a combination of negative acknowledgements, heartbeats (*last message sent*), and message sequence numbers to guarantee reliability. If a receiver determines that it is missing a message, it asks the sender to re-send the missing message, identified by its sequence number.

OrbixTalk Architecture

OrbixTalk uses the reliable multicast protocol (RMP) as the basis for building an ORB communication protocol. In the same way that ORBs use IIOP on top of TCP/IP to send a message from a client to a single servant object, OrbixTalk uses the RMP to send a multicast message from one client to many servant objects. The network and application protocols are layered as shown in Figure 7.6.

Our previous discussions of CORBA remote method invocations have all focused on making an invocation on a client proxy, which sends a message from the client to a single servant object in a specific server process. The client's proxy is associated with information that identifies the target object, the name (or IP address) of the host on which the object's server process is running, and a port number on which that server process is listening.

Assume we want to send a stock price update to three objects. With normal IIOP-based communication, this requires three remote method invocations, each of which results in an IIOP request being sent to the particular target object. This is illustrated in Figure 7.7.

Figure 7.6   OrbixTalk Transport vs. IIOP

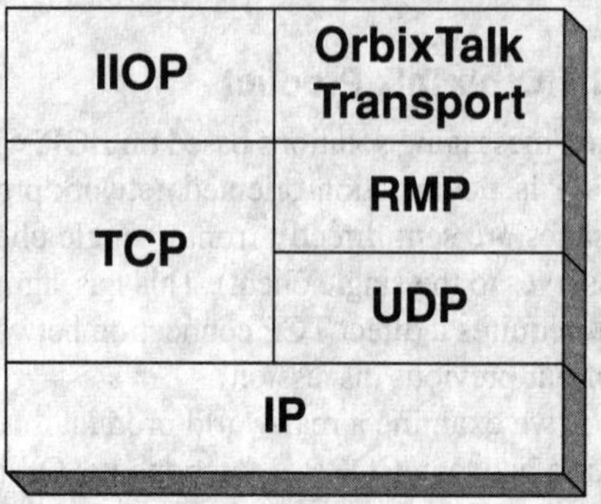

IIOP	OrbixTalk Transport
TCP	RMP
	UDP
IP	

Figure 7.7   IIOP requests via TCP/IP

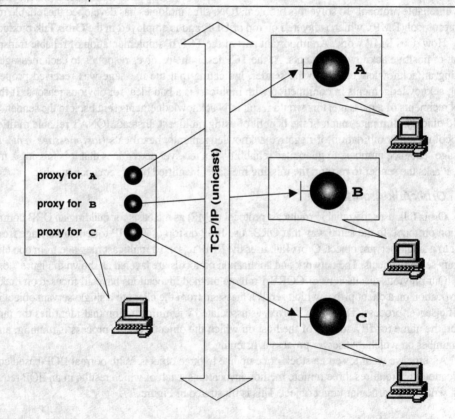

Figure 7.8 OrbixTalk requests via multicast

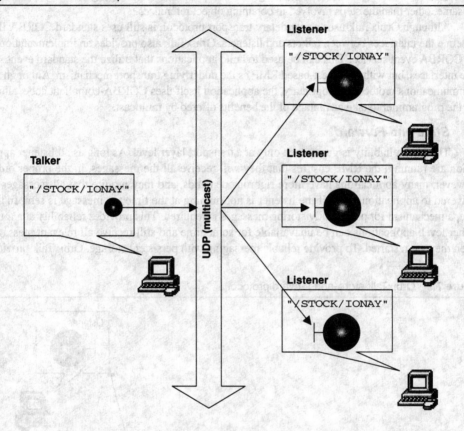

Achieving the same results with OrbixTalk and multicast is much more efficient, as shown in Figure 7.8. Sending the stock price update to the three objects is accomplished with a single multicast message.

OrbixTalk provides the same notion of proxy objects and implementation objects as in IIOP-based communication, but with two main differences. First, all the IDL interfaces must contain only oneway operations, since multicast implies that communication is unidirectional—that is, the sender does not expect a reply. Second, proxy objects are no longer associated with a specific servant object, but instead with a *topic* name which, internally, is mapped to an IP multicast address. In Figure 7.8, the topic name is " / STOCK/ IONAY". A client proxy is called a *talker*, a servant object is called a *listener*. Each talker and listener is associated with a topic. In addition to multiple listeners for a given topic, there can also be multiple talkers.

Making an invocation on a talker is a remote invocation not on a single listener, but on all listeners that are registered for the particular topic (as shown in Figure 7.8). While an invocation on a normal proxy results in a message being sent by unicast to a specific application at a specific IP address, an invocation on an OrbixTalk talker results in a message being sent using a specific IP multicast address. From an application programmer's point of view, the programming approach is the same, other than the steps involved in obtaining object references.

Although OrbixTalk uses a proprietary transport protocol, is still uses standard CORBA IDL to define the interfaces between talkers and listeners. OrbixTalk also provides an implementation of the CORBA event service. This can be used to build applications that utilize the standard event service interfaces, but with multicast-based RMP as the underlying transport mechanism. Although the communications protocol is proprietary, the application itself uses CORBA-compliant code, allowing the programmer to take advantage of the benefits offered by multicast.

Store-and-Forward

Thus far, reliability is guaranteed only at a transport layer level. As long as all listener application are running, the RMP ensures that they will receive all the messages, in the proper order. However, many applications have more rigorous demands, and may require that all messages be delivered to applications even if the listener is not running at the time the message is sent. In this case, a mechanism for persistently storing messages is required. This provides reliability at a much higher level; applications can be unavailable for some time and still receive all relevant messages when they are restarted. To provide reliable messaging with persistent storage, OrbixTalk provides

Figure 7.9   OrbixTalk store-and-forward protocol

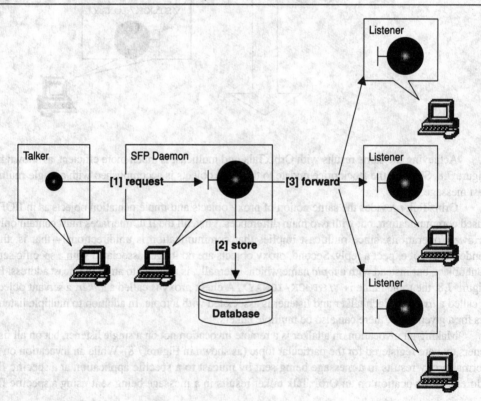

an extension to the RMP, called the store-and-forward protocol (SFP). This is illustrated in Figure 7.9. The basic idea is to have a dedicated server (the store-and-forward daemon) that receives the requests from all the talkers, stores them in persistent storage, and forwards the requests to the relevant listeners. If a listener is currently not available, it can later ask for a replay of previously sent requests. Such a request is easily accommodated with this approach, since all the messages have been stored persistently. Configuration tools allow the programmer to define administrative settings, such as how long requests should be stored in the database and how often to back up the request databases.

Summary

In this chapter we have addressed messaging, which we loosely defined as decoupled, asynchronous communication between components. We saw that our basic ORB can provide us with some degree of asynchronicity and decoupling. However, as we saw when we briefly discussed commercial message-oriented middleware products, there are many qualities of service missing from one-way and deferred synchronous requests. Some of these features are supported in the CORBA event and notification services, while other are being addressed as part of the CORBA messaging service.

For large-scale systems, multicast messaging is often an efficient mechanism for communication. Products such as OrbixTalk provide standard CORBA interfaces, while using IP multicast as a communication mechanism.

When CORBA is used to build large systems, there is often a need for elements to communicate in an asynchronous, decoupled manner. CORBA offers a variety of mechanisms to accomplish this, which vary in their complexity, robustness, and performance. Multicast communication is also an effective way to build a system requiring messaging, and will be standardized in a forthcoming CORBA specification.

Security

T̲oday's businesses depend on information technology. Enterprise systems are connected through internal networks and the public Internet. Employees access corporate data through a variety of interfaces—both internal and public. Customers make purchases via Internet-based e-commerce systems and conduct financial transactions via online banking services. But if information is so vital to companies these days, what is protecting this essential asset? In this chapter, we look at securing CORBA-based systems to protect information.

Access to a multitude of information resources is provided by CORBA servers, often through new interfaces to existing system data being introduced through the Internet. With this new arena of distributed systems and information resources, however, the inherent distributed nature of CORBA systems means there are more areas in the system at risk from attack by unauthorized users. Securing the system from internal or external attacks and violations of confidential data becomes an ever more difficult task. Distributed systems architects, developers, and administrators are faced with the challenge of securing the information when more information is being transmitted than ever before; more possible attack points are created and protection of non-public information from unauthorized users is as critical as ever before.

The OMG has recognized the importance of providing standardized security solutions for distributed systems, and has defined a set of specifications, including the CORBA security service, the network-level based security service ORB-SSL, and a CORBA firewall specification. These specifications are based on a number of existing and emergent products and technologies, and are consistent with many of the information security strategies being pursued in enterprises today. They have evolved from existing enterprise-oriented technologies such as the Kerberos protocol (a protocol for distributed authentication and encryption) and RACF (Remote Access Control Facility), which has been used successfully in mainframe environments for many years, together with more recent specifications dealing with emerging lighter-weight, Internet-focused technologies such as the Internet Engineering Task Force's (IETF) Secure Socket Layer (SSL), and firewall solutions. Each technology has its place, fitting the needs of particular distributed system environments and requirements, but often not fitting together well to create a streamlined overall picture. This chapter is aimed at discussing security solutions for enterprise and Internet CORBA systems in the real world.

Security Concepts

In the following, we introduce the core security concepts in the context of distributed systems.

Authentication

Authentication is the ability to prove the identity of an individual or a user—the proof that "you are who you say you are." The main techniques used for user authentication include :

- What you know: passwords, a secret known only to an individual
- What you have: physical key or a security pass such as an ATM card or Smart Card
- What you are: voice recognition, fingerprint analysis, retina analysis

Authentication is required to enable trust in a system. For example, if an on-line banking system requires that bank details be given to the bank account holder only, this means that the account holders will be required to authenticate themselves to the system to ensure no imposters are given confidential financial information.

Authorization

Authorization means the ability to restrict access to data to certain users only. While authentication establishes who you are, authorization establishes what you are allowed to do, given that you are who you claim to be. In most situations, especially those involving resource access across a network, security involves authentication followed by determining your authorization rights. Access Control Lists (ACLs) are used to associate an authorized user set with each resource. Much of the time-consuming work in developing a secure system is involved in the initial setup and maintenance of authorization lists using ACLs.

Encryption

Encryption means protecting data in transit via the application of cryptographic functions. Encryption is the process for producing cipher-text from plain-text by applying a cryptographic function to the data. Encryption can be either secret-key or public-key based. Public key encryption requires two keys—a private key that is only available to the user, and a public key which can be distributed freely. Secret key encryption uses just one key which, as the name implies, must be kept secret. For public key encryption, the public and private keys are inverse functions of each other—what can be encrypted with the public key can only be decrypted with the private key, and vice versa.

Public key encryption tends to be slower at runtime than secret key (the algorithms are more complex), so a common paradigm is to use a public-key handshake to establish a secret key for the session, which is then used to encrypt the remainder of the traffic in that session. This is the approach used in the Secure Socket Layer (SSL) protocol.

Systems such as the Data Encryption Standard (DES) use secret key encryption; other systems such as Rivest Shamir Adleman (RSA) encryption suites make use of public key technology.

Data Integrity

Integrity refers to the correctness of the data received and involves the protection of communications during data transmission on the wire. Data integrity features are designed to prevent data tampering while messages are in transit. To detect if communications between users has been intercepted or changed, a checksum (a piece of data used to represent a message and ensure data integrity) is applied to the encrypted data communication packets. This checksum takes the form of a message authentication code (MAC) or similar technique like a message digest (MD). The technique is repeated by both users until the communication session has ended.

Public keys can also be used to digitally sign messages—a MAC can be added to each message. This code is computed by applying a hash function to the message content. This hash code is then encrypted using the sender's private key. The receiver decrypts the message using the sender's public key, and checks to see if the MAC matches the message. If the message is corrupted during transmission, the message content will not match the MAC.

Non-repudiation

Non-repudiation is the term applied to the technique of prevention of denial that a message has been sent or received by a user. It guarantees that a user cannot deny having sent a particular message or performed a certain action. Non-repudiation can be achieved using unique digital signatures which prove a particular message was sent and received by the correct user. Public key mechanisms can be used to provide digital signatures for messages.

As an example, consider a situation shown in Figure 8.1 where user Ann is communicating with an online shopping server, and wishes to make a purchase. To do this, Ann needs to send her credit card details over to the public server (which she has already authenticated to ensure she is not communicating with an imposter). Apart from Ann wanting to be sure that her credit card details will not be observed while in transit (which can be accomplished using encryption), Ann also wants to be sure that the details cannot be altered in any way before reaching the server. The shopping server requires that Ann cannot deny at a later stage having made this purchase and that she has authorized the server to debit her credit card account. To do this, digital signatures can be used—to provide data integrity for Ann, and non-repudiation for the online shopping server. Ann can use her private key to generate and add a digital signature to the message. When the online server receives the message, it uses Ann's public key to check the digital signature, and verify that it matches the message content. If it does, then the message must have been sent by Ann, since only Ann holds her private key, thus providing non-repudiation. Checking the digital signature matches the message ensures the integrity of the message. The server can then log that the message was indeed sent by Ann.

Credentials and Delegation

A user's credentials determine what s/he is allowed to do in the system. These credentials contain the user's security attributes. Credentials typically contain two types of attributes:

- **Identity** attributes, which specify who the user is.
- **Privilege** attributes, which specify what a user can do, what groups it is a member of, what roles it plays, and what capabilities and clearances it has.

Figure 8.1 Non-repudiation

Applications may use a single user's credentials when invoking on other applications, or may use one of a set of credentials associated with it. In the latter case, different credentials (with different privilege attributes) may be used when invoking on different objects. Delegation of credentials is a common system requirement—allowing an intermediate application to take on the credentials of an invoking application in order to be able to carry out a function required by the invoking application.

Enterprise System Security Requirements and Policies

Building a secure distributed enterprise system can be thought of as consisting of three separate steps:

1. **Analysis** of the threats and risks in the system that require security and protection.
2. **Design** of a security policy to provide counter-measures to these threats.
3. **Implementation** of this policy using chosen tools and methods.

Analysis

A security policy is designed and implemented so an enterprise can protect its business assets from perceived threats, using appropriate security measures. Typically, it is enterprise management who will be responsible for the security policy design, since it is they who are responsible for business assets including business data managed by their IT systems and who therefore have ultimate responsibility for protecting the information in the system from security threats. A security *threat* is a potential system misuse that could lead to a failure in achieving system security goals. Different security threats present in a system each have appropriate countermeasures that can be taken to ensure the security of the system is maintained. For example:

THREAT	COUNTER-MEASURE
Information compromise—the deliberate or accidental disclosure of confidential data	Data confidentiality, maintained using authorization control and encryption methods
Integrity violations—the malicious or inadvertent modification or destruction of data or system resources	Data integrity, maintained using digital signatures to sign messages sent around a system
Malicious or inadvertent misuse—active or passive bypassing of controls by authorized or unauthorized users	Non-repudiation, achieved using digital signatures and logging to ensure users are held responsible for all actions they carry out in the system

The goals of designing a security policy for a system are to identify the possible threats to the system, and then choose and implement appropriate counter-measures to counteract these threats. When identifying the possible threats to a CORBA system, the following steps can serve as a guideline:

1. Conduct a risk assessment. What needs to be protected?
2. Understand the potential security threats to the organization. From what and whom do these resources need to be protected?
3. Document such risks and threats and their potential consequences.
4. Consider the roles of all individuals connected with the organization and the various levels of trust offered to each individual.

Once the threats have been identified and documented, the next step is to move on to designing a security policy to tackle these threats.

Design

A *security policy* is simply a high-level statement outlining the organization's approach to information security. It refers to a set of high-level requirements or rules an organization places on the security attributes of its assets (often independently of the use of computers). A policy determines both physical and electronic measures to protect against perceived threats, and concerns access control, authentication, secure invocations, credential delegation, and accountability. In real terms, this means dealing with questions such as:

- What information needs to be secured?
- Who should have access to "secure" information?
- How is "secure" information protected—physically (servers in a room with controlled access) and electronically (passwords, encryption, logging)?

- How should systems respond to security violations (logging, deny service, report to various people, set off alarms)?
- What are the implementation details? For example, how often must passwords be changed, etc.?

From an implementation point of view, the security policy should cover the following:

- What authentication of users and other principals is required to prove who they are.
- The security of communications between objects, including the trust required and the quality of protection of the data in transit between them.
- What logging of which security-relevant activities is needed.
- Under what conditions active entities (such as clients acting on behalf of users) may access objects.
- What active entities can do, and whether they can delegate their rights.

This information is supplied to the administrators who typically manage the secure system environment.

Implementation

Once the policy has been designed, an implementation method must be chosen, and the details of the implementation mapped out. This involves applying the security policy to the entities such as users, servers, server groups, and server objects in the CORBA system. In detail, this involves deciding:

- The users, groups and organisations that can be granted or denied access to all or to certain CORBA server objects or their operations.
- The CORBA objects and operations that can be accessed by any unknown user. Which servers and objects will be insecure?
- The level of authentication that a user or server principal requires and supports for communications with another entity to proceed. Authentication levels include no authentication, one-way authentication (client *or* server authentication), and mutual authentication.
- The quality of message protection that a user or server principal requires and supports for communications with another entity to proceed. Message protection qualities include none, data integrity, and data confidentiality. The latter two may be combined for increased protection.
- The delegation policy of a server principal. For example, if the server requires the client to communicate its security credentials to it so that the server can perform operations acting as that client.

Once defined, the next step is to choose implementation approaches and tools for the security policy. In CORBA, there are several specifications designed to focus on different security aspects and provide the kind of functionality outlined above for different types of system requirements. We discuss these specifications, and the problems they are designed to address, in the following section.

The final section looks at applying these specifications and their implementations to the security problems identified by the security policy as defined above.

CORBA Security

There are currently four security-related CORBA specifications defined by the OMG:

- The CORBA Security Service specification
- The Secure Interoperability/SecIOP specification
- The CORBA ORB—SSL integration specification
- The CORBA/Firewall specification

Each of these specifications has evolved from existing security technologies and security requirements, and addresses the different security needs of enterprise CORBA systems. We review the functionality defined by each specification with some information as to the background of the specifications and the type of system problems they seek to address.

The CORBA Security Service Specification

The first security-related CORBA specification, the CORBA security service specification, evolved from existing security technologies such as the Distributed Computing Environment (DCE) Security Service, the Kerberos protocol for distributed system authentication and encryption developed at Massachusetts Institute of Technology and the generic framework for accessing security services, the Generic Security Service API (GSS API). The CORBA security service specification covers the main aspects of enterprise system security under the following classifications:

- **Identification** and **authentication** of principals (human users and objects which need to operate under their own rights), to verify they are who they claim to be.
- **Authorization** and **access control**, to decide whether a principal can access an object, normally using the identity and/or other privilege attributes of the principal (such as role, groups, security clearance).
- **Security auditing** to make users accountable for their security-related actions. It is normally the human user who should be accountable.
- **Security of communication** between objects, involving some or all of authentication between client and target (possibly mutual), data integrity protection, and possibly data confidentiality protection of messages in transit between objects.
- **Non-repudiation** to provide irrefutable evidence of actions performed in the system to prevent against subsequent attempts to falsely deny the receiving or sending of the data.

The CORBA security service is divided into two levels of security service that can be provided in a system, CORBA level 1 and level 2. CORBA level 1 security provides a first level of security for applications which are unaware of security and for those having limited requirements to enforce their own security in terms of access control and auditing. CORBA level 2 security provides more security facilities, and allows applications to control the security provided at object invocation. It also includes administration of security policy, allowing applications administering policy to be portable.

CORBA Level 1 Security

CORBA level 1 security defines a security service that supports clients and servers that are unaware or minimally aware of the presence of the security service in the system. This level applies to all applications running under a secure ORB, whether or not they are aware of security. Non-repudiation, the provision of irrefutable evidence of actions in the system is an optional part of level 1.

The main features of CORBA security level 1 are:

- **Authentication** of principals, using usernames or other principal types.
- **Secure invocation** between client and target object, including establishment of trust using authentication, data integrity and/or confidentiality, and authorization of objects to clients. At level 1, this can be based on sets/groups of objects and groups of users. Level 1 object-level access control is provided per interface, not per object instance.
- The ability to **delegate** incoming credentials. At an intermediate object in a chain of calls, the ability to be able to either delegate the incoming credentials or use those of the intermediate object itself.
- **Auditing** of a mandatory set of security-relevant events such as principal authentication, session authentication, authorization, and changes in the security policy.

Implementations of the CORBA level 1 security service can typically be done by adding functionality to applications at the ORB interceptor level only, since this level of security is for applications that are typically unaware of the security service's presence in the system. This means that a CORBA level 1 security service could be added to an existing system without requiring any changes to existing application code. There are already implementations of the CORBA security service level 1 available—IONA's OrbixSecurity provides a full implementation of CORBA level 1 security based on the DCE security service. PeerLogic has a version of the CORBA security service available with the DAIS ORB (previously owned by ICL). Implementations are also being developed by Inprise (in partnership with DASCOM and Concept Five), and OmniORB. IONA is also currently working with Concept Five to develop a new version of OrbixSecurity using SSL as the security mechanism, to provide CORBA Level 1 functionality based on the SSL security service.

CORBA Level 2 Security

CORBA level 2 security is the functionality level which supports most of the application interfaces defined by the CORBA security service specification. Level 2 security adds these interfaces so that clients and servers can dynamically control their use of the security service, in a fine-grained manner. The CORBA level 2 security service supports the functionality in level 1 outlined above, and adds extra options and functionality for secure applications, such as:

- The ability to control the options used on security invocations, for instance, to choose the quality of protection of messages required.
- The ability to change the privileges in credentials.
- The ability to choose which (of a possible set of) credentials are to be used for object invocation.
- More delegation options are supported, but not mandatory—for instance, composite delegation where the target object can obtain *all* credentials passed along the invocation chain.
- Applications can find out what security policies apply to them—including those policies they enforce themselves and those the ORB enforces.

Most of the ORB vendors do not yet have CORBA level 2 implementations available. IONA is working with Concept Five to develop level 1 followed by a level 2 implementation built over SSL. Inprise is doing likewise with Concept Five and DASCOM. PeerLogic has an implementation of level 1 and level 2 security available with the DAIS ORB, while other vendors such as OmniORB are currently developing support as well. Security vendors such as Gradient Technologies are also developing integrations with the IONA and Inprise ORBs, to provide Kerberos-based level 1 and level 2 security service implementations.

The Secure Interoperability/SecIOP Specification

The CORBA security specification describes the CORBA level 1 and level 2 security service and also defines the secure inter-ORB protocol, SecIOP, for use with GIOP/IIOP for secure interoperability between different vendor's CORBA security service implementations.

To provide secure interoperability between ORB security services, the specification states that an IOR tag and security tokens must be used to establish a secure connection between a client and the target object. An object running under an ORB security service must provide an IOR containing a tagged component for security, giving information about the security policy of the associated object—for instance, what security service it supports, what levels of message protection it requires for communication. When a client wishes to communicate securely with this object, the IOR provides initial information about the security levels required for communication. SecIOP messages containing security tokens are then passed between client and server. These tokens contain security information such as the client/server user name, privileges, and supported security mechanisms for message confidentiality, integrity, and trust establishment/authentication. For example, the token may indicate that the client uses DCE/Kerberos for authentication and message protection, or SSL. Using the information contained in the tokens and the client and server's security policies, a security context, or secure association, can be negotiated and set up using SecIOP messages between the client and server. The chosen underlying security service (for example, SSL/Kerberos) is then used to establish authentication and provide message protection mechanisms for the remainder of the communication.

Another specification, the Common Secure Interoperability specification, builds on this SecIOP definition, adding further detail on supported authentication mechanisms, encryption algorithms, etc. The concept of level 0 security is also added in this specification, corresponding to the provision of identity-based policies without delegation—essentially what is provided by the standard SSL protocol.

Figure 8.2 ORB-SSL stack

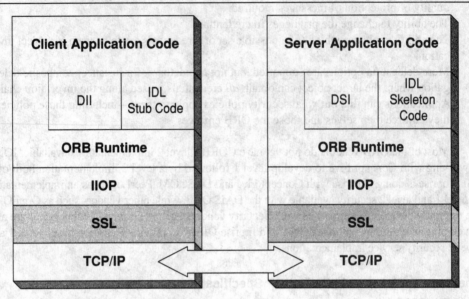

The ORB-SSL Integration Specification

At the time of specification of the CORBA security service and common security interoperability specifications, DCE and RACF security services were the most commonly used and popular system security services available. In the subsequent months and years, as Internet technologies came to the fore, so too did the Secure Socket Layer, a transport level security standard designed for Internet use. Standardized by the Internet Engineering Task Force (IETF), SSL quickly became the accepted standard for secure Internet communication. Thus followed a concise OMG specification, outlining the basic requirements for an SSL v3.0 integration with a CORBA ORB. From an IIOP/GIOP point of view, SSL security sits conceptually below the GIOP implementation (for instance, IIOP) and above TCP/IP, providing security at the socket layer—hence the name of the protocol.

The SSL specification addresses the security needs of Internet clients where a full DCE security solution might be too heavyweight to suit the thin client environment. SSL provides clients and servers with transport-level security functionality incorporating:

- **Authentication**. An SSL connection can be authenticated using asymmetric, or public key, cryptography (for example, RSA) and the IETF X.509 standard for security certificates.
- **Data Privacy**. Protects messages from being viewed while in transit, ensuring data confidentiality.
- **Data Integrity**. Ensures messages cannot be tampered with while in transit.

Commonly known as "credit card security," SSL is extremely well-suited to the security needs of Internet commerce systems. Fast, lightweight, but providing a robust and strong level of security, it is ideally suited to the Internet where public servers are common, but protection of sensitive information such as credit card details in transit is of extreme importance.

The CORBA/Firewall specification

As enterprise and Internet systems evolve, and concepts such as on-line banking become common, the need to bring CORBA systems out onto the Internet securely becomes important. Organizations providing new Internet interfaces to their systems often require the extra security provided by a firewall. However, this can cause problems with CORBA clients and servers communicating using IIOP through the firewall, since firewalls are not designed to interpret IIOP.

The CORBA/Firewall specification describes how a firewall can process IIOP to allow CORBA objects managed behind the firewall to have operations invoked on them from the outside world. It covers the issues involved in how firewall processing of IIOP can be performed to enable firewalls to process and authorize IIOP requests like any other firewall-supported protocol. This includes firewall support of the following features:

- Processing IIOP as an ordinary application protocol; determining what network traffic is expected to be IIOP (for instance, destination hosts, ports) and performing access control, deciding which IIOP traffic may pass through the firewall, and which may not.
- Protecting inside target object servers from attack by data streams that are not valid IIOP.

The specification covers three types of firewall :

- TCP/IP firewalls
- SOCKS v5.0 firewalls
- GIOP proxy firewalls, for instance, IONA's Orbix® Wonderwall™

The specification also supports the use of SSL as a transport mechanism for secure invocations through GIOP proxy firewalls, while still providing the same level of access control available to the proxy administrator regarding permitted users and permitted targets.

This incorporates support for:

- Client- and server-side authentication for proxified connections.
- Access to client and server X.509 certificates.
- Access control to firewall proxies.

The specification supports the following features for client and server side firewalls and IIOP:

- Multiple firewall enclaves (use of multiple firewalls in a system—each one must be traversed in order to reach the outside world or the server).
- For server-side firewalls:
     Information for traversal of firewalls is contained in the IOR.

Multiple entry points and inbound routes supported.
• For client-side firewalls:
Single outbound route.
Traversal information configured into ORB/firewall.

Details required for supporting this secure firewall traversal are obtained from the IOR. The specification also covers support for bi-directional GIOP where the client-server connection is reused so the server can invoke on the client's object.

There are currently no implementations of this CORBA/Firewall specification available. ORB vendors to date have provided IIOP firewall proxies, such as IONA's Wonderwall, or support for using HTTP tunnelling to mask IIOP messages and allow them pass undetected through the firewall, as supported by Inprise's Gatekeeper product. The new specification allows IIOP messages to pass through firewalls securely, without compromising the authorization and logging abilities of the firewall as tunnelling can, and with added provision for SSL connections for added security functionality. IIOP proxies such as Wonderwall already provide all the functionality of a standard firewall, without any security compromise. Support for the new specification allows vendors such as IONA to provide this functionality in a standardized manner. At the time of writing, IONA had already announced pending support for the new CORBA/Firewall specification; it is expected that other vendors such as Inprise and the firewall vendors will follow suit.

Solutions for the Real World

Probably the biggest challenge facing developers of secure systems today is trying to find a comprehensive solution that can address all of the features required of the system, while still providing room for the system to evolve and grow. The market today is showing the strains from having emerged quickly from a DCE- and RACF-dominated world into an Internet arena focused on more lightweight technologies than the established DCE or RACF solutions. There are a myriad of emerging standards, technologies, and products that solve one piece of the security puzzle or another, but do not yet interoperate well.

Enterprise systems are moving increasingly into the Internet environment, building Java frontends to existing systems, or developing new Internet-focused systems with requirements for thin client models, and therefore lightweight security libraries not typically available from, or suitable to, traditional DCE/RACF security solutions. Within this Internet-oriented world, firewall technology is understood and established, but does not solve all the issues around system and data protection. In this final section, we will look at the requirements of Enterprise CORBA systems, and the CORBA security technologies that can be used to address these security requirements.

Enterprise CORBA Security: Making It All Work Together

When choosing which CORBA technology to apply to solve particular system security issues, the problems that need to be addressed depend on the model and architecture of the distributed system. Enterprise organizations that have worldwide distributed corporate systems will have different requirements from a system with a large amount of public access and Internet availability (such as an on-line banking system, or web-commerce systems). Sometimes systems will be a combination of both, but for the purpose of this discussion, we will loosely divide the problems faced by these two types, and the CORBA technologies which can be used to address them.

From our security policy section, we learned that the main issues to be considered when moving to the step of implementing a security policy are:

- The users, groups and organisations that can be granted or denied access to all or certain CORBA server objects or their operations.
- The server objects and operations that can be accessed by any unknown user (that is, which servers will be insecure servers).
- The level of authentication (none, one-way, or mutual authentication) that a user or server principal requires and supports for communications with another entity to proceed.
- The quality of message protection (none, data integrity, and/or data confidentiality) that a user or server principal requires and supports for communications with another entity to proceed.
- The delegation policy of a server principal. For example, if the server requires the client to communicate its security credentials to it so that the server can perform operations acting as that client.
- The requirement for non-repudiation in the system to enforce accountability for actions carried out in the system.

Security Feature	Requirement	Example
Authentication	Required before any secure action takes place	For a system dealing with any kind of business data, the first step is to ensure that the communicating user is indeed an employee and not an imposter in the system. This can be done using a system login/password or user security certificate.
Authorization	Per user, department/group and organization	Accounting information may be public (within the organization) for data such as corporate process information on claiming expenses. Other data should be available only to individual employees (for example, individual salary information). Some data should be available to groups such as accountants and senior executives only (for instance, corporate revenue information)
Authorization	ACLs required per secure server, per object instance, and per operation	Depending on how business data is stored, ACLs may be required at the operation, object, or server level in the business logic

Security Feature	Requirement	Example
		layer providing access to the data—for example, an object providing an interface to corporate revenue information may have operations to read and write the information. ACLs would be required per operation in this case, allowing accountants and senior executives to read the revenue information, but allowing only accountants to revise it.
Message Protection	Data confidentiality and integrity for all highly sensitive information passed around in the system	Information on company financial revenue reports, potentially damaging if in the hands of analysts or competitors, would be highly sensitive information requiring encryption and data integrity protection at all times.
Delegation of credentials	Simple	The credential delegation requirements of this system are relatively simple. For example, the company uses an automated shipping process. Receipt and acknowledgment of a payment is registered with a financial records server, which then results in the automated shipping of a product to the customer via a product shipment server. In this case, once the financial records server is told that payment has been received, it invokes on the product shipment server to authorize the shipment. This occurs under the authority of the finance clerk who entered the payment into the system.
Logging	Required for all financial transactions	For all financial transactions such as payroll payouts, quarterly revenue reports, and expenses payouts, keeping a log to record the transactions is typically a mandatory requirement.
Non-repudiation	Required for all security related actions in the system	New, inexperienced, or devious users in the system can sometimes gain access to unauthorized resources, despite security policies being in place. Should this happen, digital signatures and logging can be used to ensure the employee in question can be tracked down and held accountable for any actions carried out in the system.

Internal Intranet System

For internal enterprise systems with many users, a typical security policy could be expected to include requirements for many user and data types, credential delegation, message protection in some situations, and logging. In the table below, we look at a sample security policy for an enterprise system, taking examples from a corporate accounting department and the security requirements of this department as a microcosm of the security needs of the system at large.

The example outlined above of the corporate financial accounting department is in many ways a microcosm of the requirements of a typical enterprise secure system. This accounting department deals with multiple data authorization levels and multiple user types. The types of data in the system will vary from individual employee financial and salary records to overall quarterly revenue figures for public companies. User types may be normal employees with permission to read only their personal data, or accountants, managers, and executive staff with broader authorization. In a system such as this, a security service capable of fine-grained control of access to the financial data is required. For instance, it must support authorization based on different user types and groups. It may even require access control lists down to the level of permitting or denying specific users access to specific operations on specific objects. For particularly sensitive information, such as company financial reports, message protection for data in transit may also be required. Other information may require little or no protection at all—for instance, data providing information on standard financial processes for all employees, such as how to claim expenses. For all financial transactions, it is expected that logging is a mandatory requirement.

For a system requiring the kind of functionality outlined above, the CORBA technology solution designed to address all of these features is an implementation of the CORBA security service. Whether an implementation of CORBA level 1 or level 2 security is required depends on the lower-level requirements of the system. In many cases, level 1 security will suffice; only in systems dealing with highly sensitive information, or complex levels of authorization, or dynamically changing security attributes, may level 2 be required.

Implementations of the CORBA security service are available from ORB vendors today. With the advent of the Internet however, many corporations are seeking the kind of functionality achieved in CORBA level 1/level 2 security, but built over a security mechanism suitable to Internet and Java environments. As a result, vendors are now building implementations of the CORBA security service over the SSL transport layer. For interoperability, the official standard for secure interoperability between CORBA security services is to use SecIOP. However, with the increasing use of SSL and SSL-based security services, providing security at a transport level lower than IIOP, this protocol has not been implemented or used as much as initially anticipated. The next example discusses the use of SSL.

External Internet System

For systems focused on providing public services via the Internet rather than connectivity and information to employees, the security requirements for the system may be somewhat different. Systems such as online banking systems, web commerce applications or Internet stock trading systems all provide a service to the public via the World Wide Web. Public servers may be located behind or

Security Feature	Requirement	Example
Authentication	Mandatory for client and server	A customer using an on-line shopping server needs to be sure that the server is not an imposter, before passing credit card details over the network to this server. Likewise, a server accepting an order from a customer, needs to be sure that the customer is who they claim to be, and not an imposter.
Data confidentiality	Required for all Internet communications	When sending credit card details to the shopping server via the Internet, encryption is required to ensure the information cannot be read (or "snooped") while in transit.
Data integrity	Required for all Internet communications	Again, when dealing with sensitive information in a public arena, we need to ensure that not only are the credit card details not observed in transit, but that the message containing them is also not tampered with. Credit card fraud is not uncommon, and the details need to be protected.
Authorization	Firewall level, per user	For a public server, application-level access control may not be a requirement, since all functionality on the server will typically be available to any users who communicate with it and are authenticated against it. Firewall-level access control will often suffice if there is a requirement for authorization at all, by providing a single point of access control for the system while still ensuring authorization of servers is maintained.
Credential Delegation	None	In a relatively simple system such as this, dealing with a small number of public servers and a group of users typically all having the same authorization level, credential delegation is not usually required.
Non-repudiation, logging	Depends on system type	For a web-commerce system taking orders for products, non-repudiation may be required as a type of customer contract so the server has proof that the customers made a purchase at a particular time or date, and authorized the server to debit their bank account. Logging may also be required to support this.

in front of a firewall. For this system design, the main security features are not focused so much on fine-grained access control measures but more on protection of data while in transit over the Internet. In these types of systems, public servers are handling users of similar if not identical authorization levels, and the focus is on providing protection of sensitive data being sent from a user to a web-commerce or shopping server. Let's look at an example, focusing on a simple web-commerce system, where an online shopping server accepts orders from customers over the Internet. Customers must pass their credit card details to the public server over the Internet in order to make the purchase.

For systems requiring this type of functionality, focusing on authentication, message protection, non-repudiation and logging, with application level access control functionality not being required, the best solution from a CORBA technology viewpoint is an implementation of the CORBA/SSL specification, perhaps in conjunction with a firewall proxy supporting the CORBA Firewall specification. The CORBA/SSL specification provides

- Authentication, mutual if required, using X.509 certificates.
- Data privacy, using encryption.
- Data integrity.

An implementation of the CORBA firewall specification, if using a GIOP proxy firewall, will add the following:

- IIOP and SSL interoperability with a GIOP proxy firewall.
- Firewall-level access control.
- Logging, if supported by the firewall.

Vendors such as IONA and Inprise have developed IIOP proxies for firewalls, and HTTP tunneling methodologies. IONA's OrbixWonderwall already provides a GIOP proxy for IIOP interoperability with firewalls, providing firewall-level access control and logging. Support for the CORBA firewall specification will additionally provide SSL interoperability as well, providing all the security required for a public system such as this. Inprise's Gatekeeper uses HTTP tunneling for firewall navigation, allowing users to navigate firewalls by piggybacking onto HTTP requests. Support for SSL is also achieved through use of the tunneling mechanism.

In all cases, using an SSL-based transport has the advantages of being suitable for both C++ and Java systems, and, when used as part of a CORBA security service, or with a CORBA firewall implementation, can provide the additional security features required for systems not available as part of the standard SSL protocol. For enterprise CORBA systems typically consisting of disparate languages and platforms, SSL is seen as a solution suitable not only for the Internet, but also to provide security across the system, even to provide integration with COBOL-based mainframe systems using RACF technologies. For this reason, ORB vendors are developing CORBA level 1 and level 2 security services based on the SSL protocol.

For large-scale systems, while CORBA has comprehensively addressed many of the functional aspects for providing security in the system, manageability and scalability issues have not been fully addressed. Problems such as distributing and updating user authentication certificates or authorization credentials, maintaining records of users that may not be permitted access to systems under any circumstances, and the implementation details of the storage of authentication information (whether to use Smart Cards, secure tokens, or login and password)—none of these issues have yet been addressed by CORBA, nor are they likely to be. Since CORBA deals with functionality specification rather than implementation detail, these issues must be solved separately outside of the CORBA security arena. There are many successful products on the market that deal with these issues, providing full support for SSL and X509 security standards, and that can be used with the CORBA security services to manage a large-scale secure distributed system.

In general, CORBA has evolved well to meet the changing demands for security in a distributed system. The technologies and methods used to provide this functionality are themselves evolving to meet the new demands posed by the Internet and distributed nature of enterprise systems today. As new technologies come to the fore, CORBA is providing new specifications to support integrations and implementations of these technologies in a standardized manner and to allow independent CORBA users and system implementors to choose the right solution to satisfy the particular needs for their secure CORBA system. There is no silver bullet, but the options are there to allow CORBA users the freedom to choose the right tools to provide full security to enterprise CORBA systems.

Database Integration and Transaction Processing

In this part of the book, we look at how to integrate CORBA with existing Database Management Systems to build CORBA-based transaction processing systems.

First of all, we give a brief introduction to object persistence in general (Chapter 9 "Object Persistence"). This introduction is not related to CORBA at all, but the following chapters make use of the techniques described there. Based on this general introduction to object persistence, we have a closer look at CORBA and database integration, and how to implement persistent CORBA objects (Chapter 10 "Database Integration"). Next, we examine the different ways transactions can be implemented in a CORBA environment (Chapter 11 "Transactions in a CORBA Environment"). One of the approaches leads directly to distributed transaction processing, which is discussed in detail (Chapter 12 "Distributed Transaction Processing"). An important technology introduced here is a CORBA-based transaction service, the object transaction service (OTS). Since OTS is such an essential technology for building CORBA-based transaction processing systems, we explain how to program with an OTS, and also how an OTS affects issues like ACID properties and concurrency control. In the same context, we also discuss advanced transaction concepts like multi transactions, sagas, and nested transactions. Related to these topics is the concept of a session. Sessions in a CORBA environment can be quite complex, and often involve additional concurrency control mechanisms on top of the standard mechanisms provided by the database. Therefore, we discuss different concurrency control mechanisms at this point, and then how database-level concurrency control can be combined with application-level concurrency control. Based on this discussion, we explore a real-world example (Chapter 13 "User Sessions").

Object Persistence

$\mathbf{T}$oday's data is stored in a variety of different formats. Common data storage mechanisms range from the hierarchical and network databases of the mainframe area to newer relational and object-oriented databases. Also, a large amount of data is stored in files, for instance, configuration files, HTML files, word processor documents, and spreadsheet files.

In this chapter we examine how these different data formats can be accessed through objects. Or, put a different way, how objects can be stored in these different data formats. We explore mappings between object models and different data models in general. The main emphasis is on object/relational mapping techniques. This reflects the fact that today in many projects object-oriented programming languages are combined with relational databases.

Notice that this chapter is not related to CORBA objects and persistence at all. Instead, it provides the foundation for the discussion of CORBA, database integration, and transactions in the following chapters.

Introduction

After a brief characterization of relational and object-oriented database management systems, this chapter examines the impedance mismatch phenomenon, and discusses how critical the impedance mismatch in a persistent object system is for the different types of DBMS. Based on this discussion, the common features of an object persistence service are defined.

Given that the impedance mismatch between the relational and the object model is usually quite drastic, we explore object/relational mapping techniques. After this, we briefly discuss object-oriented databases.

Providing support for keeping data consistent is one of the main requirements for every persistence service. Therefore, we look at data consistency, including transactions, concurrency control, and data synchronization in a distributed system.

RDBMS vs. ODBMS

As you might expect, object database management systems (ODBMS) provide the most natural way of storing objects and relationships between objects in persistent storage. The persistent state of the objects is stored in a database. Database clients provide object implementations. Since state and implementation are separated, it is the ODBMS's responsibility to provide a mechanism to amalgamate them in a way that gives the programmer the impression of dealing with real persistent objects.

Most commercially available ODBMSs are tightly coupled to a particular programming language, using a schema compiler to generate a database schema from the class definitions in the program code. An ODBMS usually implements some form of cache in the client library. Often, some form of smart pointer is used to enable clients to access persistent objects in this cache. If an invocation is made on a persistent object via such a smart pointer, the smart pointer checks if the object is in the local cache. If so, the invocation can be delegated directly to the transient instance, which represents the persistent object in the local cache. Otherwise, the object's state must be obtained from the database before the delegation can be done. Usually, persistent objects can only be accessed in the context of a transaction, and if the transaction is committed, the changes are written back from the cache to the database. Most ODBMSs provide some sort of database server which is responsible for providing database clients with the object state, as well as administrative functions such as managing an object lock table to enable concurrent access to objects. Examples of commercially available ODBMS include Versant, ObjectStore, Objectivity, and Poet.

The theoretical foundation for relational database management systems (RDBMS) is the tuple relational calculus. In an RDBMS, data is stored in tables. Each data item is represented as a row in a table. Each row can have multiple columns. Each column represents a basic data type like numbers or strings. A key identifies a row in a table. Relationships are represented using foreign keys, referencing to rows in the same or a different table. Interaction between database clients and the database server is done via SQL. Most RDBMS provide some basic language bindings which enable database clients to send SQL statements to the database server, and retrieve the result. A query result is usually a set of rows. Similar to object-oriented iterators, databases provide cursors to handle variable-length query results. Examples of commercially available RBDMSs are Oracle, Sybase, DB2 and Informix.

Relational data stores are well-suited to storing huge amounts of data, using SQL as a flexible and efficient language to access the data. Unfortunately, relationship traversal with an RDBMS is usually quite costly. This area is traditionally a domain of ODBMSs, which are highly optimized for management and navigation of complex object graphs. A key difference between RDBMS and ODBMS for relationship traversal is the way they handle caching. Compare to RDBMS, ODBMS provide more sophisticated mechanisms for optimizing application-specific caching strategies. For example, object clustering allows objects to be grouped logically to reflect application-specific dependencies between objects.

But if ODBMSs seem so well-suited for implementing persistent objects, why do so many systems use RDBMS instead? Often, the decision against an ODBMS, and for an RDBMS, is not only influenced by technical factors, but also by strategic factors. But strategic thinking is not the only reason why many projects today combine object-oriented programming languages with relational databases; another important reason is the existing investment in relational technology.

The Impedance Mismatch Problem

Traditionally, the term *impedance mismatch* is used to describe the difference between the data structures provided by the database and the data structures provided by the programming language which is used to access the database.

Systems that implement persistent objects, however, are usually based on three different models: the design object model, the implementation object model, and the persistent data model. There is often a conflict or tension between these three different models. In this book, it is this three-way tug-of-war in object-oriented systems that we refer to as the *impedance mismatch*. Figure 9.1 shows the conflict triangle, which represents the impedance mismatch in object-oriented systems. This illustrates that often, there is not only a mismatch between fundamentally different model worlds, like the object-oriented and the relational model, but also between the different object models. For example, an object design model might be based on multiple inheritance, but the implementation language may not support this. Or, even worse, the model might be object-oriented, but the programming language may not support object-orientation at all. For instance, the MOTIF GUI class library is implemented in an object-oriented fashion, but uses the non-OO language C.

Next, we discuss two examples of the impedance mismatch, one where the impedance mismatch is moderate, and one where the mismatch is quite drastic.

Let's assume we build an application from scratch, using an OO modeling language like UML, an OO programming language like C++, and an ODBMS like Versant or ObjectStore. We start with the object model. Maybe we are lucky, and our modeling tool provides a code generation feature, which can be used to generate a skeleton implementation from the object model, including class header files and empty method bodies. Maybe we are even luckier, and our modeling tool provides some sort of reverse engineering, which enables us to incorporate changes we make in the implementation model back into the design model. However, there will most likely be some minor mismatches, since usually not all the programming language features can be represented by the modeling tool, and vice versa.

Using an ODBMS, implementing the object model and specifying the persistent object schema often go hand-in-hand. However, a common problem is that an ODBMS requires us to use DBMS specific data types, which may not be supported by the modeling tool. Therefore, the imple-

Figure 9.1   OO impedance mismatch conflict triangle

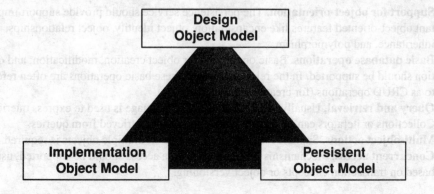

mentation model is likely to be closer to the model imposed by the ODBMS. Also, the ODBMS may not support all the features supported by the particular programming language. For example, the programming language may support multiple inheritance, but the ODBMS does not.

In this first example, there is only a small mismatch between the design model and the implementation model. The mismatch between the implementation model and the database schema will depend on how well the programming language and the ODBMS fit together. If the ODBMS is specifically designed for the particular OO programming language, there is a high likelihood that the mismatch will be very small.

The second example assumes that we use an RDBMS. We are given a strongly normalized database schema, which is not object-oriented at all. The schema describes a database which is used by an already existing application, so we cannot adapt it to the needs of our new application. We can now do an object-oriented analysis of the schema, and come out with an object model, which we think represents the database schema on the one hand, and the business object model that we want to implement on the other. From the object model, we can derive implementation classes as described above. The big problem now is that we somehow need to map our objects back to the rows in the database, and this is usually a quite difficult task, especially if the schema is highly normalized. There might be a relationship between some of the classes in the implementation model and tables in the database, but often classes and tables are orthogonal if the schema is normalized. In this case, implementing a mapping is usually situation-dependent, and finding a structured approach to bridging the mismatch is difficult.

Usually, the impedance mismatch problem is particularly drastic when using an OO programming language in conjunction with an RDBMS. For this reason, we have a closer look at how an RDBMS can be accessed from an OO programming language in the section *Accessing Relational Databases*. First, however, we define the standard features required by an object persistence service.

Features of an Object Persistence Service

There are different ways of implementing persistent objects. Sometimes a DBMS provides direct support for object persistence. In other cases, we might have some object persistence layer on top of the standard DBMS services, which bridges the impedance mismatch between the programming language's object-model and the DBMS's data model. The generally desired features of an object persistence service are:

- **Support for object-orientation.** The persistence service should provide support important object-oriented features like encapsulation, object identity, object relationships, inheritance, and polymorphism.
- **Basic database operations.** Basic operations for object creation, modification, and deletion should be supported. In the relational world, these basic operations are often referred to as CRUD operations (for create/read/update/delete).
- **Query and retrieval.** Usually, some kind of query language is used to express queries. Collections or iterators can be used to handle the results retrieved from queries.
- **Multi-object actions.** Support for composite actions on multiple objects is required.
- **Concurrent access.** Mechanisms for concurrent data access should be supported, usually based on transaction concepts or object versioning.

• **Language bindings.** Bindings for different programming languages should exist, for exemple, for C++, Smalltalk, and Java.

Accessing Relational Databases

Database clients interact with a relational database server by sending SQL queries to the server. Depending on the query, the database server may update some data or return a query result. Queries and query results are usually provided as a set of name/value pairs. Most language bindings for a relational database handle this by mapping name/value pairs to programming language variables, and vice versa. This enables the client to send queries to the server, and to process the query results. In this section we want to look at some common language bindings for relational databases.

Native SQL APIs

Most relational database vendors provide bindings for traditional programming languages such as C and COBOL. A few provide specialized bindings for OO programming languages such as C++ and Smalltalk, while fewer still provide native access through Java. Examples of native SQL access products are the Oracle Call Interface (OCI), Oracle Pro*C (for embedded SQL) and Informix ESQL (embedded SQL). Notice that call-level interfaces sometimes provide more flexibility than embedded SQL on the one hand, but are usually more difficult to program on the other. The following code fragment shows how embedded SQL provides a language binding for the C programming language:

```
// Pro*C example for embedded SQL

void db_set_stock_description(char* symbol, char* desc)
{
    EXEC SQL BEGIN DECLARE SECTION;
    char db_symbol[6];
    char db_desc[20];
    EXEC SQL END DECLARE SECTION;

      // Not shown: copy arguments to db variables

    EXEC SQL UPDATE STOCK
      SET DESCRIPTION = :db_desc
      WHERE CODE = :db_symbol;

    // Not shown: handle errors
}
```

This example shows how a function could set a new description for a given stock in our STOCK table. Recall the STOCK and STOCK_PRICE tables introduced in Chapter 4. The STOCK table has two columns, SYMBOL and DESCRIPTION. The STOCK_PRICE table refers to the STOCK table using a foreign key SYMBOL. In this chapter, we use these two tables for discussing some examples.

Table STOCK

String SYMBOL	string DESCRIPTION

Open Connectivity

Some attempts have been made to standardize the access to relational databases. The idea behind this is to define a standard API, which can be used to access relational databases, and then provide different implementations of the API for specific databases. The most popular open connectivity standard is Microsoft's Open Database Connectivity (ODBC). More recently, a similar standard for the Java programming language emerged, known as JDBC, which enables Java programs to access relational databases in a standardized way.

The programming comfort that open connectivity tools provide is somewhere between the native SQL APIs discussed in the previous section and the OO SQL wrapper classes to be covered in the following section.

OO SQL Wrapper Classes

Finally, we look at OO SQL wrapper classes. These are class libraries which model the elements of SQL as objects. However, notice that this doesn't mean that the data itself is exposed in the form of objects. In the following example using RogueWave DBTools.h++, we can see how SQL elements such as database, table, column, and result are modeled as C++ objects. The example selects all stocks with a price greater than 50, and prints out the result set.

```
// Rogue Wave DBTools.h++ example:
// Database connection details not shown
RWDBDatabase aDatabase = RWDBManager::database (...);
RWDBTable aTable = aDatabase.table("STOCK_PRICE");
RWDBSelector aSelector = aDatabase.selector();

aSelector << aTable;
aSelector.where(aTable["PRICE"] > 50f);
RWDBResult aResult = aSelector.execute(session);
RWDBReader aReader = aResult.table().reader();

float balance;
RWCString name;
while(aReader()) {
 aReader >> balance >> name;
 cout << name << ":" << balance << endl;
}
```

Object/Relational Mapping

In the discussion above we have introduced a set of different language bindings that allow us to process SQL. All of these language bindings somehow bind the elements of SQL to a programming language. In the following we introduce a technique known as *object/relational mapping* (O/R mapping). The fundamental difference between O/R mapping and the above SQL language bindings is that O/R mapping attempts to provide an object-oriented view of relational data. This means that the data itself is represented as objects.

Figure 9.2   Basic object relational mapping

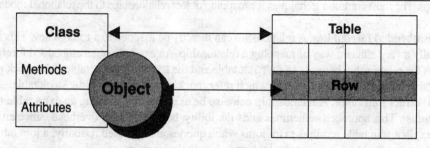

Basic Mapping Techniques

In the following we explain the basic techniques used for object/relational mapping, including a discussion of the mapping of basic object-oriented concepts like classes, relationships, and inheritance to the relational world.

Mapping Classes to Tables

The basic idea of object/relational mapping is actually quite simple: classes are mapped to tables, object instances are represented as rows, and object attributes as columns in a relational table. Figure 9.2 illustrates the basic object/relational mapping.

Often, this very simple one-to-one mapping between class and table is not sufficient. For example, if a relational schema is highly normalized, it may be better to use a class to wrap multiple tables. This means that a single object can represent multiple, related rows in different tables. We further discuss the problem of normalization in the section "Top Down vs. Bottom Up." Finally, there are sometimes cases where it may make sense to map different classes to the same table. One example for such a mapping is the unification approach for mapping inheritance, discussed below.

Object ID

Each object should have a unique ID, which should not be changed during the lifetime of the object. This can easily be accomplished by assigning each object an attribute called the object identifier (OID), usually a large integer value. In the relational world, this means that each table has a column OID. The OID column should ideally have no business meaning. A column with a business meaning can potentially change, and this will usually have effects not only on the table itself, but also on other tables using the ID as a foreign key to the first table, as well as on indexes. In general, the use of surrogate keys generated by the RDBMS for identity in all tables provides a more standard access paradigm that promotes the use of generic code and helper functions for accessing data in a relational store.

Relationships

Relationships play a very important role, both in the object world and in the relational world. In the relational world, reference relationships are realized by foreign keys. The results are bi-directional relationships, since it is always possible to find the foreign key that matches a primary key, and vice versa. Using an object-oriented programming language, the direct way of expressing relationships is to use pointers or references. Many programming languages provide list and collection types, which can be used to express one-to-many relationships. Often, hash-tables are used to implement qualified relationships. The most common techniques for mapping object relationships to the relational model are:

- **Embedded foreign key.** A relationship can directly be mapped to a foreign key. This is usually a very efficient way of mapping a relationship. An example of an embedded foreign key is the relationship between our STOCK table and the STOCK_PRICE table—the stock price table has a foreign key SYMBOL, which refers back to a single row in the stock table.
- **Distinct join table.** A relationship can also be expressed by creating an extra table (a *join table*). This approach sometimes adds flexibility, but it also adds overhead, since an explicit join table requires extra joins when queries are executed. Usually, a join table is only required to express many-to-many object relationships.
- **Folded classes.** Finally, one can combine classes by *folding* them into a single table. Usually, this is only possible for one-to-one relationships and attributes. As an example of a folded class, let's assume we want to use a new, slightly more complex type for money; A money object may have two attributes, currency and amount. A stock price has an attribute of type money. For performance reasons, we could add the two columns CURRENCY and AMOUNT to the table STOCK_PRICE directly, instead of defining a new table MONEY.

Reference and aggregation are important relationships in the object world.. While reference relationships can be easily implemented using one of the above techniques, aggregation relationships can be more difficult. In the object world, we expect a composite aggregation to propagate deletion (that is, the aggregation as a whole must be deleted, including all aggregated objects). In the relational world, we often use database triggers to propagate deletion of aggregated values.

Inheritance

The relational model does not provide the notion of inheritance. Therefore, mapping an object model's inheritance hierarchy to a relational schema is not an easy task. There are several different possibilities for mapping inheritance on the object model level to the relational model; all have certain advantages and disadvantages. For example, one can map each class to its own table, map only class fragments to tables, or map all classes into a single table. Each of these approaches has different performance characteristics, and different degrees of flexibility with regard to changes in the inheritance hierarchy.

Horizontal Partitioning

Each concrete class in the inheritance graph is mapped to a distinct table. Each of these tables contains column definitions for all attributes of the concrete class, plus all attributes of its inherited concrete and abstract base classes. Abstract classes are not mapped to their own tables. Horizontal partitioning can support multiple inheritance. Column names may be prefixed with the name of the class on which the attribute was originally defined. Horizontal partitioning provides a mapping which maintains the simple *map-each-class-to-a-table* notion and provides good performance for strongly typed data manipulation operations. The example in Figure 9.3 shows how horizontal partitioning looks for a base class stock with two specializations, option and preferred stock. A request to retrieve all the preferred stock objects requires only a single simple query that returns the entire collection; in essence,

Figure 9.3 Horizontal parttitioning

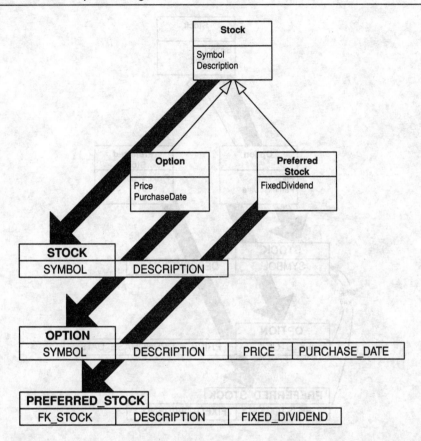

issuing a SELECT * FROM PREFERRED_STOCK SQL call. However, it also has a number of disadvantages. First, if a change is made to one of the abstract base classes or to a concrete class near the root of the inheritance graph, say to add an additional attribute, then each and every concrete class/ table that inherits from this class would have to be changed. From a query perspective, a weakly typed query will require multiple table queries followed by an aggregation of the results. For example, to retrieve all the stock objects, we would have to issue three individual SQL SELECT queries; one to retrieve all the instances of stock, a second to retrieve all the instances of option and a third to retrieve all the preferred stocks. Theses intermediate result collections would then have to be combined to create a single unified collection containing all stocks. It may be possible to define relational views that overlay a horizontal partitioned schema to make this type of query more efficient.

Vertical Partitioning

Each derived class is mapped to a new table, which contains only those attributes defined explicitly on that class. In addition, each table contains a foreign key to the table of its base class. Multiple inheritance is supported by the inclusion of multiple foreign key columns in the table for

Figure 9.4   Vertical partitioning

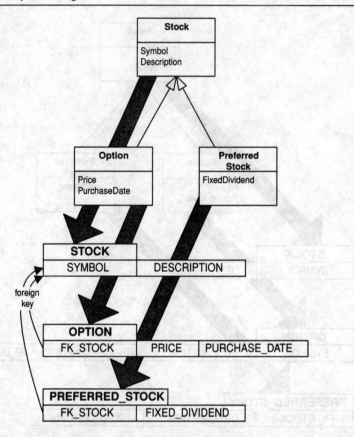

the derived class. Extensions and modifications can be easily incorporated as they require changes to be made to only one table. However, any query to retrieve instances of a derived class/ table will always require at least one join and in cases where the inheritance hierarchy is deep, multiple joins may be required. This will affect the performance of all operations that manipulate data (insert, query, update and delete). An example of the vertical partitioning method is shown in Figure 9.4.

Unification

All abstract and concrete classes within an entire root branch of the hierarchy are mapped to a single table. An additional column, referred to as the *type discriminator,* is used to identify the actual type of each row. In most cases, the actual class name can be used for this purpose. This mapping does not conform with the normalization rules endorsed by relational design. Consequently, the tables may be very sparsely populated, particularly if one leaf class had a large number of attributes defined. This mapping is most beneficial when abstract parent classes are used; that is, there are no real instances of the abstract class, although the attributes defined against it will appear in each class that inherits from it. An example of the unification method is shown in Figure 9.5.

Figure 9.5 Unification

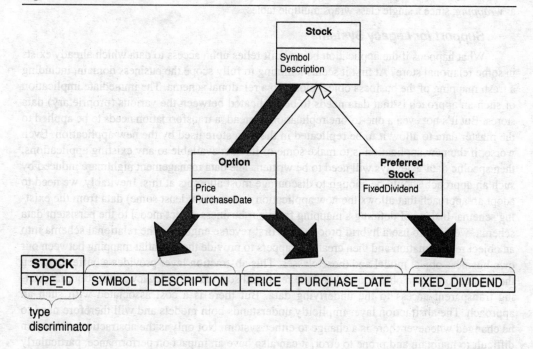

Top-Down vs. Bottom-Up

In general, there are two ways of looking at object/relational mapping: storing objects in relational tables, and accessing relational tables through objects. Often, these two approaches are referred to as top-down and bottom-up. The idea of the top-down approach is to start with an object model, and then derive a relational data schema from it. The bottom-up approach starts with a relational data schema, and derives an object model from it.

The top-down approach allows a focus on the business logic, for example using UML to describe the general model. The relational data schema can then be derived from the object model. Care must be taken that the derived relational data schema is designed in a way that ensures performance and data integrity. It is not always possible to use simple, one-to-one mappings between classes and tables. Often, the data schema must be adapted to the specifics of the relational world. For example, normalization can be an issue. Often, relational data schemas are normalized to avoid redundancy and update anomalies. However, very often extreme normalization can lead to poor performance, highly fragmented data schemas, and drastically increased complexity. This is why many people tend to avoid a too-strict normalization.

The bottom-up approach is most commonly used in cases where a relational data schema already exists, and changing the schema is not an option. In these cases, we analyze the relational schema and try to derive an object model which reflects the business logic on the one hand, and the relational schema on the other hand. This can be particularly difficult in cases where the relational schema has been normalized. In these cases we will often have to map multiple tables to a single class, so that a single object instance represents a set of data rows. Often, this approach is referred to as *wrapping*, since a single class wraps multiple tables.

Support for Legacy Systems

What happens if the application being built relies upon access to data which already exists in some relational store? At first it seems tempting to fully scope the business domain, including a fresh mapping of the business object model to a relational schema. The immediate implication of such an approach is that data needs to be replicated between the various (proprietary) data stores. But it's not even a one-to-one replication; instead, a transformation needs to be applied to the master data to allow it to be replicated in the data store used by the new application. Even worse, if the new application is to make some of its data available to any existing applications, then specific data-gateways will need to be written. The data management nightmare induced by such an approach should be enough to discourage most attempts at this. Inevitably, we need to adopt an approach that allows the new application to access (at least some) data from the existing schema. Instead of defining a mapping from our business object model to the persistent data schema, we need to use a hybrid process that first reverse engineers the relational schema into an object representation and then creates wrappers to provide the essential mapping between our own business object model and those classes. This abstraction layer provides a buffer between the application's own object model and the relational schema of the legacy application, facilitating transparent access to the underlying data. But there is a cost associated with such an approach. The abstraction layer implicitly understands both models and will therefore need to be changed whenever there is a change to either system. Not only is the abstraction code often difficult to maintain and prone to error, it can also have an impact on performance, particularly if the application business objects simply delegate to the data-access objects which represent the relational data. In general, any additional redirection will reduce both the performance and flexibility of the application.

Object/Relational Code Generation

Implementing object/relational mappings is a highly repetitive task. Code generators are ideally suited to take over this work. An object/relational code generator can either start from the relational database schema (bottom-up), or provide means to define an object model, from which the O/R access code can be generated (top-down). In either case, the code generator will require meta-information, that is, more detailed information about the mapping that we want to generate.

Examples of object/relational code generation tools include Persistence from Persistence Software and ONTOS Integrator for C++, and CocoBase for Java. The following is an example that assumes the object model for `Stock` and `StockPrice` classes are defined using the Persistence tool, mapping them to the `STOCK` and `STOCK_PRICE` tables. The Persistence tool provides a GUI for such a top-down approach, which can be used to graphically define the object model and annotate it with information about the related classes. Based on this information, the Persistence tool automatically generates a set of C++ classes. The example is for a simple application that uses the generated classes to query for stock prices and prints out the result. It is enlightening to compare this example with the one given in the section "OO SQL Wrapper Tools."

```
// Persistence O/R example
StockPriceCltn result =                                          (1)
    StockPrice::querySQLWhere ("price>50");                      (2)

for (int idx=0; idx<result.extent(); idx++)                      (3)
{
    StockPrice* sp = (*result)[idx];                             (4)
    cout << sp->getSymbol() << ": "
        << sp->getDate() << ", "
        << sp->getPrice() << endl;                               (5)
}
```

In (1), we declare an instance of a generated collection class, which is used in the following to keep a query result. In (2), we execute a query, using the querySQLWhere() function on the StockPrice class. This class is generated by the Persistence tool, and can be used to access the STOCK_PRICE table. An instance of the class represents a row in the table. In (3), we define a for loop to iterate over the result set. In (4), we access an element of the result set, using the generated bracket operator. The result is a stock price object, which represents one row of the query result. Finally, in (5) we access the specific stock price to print out some detailed information. Notice that the StockPrice class provides generated accessors and mutators (get/set methods) for each attribute.

Object Granularity

Most commercial O/R code generators implement a very straightforward object/relational mapping, where each table is directly mapped to one class. The results of this very simplistic approach are usually very fine-grained, data-centric objects. To implement our business logic, we usually have two options. We can add methods to the generated classes, to represent some business functionality. Or, as proposed in the previous section on legacy systems, we can use these fine-grained data objects to implement an additional abstraction layer, which implements the business logic. The second approach is often preferred, especially in situations with highly normalized data.

Limitations of Object/Relational Mapping

Don't be disappointed by the results of a straightforward object/relational mapping. Remember the rationale of object/relational mapping: we are trying to find a workaround for a much more fundamental problem. We are building object-oriented concepts on top of an architecture that was simply not designed to support objects. The problem is that as long as the database doesn't have the necessary object-oriented fundamentals built in, we have to deal with workarounds that will never provide the seamlessness and performance of a solution that is designed from the ground up to support object-orientation. If a system really needs seamless access to objects and high-performance navigation of complex object graphs, an RDBMS is simply the wrong choice, and an object/relational mapping is unlikely to help much. Instead, consider using an ODBMS, or one of the recently emerging object/relational databases.

Object/relational mapping results in fine-grained, data-centric objects. For the parts of an application that implements the simple CRUD (create/read/update/delete) logic, a straightforward object/relational mapping can be extremely useful, since it is much easier to use than, for example, embedded SQL.

However, using a bottom-up approach often results in meaningless objects, that is, objects that have no relationship with real-world entities. In these cases, we often need additional layers on top of the basic object/relational mapping. On the other hand, a top-down approach is often naïve from a relational point of view—for example, it often does not solve problems that are addressed by normalization or strategies for optimizing relational schemas.

In the following chapter on CORBA and database integration, we examine how CORBA IDL interfaces can help wrap complex relational database schemas, exporting services through behavior-centric CORBA business objects.

Object Databases

Object databases combine the semantics of an object-oriented programming language such as C++ with the data management and query facilities of a conventional database system. When an object-database management system (ODBMS) is integrated with an object-oriented programming language, it should be able to support the semantics of the language directly. That is, if the programming language supports inheritance, encapsulation, and polymorphism, then the ODBMS should support these features as well. Because the "in memory" representation of the data is now consistent with its "persistent" representation, the need to transform objects when saving them is greatly reduced. In effect, the impedance mismatch discussed earlier in the chapter often doesn't exist any more, or is very small. In particular, relationships established between objects in the programming language are transparently represented in the database system. Object databases don't just provide a convenient persistence mechanism for object-oriented programming languages; they add additional database features of concurrency, transactions, and query processing. With the significant advantage of a direct mapping between objects in memory and their persistent state, we would have expected to see more ODBMSs used in conjunction with object-oriented languages. Although the market for ODBMS systems has grown, it has not displaced traditional relational systems. A contributing reason is that many new application systems either use or augment an existing relational system. Nevertheless, ODBMSs have found a stable niche in many problem domains where management and traversal of extremely complex object graphs is required, for instance, in CAD/CAM systems.

ODMG

The Object Data Management Group (ODMG) was formed to define and evolve a set of standards that all vendors of object databases would endorse and implement. Before ODMG, the lack of a standard for object databases was a major limitation to their more widespread use. The success of relational database systems did not result simply from a higher level of data independence and a simpler data model than previous systems. Much of their success came from the standardization that they offer. The acceptance of the SQL standard allows a certain degree of portability and interoperability between systems, simplifies learning new relational DBMSs, and represents a wide endorsement of the relational approach. The ODMG recognized these factors and set about defining and refining the specification for object databases. The current ODMG specification level is 2.0, which incorporates a number of significant features such as the Java Persistence Standard (in addition to the C++ and Smalltalk ones that already exist), the meta-object interface and an object interchange format. The major components of the ODMG standard are the ODMG object model, object definition languages (ODL), different language bindings for ODL, and the object query language (OQL):

- **ODMG Object Model.** The ODMG object model is based upon the OMG object model. By adding an ODBMS profile to the core OMG model, the ODMG model has added support for relationships, queries, transactions, and, unsurprisingly, persistence.
- **ODL Object Definition Language.** One of the specification languages available for use with ODMG-compliant databases is ODL, the object definition language. ODL shares some similarities with the SQL-based data definition language (DDL) that is commonly used by relational databases. However, like the OMG's IDL, it is not a full programming language, but rather a specification language for interface signatures.
- **ODMG Language Mappings.** ODL provides the declarative piece of the mapping. ODL is mapped to various programming languages, such as C++, Smalltalk, and Java. From a developer's perspective, there is only one language, not two separate languages. For C++, the mapping between ODL and C++ is expressed as a class library and an extension to the standard C++ class definition grammar.
- **OQL (Object Query Language).** OQL is an SQL-like declarative language that provides a rich environment for querying objects in a database, including high-level primitives for object sets and structures. OQL provides a superset of the SQL-92 SELECT syntax. This means that most SQL SELECT statements that run on relational DBMSs work with the same syntax and semantics on ODMG collection classes. OQL also includes object extensions to support object identity, complex objects, operation invocation, and inheritance. OQL's querying capabilities include the ability to invoke operations in ODMG language bindings, and OQL may be called from within an ODMG language program.

Data Consistency

Obviously, we expect our object persistence service to make data accessible in the form of objects, providing sophisticated mechanisms for navigating relationships and executing queries. However, the most fundamental service that we expect is keeping the data in a consistent state. The object persistence service must provide mechanisms that ensure data consistency, even in the case of concurrent access to the same data.

In the following, we look at issues related to ensuring data consistency, including transactions, concurrency control, and data synchronization.

Transactions

The most natural way of ensuring data consistency is to use the concept of transactions. Almost all database management systems, including ODBMSs, are based on the concept of *transactions*. A transaction is a set of operations that are logically grouped to form an atomic action, which transforms a system's persistent data from one consistent state to another. This means that during the execution of a transaction the system's state can be inconsistent, but that the transaction mechanism guarantees that the state will be consistent again at the end of the transaction. Because the system's state can be inconsistent during execution of a transaction, it is important that transactions are isolated from each other, so that they can see their internal, inconsistent state. This is also referred to as *serialization* of transactions, since it means that even if transactions are executed concurrently, the transaction mechanism must ensure that the net effect is the same as if they were executed serially.

These are only some of the properties supported by transactions, which are examined in much more detail in Chapter 12, "Distributed Transaction Processing."

Concurrency Control

To ensure the serializability of transactions, a DBMS must provide mechanisms for isolating concurrent transactions from one another. This is also referred to as concurrency control. The most common concurrency control technique used on commercial DBMS is locking. If a transaction T_2 wants to access a certain data item, it must get a lock for the data item before accessing it. If another transaction T_1 already holds a lock to the data item which is incompatible with the lock required by T_2, then we have a locking conflict, which must be handled appropriately. The two most common types of locks are *read-locks* and *write-locks*. However, a DBMS might provide additional lock types. Concurrency control and locking are discussed in Chapter 13 "User Sessions."

Isolation levels

Locking can be quite expensive, so isolation is often a tradeoff between performance and concurrency on the one hand, and data consistency on the other. To allow a flexible adjustment that reflects the required level of performance, concurrency, and data consistency, most database management systems support different levels of isolation.

The ANSI/ISO SQL92 standard defines four levels of isolation. Nearly all commercial DBMS provide at least one of these four isolation levels; many can even be configured to use different isolation levels for different transactions. Each of these four isolation levels is related to one of three phenomena that can occur between concurrently executing transactions. These three phenomena are:

- **Dirty read.** A transaction reads data that has been modified by a transaction that has not been committed yet.
- **Non-repeatable read.** A transaction re-reads data it has previously read and finds that another committed transaction has modified or deleted the data in between.
- **Phantom read.** A transaction re-executes a query returning a set of rows that satisfy a particular search condition and finds that another committed transaction has inserted additional rows that satisfy the particular condition.

Based on these three phenomena, the SQL92 standard defines four levels of isolation. Depending on the isolation level a transaction is running on, it might be permitted to experience none, some, or all of these phenomena:

Isolation Level	Dirty Read	Non-Repeatable Read	Phantom Read
Read Uncommitted	Possible	Possible	Possible
Read Committed	Not possible	Possible	Possible
Repeatable Read	Not possible	Not possible	Possible
Serializable	Not possible	Not possible	Not possible

It is important to notice that only the *serializable* isolation level provides full isolation—that is, fully guarantees data consistency. All other isolation levels accept potential data inconsistency for the benefit of increased concurrency and performance.

Data Synchronization

Closely related to the topic of data consistency is the whole area of data synchronization. Consider a scenario where a user has a desktop and a laptop, used to read e-mail and edit documents. How does she synchronize the data between these two computers? The standard approach for documents is to manually copy files back and forth. This often results in many temporary files with slightly different names. Another problem may be that the e-mail program may use a proprietary file format, and may not support easy synchronization between the two computers. There are many tools available to help solve these particular problems, but nonetheless this discussion illustrates the general problem of data synchronization.

In the following, we examine two important parts of data synchronization, caching and replication, from the perspective of object persistence.

Caching

A major advantage that ODBMSs have over common RDBMSs is that they provide sophisticated, business-domain-specific caching. RDBMSs usually provide caching only in the database server, and these caches are based on table structures, not on business domain logic. In contrast, ODBMSs usually provide caching mechanisms on the database client side, and also allow fine-tuning of the caching mechanism on the application level. A common technique is to define clusters of logically related objects which can be managed by the caching mechanism as a group. This is a major benefit of structuring data in an object-oriented manner, since it allows the reflection of dependencies between business objects in the caching strategy. These application-specific caching strategies are a main reason why ODBMSs usually outperform RDBMSs by orders of magnitude when handling navigation of complex relationship graphs.

Some of the object/relational tools that we discussed in the section "OO Code Generation" provide object caches for the database client side. However, recall our discussion in the section "Limitations of Object/Relational Mapping": O/R tools provide workarounds, and as long as the database server does not directly support management of persistent objects, it is unlikely that the results of an O/R-based client-side cache will be comparable with a true ODBMS.

Finally, an interesting question is the extent to which the cache is related to transactions. Some caching mechanisms cache data only for the duration of a transaction. For example, most ODBMSs will allow access to objects only in the context of a transaction, and will flush all objects from the local cache at the end of the transaction.

However, some caching strategies maintain a cache across transactional boundaries. In this case, a special synchronization mechanism must be introduced that ensures data consistency. Often, a timestamp mechanism is used to compare the cached version with the version in the database in case we want to modify and write back an element from the cache. Since we usually do not deal with just a single cache, but with multiple caches, we need to consider some kind of cache synchronization mechanism. If data is changed in the database, we want to communicate this event to the relevant caches, so that they can either update or invalidate the cache entry. This way we reduce the number of potential failures due to cache inconsistencies.

Replication

The main goal of replication is usually to improve system availability and response time. We can replicate either persistent data or active server processes. In the following, we focus on data replication. An important question is how highly synchronized our replicated data should be. In the case of an FTP mirror, we don't expect the replicas to always be fully in synch with the master—it is usually sufficient if the replicas are synchronized with the master once a day, or maybe even only once a week.

On the other hand, we can have replicated systems that expect all replicas to be synchronized virtually instantaneaously. This usually requires distributed transaction processing, which we discuss in more detail in Chapter 12. A common approach is *primary/secondary* replication, where update transactions can only be executed at the primary copy, from where the changes are propagated to the secondary copies.

Replication is quite a complex topic, and we don't provide an in-depth discussion here. For a more detailed discussion on replication, refer to Bernstein (1997).

Summary

The topics covered in this chapter included the object/relational impedance mismatch, issues relationg to relational database systems (such as the limitations of the object/relational mapping approach), object databases, and data consistency. These topics are not CORBA-specific, but are relevant to many CORBA systems. An understanding of these topics essential to obtain the maximum benefit from the remaining chapters in this section, which cover database integration in CORBA systems, transaction processing, distributed transaction processing, and user sessions.

CHAPTER 10

Database Integration

CORBA and database technology can be integrated to support persistent CORBA objects. An ORB provides us with important features such as distribution, interoperability, and technology integration, but also with the benefits of object orientation, like abstraction and encapsulation. Databases, on the other hand, provide us with data persistence and data integrity, transactions, concurrent data access, and also distribution. In the following we discuss how to blend these two technologies together, to leverage each of their strengths, without diminishing the other's benefits. After a general discussion of system architectures, we look at the current CORBA standards, followed by general aspects of integration.

System Architectures

Before discussing the systems architectures that result from an integration of CORBA and databases, we briefly examine each on its own. The CORBA messaging paradigm is relatively simple: CORBA is designed to enable clients to send requests to objects, and possibly receive a reply. Similarly, most databases provide APIs that enable database clients to send queries to a database server. The database server will execute the query, and send some kind of reply. From an integration point of view, there seem to be two obvious possibilities: either the database itself provides a tight integration with CORBA by exporting services using CORBA interfaces, or the integration happens on the application level. Lack of commercially available integrated products usually forces us to do the integration on the application level.[1] Such an application level integration leads quite naturally to system with a three-tier architecture.

Three-Tier Architectures

The basic elements of a three-tier architecture are clients, application servers, and database servers. Clients access application servers via the IDL interfaces exported by the application servers.

---

[1] The recently announced Oracle 8i product promises to support Enterprise Java Beans and IIOP communication. This is an interesting and encouraging development, and we look forward to using this product when it is released.

Figure 10.1 Three-tier CORBA architecture

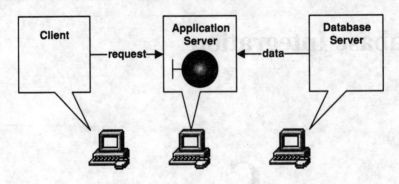

Application servers play a dual role as CORBA servers on the one hand, and database clients on the other, accessing database servers to get persistent state information. The three tiers of such an architecture, as shown in Figure 10.1, are usually defined as

Client	Graphical User Interface
Application server	Business logic
Database server	Data management

N-Tier Architectures

Three-tier only forms the basis for real component-based computing, often referred to as N-tier computing. The user interface tier is only one part of N-tier computing, illustrated in Figure 10.2. The middle tier itself is usually provided as a set of interacting components, where one component can access the services of another component via well-defined CORBA interfaces. Each component is unaware of any other component's internal implementation details, database access mechanisms or persistent data schema. Encapsulating this component-internal complexity and exporting only well-defined, IDL-based component interfaces, is often the main aim of integrating CORBA and database technology. In the following, we see that this is often not an easy, straightforward task. Hopefully the benefits will justify the additional cost for the componentization.

Related OMG Work

There are many CORBA specifications that are directly or indirectly related to the are a of CORBA and database integration—for example, the *object transaction service* and the *concurrency control service*, and also services like the *query service*, the *relationship service* and the *lifecycle service*, and the *objects by value service* and the *portable object adapter* specification. However, none of these services directly address the issue of CORBA and database integration. The first service that addressed this issue was the *CORBA persistent object service (POS)*. Unfortunately, the POS has some major drawbacks. Management of persistent state is directly exposed to CORBA clients. The POS lacks encapsulation, has a very complex internal architecture, and is not particularly well suited

Figure 10.2 N-tier architecture

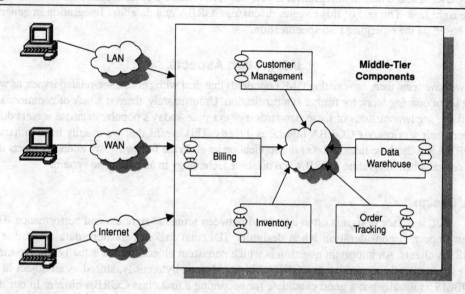

to integrating existing storage facilities. No commercial implementation of the POS is available today. An interesting discussion of problems with implementing the POS can be found in Plasil, Kleindienst and Tuma (1996).[2] For these reasons, the OMG decided to rewrite the persistent object service completely. This will result in an entirely new specification, which will even have a different name: *CORBA persistent state service (PSS)*.

The specification of the PSS is still in progress, but it is clear that the new PSS will be a more server-oriented framework, which does not expose object persistence mechanisms to CORBA clients. Some of the main features will be:

- **Persistent values.** The PSS will provide support for storing persistent values, based on the objects-by-value specification (see Chapter 5, "Performance Considerations," section "Objects-by-Value"). The API will be data-store independent, and based on the language mappings of the object-by-value specification.
- **POA integration.** The PSS will be tightly integrated with the CORBA portable object adapter (See Chapter 2, "CORBA Revisited").
- **Transaction management.** The PSS will support both distributed and non-distributed transactions. For distributed transactions, the PSS will provide mechanisms for interoperation with the CORBA object transaction service.

Because the PSS specification is not yet finalized, it may take some time before commercial implementations of the persistent state service are available. Since there is a great demand

---

[2] Plasil, F., Kleindienst, J., and Tuma, P., "Lessons Learned from Implementing the CORBA Persistent Object Service," Proceedings from OOPSLA '96, ACM, October, 1996.

for CORBA and database integration today, we need to have a look at solutions that are available right now. The rest of this chapter discusses CORBA and database integration in general, not based on the emerging PSS specification.

Integration Aspects

As we have seen, there are existing OMG standards that deal with persistence-related issues, as well as a lot of ongoing work for further standardization. Unfortunately, there is a lack of commercially available implementations of these standards. For example, today's popular database servers don't export their services via CORBA interfaces directly. This means that we usually have to handle CORBA and database integration at the application level. In the following, we address aspects that are critical when integrating CORBA and database technology in an enterprise system.

IDL Design

IDL interface design is often a tradeoff between semantic richness and performance. This is an important consideration when designing IDL that makes persistent data accessible to CORBA clients. An important question is which persistent objects do we actually want to make accessible directly as persistent CORBA objects. A four-byte entity, stored as an object in an ODBMS, is usually not a good candidate for becoming a first class CORBA citizen. In our discussion of object/relational mapping we identified the characteristics of the objects that result from such a mapping; they are usually very fine-grained data objects. A too-direct mapping is particularly problematic if the relational schema is highly normalized. On the other hand, CORBA objects are usually very behavior-centric, due to the nature of the CORBA architecture: CORBA is an architecture for message passing, and does not have a notion of state; for instance IDL attributes imply but don't require that the implementation has member variables equivalent to the IDL attributes. Next, we discuss three different approaches to making persistent data accessible through IDL: direct database access, front-ending, and CORBA business objects. In most systems, a combination of front-ending and business objects are used.

Direct database access

To make persistent data directly accessible through IDL, we usually use some kind of query processor interface, which takes a single query string as an argument and returns the results in some form of sequence of string or structures. For example, the following IDL could be used:

```
struct NameValue {
    string m_name;
    string m_value;
}
typedef sequence<NameValue> NameValueSeq;

interface QueryProcessor {
    NameValueSeq processQuery (in string queryExpression);
};
```

In this example, query results are passed back as a sequence of name/value pairs. Another solution would be to pass back a sequence of type `any`, where each `any` holds an element of the result set. This would allow us to pass back results without converting them into string format. However, providing direct database access does not use CORBA to its full strength; the results are data structures, which could also be obtained using a standard database access mechanism like embedded SQL, or a SQL wrapper tool as discussed previously. One of the main benefits of CORBA is that it provides behavior-centric objects. Next, we examine how IDL can be used to leverage this strength, using front-ends and business objects.

Front-ending

The idea of front-ending is to provide CORBA objects that act as a front-end to some persistent data, so that the data can be manipulated via the front-end. The front-end type of IDL interfaces is similar to RPC style interfaces, that is, very procedural. For example, a front-end that allows us to manipulate portfolio objects could look like the following:

```
typedef string ID;

interface PortfolioFrontend {
    // Portfolio lifecycle events:
    ID createPortfolio (in string Name);
    void deletePortfolio (in ID portfolioID);

    // Portfolio manipulation:
    Money getCurrentValue (in ID portfolioID);
    ...
};
```

Usually, a front-end provides procedure-style operations that allow clients to manipulate data or objects by passing the ID of the target object to be manipulated. The front-ending approach can have significant benefits. For example, it might provide better performance under certain circumstance. Remember our discussion on secondary OIDs in Chapter 5, "Performance Considerations." In essence, a front-end can be implemented as a stateless servant. This makes it very easy to implement front-ends from a memory management point of view. However, the drawback of this very procedural approach is that it lacks semantic expressiveness, as well as the other benefits of a clear, object-oriented design.

CORBA Business Objects

The answer to the question "What is a business object?" is nearly as difficult to find as the answer to the question "What is a CORBA object?"—it is somewhat abstract. We use the notion of business objects to refer to objects that have some meaning in the business domain that we are dealing with. A CORBA business object can map to a single persistent object, or a single row in a relational database. However, the likelihood is that it actually maps to a more complex persistent data structure, especially if we deal with a normalized data schema.

As discussed in Chapter 5, "Performance Considerations," it is not always easy to determine which objects should become first class CORBA citizens. Similarly, it is not always easy to determine which business objects we want to model on the IDL level to offer access to persistent data structures. The following example describes how we could model portfolio objects as proper CORBA objects:

```
interface Portfolio
{
    void delete ();
    Money getCurrentValue ();
    ...
};
```

This interface should not be surprising. Notice that we now can manipulate a portfolio object by directly invoking on it, rather then passing an identifier to an operation in a front-end object. Usually, business objects require some kind of manager object that helps handle object creation and operations on sets of business objects, for instance, query operations. For our portfolios, we need such a manager, which has a little bit of the character of a front-end:

```
Interface PortfolioManager
{
 Portfolio createPortfolio (in string Name);
};
```

Impedance Mismatch

There is not only an impedance mismatch between persistent data schema and database client programming languages, but also between persistent objects and CORBA objects. On the IDL level, we are often able to observe a shift in the interface hierarchy, compared to the underlying class hierarchy. This leads to what we call an *up-shift in the aggregation hierarchy*—many persistent object graphs form some kind of aggregation hierarchy, expressed by the hierarchy of the classes that implement the graph.

Figure 10.3 gives an example of such an up-shift. Recall the database schema for stock and stock price information: stock prices are associated with stocks via the stock's primary key. For example, using an Object/Relational code generator, we would get classes Stock and StockPrice as a result of the direct mapping. However, for performance reasons, it doesn't make sense to export stock price objects as first class CORBA citizens. Instead, we need to introduce a manager interface at the IDL level (StockWatch). This example shows how the front-ending and the business object approach can be combined: our persistent stock objects became first class CORBA business objects. Our persistent stock price objects are only represented as IDL data structures, accessible via stocks (that is, stocks are acting as front-ends for stock prices). Such an up-shift is very common in the real world: CORBA business objects are often assembled from finer-grained data objects.

However, this up-shift is only one example of the effects of the mismatch between CORBA objects and their relational representations. It is likely that the impedance mismatch will have a

Figure 10.3 Example of up-shift in aggregation hierarchy

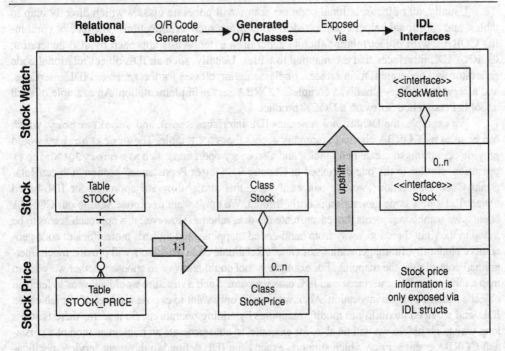

Figure 10.4 Example of strong impedance mismatch

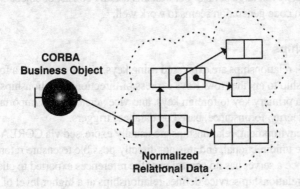

much stronger impact than a simple hierarchy up-shift, especially in cases where relational data is strongly normalized. As indicated in Figure 10.4, we often have the case where a CORBA business object is related to a set of rows. In cases like this, it is questionable how much a straightforward object/relational mapping on the sever-side is really helpful for implementing the CORBA business object.

Object/Relational Code Generation

Usually, an object/relational code generator will generate classes which directly map to tables, and additional helper classes to deal with things such as collections. The idea of combining CORBA with object/relational code generation extends this approach by also generating CORBA IDL interfaces that are mapped to tables. Usually, such an IDL object/relational code generator will generate IDL interfaces, implementation classes for the generated IDL interfaces, and a server mainline—that is, a complete CORBA server implementation. An example of such a tool is Persistence Software's DOCK product.

For example, the DOCK tool generates IDL interfaces `Stock` and `StockFactory`, which can be used by CORBA clients to remotely access the `STOCK` table. The `StockFactory` would provide operations to create new stocks, and also query operations such as a `querySQLWhere()` operation, similar to the one discussed in Chapter 9, "Object Persistence," section "Object/Relational Code Generation." As we can easily see, this straightforward approach for IDL-based Object/Relational code generation is fairly limited. We don't want to expose SQL to our CORBA clients; we want components that encapsulate the data schema. However, this approach seems to be a step in the right direction, away from hand-coded mappings and towards more efficient code generation. Hopefully, future generations of Object/Relational code generators will provide much finergrained control over the mapping. For example, a tool could allow us to choose whether we want to map a table to an IDL interface or an IDL data structure. Such a structure would allow us to fetch an object's state in a single invocation. Also, we usually only want to expose a subset of our tables via IDL, and we need flexibility to modify mappings by adding operations. So it seems there is still a long way to go before we will be able, for example, to auto-generate an implementation of a persistent CORBA event service which supports exactly the IDL defined in the event service specification. It is questionable if we will ever reach this goal for those parts of a system that require highly normalized tables. However, large parts of our systems usually consist of objects with simple CRUD operations, for which code generation seems to work well.

Object Relationships

In an RDBMS, relationships are expressed using keys. A row may have a foreign key attribute to express a relationship to another row. Keys express bi-directional relationships, since it is always possible to go from a primary key to foreign keys, and vice versa. This is important in being able to ensure referential integrity, for instance, based on database triggers.

In a CORBA environment, relationships are usually expressed via CORBA object references. Object references are unidirectional, and it is not directly possible to ensure referential integrity for object references, since a server has no control over the references exported to clients.

The CORBA relationship service defines relationships at a higher level of abstraction. Relationships are explicitly modeled as CORBA objects. This means relationships and the participants in a relationship are expressed as IDL interfaces. The Relationship Service supports bi-directional relationships, which can be traversed by the normal means of CORBA remote method invocations. The problem is that the CORBA relationship service deals with relationships on the second and third tier, and the question is how well this service will perform if large numbers of relationships must be navigated. We take a closer look at this problem by comparing how an ODBMS and the relationship service differ in their approaches to implementing the traversal of an object graph.

ODBMS

ODBMSs provide highly optimized ways of traversing object relationships by implementing sophisticated caching strategies, and often by providing ways of grouping objects into clusters to enable the application to optimize cache utilization.

Figure 10.5 illustrates how a typical ODBMS client traverses an object graph: The first time a client accesses an object, the ODBMS fetches the object's state into the client-side cache, which is managed by the ODBMS. Most ODBMSs are optimized to reduce the number of times that data needs to be loaded from the database server by not only loading the requested object, but also state and relationship information for other objects which are likely to be accessed next.

In our example, the client's access to the first object (1a) results in a group fetch which brings a whole group of related objects into the cache (1b). If the client now wants to navigate a relationship (2) to access a related object (3), which is also active in the cache, this is done without another request to the database server. The better the clustering technique provided by the ODBMS, the better the cache utilization will be. This is important for ensuring high performance when navigating complex object graphs.

CORBA Relationship Service

The CORBA relationship service represents relationships using IDL: the relationship between two CORBA objects is expressed by CORBA objects that implement the interfaces `Relationship` and `Role`. The problem with navigating an object relationship that is expressed in IDL is that each step in the navigation (1-3) is a remote invocation, and each remote invocation imposes some overhead. Plus, relationships involve too many relatively heavyweight CORBA objects. Therefore, traversing a relationship that is expressed via the CORBA relationship service will be slower by orders of magnitude than traversing a relationship using an ODBMS with a highly optimized caching and clustering mechanism. The specification addresses this problem vaguely. For example, the specifi-

Figure 10.5   ODBMS object graph navigation

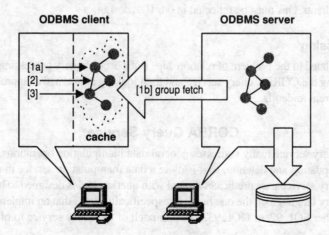

Figure 10.6   Traversing a relationship using the relationship service.

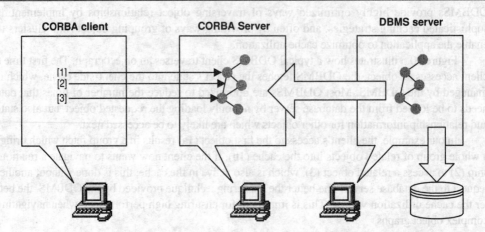

cation states that the `get_other_related_object()` operation can be "implemented by caching object references to other roles and related objects." This doesn't really address how to manage caching of relationship information for clusters of related objects. The specification vaguely proposes to manage clustering by the choice of object factories, but doesn't address how clustered relationship information can actually be cached in a single action. Finally, even if the specification allowed for implementing an efficient caching and clustering mechanism, the standard stubs generated by an IDL compiler wouldn't be sufficient: we would need a client-specific solution to implement the cache management.

So it seems like the CORBA relationship service is mainly useful for systems that need data-store independent access to relationships and a high level of abstraction, without having high requirements for performance and scalability. In cases where performance and scalability play an important role, it will be difficult to find a way to efficiently traverse relationships from the third tier using CORBA clients. This must be reflected in our IDL design.

Query Processing

Closely related to the problem of relationships is the area of query processing. We address this by first discussing the CORBA query service and then looking at alternative approaches before discussing the different tradeoffs.

CORBA Query Service

The CORBA query service really addresses general data manipulation operations, including selection, insertion, updating and deletion, so it is more a data manipulation service than a simple query service. The query service uses predicates to deal with queries, and is designed to be independent of any specific query language on the one hand, but specifically states that an implementation must at least support either SQL 92, or OQL 93. The approach of the query service to offer manipulation operations on collections that can be executed on the server side seems to be very promising, especially with respect to our discussion on the problems with remotely navigating relationships. Ideally, an implementation of the query service would be tightly integrated into a DBMS. Unfortunately, there is a lack of commercially available implementations of the query service.

Application-Specific Solutions

It is not only the lack of commercially available implementations of the query service that leads to application-specific solutions to the problem. Often, much simpler solutions are required, where a query service would simply add too much overhead and complexity. An example of an extremely simple application-specific solution is implemented by our `StockWatch` interface, which provides an operation `getStockBySymbol()`—this is a typical, very simple form of a query interface . A slightly more complicated query operation would allow a string to be passed that contains wildcards, returning a set of matches. A common approach is to have the query operation accept a sequence of string name/value pairs, which act as the query's WHERE clause. The CORBA trading object service, as discussed in Chapter 6 "Object Location," provides another interesting approach that enables clients to query for objects.

Very often, query processing for a certain type of business object is dealt with on two different levels: The business object itself provides operations to access and modify its state, while query operations on collections of business objects are offered by a manager object that acts as a front-end to the collection.

Tradeoffs

As usual, there are tradeoffs associated with the different solutions. The approach that best encapsulates our underlying data schema will make it accessible by exporting interfaces to business objects and their relationships, so that clients can query and navigate them using the normal CORBA means of accessing remote objects. Although providing a high level of encapsulation and flexibility, unfortunately this approach is not very scalable, so that it is unlikely to be usable for large numbers of objects and complex relationships.

We often have to provide specialized query operations which work around the performance problem by delegating the work to the server side. Although this approach seems to be more scalable, it is also less flexible, since it restricts clients to the functionality offered by the specialized query operations, possible weakening encapsulation by exposing specifics that are internal to the objects.

SQL and OQL enable a client to send queries to a server so they can be executed on the server side. The benefit of this approach is that it will most likely provide the best performance. Unfortunately, this approach also fully exposes the internal structure of our data to the client. Exposing the data schema to CORBA clients is contrary to the idea of using CORBA for encapsulating this complexity. These tradeoffs are illustrated in Figure 10.7.

Which Tier is Doing the Real Work?

One question that arises in the design process is that of where the real work should be executed. Relational database management systems are designed to execute all the work in the first tier: clients send queries and receive results, but the real work is done in the database server. Object data-

Figure 10.7   Tradeoffs for object querying via CORBA

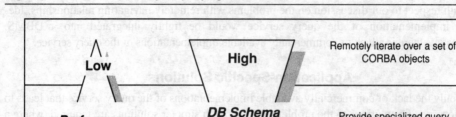

base management systems implement sophisticated caching and clustering mechanisms to enable clients to traverse highly complex object graphs efficiently in the second tier. ODBMSs are often used when an application has complex logic that requires a lot of navigation on object graphs, which couldn't be expressed in a more static data manipulation language like SQL. Notice that, in addition to the client-side object navigation functionality, most ODBMSs provide a query language like OQL, which can be used to send queries to the database server, so they can be executed in the first tier. An important difference between OQL and SQL is that OQL can return references to objects, whereas SQL always returns only data.

As we can see, there are some conflicting requirements here. Executing the work in the first tier is typically the most efficient way, since the first tier has direct access to the storage volumes. Executing work in the second tier involves inter-process communication with the first tier, which adds a performance overhead. Traditionally, application-specific business logic is executed in the second tier, separating database server functionality from application functionality. Relational database vendors are currently trying to enable a tighter integration between data server logic and application logic. Oracle's cartridges are an example of enabling more flexible queries in the second tier, whereas Informix's data blades open the first tier to the application.

Alternatively to these object/relational hybrid solutions, object/relational code generators are sometimes used to bridge the object/relational mismatch. Some of these object/relational code generators provide caching mechanisms that attempt to provide clients with a data access and navigation mechanism than performs better than plain SQL. The problem is that these tools have to work with a relational database server that is not optimized for these purposes, so that they are unlikely to perform as well as an ODBMS or an object/relational hybrid, where the database server provides specialized logic to support client-side caching.

As long as commercial databases do not offer direct support for CORBA services like the relationship service or the query service, we have to handle this at the application level, that is, on the second and third tier. It seems obvious that shifting up solutions to the second and third tier will most likely have negative impacts on performance and scalability. However, there are many situations where data-store-independent access to business objects is extremely important. For example, many enterprise resource planning (ERP) systems are starting to open up their interfaces, exporting the business objects and their relationships via CORBA. If an application needs to execute a business transaction across two such ERP systems, such as SAP and BAAN, it would be ideal if these systems would export the required objects and relationships as CORBA objects. Obviously, the design of the interfaces must be done very carefully, to ensure that the approach will scale.

Transactions and Concurrency

The example of accessing business objects residing in SAP and BAAN components in a single business transaction leads directly to the more general question of how to deal with transactions in the context of CORBA and database integration. Chapter 11, "Transactions in a CORBA Environment," addresses transactions in general, before we focus on distributed transaction processing in Chapter 12, "Distributed Transaction Processing" and long lived transactions in Chapter 13, "User Sessions." These chapters also discuss concurrency issues from different viewpoints.

Object Identity

Our previous discussion on IDL design issues related to database integration assumed some kind of object identity. In the front-ending example we used secondary OIDs to identify a portfolio. For the business object example we simply assumed that CORBA's concept of an object solves the problem of the object's identity.

Identity really is a key element of persistence. Relational database management systems use database keys to deal with identity. Object database management systems usually provide system-generated object identifiers (OIDs). The problem is that CORBA doesn't provide a strong model for object identity, at least from a database point of view. CORBA object references (IORs) contain identification data, but this only identifies an object relative to a server (or an object adapter). Also, an IOR can represent multiple CORBA objects (in the case of one-to-many communication) and a CORBA object can be represented by multiple, different IORs.

At the least, most ORBs provide a means of letting the application define some identification data for a CORBA object, which will be encapsulated in the object's IOR. This gives us the chance to embed enough information in an IOR to uniquely identify the persistent data for a CORBA business object in the whole system. Notice that it is important to choose a schema for the application-level object identifiers that is unique on the global system level: it doesn't make sense to rely on other information that is encapsulated in an IOR, like host names, or port numbers, since these are likely to change. So even if object identifiers are only interpreted on the server side, they need to be server-independent in the context of a system.

Servant Management

Object IDs that identify the targets of incoming requests can be efficiently mapped to servants that implement the requests using a servant pool pattern, as discussed in Chapter 2, "CORBA Revisited." In addition to general resource management and cleanup, the pool pattern helps to reduce the number of object faults by keeping frequently used objects in the pool. A database can contain potentially billions of objects (or data structures that represent the state of our CORBA objects).

There are obvious reasons why we don't want to keep all these objects in memory. First of all, we want to keep the size of our processes to a minimum, avoiding page swapping and unnecessary consumption of virtual memory. Also, loading large numbers of objects from a database into memory will have negative consequences for the concurrency behavior of the application if it is done without a sophisticated synchronization mechanism.

Stateless Servants

A stateless servant acts as a transient capsule that delegates incoming IIOP requests to a database server, for instance, using SQL. This means that the stateless servant provides some kind of transformation between the semantics of the IDL interface operation and an SQL query.

Many BOA generation ORBs don't provide very good support for stateless servants, since they implement a one-to-one mapping between OIDs and servants; that is, a servant can process requests only for a specific CORBA object. Whether it is worth it to use the object pool pattern to reduce the number of object faults will depend on the cost of servant activation and deactivation. If the ORB runtime does not very efficiently manage servant activation and deactivation, it might make sense to keep stateless servants in a pool to reduce the frequency of object activation and deactivation. If the ORB runtime doesn't impose a big overhead, we might be better off activating and deactivating servants on a per-request basis, reducing the overhead of pool management.

With a POA-generation ORB, it is easier to manage stateless servants, for example using a default servant that can handle requests for all incoming requests, independent of the target object's identity. The default servant obtains the target object's identity from the POA, and uses it to construct the appropriate query for the database server.

Stateless servants are a very common way of using CORBA to export services that are implemented using an underlying database. Compare the approach that is used today by thousands of Internet applications which use a combination of HTML, HTTP and CGI: the Internet client sends a HTTP request to a HTTP server, which activates a CGI script to execute the request. The CGI script is typically stateless, and delegates the HTTP request to a database server using SQL. Using stateless servants with CORBA is similar in spirit to this approach, but also provides all the other benefits of CORBA, including the powerful abstractions provided by an object-oriented system, the higher-level framework of CORBA services, and automatic marshalling and unmarshalling of request arguments.

Stateful Servants

When using stateful servants, the first important question is whether the state of the servants is tied to transaction boundaries. If the state of servants is maintained in memory only for the duration of a single transaction, this approach is less problematic. If we intend to keep state information in memory outside of a transaction, it can become very difficult. Usually, this approach requires a sophisticated cache synchronization mechanism. Unfortunately, few commercial databases are suited to support cross-transactions cache synchronization—for example, by offering efficient triggering mechanisms that could be used to synchronize caches.

In addition to transaction boundaries, we also have to look at process boundaries. On the process level, we have to ensure that caches are synchronized between application servers: many enterprise CORBA systems will have replicated application servers. There are many different approaches to cache synchronization, such as using multicast technology to publish updates.

Sometimes it is possible to achieve significant performance gains by implementing a very simple caching strategy that only caches read-only values, or values that are only changed very infrequently. For example, our stock object implementation could keep the stock's symbol in a cache, since stock symbols will only change very infrequently, for instance, in the case of a corporate merger. In this case, the caches could be managed administratively, for instance, by simply invalidating all the caches in the application in the case of a change.

Our object pool pattern is called an object pool because its purpose is really not to maintain an object cache, but to address the problem of resource management. Even though the pattern could be used to implement an application-specific caching strategy for persistent objects, this seems to be a complex task, especially if a fine-grained cache synchronization for frequently changing values is required. In the following, we briefly discuss how an ORB can be integrated with an ODBMS, so that we don't have to deal with caching on the application level, but can rely on the ODBMSs cache management.

Database Adapters

Some ORB vendors address the lack of a CORBA standard that specifies the architecture of an object database adapter by providing their own, proprietary database adapters. For example, IONA Technologies provides a generic framework for building database adapters, which is used to integrate the Orbix ORB with ODBMSs like Versant and ObjectStore. A key concept of the framework is to separate the CORBA object implementation and the persistent object: the ORB dispatches incoming calls to a transient servant. The servant only has one member variable, a *smart pointer*. The servant simply delegates each call to the persistent object using the smart pointer. Most ODBMSs support the idea of a smart pointer, which is responsible for ensuring that the target object is in the local cache, before invoking on the cached object.[3] This is illustrated in Figure 10.8.

The clean separation between transient servant and persistent object is important, avoiding problems with transient, ORB-specific data members in persistent objects. The solution described here can basically be used with any ORB, the question is only how the servants are implemented: are they written by hand, or does the database adapter provide a means of auto-generating them? Another issue that needs to be addressed by an object database adapter is the mapping between CORBA object identifiers, and smart pointers: usually the adapter will support late binding, so the adapter must be able to convert a CORBA object identifier into a smart database pointer. Fortunately, most ODBMSs provide a means of converting smart pointers to strings, and vice versa. Such a stringified ODBMS object id can be embedded into a CORBA object ID. Finally, the object

---

[3] Notice that ObjectStore is an exception here. ObjectStore's Virtual Management Architecture allows applications to access persistent objects using standard virtual memory pointers, which is the standard way of using ObjectStore. In case of a page fault, it is ObjectStore's responsibility to catch this fault, and load in the required page. But ObjectStore also supports smart pointers, which can be used for cases like the one described above.

Figure 10.8   ORB/ODBMS integration

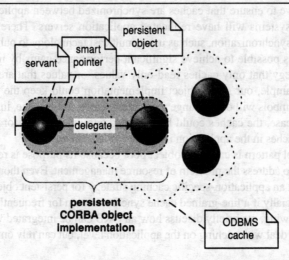

adapter needs to deal with transactions. Usually, an ODBMS does not allow an application to invoke on an object outside a transaction. Therefore, the adapter must manage transactions. We will have a closer look at different styles of transaction processing in Chapter 12, "Distributed Transaction Processing."

CORBA database adapters help us to integrate persistent objects and CORBA object implementations to build persistent CORBA objects. However, this is really only a small piece of the much bigger problem of integrating CORBA and databases. For example, such a CORBA database adapter as discussed here does not solve the problem of how to map CORBA IDL data types to data types that can be stored in a DBMS, and vice versa. This is a problem that is being addressed by the upcoming persistent state service.

The Billion-Object CORBA System

Enterprise systems often need to support gigabytes of data (or, in CORBA parlance, billions of objects). An ORB can be a powerful tool for encapsulating the internal data structure and making the data accessible at a higher level of abstraction, for example in the form of CORBA business objects. Technically, most ORBs can easily cope with the requirement of supporting billions of objects, simply by using late binding. In particular, the POA support for default servants makes it straightforward to make large amounts of data accessible via CORBA using stateless servants. For stateful servants, systems should rely on an efficient object pool implementation, which keeps frequently used objects in memory, and evicts less frequently used objects to avoid application server processes growing to gigantic sizes.

The secret of succeeding with a billion-object CORBA system often lies in the right IDL design. The IDL should provide the right combination of business objects and front-end style service objects, which allow clients to execute operations on collections of business objects. Recall the discussion of the overhead of a CORBA remote invocation and the performance impacts on access patterns in Chapter 5, "Performance Considerations." Keeping this in mind when designing IDL for systems that need to make gigabytes of data accessible is often more important than sophisticated server-side object pool and caching strategies. Try to design IDL that enables CORBA clients to do their work with a reasonable number of remote invocations. Also, try to rely on the scalability and query power provided by the database server as much as possible.

CHAPTER 11

Server-Controlled Transactions

Transactions in a CORBA Environment

Transactions are essential for building reliable, large-scale enterprise CORBA systems. In this chapter, we explore how and where transactions can fit into a CORBA system.

Two-Tier vs. Three-Tier Architectures

Most traditional database systems are designed with two-tier architectures in mind: a database client accesses a database server via some mechanism provided by the DBMS, for instance, embedded SQL or ODBC. The access mechanism is usually responsible for providing some means of beginning a transaction, enabling the client to issue queries and updates in the context of the transaction, and finally to end the transaction.

Systems that combine CORBA and database technology are usually three-tier: a CORBA client interacts with an application server, which plays a dual role as CORBA server and database client. The interesting question is how CORBA remote invocations and database transactions fit together. In the following, we discuss two fundamentally different approaches to transactions in a CORBA environment, client controlled transactions and server controlled transactions.

Client-Controlled vs. Server-Controlled Transactions

In a CORBA environment, transaction logic can either be encapsulated by the server or be exposed to the client via CORBA IDL. The first case is often referred to as *server-controlled transactions*, because the server has full control over transactions. The second case is often referred to as *client-controlled transactions*, because the client controls transactions directly. Let's assume we have a simple IDL interface for account objects, like the following:

```
interface Account {
    long getBalance ();
    void setBalance (in long newBalance);
};
```

A CORBA client could use variations of this interface to perform a simple *increment* operation, which reads the current value, adds a constant value, and stores back the result. We discuss different ways to use database transactions to ensure that the increment operation results in data consistency.

Server-Controlled Transactions

With server-controlled transactions, transactions are not exposed to the client either via IDL or another API; control over transactions remains with the server. The most straightforward implementation of server-controlled transaction processing is the *per-operation transaction model*, where each operation implements its own transaction. The second model, called *phased transaction model*, allows a transaction to span multiple remote invocations.

Per-Operation Transaction Model

The idea of the per-operation transaction model is that each CORBA remote invocation executes its own transaction. With SQL, this is relatively straightforward; each method implementation begins a transaction, issues queries and updates, commits the transaction, and returns to the calling CORBA client.

Figure 11.1 describes the use of the per-operation transaction model to implement the increment logic: A client invokes getBalance() to query an account's balance. The account implementation executes a transaction to query the account's balance. Next, the client issues a setBalance(), passing the new value. This is mapped to a new transaction on the server side, executing an update. Obviously, this is a risky way of implementing the increment logic, since there is no mechanism for handling collisions with other clients, which can potentially access the account

Figure 11.1   Per-operation transaction model

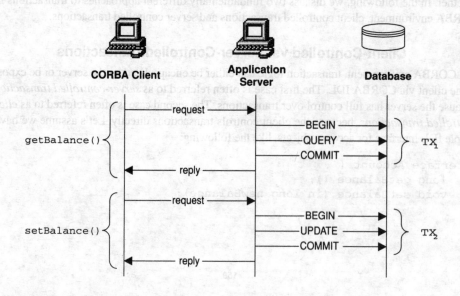

at the same time. Let's say, for example, a second client modifies the account's balance after we got the balance, but before we set the new, incremented value. In this case, our `setBalance()` would overwrite the second client's update. This simple example shows that the per-operation model cannot be used to implement the increment using the given IDL. If we are restricted to the per-operation model, we have to look for a different solution. We could move the increment logic to the server side, making it accessible to clients by adding an operation `incrementBalance()` to the `Account` interface. This would ensure that the increment is executed as an atomic action in a single, server-side database transaction.

Although the per-operation model appears to be very simple and of limited usability, it is still one of the most widely used transaction models. Many thousands of HTTP/HTML based Internet applications follow this principle: each HTTP request is mapped to a separate database transaction. This approach works for a large number of applications, where there is no need for a transaction to span multiple requests

Usually, the transaction per-operation approach results in *stateless servers*; that is, the state is managed in the database server, and the CORBA server is only a transient interface to the database. Stateless servers are easy to implement, since there is no need for synchronization at the application level. All synchronization aspects are managed by the database server. This means one can have multiple instances of application servers for load balancing or fault tolerance purposes, without worrying about how the access to the data by multiple clients is synchronized.

RDBMS vs. ODBMS

For an RDBMS, the per-operation mode is really simple to implement. Transaction control is implemented by each method implementation. However, for an ODBMS, this looks slightly different: in the case of a tight integration the target of the remote invocation is a persistent object. The problem is that with most ODBMSs, persistent objects can be invoked upon only in the context of a transaction. This means the object itself cannot begin and end the transaction. Therefore, a solution must be found where the transaction is started before the request is dispatched to the object and ended after the request returns. To solve this problem, we could simply use interceptors to control transactions. This would de-couple transaction control and object access.

Phased Transaction Model

The phased transaction model is somewhat of a hybrid of the simple per-operation transaction model and client-controlled transactions. With the phased transaction model, the idea is that a transaction can span multiple remote invocations, but without exposing the transaction logic directly to the client.

Figure 11.2 shows how to use the phased transaction model to implement the increment logic: A client invokes `getBalance()` to query an account's balance. The account implementation starts a new transaction, and queries the account's balance. Notice that the query should acquire a lock on the account. Next, the client issues the `setBalance()`, passing the new value. This is mapped on the server side to the same transaction that was used before. Since we are using the same transaction to query and update the balance, and we are using an appropriate locking mechanism, we are not in danger of ending up with data inconsistencies, as in the per-operation example before.

Figure 11.2 Phased transaction model

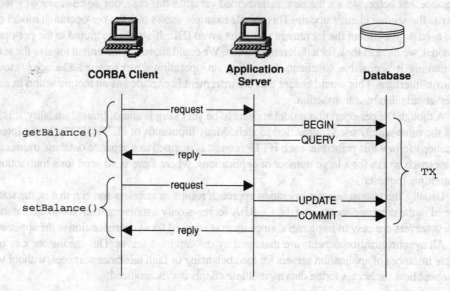

However, the problem with the phased approach is that it makes sense only under some very restricted circumstances. For example, the basic phased model makes sense only for a single CORBA client. This is not acceptable to most CORBA systems. In addition, the CORBA client will usually have to have some knowledge of the order in which operations must be invoked. Thus, our initial goal of fully encapsulating the complexity of transaction processing is not reached.

One way to work around the "single client" limitation is to have some logic on the server side, which is responsible for multiplexing between clients and transactions, for instance, by mapping client file descriptors to active transactions for incoming requests. The problem with this approach is that it is complex and error prone.

Another problem is that the client usually has to have some idea of the order in which operations are to be called. This problem could be overcome by having something like an explicit saveChanges() operation, which ends the transaction. However, this begins to expose at least some basic transaction logic to the client.

Client-Controlled Transactions

The problems associated with using the phased approach lead quite naturally to client-controlled transactions. Client-controlled usually means that there is some kind of *transaction manager* (TM), which can be used by the client to control transactions explicitly. Also, a mechanism is required to associate outgoing requests with the current transaction. Usually this is done by adding information about the transaction to the outgoing request. This can be done either as an explicit argument to the operation, or via an implicit request context (see Chapter 2, "CORBA Revisited, section Invocation Lifecycle"). An out-of-the-box implementation of client-controlled transactions is provided by the CORBA object transaction service, discussed in the following chapter.

Figure 11.3   Client-controlled transaction model

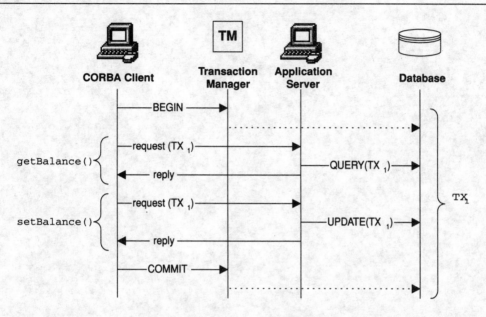

Figure 11.3 describes how a client can use a transaction manager to explicitly control the boundaries of the increment transaction. First, the client begins a new transaction TX_1. Next, the client invokes `getBalance()` and `setBalance()`, passing a transaction context with each remote invocation. The application server uses the transaction context to indicate to the database server the transaction that is to be used as the context for the queries and updates. Obviously, we still need to implement the correct locking strategy to make this example work safely.

The benefit of the client-controlled approach to transaction processing is that it enables a client to define the boundaries of transactions itself, rather then having the server side guessing what the client might want to do.

Summary

The per-operation transaction model has its limitations, but is still a very popular approach, mainly due to its simplicity. The usefulness of the phased transaction model is retricted to more specific situations. It is possible to overcome some of the limitations of the phased appraoch, in particular by mapping clients to transactions using file descriptors, but in general these methods result in complex, application-specific solutions. In cases where server-controlled transactions are not sufficient, a client-controlled model using the CORBA object transaction service is recommended.

CHAPTER 12

Distributed Transaction Processing

In this chapter we take a close look at distributed transaction processing in a CORBA environment. The OMG has defined the CORBA Object Transaction Service (OTS), which obviously plays a key role in CORBA-based distributed transaction processing.

Before we explore the CORBA OTS, we look at distributed transaction processing in general, including transaction processing systems (TP systems) and transaction processing monitors (TP monitors), as well as ACID transactions and the two-phase commit protocol. These form the basis for the introduction of the CORBA OTS. Finally, we look at how CORBA and OTS can be combined with advanced transaction models like sagas and multi-transactions to support complex enterprise workflows.

Transaction Processing

The term *transaction* is overloaded—different people have different understandings of what a transaction is. In the real world, a transaction is an interaction that usually involves the exchange of things such as money, goods, services, or information. We use the term *business transaction* to designate such a real-world task. This is quite different from the concept of a transaction in a computer system.

A classic example of a business transaction is the processing of an order. Imagine a telephone sales agent, taking our order for a new CD writer. The sales agent starts entering the order, possibly setting us up as a new customer. Initially, the order conatins one item—the CD writer. We then ask the sales agent to check what kind of cable we need to connect the CD writer to our PC, and ask him to call us back with the result. In the second conversation, we decide to order the recommended cable, and the sales agent adds this to the order. An hour later, we call the agent again to add 5 boxes of blank CDs to the order. At the end of this sequence of activities, the order is complete. This order is one business transaction, and corresponds to one shipment and one invoice.

Viewing the process from the perspective of the underlying application and database system, the business transaction "order entry" is decomposable. The order, as it is compiled over the course of a day or two, must be *consistent* at each stage. This means that even if the order is not finished and authorized, it must always make sense to the sales application and database. Each step from one consistent state to a new consistent state is performed by what we call a *system transaction*, or *trans-*

action for short. Our definition of a transaction is: *a set of operations that are guaranteed to transform the shared state of a system from one consistent state to another consistent state*. This guarantee provides the bedrock on which we can build large and complex systems. Next, we examine some important aspects of transaction processing systems.

Transaction Processing Systems

A TP System is a computer system that automates the execution of business transactions. Usually the term TP system includes both hardware and software.

One of the first TP systems was the SABRE airline reservation system, built in the 1960s, and still in use today. It connects more than 300,000 devices world-wide, and is able to handle a peak load of up to 4,000 messages per second, handling arline-related data such as flight bookings, seat reservations, and mileage bonuses.

Another good example of a TP system is a money transfer system. A money transfer system usually involves a central clearinghouse, such as CHIPS (Clearing House Interbank Payments System). The benefit of a clearinghouse is that each bank only interacts with a central entity, instead of being connected to hundreds of other banks. The clearinghouse accepts incoming payment requests and forwards them to the beneficiary banks. For each participating bank, the clearinghouse manages a different account, a *position*. During the day, no real money is transferred. Each transfer is booked to the bank's position managed by the clearinghouse. During the *end-of-day settlement*, the clearinghouse checks the balance of each bank, and settles the difference. Even if over the day hundreds of millions of dollars have been virtually transferred between all of the banks, the total amount of real money that needs to be transferred at the end of the day is usually much smaller, since each bank sends and receives many payments over the day. Thus, the central clearinghouse not only reduces the overhead of connecting all the different banks with each other, but it also helps reduce the amount of money that really needs to be transferred. In addition, a clearinghouse reduces the associated risk in exchange-based trading systems by acting as a central counterpart. Every member of the clearinghouse has to deposit money proportional to the value of its deals with the clearinghouse over time. The clearinghouse also maintains a pool of money derived from its membership and transaction fees, which is used to insure every party against the failure of another exchange member.

As we can see, TP systems are often critical for the day-to-day business of an organization. They frequently involve the transfer of ownership of things of value. Failure or loss of service from a TP system may be damaging enough to bankrupt a company. Therefore, a TP system must be reliable and accurate. It must not corrupt, lose, or repeat data. It must be highly resilient to system failure. Finally, and maybe most importantly, it must be able to recover in the unlikely case that a failure occurs.

Transaction Processing Monitors

TP monitors provide the technical framework for building, executing, and managing TP system software. This means the TP monitor usually provides a set of tools and libraries that can be used to build transactional applications, an environment in which these applications can be executed, and a set of tools for managing the active system.

A common description of the functionality of a TP monitor, is difficult because there is a great variety in the functionality offered by the different TP monitor products. Traditional mainframe TP monitors manage key resources, provide display services, and offer programming interfaces to system resources like database management systems and communication systems. Typically, these TP monitors are tightly integrated with the operating system. Examples of mainframe TP monitors are IBM's CICS and IMS products.

Distributed TP monitors support transaction processing in an environment where applications and resources are distributed among multiple nodes. In a distributed environment, it is of particular importance that the TP monitor supports such things as workflow control, security, load balancing, administration, and management of the distributed system components. Examples of distributed TP monitors include Transarc's Encina and BEA Systems' TUXEDO.

Object Transaction Monitors

Distributed transaction management is a key feature of a distributed TP monitor. In the CORBA world, OTS is used to manage distributed transactions, as we will see later. However, an OTS alone does not make a TP monitor. As we said earlier, a distributed TP monitor must support workflow control, security, load balancing, administration, and management of the distributed system components. Traditional TP monitors like Encina and TUXEDO provide frameworks for dealing with these requirements. The CORBA architecture does not directly provide anything like a TP monitor. Interestingly, we can see that CORBA vendors as well as TP monitor vendors are now integrating CORBA and TP monitor technology and marketing the resulting products as Object Transaction Monitors (OTMs). Prominent examples include IONA Technologies' OrbixOTM, Transarc's Encina++, and BEA Systems' M3. Some of these OTMs are more CORBA-centric, bundling CORBA services and OTS-based transaction management, while others add CORBA-based communication to an already existing TP monitor framework.

Since this book has a general focus, you will not find a dedicated chapter on Object Transaction Monitors. However, we believe that we cover most of the features provided by TP monitors. In this chapter, we discuss distributed transaction processing and workflow control. In Chapter 8, we discuss security in a CORBA environment. System management and monitoring is covered in Chapter 17. Finally, some OTMs provide concentrators to overcome the NxM connection problem and to facilitate load-balancing. We discuss connection management and concentratotrs in Chapter 14, and load balancing in Chapter 15.

ACID Transactions

We define a transaction as *a set of operations that are guaranteed to transform the shared state of a system from one consistent state to another consistent state*. We deconstruct this definition in the following.

A transaction comprises a *set of operations* because we need to capture the fact that transactions group individual operations into a single higher-level action. Obviously, we expect our system to operate only on state values that are *consistent*. State transformation must be *guaranteed* because we need to capture the fact that a transaction processing system must put in place safeguards that ensure either that a defined state transformation from S to S' occurs, or that the state remains unchanged in the case of a failure.

When we talk about transactions, we can divide the state of a system onto significant state and insignificant state. Significant state is usually *shared state*, in the sense of state values that are potentially accessible by multiple actors, whether human or computer entities. An example of insignificant state is data cached in a user interface. This kind of data is not generally deemed to be worthy of transaction maintenance. It is not shared, that is, it won't feed back into the understanding or actions of other actors. Thus, only *shared state* is usually maintained by transactions.

To ensure that a transaction conforms to our above definition, we usually require that it possess a set of properties called the *ACID properties*, where ACID stands for *Atomicity, Consistency, Isolation,* and *Durability*. We examine each of these four properties next.

Atomicity

ACID transactions are atomic operation; that is, a transaction is either executed as a whole, or not at all. This means a transaction is never executed partially.

A typical example of an ACID transaction is a money transfer: one account must be debited, another account must be credited. This must be executed as an atomic action; both the debit and the credit are executed successfully, or no account is updated at all.

Consistency

ACID transactions transform data from one consistent state to another. If a database contains consistent data at the beginning of the transaction, the data in the database must be again consistent at the end of the transaction.

For example, in a double-entry bookkeeping system, the sum of all accounts must always be zero. If we debit money from one account without crediting the same amount of money to another account, the total sum of all accounts wouldn't be zero any more, and thus we would have violated the consistency property.

Isolation

ACID transactions are isolated; that is, no transaction sees another transaction's work in progress.

For example, if our money transfer transaction executes the debit first, and then the credit, there would be a moment during our transaction where the data is inconsistent from a double bookkeeping point of view: after the debit, and before the credit the total balance of the system wouldn't be zero. The isolation property means that this inconsistency shouldn't be visible to any transaction except the one we are currently in. Usually, the isolation property is enforced using locking techniques. However, recall our previous discussion of the different isolation levels: many database management systems allow relaxation of the isolation property, which in essence means accepting potential data inconsistencies in order to obtain the benefit of performance gains.

Durability

The results of committed ACID transactions are durable, that is, stored in a way that will survive a failure of the TP system.

Usually, this means that the results of a transaction must be written to a disk at the end of a transaction. However, durability is a fairly generic term. Usually, a single disk is not considered to be reliable enough. Therefore, additional safety measures such as disk mirroring and regular back-ups are often used to ensure that information is not lost.

Transaction Management

We are used to executing atomic transaction with a single DBMS, for instance, using SQL. Some DBMSs even allow us to access tables from different databases in a single, atomic transaction. However, in a real distributed system we often face heterogeneous databases from different vendors, or other types of resource managers like persistent queue managers or transactional file systems. In addition, in a distributed system we usually want to propagate transactions via inter-process communication (IPC), so that multiple processes can execute work on behalf of the same transaction. How can we guarantee the atomicity of our transactions in such a distributed, heterogeneous environment? The most common solution is to introduce a transaction manager, which plays a central role in ensuring the atomicity of our distributed transaction.

We have now identified the three central roles in a distributed TP system: *application*, *resource manager*, and *transaction manager*. Figure 12.1 shows the interactions between the different components of a distributed TP system, and the roles that they assume. The application uses the transaction manager to begin and end transactions. Resource managers provide interfaces to the application that allow the execution of the operations that form the transaction, for instance queries and updates. When the application ends the transaction, the transaction manager interacts with the different resource managers to end the transaction in a way that ensures its atomicity.

If a transaction involves updates to two (or more) different resource managers, extra measures are necessary to ensure the atomicity of an ACID transaction, since each resource manager might independently fail to commit. If the first resource manager successfully commits the transaction, but the second resource manager fails to commit the changes, we have violated the atomicity of the global transaction, since it was only partially executed. To overcome this problem, we use the *two-phase commit protocol* (2 PC). The two-phase commit protocol is coordinated by the transaction manager, as shown in Figure 12.2.

Figure 12.1   Components of a distributed transaction processing system

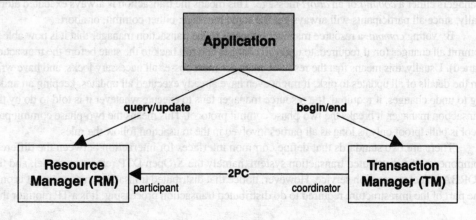

Figure 12.2   Two-phase commit protocol

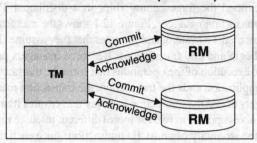

In the first phase, the transaction manager holds a vote. The participants in the vote are the resource managers. Each resource manager has a veto right; that is, each individual resource manager has the right to *abort* the transaction as a whole. If a resource manager votes *commit*, that indicates to the transaction manager that it is now prepared to go ahead with a commit of the transaction. Therefore, the first phase is also called the *prepare phase*.

Depending on the outcome of the prepare phase, the transaction manager sends all resource managers either a *commit* or an *abort* message. This means the transaction is always executed atomically, since all participants will always get the same message: either commit, or abort.

By voting *commit*, a resource manager indicates to the transaction manager that it is now able to commit all changes (or, if required, to undo all changes and roll back to the state before the transaction started). Usually, this means that the resource manager must posses all necessary locks, and have written the details of all updates to disk. It might even have already executed all updates, keeping an undo-log to undo changes, if required. If a resource manager fails to execute whatever it is told to do by the transaction manager, it breaks the two-phase commit protocol. This means the two-phase commit protocol is bulletproof only as long as all parties involved in the transaction follow the rules.

There are two standards that define common interfaces for interaction between the different components of a distributed transaction system, namely the X/Open DTP reference model, and the CORBA object transaction service. However, notice that distributed transaction management is only one part of the infrastructure required to do distributed transaction processing. It is a TP monitor that usually provides a framework for TP systems, and transaction management is only one part of this framework.

X/Open DTP

The X/Open Reference Model for Distributed Transaction Processing (DTP) defines standard interfaces for the interaction between the components of a distributed TP System, as shown in in Figure 12.3:

- **Transaction manager (TM).** Transaction managers enable clients to begin and end transactions, and are responsible for executing the two-phase commit protocol.
- **Resource manager (RM).** A resource manager manages transactional resources. Typically, the term resource manager refers to a database management system, but other examples for resource managers include persistent queue managers and transactional file systems.
- **Communications resource manager (CRM).** A communications resource manager provides remote transactional communication. For example, a CRM can be based on DCE remote procedure calls.

Applications interact with a transaction manager to begin and end transactions using the TX interface. Interaction between application and resource manager is not standardized by the X/Open DTP model. Remote transactional communication can be done, for example, using the CRM interface TxRPC for transactional RPCs. When a transaction is to be ended, it is the transaction manager's responsibility to execute the two-phase commit protocol, integrating all resource managers that are involved in the particular transaction. A transaction manager uses the XA interface to interact with a resource manager.

Figure 12.3   X/Open DTP model

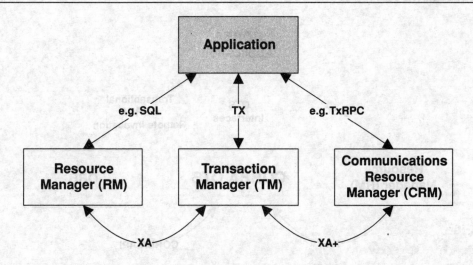

The X/Open DTP model is a widely accepted standard, supported by a variety of TP monitor and resource manager products. X/Open is now part of The Open Group, Inc. The initial version of the X/Open DTP model was released in 1991, including the TX and XA interfaces described above. X/Open DTP interfaces such as TX and XA are defined using the C programming language.

CORBA Object Transaction Service

In the IT world, the last decade has brought two important paradigm shifts: from centralized computing towards client/server computing, and from procedural programming towards object-orientation. The combination of these has led to distributed object technology like CORBA. We can observe how the TP system area follows this trend, for reference models as well as for commercial products.

While the X/Open DTP model defines *procedural interfaces* restricted to *process level* access, the CORBA object transaction service (OTS) defines *distributed*, *object-oriented interfaces* for the components of a TP systems.

Commercial TP monitor products follow this trend by building CORBA-based object transaction monitors on top of existing, X/Open-based TP monitor technology. For example, IONA Technologies' OrbixOTS implementation is based on Transarc's Encina, and BEA's M3 middleware is based on TUXEDO.

The CORBA OTS specification is explicitly designed to be compatible with the X/Open model so that technology innovation can happen as an evolutionary process, not replacing but integrating existing technology. Thus, CORBA OTS implementations allow us to leverage the strengths of existing, well-proven TP monitor technology in a modern, object-based CORBA environment.

Figure 12.4 describes the CORBA OTS model, and also shows how an X/Open-compliant resource manager can be used with CORBA OTS. Compare this diagram to Figure 12.3, where the X/Open DTP model is described: applications can now make use of clean CORBA-based interfaces

Figure 12.4   CORBA OTS and X/Open-compliant resource managers

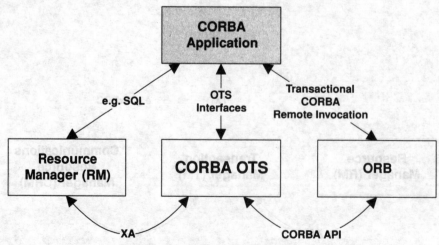

to build distributed TP systems, while under the hood the OTS interacts with existing resource managers via the XA interface. A CORBA OTS-based application uses the CORBA OTS interfaces to manage a transaction instead of the X/Open TX interface. Also, transactional remote invocations use the normal CORBA mechanism for making remote invocations, instead of the X/Open TxRPC interface. An OTS implementation uses the standard CORBA API to interact with the ORB. An important role of CORBA OTS is to act as a transaction manager. In this role, an OTS can use X/Open's XA interface to interact with a resource manager. This means that any X/Open-compliant resource manager can be used with CORBA OTS out of the box.

Overview

The OTS specification defines two different ways of propagating transactions: *implicit* and *explicit*. With the implicit model, transactional remote invocations carry with them a transaction context sent in addition to the IDL-specified arguments for an invocation. With the explicit model, a transaction context is represented as an IDL data structure, and listed among the invocation's arguments in IDL.

Also, the OTS specification defines two different ways for an application to manage transactions: *direct* and *indirect*. With the direct way of managing transactions, a transaction factory is used to create new transactions. Transactions are represented as CORBA objects. With the indirect way of managing transactions, the application has no direct exposure to transactions. OTS defines the Current interface, which represents the current thread from an OTS point of view. This interface is used to indirectly manage transactions: an application calls begin() on the Current object, and the OTS associates the current thread with a new transaction. Usually, indirect transaction management is combined with implicit transaction propagation: the indirectly created transaction is implicitly propagated with each transactional remote invocation. The indirect/implicit usage model is the most common way of using OTS.

In addition to the interfaces required for an application to manage transactions, the OTS also defines a set of interfaces that deal with resource management, recovery, and nested transactions. However, in this book, we focus on applying the indirect/implicit usage model. The next section gives an introduction to programming with the indirect/implicit usage model, followed by a section that describes the general architecture of an OTS-based TP system.

Programming with OTS

The easiest way to explain how to use an OTS is by comparing an OTS-based application with a standard two-tier database application, as shown in Figure 12.5. In most cases, such a two-tier application would use some kind of database client library to talk to a database server. The database client program would have two main parts:

- **Database initialization.** Usually, the database client library needs to be initialized, requiring information like database name and location, user name and password.
- **Transaction implementation.** A normal program would have some application logic that calls some transaction implementations. Such a transaction implementation would use the database client API to begin a transaction, execute queries and updates, and finally commit the transaction.

Figure 12.5 Standard two-tier database client

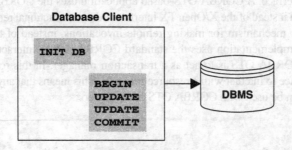

Now we compare this to a simple three-tier OTS-based application. Using the implicit/indirect mode (the standard way of using OTS), we have to do the following to change our two-tier database application to a three-tier OTS application:

- To implement transactional CORBA objects, we start by defining a CORBA IDL interface that inherits from the IDL interface `TransactionalObject`.
- We implement the new CORBA IDL interface, and link the new implementation class to our application server.
- Our application server plays a dual role: acting as a database client on the one hand, and providing CORBA object implementations on the other.
- Instead of directly initializing the database client library, we register it with the OTS. It is the OTS's responsibility to initialize the database client library.
- In an OTS application, we are not supposed to use native database client APIs to begin and end transactions. Therefore, if we want to reuse the existing transaction logic in our new transactional CORBA object implementation, we have to delete the original BEGIN and COMMIT calls.
- We add a new process to our system, which acts as a client of our implementation server. It is this client's responsibility to begin and end transactions, using the standard OTS interfaces. In our simple example, the client begins a transaction, makes transactional remote invocations on transactional CORBA objects (which, in turn, update the database), and finally commits the transaction.

To summarize: we have to add the CORBA client and server logic, remove the database client API-based BEGIN and COMMIT calls from our transaction implementations, and register the database with OTS, instead of initializing the database ourselves. Figure 12.6 shows how a two-tier application can evolve to a three-tier CORBA application.

To use a CORBA object with the implicit/indirect mode, the object's interface must inherit from the IDL interface `TransactionalObject`. (This interface is defined as part of the OMG's common object services (COS) specification, in the `CosTransactions` module.) This is an empty interface which is used merely as a marker, indicating that each operation of the interfaces must be called in the context of a transaction:

Figure 12.6   Three-tier application with OTS

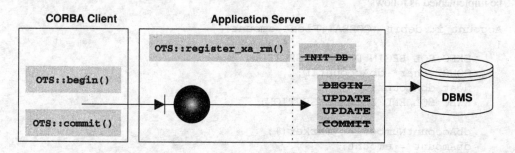

```
interface Account : CosTransactions::TransactionalObject
{
    void debit (in float amount);
    void credit (in float amount);
}
```

A client could use the interface like the following:

```
Account_var firstAccount = ... // Get first account
Account_var secondAccount = ... // Get second account
Current_var current = ... // Get OTS current

current->begin();
{
    firstAccount->debit (100.0);
    secondAccount->credit (100.0);
}
current->commit();
```

The client uses the Current interface to deal with transactions implicitly. The Current interface is a pseudo interface (that is, not distributed) and represents the current transaction context. The current thread creates a new transaction using Current::begin(). The client's OTS library associates this new transaction with the current thread. If this thread now makes a remote invocation, the client's OTS library intercepts the outgoing request, and checks if the interface of the target object inherits from TransactionalObject. If so, the OTS adds a transaction context to the outgoing request. On the server side, the same happens: if an incoming request carries with it a transaction context, the server's OTS library takes the transaction context, and associates a thread with the transaction. This thread is then used to invoke on the target object. If the object accesses a database, this is now done on behalf of the transaction which was passed implicitly by the client.

An object's implementation must operate on the appropriate row in the underlying database table. Applications can embed this primary key information in an object's identifier. For example, with Orbix, an implementation could use the object's marker as the primary key for an account table (_marker is an Orbix-specific method). With embedded SQL, the debit() operation might be implemented as follows:

```
Account_i::debit (CORBA::Float amount)
{
    EXEC SQL BEGIN DECLARE SECTION;
    CONST char* dbAccountID;
    float dbAmount;
    EXEC SQL END DECLARE SECTION;

    dbAccountNumber = _marker();
    dbAmount = amount;

    EXEC SQL UPDATE account
    SET balance = balance - :dbAmount
    WHERE account_id = :dbAccountID;
}
```

Finally, our client calls Current::commit() to commit the transaction which is associated with the current thread. The OTS must now execute the two-phase commit protocol, preparing and committing all resource managers that were previously accessed in the context of the current transaction.

Transactional Resources

The OTS provides two different approaches for integrating resource managers into a TP system. The first approach is based on the X/Open XA interface, as discussed in section "X/Open DTP."

X/Open DTP-compliant resource managers which can be used with OTS out-of-the-box include Oracle, Sybase, Informix, and IBM's MQSeries. Many ODBMS vendors like Versant and Object Design have announced X/Open DTP support for upcoming releases, or have already delivered first releases. The same applies for database access tool vendors like RogueWave (DBTools.h++) and Persistence Software.

The second approach is based on an IDL interface Resource. An application can implement a resource object, and register it with a particular transaction. OTS will then ensure that the resource object is integrated into the two-phase commit. The Resource interface is often used for application-specific solutions, for instance, integrating legacy systems and resource managers that don't provide an XA interface.

The difference between the OTS Resource interface and the X/Open DTP XA switch is that a resource object represents a particular resource in the context of a transactions, whereas the XA switch represents the whole resource manager, and is usually registered with the OTS for the lifetime of a process. Also, a Resource is a distributed CORBA object, whereas the XA switch can only be accessed locally.

Recall that in most cases, interaction between the OTS and the resource manager is completely transparent for the application programmer. Therefore, there shouldn't be a difference between XA and the native resource interface from an application programmer's point of view.

Recovery

An important feature of a TP system is that it must always be able to recover from a failure, at any point in time. To ensure the atomicity of a transaction, we must be able either to undo all updates that have been executed before the failure, or to finish the transaction. In an OTS-based system, the responsibility for recovery is shared between the OTS as the transaction manager, and the resource managers. A common technique is to use logs. The resource managers keep information about all updates in persistent logs. The transaction manager keeps a log file that contains information about the transaction and its current state. For example, the log for a particular transaction might contain the status *prepared*, and the identity of the transaction's participants. However, notice that the recovery log of the transaction manager does not contain any information about the data that was accessed by the transaction.

In an OTS environment, a server that can log transaction state information (that is, the state of the transaction, but not the state of the data accessed by the transaction) is referred to as a *recoverable server*. Only a recoverable server can act as a transaction coordinator. Often, OTS clients are not recoverable, and therefore defer the coordinator role to a recoverable server that participates in the transaction.

OTS Architecture

The following gives an overview of the OTS architecture. We explain how transaction information is implicitly transferred with CORBA remote invocations, and how the OTS interacts with the resource manger. Note, however, that all this is fully transparent for the application programmer: With the implicit/indirect OTS usage model, the application has no direct exposure to transactions.

An important concept of the implicit/indirect OTS usage model is that of *transaction/thread* association. If a client begins a new transaction using the Current interface, the OTS will associate the client thread implicitly with a transaction context. Only the OTS is aware of this thread/transaction association. If this client now makes a transactional remote invocation, it is the OTS's responsibility to implicitly transfer the transaction context to the server side and recreate the transaction/thread association on the server side. This is important because it enables the thread that is executing the request on the server side to access resource managers on behalf of the transaction that was initially started by the remote client.

Figure 12.7 describes how transaction/thread association is done for an incoming request (1) in an application server. The OTS intercepts the request (2) and checks if the target is a transactional object. If so, the request carries with it a transaction context, which is extracted by the OTS. The OTS selects a thread to execute the request, and updates the OTS internal thread/transaction mapping (3).

Next, the OTS must inform the database client library about the transaction that came in, and also which thread will do work on behalf of this transaction. The OTS interacts with the database client library using the *XA switch* (4). The XA switch is an object provided by the RM which implements the XA interface. It is the application's responsibility to register the TM's XA switch with the OTS, so the OTS can later interact with the TM via the XA switch. The OTS calls the database client library via the XA switch, passing the ID of the transaction. The database client library updates its internal transaction/thread mapping.

Figure 12.7 OTS server with XA resource manager

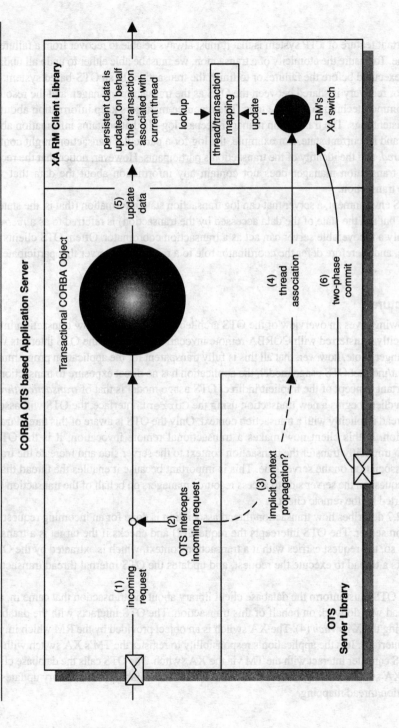

Having informed the database about the current transaction, the OTS tells the ORB server runtime to continue dispatching the request, using the thread selected previously by OTS. The ORB will invoke the appropriate method on the transactional target CORBA object, for instance, an `Account_i` object in our example above. The object updates data by calling the database client library, executing a SQL statement (5). The database client library checks the internal transaction/ thread mapping, so that the SQL code can be executed in the context of the correct transaction (an SQL request containing the correct transaction identifier is send to the database server). When the object's method implementation returns, the OTS invokes on the XA switch again, to end the current transaction/thread association.

Finally, the CORBA client calls `Current::commit()` to end the transaction. The OTS now starts executing the two-phase commit across all participating OTS servers. The OTS servers use their local XA switches to issue `prepare()` and `commit()` (or `rollback()`) calls to the databases and other resource managers (6).

Figure 12.8 gives an example of how an OTS could implement the execution and resolution of a distributed transaction. A client starts a transaction via the OTS. OTS creates a transaction context and associates it with the calling thread in the client. The client makes a first remote invocation in the context of the new transaction ($txRMI_1$). On the server side, the OTS recreates the transaction/thread association, so that the client can update some data on behalf of the transaction (SQL_1). After this, the client makes a second remote invocation ($txRMI_1$), which in turn results in a database update (SQL_2). Now the client commits the transaction.

The client's OTS library might decide to delegate the coordination of the two-phase commit to the first recoverable server.[1] In our example, the first server (or, more precisely, the server's OTS

Figure 12.8 Example of OTS transaction

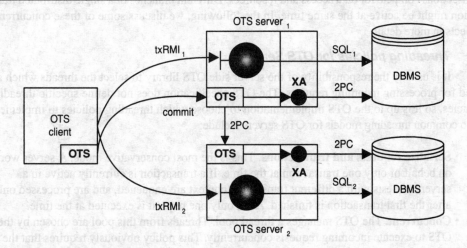

---

[1] Recall that an OTS must keep a log of each transaction and its current state, so that a recovery in case of a failure can be executed. Usually, a client will not have a log file, so that the client-side OTS library will normally decide to delegate the coordination of the two-phase commit to the first recoverable server. In our example, we assume that both servers have an OTS log file, so the client will simply choose the first server as the coordinator.

library) acts as the coordinator. From the coordinator's point of view, there are two participants in the transaction: a resource manager represented by a local XA switch, and a participant in the form of a remote OTS server. Both must be included in the two-phase commit. The second server's OTS library acts as a sub-coordinator, forwarding the incoming messages related to the two-phase commit to the local XA switch. The XA switch, in turn, will forward them to the database server.

In this example, we can see that a distributed transaction includes two types of communication: in-band, and out-of-band. We call normal application level communication *in-band*, while OTS internal communication (for instance, for the two-phase commit) is called *out-of-band*. Also, it is important to notice that the way the out-of-band communication is explained in our example is only one possible way of executing the two-phase commit. Many other ways of transaction resolution are possible—for instance, having a centralized server that acts as the coordinator for all recoverable servers involved in a transaction. In our example, we assume that transaction coordination is really distributed; that is, we form a transaction resolution tree of coordinators and sub-coordinators (each sub-coordinator plays two roles: participant and coordinator).

Concurrency

Managing concurrent access to shared data by distributed transactions is often the most difficult part of building a TP system.

Concurrency can occur at different levels in a distributed system. Multiple clients are likely to access a single application server at the same time. An application server might have multiple threads running concurrently, using classical techniques like mutexes and semaphores to synchronize access to shared data structures. Multiple application servers are likely to access a single database server at the same time, competing for access to the same persistent data. Multiple concurrent transactions compete for data access and resources. Different branches of a single distributed transaction might be active at the same time. In the following, we discuss some of these concurrency aspects in more detail.

Threading policies for OTS Servers

It is usually the responsibility of the server side OTS library to select the threads which are used for processing incoming requests. The OTS specification does not define specific threading policies, so it is up to the OTS implementation to choose which threading policies to implement. Two common threading models for OTS servers include:

- **Serialize requests and transactions.** This is the most conservative mode. A server works on behalf of only one transaction at the time. If a transaction is currently active in a server, requests with a different transaction context are enqueued, and are processed only after the first transaction is finished. Also, only one request is executed at the time.
- **Concurrent.** The OTS manages a thread pool. Threads from this pool are chosen by the OTS to execute incoming requests concurrently. This policy obviously requires that the resource manager is capable of handling multiple concurrent threads, and the application code must be thread-safe as well.

Loosely coupled vs. tightly coupled concurrency

A distributed transaction forms a tree of related nodes (processes and threads) which are participating in the transaction. These nodes are sometimes also referred to as *transaction branches*.

The question is, what happens if two branches of the same distributed transaction try to access the same data? Should they share all locks, because they belong to the same transaction, or should they be isolated from each other?

X/Open and OSI TP both support *loosely coupled* transactions; that is, different transaction branches are isolated from each other. However, CORBA OTS assumes *tightly coupled* concurrency; that is, a lock held by a transaction may be accessed by any branch of this transaction. If OTS exchanges transaction identifiers with an X/Open resource manager, the X/Open transaction identifier will not contain a branch qualifier. Therefore, care must be taken when combining transaction managers and resource managers that couple transactions differently.

Object Concurrency Control Service

The CORBA object concurrency service (OCCS) defines a set of IDL interfaces that support management of distributed locks. In addition, the OCCS is tightly integrated with the OTS specification, for example, providing a special `TransactionalLockSet` interface for managing locks in a transactional environment.

However, managing concurrency control is traditionally a domain of the resource managers. Most commercial databases implement concurrency control via internal locking mechanisms. Also, a database can implement different levels of isolation, as discussed in Chapter 9, "Object Persistence," section "Isolation Levels."

Therefore, the OCCS seems to be of most interest to someone implementing a resource manager. Normal application programmers that work with standard resource managers, such as relational databases, are unlikely to need an OCCS implementation.

How much ACID does OTS give you?

To what extent can an OTS ensure the ACID properties of a distributed transactions? Using the double bookkeeping accounting system as an example, a simple transaction in such a system transfers money from one account to another. It is important that such a transaction be atomic, because the total balance of all the accounts in the system must always be zero. If an entry were only executed halfway, the balance of the system would be uneven. This means an important consistency requirement is that the total balance of the system is zero. Obviously, a transaction must be isolated from other transactions, since during such a transaction the system's balance can be uneven (for instance, after the debit, but before the credit). And finally, we need to ensure that all the changes are stored persistently.

It is the responsibility of the transaction manager (that is, OTS) to ensure the atomicity of the transaction by executing the two-phase commit at the end of the transaction. Each resourse manager makes its own decision in the prepare phase, but by coordinating this process OTS ensures that all resource managers either commit or abort their work, thereby achieving atomicity.

The responsibility for ensuring the consistency property is usually shared by the application logic and the resource manager. For example, the application logic is responsible for ensuring that the entries make sense from a business point of view—the correct accounts are used, and the correct amount is transferred. Often, a resource manager provides mechanisms to help an application ensure that the consistency requirements are met. For example, many RDBMSs provide a way to declare that a certain column may not contain null values; that is, a record is only consistent if the column contains a non-null value. Or, the RBDMS provides a trigger mechanism, which can be used to ensure post-conditions. It is the application's responsibility to define these post-conditions, but they are enforced by the DBMS's trigger mechanism. As we can see, the application logic plays an important role in enforcing the consistency property. Application logic in this case can be either code stored by the database server (for instance, in the form of triggers, or stored procedures) or some logic implemented by the application server (the database client).

Isolation is usually enforced by the resource manager. The most common technique is to use a locking mechanism implemented by the database. An alternative solution would be the use of an application-level approach, such as a timestamp. Recall that most resource managers provide different levels of isolation, ranging from the very weak dirty read, up to repeatable read which ensures full serializability.

The responsibility for ensuring the durability property is shared by the transaction manager (OTS), and the resource managers. The transaction manger must write information describing the state of the transaction to durable storage at certain stages of the transaction. This information usually contains the IDs of the transaction's participants and the current state. For example, if the outcome of the transaction is "commit," the transaction manager must write this information to durable storage, before starting to send commit messages to the participants. This ensures that the transaction manager can continue committing the transaction even after a failure. However, it is not the transaction manager's responsibility to store any information about the updates executed by the transaction. This is up to the resource managers. For example, during the prepare phase the resource manager writes enough information to durable storage that enables either execution of all changes or undoing of all changes. This usually includes keeping locks on all data that must be updated. A common technique is to use *undo logs*: the resource manager applies all the changes during the prepare phase, holds locks on the data, and keeps information about all the changes in an undo log. Should the outcome of the transaction be abort, the resource manager could undo all the changes based on the information in the undo log.

As we can see, ensuring ACID properties for a distributed transaction is a complex task that is up to not only the OTS, but requires seamless interaction of transaction manger, resource manager, and application logic.

How much ACID is good for you?

All transaction systems are faced with striking a balance between the competing demands of *currency* and *concurrency*. This relates to two key demands of most TP systems: guarantees (with tolerances) of *throughput* and *responsiveness*.

Given that our computing resources are usually limited, the needs of our applications often force us to improve concurrency at the expense of currency. For example, many banking systems take stale data (yesterday's balance) as their starting point. The results may be unauthorized overdrafts, but banks often don't care about that because they hope that a system of limits will prevent unacceptable amounts of unrecoverable debt piling up. If we attempted to provide real-time balances that reflect intra-day transactions, the complexity of the banking system would rise significantly. Whether the resulting cost for developing and maintaining such an advanced system is justi-fiable or not depends on business judgements about the reduction of bad debt that could be achieved. So, the more current a system's data, the less concurrent a system can be. A fully current system requires fully serialized transactions.

The question of how much ACIDity is needed in a system strongly depends on the business requirements. In some businesses, reliability is only important up to a certain level. Let's take for example a system that executes millions of transactions every day, but the value of the items affected by the transaction is very small—for example, an Automatic Teller Machine (ATM). On average, the value of each transaction might be something like US $100. On the other hand, let's say we earn US $1 with each ATM transaction. If an average of one out of 10,000 transactions fails, this means that we have an average loss of 0.01%, or US $100 per US $10,000 earned. If we are willing to accept this, we might be able to relax our requirements for the system's reliability, and live with it. It might turn out to be more expensive to increase the system's reliability than the actual gain would be. Customers are unlikely to complain if we don't debit their account for each 10,000th ATM trans-action. On the other hand, a business's reputation is also valuable. If the result of lost transactions is that customers lose faith in the bank, this may in fact be very costly for the bank in the long run. Also, the cost of manually fixing data inconsistencies shouldn't be underestimated. For all these rea-sons, it is questionable if the true cost of a lost transaction in the above example is really only the $100 cash we lose; it could be much higher due to these hidden costs.

Another interesting example is a flight reservation system, like the SABRE system discussed earlier. Most airlines accept more reservations for a particular flight than seats that are available, because the airlines calculate that a certain number of reservations will be canceled before the flight or that the reservation-holders will not show up. This means that we may end up with a situation where we have an inconsistency between the number of available seats and the number of flight reservations. But does this mean that a transaction, which overbooks a flight, is breaking the consis-tency property? Taking on board risks like overdrafts and overbooked flights does not produce inconsistent data so much as meaningful data reflecting a risk. Managing such risks in a consistent manner can be critical to a business. For an airline it is essential to handle the problem of no-shows in an effective manner—underbooking airplanes can be extremely costly. Nevertheless, the airline requires a system that accurately manages the risk by keeping track of all existing reservations in a reliable and consistent manner.

Finally, recall our discussion on the different isolation levels in Chapter 10, "Database Inte-gration." Many databases allow us to relax isolation for the benefit of higher performance. In effect, this means compromising the serialization of transactions, accepting potential data inconsistencies. Relaxing the isolation level can make sense in many situations, where currency or consistency don't play such an important role, for example for pure read-only queries. However, taking potentially inconsistent data as the input for update operation is dangerous, since it can result in corrupted data. Typical TP systems will rarely compromise true serializability in the area of update activity.

Classification of Transaction Distribution

The natural result of combining CORBA with database technology is a three-tier architecture, where CORBA clients invoke on application servers which in turn act as database clients. From an architectural viewpoint, this doesn't look much different with the addition of OTS. The most significant difference is that we now have client-controlled transactions. Our transaction is now distributed over the CORBA client, the application server, and the database server. We refer to this kind of distribution as *vertical distribution*.

N-tier, component-based systems are the ultimate goal of encapsulating databases and application logic with CORBA interfaces. OTS provides the glue that can help us to have atomic transactions which span activities in multiple components.

For example, let's say a company uses two different enterprise resource planning (ERP) systems, like SAP and Baan. One ERP system is used for manufacturing, the other for supply-chain management. It seems quite obvious that we have to integrate these two ERP systems to ensure that we have a seamless supply of goods required for the manufacturing process. If both ERP systems make their business objects available as transactional CORBA objects, we can easily build new components that integrate supply-chain management and manufacturing in a manner that ensures the transactional integrity of the system as a whole. We refer to this kind of distribution as *horizontal distribution*. These types of transaction distribution are discussed next.

Vertical Distribution

Figure 12.9 shows a simple three-tier system as an example of a vertically distributed transaction. In the case of a transaction which is only distributed vertically, with only a single resource manager involved in the transaction, we don't need a two-phase commit for transaction resolution. The OTS specification efficiently handles this special case: a single commit phase is sufficient to commit a transaction, and no recovery from an OTS point of view is required. In the case of a single resource manager, the OTS is used only to give transaction control to the CORBA client—that is, to realize vertical distribution of the transaction. This is a feature of OTS which shouldn't be underestimated. Implementing a solution for client-controlled transactions in a CORBA environment is

Figure 12.9   Example of vertically distributed transaction

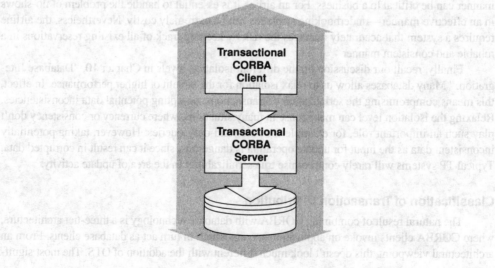

non-trivial. In Chapter 13, "User Sessions," we discuss how OTS can be used to support user sessions in a three-tier environment as a practical example of the usefulness of OTS support for vertical distribution.

Horizontal Distribution

Figure 12.10 gives an example of a horizontally distributed transaction. Our manufacturing system integrates an SAP and a Baan component, and executes transactions horizontally across these components.

Of course, this separation into horizontal and vertical is slightly artificial, and will not typically be so distinct in the real world. An N-tier component is usually not a matrix with a horizontal and a vertical axis. However, we think that this classification adds value to the discussion, since it helps us visualize the distribution characteristics of a transactional CORBA system architecture.

Performance

One important consequence of applying these transaction distribution models is the impact they have on a system's performance. In general, horizontal distribution has significantly more performance overhead than vertical distribution. Let's examine this in more detail. What is the performance overhead of distributed transaction processing with OTS?

First, there is transaction administration and propagation: transaction contexts must be created and associated with the current thread. In the case of a remote invocation, we have an additional argument with each transaction request, and the transaction/thread association must be recreated on the server side. In addition, an OTS must ensure that all participants are inter-linked, so that they can be included in the two-phase commit. This process is usually referred to as *interpositioning*. Supporting transactions via the XA interface might also involve overhead from a database's point of view.

Second, transactions are resolved by executing the two-phase commit protocol, which also adds to the cost of executing a distributed transaction. From a performance point of view, two-phase

Figure 12.10   Example of horizontally distributed transaction

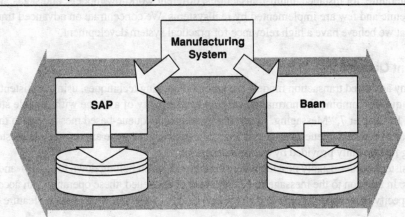

commit involves two significant cost factors: the remote communication for the two-phase commit, and file access for logging recovery information.

The additional cost for the two-phase commit is usually considered to be the most significant cost factor in executing a distributed transaction. Usually, the more distributed a transaction is, the higher the cost for the two-phase commit.

A transaction that is distributed only vertically usually only adds a small overhead. If the OTS implementation and the resource managers support the one-phase commit protocol, there is no overhead for two-phase commit. But even if the one-phase commit is not explicitly supported, pure vertical distribution is usually considered to be relatively cheap.

If performance is key, an important question that we have to ask is, do we really have to distribute the transaction? In many cases, for performance reasons we have to find a way to implement a transaction as a non-distributed transaction, since the additional cost of the two-phase commit affects performance too severely.

However, there are many cases where we can't avoid distributing transactions. One good reason is the physical distribution of resources. This is illustrated by the clearinghouse example, where a transaction is executed partly by a bank and partly by a clearinghouse. Another example is component integration, like the system discussed above, which combines SAP and Baan to build a new manufacturing system. CORBA OTS provides a generic way of implementing transactions across independent components.

Advanced Transaction Models

We have previously differentiated between *business transactions* and *system transactions*. We also introduced the ACID properties, pointing out that many system transactions are not executed as full-fledged ACID transactions; for instance, a transaction might use a weaker isolation level to gain performance and reduce lock contention.

An interesting question is how business transactions can be implemented using system transactions, and the extent to which ACID properties apply to business transactions. Often, we find that business transactions are very complex workflows, too complex to map to our very simple concept of ACID-oriented system transactions. There are many advanced transaction models described in industry literature, for instance, multi-transactions, different workflow models, and sagas. Many are very academic and few are implemented by real systems. We concentrate on advanced transaction models that we believe have a high relevance for practical system development.

Persistent Queues

Many advanced transaction models are based on queuing techniques, using persistent queues. Persistent queues combine the normal messaging functionality of a queue with durable storage of messages. In Chapter 7, "Messaging," there is a discussion of queue-based messaging. In this chapter, we treat a persistent queue as a special form of a database; here we are not very interested in the messaging functionality provided by queue managers.

Persistent queues usually provide a very simple API, often boiling down to get() and put() operations. In addition to the message to be enqueued or dequeued, these operation can accept arguments to specify other aspects, such as the required quality of service. An interesting feature of many persistent queues is that they can be used in the context of a transaction. Many queue managers implement the X/Open XA interface. This enables us to build applications which integrate persistent queues into OTS-based applications.

Persistent queues are often used to break up complex business transactions into shorter duration, less complex system transactions. The following code sample illustrates this:

```
// Example of queue based transaction:
current->begin();
{
    data = inQ->get();                              (1)
    result = remoteObj->process(data);              (2)
    outQ->put(result);                              (3)
}
current->commit();
```

A typical queue-based transaction would get some data from an input queue (1), process the data by sending it to an object in a remote component (2), and enqueue the result in an output queue (3). The important thing is that the dequeuing of the input data and the further processing of the data are executed as an atomic action. If the processing fails, we abort the transaction as a whole. This means we don't lose the data in the input queue in the case of a failure.

Workflows and Multi-transactions

Many business processes can be described as workflows. Often, a workflow is depicted as a graph in which nodes represent activities and edges represent the flow of control and data among the different activities. Usually, one node is the dedicated starting point, and often different end results are possible.

So, where do system transactions fit into the picture? The individual activities of a workflow could be implemented as system transactions. The output of the transaction could be the input for the next transaction. Some kind of workflow controller would be needed which determines the next transaction to be started, based on the output of the previous transaction. A transaction is executed and, before the transaction commits, the transaction's result is enqueued in a persistent queue. The next transaction would dequeue the result and execute the next activity. The next activity is determined by the queue in which the result of the previous transaction was enqueued. Thus, each edge in the workflow graph could be mapped to an individual queue.

Figure 12.11 gives an example: the workflow graph describes how a software company handles problem reports (PRs). The first transaction captures the PR, stores it in a standard format, and enqueues a message in the queue "pending PRs." The workflow controller dequeues the message in a new transaction and starts the activity "check PR." If the PR really describes a bug, the transaction will enqueue a message in the "pending bug reports" queue. Otherwise, the transaction will enqueue a message in the "customer replies" queue, explaining why the PR is not a bug.

What are the benefits of breaking up our business transaction or workflow into many different system transactions? Often, it is a bad idea in general to have long-lived system transactions. They consume system resources unnecessarily and increase the likelihood of locking conflicts. Therefore, one must usually try to avoid implementing long-lived transactions as system transactions. In par-

Figure 12.11   Example for workflow graph

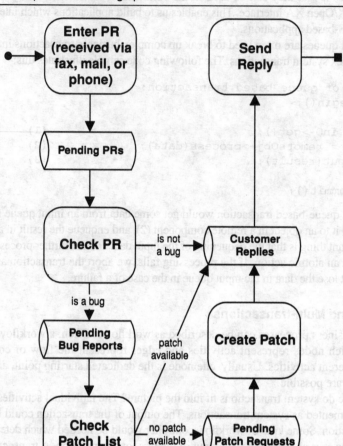

ticular, it is often a bad idea to implement a system transaction that requires user input. It is usually it is a better idea to collect the user input in advance, and then feed this input into a short-lived transaction. Also, the likelihood of failure increases with the lifetime of a transaction. A failure in a long-lived transaction might result in unnecessary loss of work done previously. If, for example, the above workflow were implemented as a single system transaction and a failure occurred in the "check patch list" part, we would have to abort the transaction as a whole, throwing away the useful results from the "enter PR" and "check PR" activities.

The implementation of a workflow graph using multiple transactions is also sometimes referred to as a *multi-transaction*. The interesting question is the extent to which it is possible to implement multi-transactions with ACID properties. We discuss each of the ACID properties based on the above example:

- **Atomicity.** Obviously, the workflow for handling a PR is not an "all or nothing" transaction. A failure or deliberate rollback in the "create patch" transaction does not, for example, result in the deletion of the PR in the PR database. In this example, this behavior is not only acceptable, but desirable. Thus, workflows implemented as multi-transactions do not enforce the atomicity property across the individual transactions that form the multi-transaction.
- **Consistency.** Each single transaction leaves the overall system in a consistent state. Multi-transactions usually enforce the consistency property.
- **Isolation.** A multi-transaction is not executed in isolation: while we are still trying to create a patch, another workflow might see the problem description which we created in the first workflow. Only the single transactions that make up the multi-transaction are executed in isolation.
- **Durability.** No problem here; we always store our partial results persistently at the end of each activity.

Persistent queue managers help enforce the consistency and durability properties: part of the system's state is usually stored in persistent queues. We have to see consistency of databases always with respect to the messages contained by the persistent queues. We are also not in danger of losing any state information between transactions, since state transition information is stored persistently in queues.

Sagas

The lack of atomicity in multi-transactions is not acceptable for many business transactions. In our money transfer system, we couldn't accept a situation where the originating account is debited, but the beneficiary account is never credited.

The idea behind sagas is to enforce atomicity for multi-transactions by associating each individual transaction with a *compensating transaction*. A compensating transaction is a transaction that logically undoes the effects of another transaction. For example, the compensating transaction for a "debit" would be a "credit." This means a compensating transaction can be executed after the original transaction was committed, to undo the work done by the original transaction. Notice that this is very different from rolling back the original transaction itself. The original and the compensating transaction are not executed in isolation; that is, any other transaction can see the changes from the end of the original transaction until the end of the compensating transaction. If another transaction is executed before the compensating transaction, it may no longer be possible to successfully execute the compensating transaction. For example, if we want to debit an account that was mistakenly credited previously, somebody else might already have debited that money, so that we are unable to execute the compensating transaction.

A saga is defined as a chain of transactions, where each transaction is associated with a compensating transaction. Theoretically, there are two possibilities. In the first case, we can successfully execute the chain of transactions. In the second case, a failure occurs after N transactions. This means we now have to execute N compensating transactions to rollback the saga. In reality, there is often a third possibility: a failure occurs executing the chain of transactions, and then another failure occurs while trying to undo the saga. In this case, manual intervention is usually required to solve the problem.

Figure 12.12 illustrates a money transfer system as an example of a saga. Recall our discussion on money transfer systems and clearing houses in the introduction of this chapter. Instead of transferring money directly from bank to bank, we use a central clearing house to connect all participating banks.

The money transfer saga is implemented as a chain of transactions. Each transaction in the chain is called a *step*. Each step is associated with a compensating transaction. Each step would usually process a payment instruction, and then enqueue the payment instruction for processing by the next step. However, a step might sometimes run into problems processing a payment instruction. For example, in step 3 the beneficiary bank might not recognize the account number given by the payment instruction to identify the beneficiary account. In this case, step 3 could not successfully process the payment instruction. Instead, step 3 would maybe enqueue a message into an error queue, containing an error number. The compensating transaction for step 3 would take this error number, create a problem report, and enqueue the problem report to the clearinghouse's error queue. The clearinghouse uses the error queue as the input source for compensation 2 (the compensating transaction for step 2), which simply forwards the problem report to the originating bank. Finally, compensation 1 must undo step 1 by executing a "credit" on the originating account, and send a letter to the customer describing the problem.

Nested Transactions

The nested transaction model adds a nesting capability to transaction processing by enabling transactions to start sub-transactions. Nested transactions form a tree of related transactions, starting with a top-level transactions, and any number of child transactions. Such a tree of related transactions is also called a *transaction family*.

Child transactions are always committed relative to the parent transaction. For example, if a child transaction commits, but the parent transaction later aborts, this will undo the child transaction's changes. On the other hand, the failure of a child transaction does not affect the parent transaction. The transaction as a whole is still isolated from any other transaction that is not part of the same family. However, the different nodes of the transaction tree are usually not completely isolated from each other. For example, if a child transaction commits, these changes would be visible to the parent transaction (and possibly other members of the family), but not to any entity outside the transaction family.

Implementing nested transactions is very difficult from a resource manager's point of view. A resource manager needs an isolation mechanism that differentiates between related transactions and non-related transactions. It also needs a mechanism for committing transactions relative to parent transactions, and support for undoing a transaction's changes in case a parent transaction aborts. The X/Open DTP model does not include the concept of nested transactions, nor do most commercially available DBMSs support nested transactions. From a transaction manager's point of view, supporting nested transactions is much simpler, since a transaction manager does not have to deal with the complexity of isolation. The CORBA object transaction service specification includes the concept of nested transactions.

But what is the benefit of having a CORBA OTS with nested transactions if an OTS can't communicate its notion of nested transaction management to the resource managers via the X/Open XA interface? Many OTS implementations provide a mapping between nested OTS transactions

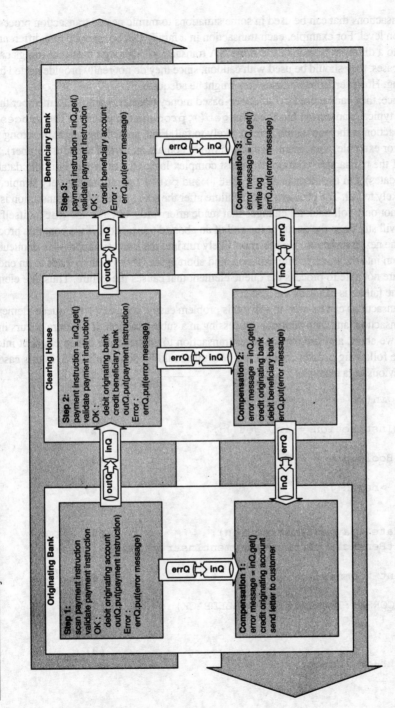

Figure 12.12 Example of a saga: money transfer

191

and flat XA transactions that can be used in some situations to mimic nested transaction processing at the application level. For example, each transaction in a family can be mapped to a different XA transaction, or to a different branch of the same XA transaction. Although these mappings can be useful in some cases, they should be used with caution, since they do not really provide nested transaction processing. However, in some cases they might be adequate.

For instance, they can be used in our queue-based money transfer example. Remember that in this example, a typical transaction has the form `get(); process(); put();`. The `process()` part of the transaction is the one which is most likely to fail. First, something might be wrong with the input data (for example, a payment instruction might contain an invalid account number). Second, this part of the transaction contains the most complex logic (for example, multiple database lookups and updates). On the other hand, the `get()` and `put()` operations are very simple, and therefore less likely to fail. The problem with a failure after the `get()` part of the transaction is that a rollback will not only roll back all changes that made afterwards, but also the `get()` itself; the queue element will still be in the queue at the end of an aborted transaction. If we continue processing by starting the next transaction, we will most likely run into the same situation—we dequeue the same element, run into the same failure situation, and abort again. This situation leads to an endless loop, since we are not able to process the queue element that causes the failure. Thus, the element that is causing the failure is blocking the system.

Nested transactions can be used to solve this problem easily: we `get()` the queue element in the top-level transaction, and then continue processing in a subtransaction. If a failure occurs in the subtransaction, we abort, and use the top-level transaction to enqueue the queue element into an error queue. The following pseudo code shows how this could be done with OTS, in this case for step 3 of our previous saga example:

```
current->begin();                                         (1)
{
    paymentInstruction = inQ.get();                       (2)

    CORBA::Boolean err = 0;                               (3)

    current->begin();                                     (4)
    try
    {
      validate (paymentInstruction);                      (5)
      creditBeneficiaryAccount(paymentInstruction);

      current->commit();                                  (6)
    }
    catch (CORBA::TRANSACTION_ROLLEDBACK) {               (7)
      err = 1;
    }
    catch (...) {                                         (8)
      current->rollback();
      err = 1;
    }
```

```
    if (err) {                                              (9)
        errQ.put(paymentInstruction);
    }
}
current->commit();                                           (10)
```

In this example, we start a top-level transaction (1), and get a payment instruction from the input queue (2). We declare and initialize a variable `err`, which is used to indicate an error situation (3). We start a new transaction (4). Since the current thread is already associated with the transaction started in (1), the new transaction automatically becomes a subtransaction of the top-level transaction. Within this subtransaction, we process the payment instruction (5); that is, we validate the payment instruction, and credit the beneficiary account. If everything is OK, we commit the subtransaction (6). The program flow would then come to the point where the top-level transaction is committed (10). In the case of a failure, an exception would be thrown. In the case of a `TRANSACTION_ROLLEDBACK` exception, the subtransaction has already been rolled back, so we only have to set the error variable `err` (7). In the case of any other exception, we need to roll back the subtransaction explicitly, and then set the error variable `err` (8). If the error variable is set in (9), we can assume that the subtransaction is rolled back, and we can enqueue the payment instruction into an error queue in the top-level transaction. The top-level transaction is always committed (10).

This example of using nested transactions seems very logical. However, it is not trivial: remember that the XA standard does not support nested transactions. How can an OTS support nested transactions on the programming level, if the participating resource managers do not support nested transactions? There are different ways an OTS can map nested transactions to XA transactions. The easiest solution is to map each transaction in a transaction family to its own, unique XA transaction, and end all transactions when the top-level transaction is ended. This mapping works reasonably well if the different transactions do not share any data. In our example, there are two possibilities from a subtransaction point of view.

If no application error occurred, we try to commit both the sub-transaction and the top-level transaction. The OTS prepares the two independent XA transactions. If the outcome of both prepares is OK, both transactions will be committed. Otherwise, both will be rolled back.[2]

If we encounter an application error in the subtransaction, we roll back the subtransaction, enqueue the element into the error queue, and commit the top-level transaction. This means the OTS must roll back the XA transaction that maps to the OTS subtransaction, and commit the OTS top-level transaction.

---

[2] Notice that a failure to commit in this situation can result in the same problem that we discussed earlier: even though we didn't encounter an application error, we have a situation where one of the two resource managers fails to commit. This means our element is still in the input queue. If this situation repeats, we are once again stuck in a loop. However, this is a much less likely situation, so our example is still valid.

There are other models for mapping OTS nested transactions to XA transactions which are more sophisticated. The important point is that however OTS nested transactions are mapped to XA transactions, the mapping will never be completely satisfactory. Therefore, care must always be taken when using OTS nested transactions with an XA resource manager, especially with respect to sharing data across the boundaries of nested transactions.

Summary

Important concepts related to distributed transaction processing are transaction, TP system, and TP monitor. TP monitors provide the technical framework for building, executing, and managing TP system software. TP monitors are used to build TP systems, which are computer systems that process transactions to automate the execution of business transactions. A transaction is a set of operations that is guaranteed to transform the shared state of a system from one consistent state to another consistent state. To ensure that a transaction conforms to this definition, we usually require that it possess the ACID properties. However, we also discussed that there are certain costs associated with ACID transaction processing, and that sometimes we might choose to relax these ACID properties, accepting potential data inconsistencies in exchange for benefits such as increased performance or reduced development costs.

To ensure ACID properties for distributed transactions, we usually use the two-phase commit protocol. The components of a distributed transaction include application, resource manager, and transaction manager. At the point in time where the application ends the transaction, the two-phase commit protocol is executed between the transaction manager and the participating resource managers. Usually, this is done via the X/Open XA interface. The CORBA OTS supports the X/Open XA interface, allowing to integrate any X/Open compliant resource manager. However, this is usually not visible from an application point of view: the OTS offers proper IDL interfaces to the application.

The OTS is most commonly used in implicit/indirect mode. CORBA interfaces are made transactional simply by inheriting from the `TransactionalObject` interface. It is the OTS's responsibility to propagate transactions implicitly with remote invocations, and to ensure that CORBA server-side database access is executed in the context of the right transaction.

Business transactions and workflows are often long-lived and quite complex. Usually, this means that such a business transaction can not be implemented as a simple, single ACID/OTS transaction. In these cases, advanced transaction concepts can be used, such as multi-transactions, sagas, or nested transactions.

CHAPTER 13

User Sessions

Database sessions with user input can be a complicated issue from a transaction point of view. The problem is that a session which requires user input can potentially last for a very long time. The user might take a break while working, go to lunch, or even go on vacation without ending the session. The potentially long duration of user sessions has consequences for how transactions are used to implement user sessions. In this chapter we explore these problems, and also look at a case study which solves many of these problems. We classify the different transaction types as short-lived and long-lived transactions. One point of focus is the problem of long-lived transactions from a database point of view. We explore how optimistic approaches to concurrency control can be used to help increase a system's concurrency. In this context, we also discuss how object versioning can be handled in a session-based CORBA system.

Short-Lived and Long-Lived Transactions

The duration of transactions has significant effects on a system's behavior. An important issue is concurrency, but we also have to think about database resource utilization. Many transactions in a system are short-lived, simple create/read/update/delete (CRUD) transactions. At the other extreme, we have potentially long-lived transactions for things such as decision support systems, batch processing, and online analytical processing (OLAP). And finally, we have transactions that require user input, which are the most difficult, because it is not at all possible to predict how long it will take a user to provide the input. Thus, we have two classes of long-lived transactions: transactions that are long-lived because they execute extremely complex queries and updates, and transactions that are potentially long-lived because they rely on user input. While simple transactions are executed in a fraction of a second, the duration of a long-lived transaction can be measured in days or even months.

Since this chapter is about session concepts, we concentrate on long-lived transactions in the following, and on the problems that are associated with them.

Problems with Long-Lived Transactions

Two important issues with respect to transaction duration are concurrency and resource utilization. We explore both aspects below.

Concurrency Issues

From a concurrency point of view, the problem is that the longer a transaction runs, the higher the likelihood that this transaction will interfere with another transaction. If a long-lived transaction holds locks for a long time, this obviously means that this has an effect on other transactions, which try to access the same data. Even worse, a long-lived transaction might lock out another transaction which is not trying to access the same logical data: many databases implement locking at different levels of granularity, for instance, row-level locking, page-level locking, or table-locking. For example, a long-lived transaction might access a row, which results in locking a whole page. This potentially shuts out another transaction which may be trying to access a different row on the same page. Even if a database supports row-level locking, there is no guarantee that the database will never escalate a row-lock to a page-lock under certain circumstances.

On the other hand, a long-lived transaction might be implemented using an optimistic approach to concurrency control. In this case, there would be no risk of the long-lived transaction locking out other transactions.[1] However, the optimistic approach is also not ideally suited for long-lived transactions: it assumes that nothing will go wrong—that there will be no collision between transactions. In case of a collision, the optimistic approach requires an abort. Obviously, the likelihood of a collision increases with the lifetime of a transaction.

Database Resource Utilization

In addition to these concurrency issues, there is a problem with long-lived transactions at the database level. Databases must keep snapshots of the data they access for the lifetime of transactions. Maintaining different views of data for a long time is likely to lead to problems. It can cause the database's log-files to grow to unreasonable sizes, and will also affect the amount of memory used by the database server.

For example, the Oracle 7 DBMS uses multiple rollback segments. The same rollback segment can be shared by multiple transactions, but all undo information for a given transaction must fit into a single rollback segment. For long-lived transactions, this means that there must be enough rollback segments, and each of them must be large enough, to support the largest possible transaction. If a system mixes long- and short-lived transactions, this can cause problems with Oracle, because these two different types of transactions have different requirements for the structure of rollback segments.[2]

In general, we can see that there are good reasons to avoid long-lived transactions: these transactions can significantly reduce a system's concurrency, and can also cause problems on the database level, due to resource utilization issues internal to the database.

---

[1] A notable exception to the classic exclusive write lock approach is implemented by Oracle. Oracle can allow read access to data even if the data is currently write-locked by another transaction. Technically, this is done by looking up the old version of the data in the Oracle rollback segments. However, this approach can lead to the "snapshot too old" problem, especially for long-lived transactions.

[2] This particular problem can be solved by explicitly allocating rollback segments to transactions. Nevertheless, the example shows the complexity of long-lived transactions.

Concurrency Control

Concurrency is also an important issue for long-lived transactions. Therefore, we recap here the different concurrency control mechanisms, and analyze how they can affect long-lived transactions.

Locking

The most common technique for concurrency control is locking. Before a transaction can access a particular data item, the transaction must acquire the corresponding lock. Locking can be done at different levels of granularity—row, page, table or database. There are two different kinds of locks: exclusive locks and shared locks. The most common approach is to use shared read locks and exclusive write locks. That means that multiple transactions can read the same data item at the same time, since they can share the data item's read lock. Write access is exclusive; only one transaction at the time can have write access to the data item. Also, read and write locks are incompatible; a writing transaction locks out reading transactions, and vice versa. A common problem with locking is deadlock situations; two transactions are concurrently trying to access the same data items, and each is waiting for the other to release the lock on an item. The most common deadlock situations are upgrade conflicts; two transactions hold a read lock on a data item, and then try to upgrade to a write lock. To avoid this kind of problem, additional lock types can be introduced, for instance intention-write locks or upgrade locks.

Timestamp Ordering

Another technique for concurrency control is based on timestamps (although this is less commonly implemented by commercial database management systems). Timestamps typically reflect the transaction start time; they are usually generated by the system in the order of transaction creation. The basic idea of the timestamp ordering protocol is to associate each data item with two timestamps, a read and a write timestamp. Each of them reflects the timestamp of the latest transaction that was successful in accessing the data item. Whenever a transaction accesses a data item, the system must compare the transaction's timestamp with the read and write timestamp of the data item. If the system detects a timestamp ordering violation, it must abort the transaction. Also, all transactions that accessed a data item after the aborted transaction wrote the data item must be aborted in turn. This is called a cascading rollback.

Optimistic Concurrency Control

There are two primary ways of approaching concurrency control: optimistic and pessimistic. Optimistic approaches assume that the likelihood of a conflict is relatively small. This "optimism" allows them to be less restrictive about concurrency control; they simply accept the need to abort one transaction in the unlikely event of a conflict. Pessimistic approaches on the other hand are much more restrictive about concurrency control; a certain degree of checking is done *before* a data item is accessed. With the locking approach, we need to check for existing locks before a lock can be granted that allows the transaction to access the data item. With the timestamp ordering approach, the transaction's timestamp must be compared with the read and write timestamps of the data item before the data item can be accessed by the transaction.

The idea of optimistic concurrency control is to defer this checking to the very end of the transaction. On one hand, this reduces the overhead during transaction execution, resulting in shorter running transactions. On the other, the risk is that a transaction must be aborted in the case of a conflict. Since transactions can run more quickly, the risk is also reduced in comparison to the pessimistic approaches. However, the optimistic approach will only pay off if there really is only a small chance of conflicts.

The most common technique for implementing optimistic concurrency control is to defer all database updates until the end of the transaction. This means that all updates during transaction execution must be applied to temporary copies of the data items. At the end of transaction execution, a validation phase checks for conflicts with other transactions. This means that with this approach, a transaction is executed in three phases:

- **Read phase.** During the first phase, only read-access to database items is allowed. All updates must be applied to temporary copies of the database items.
- **Validation phase.** During the validation phase, potential conflicts with other transactions are determined.
- **Write phase.** If there are no conflicts, the updates that were previously applied to the temporary copies are now applied to the real database items. In the case of a conflict, all changes must be discarded, and the transaction is aborted. This may result in the transaction being re-run.

With optimistic concurrency control, all checks are deferred until the validation phase, where they are all executed at once. Deferring validation to the end of the transaction effectively reduces to a minimum the time for which a transaction needs to hold locks.

Optimistic Concurrency Control and Commercial DBMSs

Most commercial DBMSs do not support optimistic locking directly. Notice that in the context of Oracle 7 the term *optimistic locking* is sometimes used to refer to the fact that Oracle will not read-lock data in SELECT statements, unless SELECT ... FOR UPDATE is used to explicitly request read-locks. This is somewhat optimistic in that it assumes that things will work out fine, but it effectively means that we risk data inconsistencies if we use data that is not locked as input to update statements.

So how can optimistic concurrency control be realized if the DBMS does not directly support it? In this case, the three phases we discussed earlier on must be implemented at the application level; in the read phase, the application reads data without acquiring locks. Changes are applied to local in-memory copies. In the validation phase, the data is re-read from the database, this time with locks. If the validation indicates that there was no conflict with another transaction, then the changes are written back to the database, and the transaction is committed. Figure 13.1 describes how optimistic locking can be implemented with a DBMS that does not directly support optimistic concurrency control.

The remaining question is how the validation mechanism can be implemented. With an RDBMS, there are different possibilities. Some RDBMSs may internally have the concept of a system commit number (SCN), which indicates when data was written last. If the database provides a public API to such an SCN, the SCN can be used to implement a simple timestamp ordering mech-

Figure 13.1   Optimistic locking

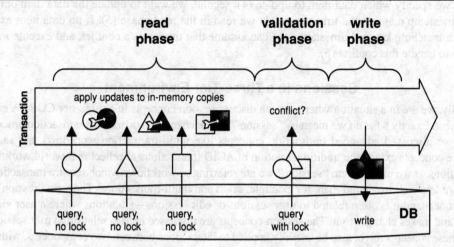

anism. In the read phase, the SCN of each data item is obtained along with the data item's value. In the validation phase, the data item is locked, and the current SCN is obtained. If the current SCN is larger than the SCN obtained in the read phase, this means that another transaction has written to the data item after this transaction read it. This means that the current transaction must be aborted.

If the DBMS does not provide SCNs, we must implement timestamps at the application level—for each data item, we need to add a timestamp attribute. This timestamp attribute is used in the validation phase to detect conflicts. If there is no conflict, we set the timestamp in the write phase to the current transaction's timestamp. Note that so far we have assumed that the validation phase and the write phase are implemented separately. An optimized implementation would group the validation and write phase into a single database operation. The following pseudo code shows how this could be done using SQL:

```
UPDATE data_table                                     (1)
SET
    data_item      = new_value,                       (2)
    timestamp      = current_timestamp                (3)
WHERE
  primary_key      = some_key                         (4)
  AND
  timestamp        = read_timestamp;                  (5)

IF SQL%ROWCOUNT = 0 THEN                              (6)
  RAISE EXCEPTION timestamp_failure
END IF;
```

The update statement shown above combines the validation and write phase. We want to set a new value (2) to a data item (1). In addition, we want to set the data item's timestamp to the current transaction's timestamp (3), if the update succeeds. The condition we use has two parts: first, we specify which data item to update (4); second, we want to update the data item only if its timestamp matches the timestamp that we read in the read phase (5). If no data item exists with a matching key and timestamp, we can assume that there was a conflict, and execute some logic to handle this conflict (6).

Sessions in a Three-Tier Environment

Finally, we are in a situation where we can discuss session concepts in a three-tier CORBA environment. Exactly what do we mean by "session"? In the chapter on distributed transaction processing, we discussed advanced transaction concepts like multi-transaction workflows and sagas. These concepts extend the traditional notion of ACID transactions to reflect real-world workflow situations. If we use the term "session," we are referring to workflows which require transactions, but are less well structured than, for example, sagas and multi-transactions. The term "session" as we understand it is often related to user sessions or edit sessions—situations where a user views data and makes changes to it. The session concepts are discussed here in relation to user sessions, but these concepts might also be usefully applied to interactions between two components, without direct user interaction.

When designing the workflow of an edit session, one of the decisions we have to make is to choose between optimistic and pessimistic concurrency control. This decision will have a major impact on the design and implementation of the system. From a user point of view, both approaches have their pros and cons. A more pessimistic approach prevents the situation where users have to discard their changes because a conflict was detected too late. On the other hand, a pessimistic approach often has the disadvantage that one user can lock out other users. This can cause long waiting times, where users have to stop working until another user has finished, or until we have finally tracked down the colleague who has left a session open—but instead of working on the session he is working on his beach-ball skills somewhere in Hawaii. An example of a two-tier editing environment with pessimistic behavior is Oracle Forms: In pessimistic mode, a record is locked as soon as the user modifies any character in the corresponding field of a form. The lock is not released until the user either saves the changes or aborts. Also, if the database does not release locks in the case of abnormal client termination, this can lead to dangling locks.

For all these reasons, one will very often prefer an optimistic approach over a pessimistic approach. Especially in an environment where users are cooperatively working on the same piece of work, it is often okay to be optimistic that the people will cooperate and communicate to reduce the frequency of sharing conflicts.

In the following, we describe how sessions can be implemented in a three-tier CORBA environment, distinguishing between client controlled and server controlled transactions (per-operation and phased).

Client-Controlled Transactions: OTS

If a pessimistic concurrency control style is chosen, sessions can be implemented relatively easily with the CORBA object transaction service. The clients that present the interface to the user also control transactions. Each persistent object that can be edited in the context of a session should be transactional—that is, changes to the object should only be permitted within a transaction. Operations that return data read the data from the database and acquire the necessary lock. If another operation writes back a change to the data, this will be done on behalf of the same transaction. The user will click some kind of "save" button to submit changes, which will result in the commitment of an OTS transaction.

If the database provides optimistic locking out of the box, OTS can even be used to implement sessions with an optimistic locking behavior. The principle is the same as described before, only the database behaves differently because a different database locking mode has been chosen.

However, if CORBA OTS is used to implement user sessions, keep in mind that this will automatically result in long-lived transactions at the database level: each edit session is mapped to an OTS transaction. Make sure the datablse being used can be configured to avoid the resource utilization problems discussed previously.

Server-Controlled Transactions: Per-Operation

In the common per-operation approach used for handling transactions in a three-tier CORBA environment, each CORBA operation is implemented by executing a transaction; that is, transactions don't span multiple remote invocations. This is the most straightforward use of transactions in a CORBA environment.

The most important consequence of choosing the per-operation approach here is that a session is always mapped to multiple transactions. Since databases do not commonly support concurrency control across transaction boundaries, this means that with this approach we must deal with concurrency control at the application level. Both approaches are possible, optimistic and pessimistic, and both usually require that we add additional attributes to our data items, timestamps or "lock attributes," which indicate that a data item is locked at the application level. Here, we concentrate on the optimistic approach.

We have previously described how optimistic locking can be implemented with a DBMS that does not explicitly support optimistic locking. We apply those concepts here. Since our implementation will map a session to multiple transactions, it doesn't matter whether our database supports optimistic locking or not; we have to handle it at the application level in any case. The only difference to the approach described previously is that the read/validate/write phases are not implemented by the same transaction, but by using multiple, independent transactions instead.

In Figure 13.2, we illustrate the basic idea of implementing sessions using multiple transactions. Every time a client invokes an operation on a CORBA object to get some data, this is mapped to a new transaction to read the data from the database. The client can also invoke operations that update a CORBA object. These updates are kept in memory. For the sake of simplicity, let us assume for the moment that each client has its own set of CORBA objects in a private working area in the application server. Furthermore, let us assume that there is some kind of "save()" functionality provided at IDL level. From a transaction point of view, the important thing is that all changes are saved back to the database by the transaction that is triggered by the "save()" operation. This "save" transaction will usually combine the validation and write functionality into a single operation, as shown previously in SQL pseudo code.

Figure 13.2 Session implemented using multiple transactions

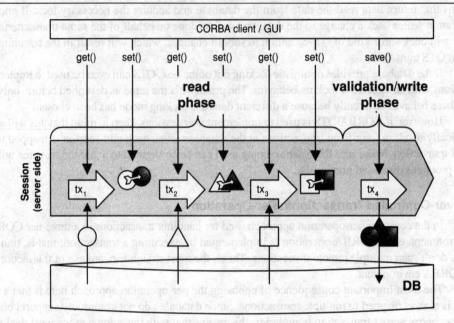

Server-Controlled Transactions: Phased

Using the phased approach to handling transactions in a three-tier CORBA environment, transactions can span multiple remote invocations without explicitly exposing transaction management to clients.

In the previous section, we described how to separate transactions and sessions, implementing a session as a series of read-only transactions, followed by an update transaction. We could combine this decoupling of transaction logic and session logic with the phased approach, as in following: The same transaction is used for read-only access by multiple sessions. As soon as a session requests a save of its changes, the transaction becomes an update transaction, executes the validation/write to end the session, and commits. The next incoming request will start a new transaction, which again can be shared by multiple sessions until another "save" is requested. This is illustrated in Figure 13.3.

What is the benefit of this approach? On one hand, it reduces the average number of transactions that are executed. Since creating and ending transactions can be quite costly, this is a strong argument for this approach. However, this brings us back to the problem of long-lived database transactions. The per-operation approach is completely based on short-lived transactions, while the phased approach described here can again result in long-lived transactions. So the decision between the per-operation and the phased approach is a tradeoff between design complexity and the cost of creating and ending transactions on one hand, and the problems of long-lived transactions on the other. If there are no problems to be expected with long-lived transactions with respect to concur-

Figure 13.3 Concurrent sessions sharing transactions

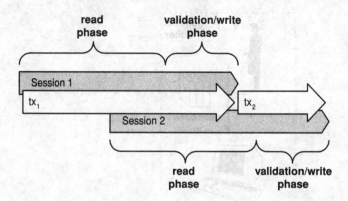

rency and database resource utilization, then the phased approach might be a good idea. Otherwise, the per-operation approach should be used.

Case Study: Insurance Contract Manager

In the following, we use a case study to explore how to design and implement session concepts in a CORBA environment. A large insurance company with many thousands of employees must manage many different kinds of insurance contracts, serving a large number of customers. Some insurance contracts can be extremely complex: compare your personal car insurance with insurance for an airplane, or a fleet of airplanes. Or, consider insurance for an open-air rock concert with hundreds of thousands of visitors. As we can see, an insurance contract can be a complex document, containing a large amount of detailed information. On a very abstract level, an insurance contract can be seen as a collection of questions and answers. Depending on the answer to a particular question, a set of new questions might arise. For example, one question may be whether an airplane has a jet engine or a propeller. If it has a propeller, a following question may ask for the number of rotor blades. Each answer can have a different type—a textual description, a number, a date, or yes or no.

Our insurance company has a large legacy application that manages insurance contracts and automates the billing and claim processing. Users can create, view, and update insurance contracts via terminals. The application runs on a mainframe where contract details are stored in flat VSAM records. The contract editor application is implemented in COBOL, and the COBOL code is responsible for marshalling and unmarshalling the information to and from the flat VSAM record format, so that it can be displayed on the screen. To actually understand the information displayed on the screen, the user must use a handbook, which describes the meaning of the different screens, on many pages. This means information about specific contract types is stored in two places: implicitly in the COBOL routines, and explicitly in the handbook.

There are many problems with this application: the information stored explicitly in the handbook and implicitly in the COBOL code is often out of synch, it is complicated to extend the application's functionality, and the maintenance cost is high. Therefore, the insurance company's IT department starts a project to eventually replace the existing application with a new, modern appli-

Figure 13.4 Contract Management System

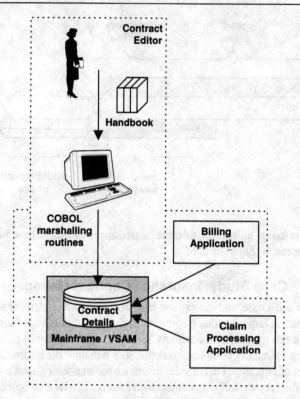

cation that should help to solve all these problems. Since the existing system is very complex, and many people are involved, the new application can't simply replace the existing application all at once. It is important that the two systems be able to co-exist, so that the new system can replace the existing system step by step. The first sub-system that is to be re-implemented is the contract editor, now called the *advanced editor*.

System Requirements

Management has defined the following requirements for the advanced editor:

- The advanced editor must support an Internet-based GUI.
- Since a contract can be an extremely complex document, it must be possible for multiple users to work on the same contract at the same time. It can be assumed that these users are working closely together: conflicting updates must be detected by the system, but the users will interact directly to solve conflicts.
- All contract-specific information must be stored in a relational database. No contract-specific information should be hidden in the application logic or the GUI implementation. In particular, no textual information displayed by the GUI is to be hard-coded.

- The GUI and application server implementations must be completely generic—a change to a contract type should not have an affect on the implementation. That means the company should be able to modify and create insurance products without modifying the application.
- The new system must use a modern, relational database. The information stored in the relational database must be synchronized periodically with the information in the VSAM database.
- The application must be component-based. Future components should be able to reuse parts of the existing functionality. For example, the claim processing application and the advanced editor should share the component that reads and writes the contract details from the relational database.

The team responsible for the re-engineering project defines the following design requirements for the advanced editor:

- To support component-based software reuse and ease of distribution, the application interfaces should be defined in CORBA IDL.
- The advanced editor and the claim processing application will share a component that provides an abstract, object-oriented view of contracts.
- A contract is modeled in an object-oriented manner. The main objects are *question* and *answer*.
- The concept of a *question block* is introduced to logically group questions. This logical grouping has two benefits: first, it makes it easy to implement a generic GUI, for instance, by mapping a question block to a form; second, a question block can be used as the unit of locking—that is, concurrent access to a contract can be enabled on a per-block basis.
- The advanced editor will be implemented in Java, accessing question and answer objects via CORBA remote invocations.

Each department has different types of contracts. For instance, the health insurance department uses different contract types from the life insurance department, and an insurance contract for cars is different from an insurance contract for airplanes. Each specific contract can be described as a tree of questions: a question can be annotated with an answer, and the child-questions of a parent question depend on the answer. The logic to derive new questions from a given answer is driven by a generic state machine, which is used for all the different contract types. The state machine reads state-transition information from a database containing metadata. The same database also contains a detailed textual description of each question and the possible answers. The separation between state-machine implementation and state-transition information allows us to store all contract-specific information in a central database, which contains all metadata that is specific for particular contract types. This information was previously hidden in COBOL application code and a set of handbooks. There will be an editor for the contract catalogue, which enables operations such as the definition of new contract types and modification of existing contract types. However, we do not focus on this editor here.

The actual contract details are stored in a separate database. The information in this database consists of a tree of question identifiers, annotated with concrete answers. It is this database which must be synchronized with the existing VSAM database for as long as other legacy applications get their input data from the VSAM database.

Design

One of the main problems in the system is how to manage modifications to existing contracts. Once they are approved, contracts reside in the production system, where they are used as input for other applications like billing and claim processing. Creating or modifying a contract can be quite a lengthy process. Thus, a mechanism must be implemented to allow users to save changes before they are made visible in the production system. Also, as we said before, multiple users can edit a particular contract at the same time. This means we have to handle two problems: multiple versions, and concurrent access. The solution that we describe here deals with versioning on a very simple level (no history of contract changes is maintained). There will be a master copy of the contract residing in the production database.[3] A second, similarly structured database will act as a workspace for new contracts, and contracts which need to be modified.[4] A manager must explicitly approve moving a contract from the workspace database to the production database.

For editing a contract, the system introduces the concept of an *edit session*. An edit session is very different from a login session, which deals with such issues as authorization and authentication. An edit session is independent of login sessions and can potentially span multiple login sessions. Multiple users can participate in the same edit session. To edit a contract, a user must *enter* a session. If no current edit session for the contract exists, the system will create a new session, and copy the current version of the contract from the production database to the workspace database. Other users can participate in the edit session by issuing an *enter session*. Notice that there will always be only one working version of a particular contract stored in the workspace—users may be concurrently working on the same contract. An optimistic concurrency control policy is chosen for edit sessions. Users indicate that they are finished with their modifications by issuing a *leave session*. Only if all users who previously issued an *enter session* have issued the corresponding *leave session* can the changes be approved by a manager. Once the changes have been approved, they can be propagated to the production system.

Example Session

In the following, we give an example of a simple edit session. Two users are working cooperatively to apply some changes to a contract. At the end, a manager will approve the changes. All interactions with the system are done via a GUI that acts as a CORBA client to the advanced editor application server. The application server accesses the workspace database, the metadata database (not shown), and the production data.

Figure 13.5 describes the sequence of interactions for two users entering the same session. In [1], the first user implicitly creates a new session by issuing an *enter session* for a particular contract. The application server checks out the contract [2], copies the contract from the production data to the workspace, and adds the user to the contract's session [3]. When the second user enters the

---

[3] As long as other legacy components require the VSAM database, this production database must be synchronized with the VSAM database.

[4] Of course, it is not strictly necessary to have two separate databases for the production system and the workspace. Independent tables in the same database would do the job, or an additional attribute for each data item could be used to differentiate between work and production versions. However, for our discussion it is easier to assume we have two independent databases.

edit session in [4], the contract is already checked out. Therefore, all that needs to be done is to add the user to the existing session [5].

Figure 13.6 describes an example of browsing the contract. If an attribute of the contract is to be displayed in the GUI (for example, the answer to a particular question), the value needs

Figure 13.5   Entering a session for an existing contract

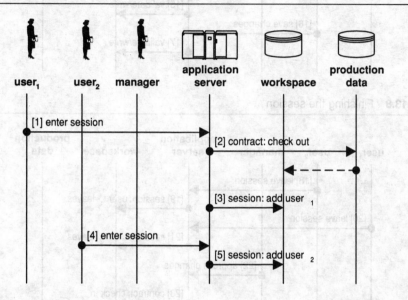

Figure 13.6   Browsing the contract

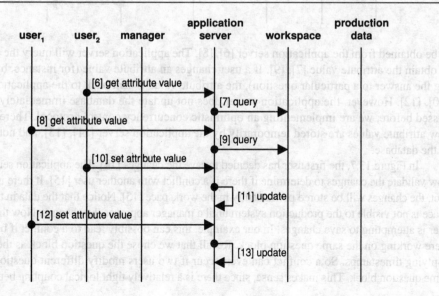

to be obtained from the application server [6] [8]. The application server will query the database to obtain the attribute value [7] [9]. If a user changes an attribute value (for instance by changing the answer to a particular question), the change needs to be sent to the application server [10] [12]. However, the application server does not update the database immediately, as discussed before; we are implementing an optimistic concurrency control scheme. Therefore, the new attribute values are stored "among" the application server values; they are not stored directly in the database.

In Figure 13.7, the feature is described in more detail. The application server must first validate the changes to determine if there is a conflict with another user [15]. If there is no conflict, the changes will be stored among the network data [3]. Note that the changes to the workspace is not visible to the production system or to the master; we allow them to follow the second user to attempt to save changes. In our system, or to display, can only be consistent if both users were working on the same contract [4]. Then, if we change the fields' question blocks; the unit for applying timestamps. So a contract can even contain blocks in different locations in the same session block. This model is used; since each is relatively tightly locked during the change between the

Figure 13.7 Saving the changes

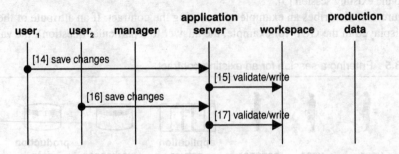

Figure 13.8 Finishing the session

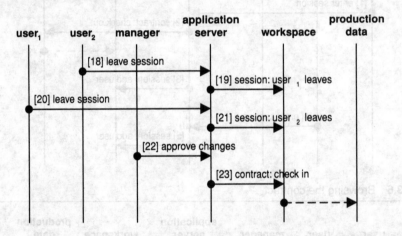

to be obtained from the application server [6], [8]. The application server will query the database to obtain the attribute value [7], [9]. If a user changes an attribute value (for instance, by changing the answer to a particular question), the attribute value is sent back to the application server [10], [12]. However, the application server does not update the database immediately. As discussed before, we are implementing an optimistic concurrency control protocol. Therefore, the new attribute values are stored temporarily by the application server [11], [13], and not directly in the database.

In Figure 13.7, the first user has decided to save the changes [14]. The application server must now validate the changes to determine if there is a conflict with another user [15]. If there is no conflict, the changes will be stored permanently in the workspace [15]. Notice that the data in the workspace is not visible to the production system until a manager approves the changes. Now the second user is attempting to save changes. In our example, this can possibly lead to a conflict if both users were working on the same question block. Recall that we chose the question block as the unit for applying timestamps. So a conflict can even occur if two users modify different questions in the same question block. This makes sense, since there is a relatively tight logical coupling between the questions in the same question block. If a conflict is determined in [17], the changes of the first user will be discarded. The user should be told that there was a conflict, and that the question block can be read again if desired.

As shown in Figure 13.8 if our users have decided that they are finished with the modifications they wanted to apply to the contract, they should leave the edit session [18], [20]. The application server removes the user from the contract's edit session [19], [21]. Finally, a manager attempts to approve the changes that were done by our two users [22]. The approval logic must ensure there are no more users actively editing the contract (all users have left the edit session). If this is the case, the data in the workspace is checked back into the production database so that it becomes visible to the production system [23].

Object Model

Figure 13.9 shows the object model for a contract. Basically, a contract is described as a tree of questions, associated with answers. Questions are logically grouped into question blocks, which may contain other question blocks.

Figure 13.9 Object model

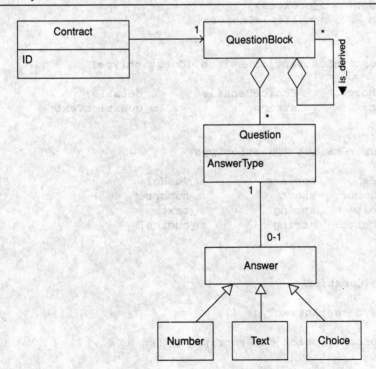

IDL Interfaces

Next, we describe two IDL modules. The first module defines interfaces that are shared by all components of the contract management system. The interfaces defined in this module give a read-only view of objects. The second module extends the first module to define specialized interfaces for the advanced editor, which requires update functionality.

Remember that component reuse was one of the main goals stated in the requirements. Even if the first phase of the re-engineering project concentrates on the advanced editor, it is important that future applications like billing and claim processing be able to reuse parts of the initial system. Therefore, the IDL is split into two parts: one part that is considered to be generic enough for reuse by other components, and one part specific to the advanced editor.

```
// IDL for Contract Management System
module CMS {

... // Type declarations (not shown here)

enum QuestionType {
  YesNo, Number, Text, Choice, ...
}

struct ChoiceDetails {
  string        m_questionText;
  StringSeq     m_choices;
  boolean       m_multipleChoices;
};

union QuestionDescription switch (QuestionType)
{
  case Choice:      ChoiceDetails       m_details;
  default:          string              m_questionText;
};

union Answer switch (QuestionType)
{
  case YesNo:    boolean       m_yesNo;
  case Number:   short         m_number;
  case Text:     string        m_text;
  case Choice:   string        m_choice;
  ...
};

interface Question
{
  AnswerType getAnswerType ();

  QuestionDescription getDescription ();
```

```
  Answer getAnswer ()
    raises (NoAnswerAvailable);
};

interface QuestionBlock
{
  QuestionSeq getQuestions ();

  QuestionBlockSeq getDerivedQuestionBlocks ();
};

typedef string ContractID;
interface Contract
{
  ContractID getContractID ();

  QuestionBlock getFirstQuestionBlock ();
  ...
};

interface ContractBrowser
{
  Contract getProductionVersion (in ContractID id)
    raises (InvalidContractID);
  ...
};

}; // end module
```

At the IDL level, questions are mapped to interfaces, and answers are mapped to unions. The questions themselves are fairly simple; they allow us to find out about the particular answer type, and to get the actual answer.[5] This makes sense, given that a contract is a tree of questions, annotated with answers. Notice that there is no operation to set an answer; these modules provide a read-only view of contracts.

A block contains a set of questions that have some logical relationship. This makes it easier, for example, to implement a generic GUI which can be used to display and edit arbitrarily complex trees of questions. The GUI could simply use one form per question block, popping up new forms for derived question blocks.[6] Also, as we will see later, a question block becomes a unit of work for the end users who are editing contracts.

---

[5] Notice the choice of operations over attributes for the get/set functionality, since only operations can raise user-defined exceptions.

[6] A more realistic example might introduce a more sophisticated structuring mechanism, but we want to keep the example as simple as possible.

```
#include <CMS.idl>

module AdvancedEditor {

... // Exceptions, type definitions,etc. (not shown)

interface UpdateableQuestion : CMS::Question
{
    void setAnswer (in CMS::Answer a)
      raises (UpdateConflict, NotCheckedOut);
};

interface UpdateableQuestionBlock : CMS::QuestionBlock
{
    void refresh ()
      raises ();

    void saveUpdates ()
      raises (UpdateConflict);
};

interface ContractEditor : CMS::ContractBrowser
{
    CMS::Contract createNewContract ();

    CMS::Contract enterSession (in CMS::ContractID c);

    void leaveSession (in CMS::ContractID c);

    CMS::Contract getWorkingVersion (in CMS::ContractID c)
      raises (NotCheckedOut);

    void approveChanges (in CMS::ContractID c)
      raises (ActiveSession);
};

}; // End module
```

The second module uses inheritance to extend the read-only IDL of the CMS module, adding operations to interfaces that need update functionality. This means that a client trying to update objects needs to narrow the interface to the required update type. For example, a client might obtain a set of questions from a question block. If the client intends to set a new answer to the question, the client must narrow the Question object reference to the type Updatable-Question to be able to invoke the setAnswer() operation. In the description of the system architecture below, clients do not share question objects. Therefore, there is no danger that a user who is not a member of an edit session for a given contract will attempt to make an update; the narrow would fail if the target object is not updatable.

The `ContractEditor` interface is used to enable users to enter edit sessions using `enterSession()`. Recall that the edit session and the login session are not tightly coupled. Users can enter a session, and then log out and log in again. In this case, they would use `getWorkingVersion()` to continue their work. Finally, a client calls `leaveSession()` to indicate all the required changes are complete. A manager can check the current working version without entering a session, using `getWorkingVersion()`, before approving the contract using `approveChanges()`.

The benefit of splitting the read-only and the write-access part of the system into two different IDL modules is that applications with read-only behavior, like the billing and claim processing components, have a simplified view of the system. The drawback is the slightly increased complexity for clients with update intention.

Architecture

Figure 13.10 shows the architecture of the contract management system, including the advanced editor. An important feature of the architecture is that we extend the servant pool pattern, so that there are now different types of servant pools. A *shared servant pool* contains the servants that are accessible by all clients. In addition, each client has a private *client servant pool*, which contains servants that are only accessible by the particular client. The idea of a private servant pool is important, since it helps isolate clients from one another by ensuring that one client can't see the temporary updates performed by another client before they are written to the database.

All clients share the `ContractEditor` and the `ContractBrowser` singletons. Also, the `ContractBrowser::getProductionVersion()` operation returns a read-only view of the current version of the contract in the production system. Since this is a read-only view, all objects in this view of can be shared as well. If a client uses the `ContractEditor` interface to access a contract, the servants representing the contract will not be shared with other clients; those servants will reside in the client's private servant pool. The `ContractEditor::getWorkingVersion()` operation also returns a private view.

Figure 13.10 Architecture of the contract management system

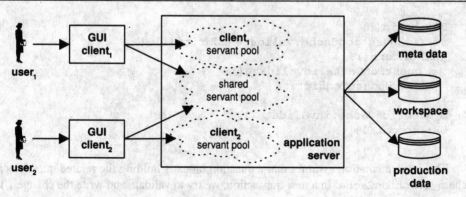

Implementation

Next, we discuss how to implement the IDL on the server side. We focus on the `getAn-swer()`/`setAnswer()` operations and the related `saveChanges()` and `refresh()` operations.

A key process in implementing an optimistic concurrency control mechanism on top of pessimistic database transactions is synchronizing the working data stored in application memory with the data in the database. We could implement sophisticated synchronization mechanisms, trying to ensure that working data is synchronized as much possible with the database. However, in our example we assume a very simple, client-controlled synchronization mechanism. Clients must call `refresh()` on a question block to synchronize the servant with the current database contents. In our example, this simple approach makes sense, since we do not expect many conflicts. The refresh operations will re-read the answers to the related questions from the database. In addition, the database provides a timestamp value for the question block, which must also be stored in memory. In some cases, the refresh operation will detect that the question block no longer exists in the database. This can be the case if the current question block is contained in another question block, and the containing question block is changed by another user, deleting some of the contained question blocks. In this case, the refresh operation would raise an exception. Afterwards, the servant that implements the question block could be evicted. Further attempts to invoke on the now exterminated question block would fail, which seems reasonable.

A question has a member `m_answer` to store the current answer, and a member `m_isChanged`, which is used to indicate whether the question has been modified by a client. The `getAnswer()` operation will simply return the value of `m_answer`. The `setAnswer()` operation is also very simple, and could look like the following:

```
void UpdatableQuestion_i::setAnswer(CMS::Answer& a)
{
    delete m_answer;
    m_answer = new CMS::Answer (a);
    m_isChanged = 1;
}
```

Finally, we save the changes:

```
void UpdatableQuestionBlock_i::saveChanges()
{
    DB::begin();
    if (!m_questionCache.validateAndWrite()) {
      DB::abort();
      m_questionCache.invalidate();
      throw UpdateConflict;
    }
    m_questionCache.invalidate();
    DB::commit();
}
```

This implementation assumes that a question block is holding the related questions in a cache `m_questionCache`. In a new transaction, we try to validate and write the changes. This means the `validateAndWrite()` method must check each question in the cache. If at least one question was modified we must compare the timestamp of the question's cache with the timestamp in the database. If there is no conflict, we write the changes and the current transaction's timestamp. If we encounter a conflict while iterating over the relevant questions, we have to abort. Only if we can make all the changes do we commit. Notice that the cache must be invalidated in either case.

Versioning Granularity

Notice that in the above example we assume that questions themselves are associated with timestamps. However, this is not really necessary. We said that a question block is the unit of concurrency control in our system. Therefore, it would be sufficient to add a timestamp column to the question block table.

The ObjectStore ODBMS introduces the notion of a *configuration* to logically group objects for versioning purposes. Versions are not created on a per-object basis, but rather on a per-group basis. This is a very interesting approach, since it reduces the complexity of versioning. A question block in our example would be the equivalent of a configuration.

Which tier should manage versions?

Finally, we discuss versions and timestamps in a three-tier system. The advanced editor manages different versions of data on two levels. First, we have two databases, one for the production version of data, and one for the current working versions. Second, an application server implements a very simple cache to temporarily store a user's changes in memory, before the user commits the changes (`saveChanges()`). We focus on the latter. In our implementation, we assume that a user's working version is not visible to other users by ensuring that users work with their private set of objects. This means that each user has a set of objects in the application server that are only visible to that user and changes to the state of these objects are private until they are saved.

We use the idea of "private" objects to solve the problem of having multiple object versions. But is this the only feasible approach? What else could we do to enable users to have views of different versions of an object? One approach would be to have single, shared object instances that behave differently for each client. For example, an object could know which client should see which version of the object, returning different versions of data depending on the client. In general, this is a bad idea. If the ORB provides an infrastructure that can be used to ensure that each client only sees a certain subset of objects, why should we re-invent the wheel?

Another idea is to embed version or timestamp information into the data that is passed to the client. For example, each data structure could have a timestamp field. If the client modifies the data and returns it to the server, the server could use the timestamp information that was passed back from the client to detect any conflicts. An example of such a data structure is shown below.

```
struct VersionedAnswer {
    Answer m_answer;
// conceptually private:
    unsigned short m_version
};
```

This approach requires that clients don't modify the timestamp information; the timestamp should be a private member. IDL data structures don't support the concept of private members, but the future "object by value" specification does.

The benefit of this approach is that clients can share objects. However, it seems that this benefit is outweighed by the increased complexity for the client. Basically, each data item passed to clients must be versioned, which tends to make the IDL ugly. Also, what about relationships? Would object references be versioned as well? These additional questions are equally difficult to answer.

It seems that the approach of using private servant pools on the server side is the best solution to the problem of managing version or timestamp information.

Summary

In this chapter we examined common problems with user sessions, and proposed approaches to overcome these problems. Some of the problems are due to the three-tier nature of CORBA-based systems, but many of the problems also appear when using traditional two-tier approaches based on forms, or a 4GL.

The fundamental problem is that most commercial DBMSs are not designed to manage long-lived transactions. There are two major problems with long-lived transactions: concurrency issues, and database resource utilization. We addressed the issue of concurrency control, with a focus on optimistic concurrency control. We described a way of implementing an optimistic concurrency control mechanism on top of pessimistic database transactions by de-coupling sessions from database transactions, essentially implementing the session management at the application level. This approach of de-coupling sessions and transactions addresses the problems of database resource utilization, and also addresses the concurrency problem, due to its inherently optimistic nature.

Next, we briefly discuss two different approaches to implementing CORBA-based user sessions, using either client-or-server controlled transactions.

Using client-controlled transactions (OTS) implies that we have a tight coupling between sessions and transactions. This means we have to face the concurrency and resource utilization problems caused by the long-lived nature of sessions. The OTS-based approach is feasible only if we can find satisfactory solutions to these problems. If we manage to solve these problems, using OTS can actually be quite an elegant solution, since it means that we use out-of-the-box transaction and concurrency control mechanisms and don't have to handle concurrency control on the application level.

Using server-controlled transactions usually implies that we de-couple sessions and transactions, often implementing an application-level-based optimistic concurrency control mechanism. With the per-operation mode, this means that each session uses a transaction per query, and a final transaction for verification and update. The phased approach seems less applicable since it means we have to face the database resource utilization problem again. Although the approach of de-coupling sessions and transactions solves most of our problems, it also has a major drawback. Basically, it means that we must implement a concurrency control mechanism at the application level. Ideally, we would use common off-the-shelf solutions.

In our insurance contract case study, we examined an example of server-controlled transactions in more detail. The benefits of choosing a CORBA-based, three-tier approach in this example is that we provide a re-usable component, which encapsulates the database schema. The initial component exported a read-only view of the system, so that we had to add a second, specialized component interface for update operations. Separating the read-only and the update view has the benefit of reduced complexity for read-only clients, but also imposes slightly increased complexity for update clients. In addition to reuse and encapsulation, the three-tier approach also allows us to build a lightweight presentation layer that doesn't have complex application logic built in. This is important, for example, for Internet clients using Java-based GUIs.

Scalability Issues

When designing a small-scale CORBA system, there are many issues that can be safely ignored, due to the nature of the system. Such systems typically support a relatively small number of users, and are typically less critical to a business, so they have more relaxed uptime and performance requirements. These types of systems are ideal for a first CORBA project. Developers have the opportunity to learn new technology without the pressure of also delivering a highly robust, high-performance system.

Developing a large-scale CORBA system is more difficult. These systems are generally expected to deliver 24 × 7 uptime, along with robust, high-performance services. When developing such a system, the issues discussed in this section become critical.

Chapter 14, "Managing Server Resources," discusses three elements that must be controlled in servers: memory, connections, and threads. No distributed system will be able to scale without addressing these topics.

Two related topics are covered in Chapters 15, "Load Balancing," and 16, "Fault Tolerance." These are distinct goals, but often their solutions are closely tied together. Any system that is going to deliver high performance and high availability must be designed with these principles in mind.

Chapter 17, "System Management And Maintenance," discusses the issues surrounding infrastructure and CORBA applications in production. Topics addressed include the management of distributed components, and handling changes to IDL.

CHAPTER 14

Managing Server Resources

Resource management is an important topic. If we are going to build robust, large-scale systems, our processes must carefully manage their use of resources. This is especially true in a CORBA environment, where the application logic is distributed among clients and servers. The difficulty is that servers often manage resources on behalf of remote clients, but it is not always perfectly clear how long a client requires these resources. We discuss three topics here, which are important from a server's perspective: memory management, connection management, and thread management. Memory management focuses on server-side control of servant objects. Connection management addresses the use of network connections between components and the scalability issues associated with them. Thread management discusses multithreading in CORBA applications, focusing on approaches to multithreading in CORBA servers.

Memory Management

Memory management is essential for all but the most trivial of servers. If our server is going to provide a stable service, it cannot leak memory, and it should limit its memory usage, so that the process size does not bloat. These are the two goals of server memory management:

- Ensure that all memory is eventually freed.
- Limit server memory usage.

The first memory management goal ensures that our server never leaks memory. If an object is instantiated, we need to ensure that it will eventually be freed. This goal is easily measured, and is clearly beneficial for our server. The second memory management goal is more subtle. Limiting the amount of memory used by a server process is worthwhile, but only to a degree. By freeing memory, we reduce the size of our server process. Preventing processes from bloating helps ensure that the server and the operating system run more smoothly. In a CORBA system, we typically accomplish this by deactivating idle servant objects. This imposes a performance cost, since any persistent state associated with objects must be written, and read in again when the object is activited.

Servers use many types of resources, such as memory, files, database connections, and mutexes. Throughout this section we refer to management of servant objects, but the discussion applies equally to other resources used by servers.

Object Classifications

In Chapter 2, "CORBA Revisited," we introduced the basic classification of CORBA objects, from a servant memory management perspective. We defined these as

- Static CORBA objects
- Transient CORBA objects
- Persistent CORBA objects

Static CORBA objects exist for the lifetime of a system. They are always available for clients to use, and are often published as component entry points. Usually, these static CORBA objects are implemented by servant objects which are instantiated each time a server process starts up, and are immediately bound to their associated CORBA object. As such, there are really no interesting lifecycle events for this type of object.

Transient CORBA objects are not associated with any persistent state, and are typically implemented by stateful servant objects. Thus, the CORBA object's lifetime is identical to that of its associated servant object. This means that deactivation of this CORBA object results in the immediate deletion of the servant object, and permanent loss of the associated state. These are therefore interesting objects, since we should only deactivate them when clients have finished using them.

Persistent CORBA objects are associated with some persistent state. While these CORBA objects are active, their state may be stored in the associated servant object. (These servants may actually be stateless, and simply delegate all operations to the underlying persistent storage mechanism. That is, we can have stateful, persistent CORBA objects implemented by stateless servants.) When these objects are deactivated, any state is written to the underlying persistent storage. Therefore, we can safely deactivate the servant object at any time without affecting the associated CORBA object. If we receive a request for an inactive CORBA object, we simply activate it by instantiating a servant object and restoring any state from the persistent store. This type of object provides us with the most flexibility from a memory management perspective, since we can freely deactivate it at any time with no danger of losing any state.

Note that the servant objects discussed previously are assumed to have state. That is, they are stateful servants. Stateless servants can be treated somewhat differently with a ORB supporting the POA. Recall that under the POA, all stateless servants of a particular interface can be handled by a single default instance. With a BOA ORB, however, each stateless servant must be handled by a dedicated programming language object. In this case, the object lifecycle events discussed below do apply to stateless servant objects.

Object Lifecycle Events

CORBA objects, which are abstract entities, have the following lifecycle events:

- Creation
- Deletion

A CORBA object's lifecycle begins when it is created, typically by a client making an invocation on a factory object. For instance, the `PortfolioManager::createNewPortfolio()` method creates a new CORBA object.

A CORBA object's lifecycle ends when it is deleted. Sometimes, this is performed by a `delete()` method in the object's IDL interface, or by a similar method in the object's factory.

As server programmers, however, we do not work with these abstract CORBA objects. We work with concrete servant objects, which implement CORBA objects. Creation and deletion of CORBA objects are relatively uninteresting events from a memory management perspective. When a CORBA object is created, we typically perform early binding, and instantiate the associated servant object at that time. When a CORBA object is deleted, we will usually also delete its associated servant object.

There are two additional lifecycle events which apply to CORBA objects.

- Activation
- Deactivation

The activation event occurs when a servant object becomes associated with a particular CORBA object. Typically, this coincides with the instantiation of the servant object. (The POA specification distinguishes between these steps, but for this discussion we assume that they occur at the same time.) Activation is largely driven by the late binding approach discussed earlier. CORBA objects are activated (and their associated servant objects are instantiated) when a client makes an invocation on them. Therefore, from a memory management perspective, this is not a particularly interesting event either.

CORBA object deactivation occurs when a servant object is disassociated from its CORBA object. Typically, this occurs when the servant object is deleted. (Again, the POA specification distinguishes between these steps, but we will treat them as occurring simultaneously). From a memory management perspective, this is the only interesting lifecycle event. In some cases, deactivation occurs when a client invokes a method (such as `done()`) on an object. This explicitly indicates to the server that the client is finished using this object, and that it may be deactivated. In this case, memory management is very straightforward. In other cases, however, determining the proper time to deactivate an object can be difficult. Next, we discuss a pattern for accomplishing this.

The Servant Pool Pattern

The servant pool pattern can be applied to many different servant management strategies. The basic idea is to maintain a pool of active servants which can execute incoming requests. We call this a *pool*, rather than a *cache*, since there is no requirement that the servants maintained by the pool get their state from persistent storage. Servants that need to be managed are added to the pool upon activation, and the pool takes responsibility for the servant, deactivating it some time later to free up resources.

The central element of the pattern is a pool manager. The pool manager accepts offers to keep a servant for a certain time, before the servant is evicted by the pool manager. When offering a servant to the pool manager, an eviction policy is passed as an additional argument. The pool manager uses the eviction policy to determine the lifetime of the servant. Obviously, different types of CORBA object implementations need different types of eviction policies. For example, a transient iterator object might be associated with a policy that ties eviction to an event like connection closure, whereas a persistent object can be associated with a simple timeout policy, since it can be reactivated at any time.

An eviction trigger is responsible for starting the eviction. During eviction, the pool manager sweeps its servants and evicts some according to their eviction policy. The evictor frees objects by invoking CORBA::release() on them, which deletes the servant object, thereby deactivating the associated CORBA object.[1] Two key roles played by the servant manager are:

- **Keeper.** The servant manager acts as a keeper of servants. Different types of servants should be kept in memory differently. For example, a transient object like an iterator should be kept in memory until it has performed its duty. It is the eviction policy that defines when this is the case. For a persistent object, it is not as important to keep servants in memory, since we can reactivate them using late binding. However, often it can be quite costly to activate a servant, in particular if it is a stateful servant that reads information from a database. In this case, reducing the frequency of activation and deactivation by keeping these objects alive in a pool will help improve performance.
- **Evictor.** Obviously we don't have unlimited system resources, and we need to free up resources from time to time. The eviction policy controls which objects are freed, while the eviction trigger controls when this is done. Common eviction policies and triggers are discussed in detail below.

A complete discussion of a pattern similar to this for Orbix, accompanied by source code, is available from the IONA website, www.iona.com/support/cookbook/evictor/evictor.html)

The key to the effectiveness of the servant pool is the proper choice of eviction triggers and eviction policies. Eviction triggers determine what sparks the eviction process. Eviction policies determine which objects will be evicted at that time.

In order to discuss this pattern, we must introduce some terms. An *idle* servant object has not been used by a client for some period of time. How long it takes before an object is considered idle is dependent on the specific application's usage patterns, and on the type of object. In some cases, an object may be considered idle if a client has not invoked on it in one minute. In other cases, we may decide that ten minutes is a more reasonable threshold. An *orphaned* servant is one that is idle and that will never have another invocation made on it. Clearly, this distinction can only be made at an application level, with an understanding of how the different types of CORBA objects are used.

---

[1] CORBA::release() will decrement the reference count for the object. If there are no other local references to this CORBA object, then the servant object will be deleted. If another part of this application has a reference to this object, then the CORBA object will not be deactivated; its reference count will just be decremented.

Eviction Triggers

When an eviction trigger occurs, the pool manager performs an eviction. It sweeps through the servant objects in its pool, searching for objects to be evicted. The set of objects chosen for eviction is dependent on both the eviction trigger and each object's eviction policy.

Common Eviction Triggers. Now we discuss some common triggers, in order of increasing generality.

Explicit call. An explicit call trigger occurs when a client application makes an invocation which tells the server that it has finished using a particular object, and that the object can be deactivated. This type of trigger can apply to both transient and persistent CORBA objects. For instance, our client may be using a transient iterator. When it has finished retrieving all the data that it needs, it invokes a method such as `done()` on the iterator. This indicates to the server that this CORBA object can be safely deactivated (which for transient objects is the same as deletion). If our client is using a persistent object (such as a `Portfolio`), this method indicates that the client application has finished using this object for the time being. The server may safely deactivate this persistent CORBA object by writing any state to persistent storage and by deleting the servant object. One interesting approach is to use a custom proxy on the client side. When the custom proxy is being deleted (because the client application has released the object) it invokes the `done()` method on the corresponding object.

Connection closure. A connection closure trigger occurs when the application detects that the network connection to a client has closed. Typically, this means that the client process has terminated, and that the server should clean up any resources allocated on behalf of the client. For the servant pool manager, this trigger indicates that it is safe to deactivate all active CORBA objects dedicated to this client.

The explicit call trigger only affects a single object; client connection closure affects all objects associated with a particular client. These two triggers are used for achieving the first goal of memory management—eliminating resource leaks. The remaining triggers can affect any of the active CORBA objects in the server, and are used for achieving the second goal of memory management—reducing server resource usage.

Periodic eviction. A periodic policy triggers eviction regularly, after a specified amount of time has elapsed. Every time the trigger fires, the evictor sweeps through its pool, searching for objects that are candidates for deactivation.

Object threshold. An object threshold trigger is fired when a server process contains more than a configurable number of active objects. Each time a CORBA object is activated, the server's object count is incremented. If this count has exceeded a configurable threshold, eviction is triggered. This may deactivate some objects and reduce the active object count.

Object activation. A similar policy is the object activation trigger. Each time a CORBA object is activated, the eviction is triggered. The pool manager searches for candidates, deactivating any matching objects.

External trigger. With an external trigger policy, eviction is triggered by some external agent making an invocation on the servant manager. For instance, this may be performed by another part of the server application, or by an external administrative tool invoking an IDL method. When this invocation is made, the pool manager performs an eviction.

Selecting Eviction Triggers.   Choosing which eviction triggers to use in a server requires a careful balance. If objects are frequently evicted, the server can reduce its memory usage. However, performing eviction slows down the server, especially if it causes frequent re-activation of objects. Also, transient and persistent objects must be treated differently. Once a transient object is deactivated, it cannot be restored. Persistent objects can be reactivated at any time, without any loss of state.

The ideal eviction trigger for eliminating resource leaks is the explicit call. If client applications inform the server when they have finished using an object, that object can be immediately deactivated. This approach can be very effectively used for both transient and persistent CORBA objects. However, it is typically combined with other triggers, due to its weaknesses. It relies on the client application to behave correctly. If the client is incorrectly written, it may fail to inform the server when it has finished using an object. If the client program terminates unexpectedly, or a network failure severs the communication link, then the server will never be explicitly informed that these resources should be freed. In order to meet the goal of having no resource leaks, we often combine different eviction triggers in our servers.

Client connection closure is a trigger that is commonly used in combination with the explicit call trigger. By detecting when the network connection to a client application closes, the server can then free up any resources that it had allocated on behalf of the client. This approach relies on the ORB to provide the application with an indication of when client connections have closed, as well as a means of associating connections and clients (typically by using the connection's unique file descriptor). However, this approach does not free any resources until the client application has completed, which may take a considerable period of time.

Periodic eviction is a good general choice for eviction. By performing eviction regularly, we can ensure that objects do not remain idle or orphaned for an extended period of time. Also, it is the simplest of the remaining policies, so it can be easily implemented.

Evicting when an object count threshold is crossed is a relatively simple approach, but suffers from two potential problems. First, no eviction occurs until the threshold is reached. This means that our server will contain idle or orphaned objects unnecessarily, until the threshold is reached. If the threshold is high, it may take a considerable amount of time for this to occur. Second, if our threshold is set too low (or our server is extremely busy), the server may continually exceed the threshold. This will cause eviction to occur frequently, and impose an unnecessary overhead.

Performing eviction each time an object is activated suffers from similar limitations. The overhead of an eviction is imposed each time an object is activated, which may occur frequently. Also, if our server stops activating objects, eviction will never occur again. Once all clients complete their work, no further evictions will be triggered until a new client causes an object to be activated. The server can end up maintaining resources in memory unnecessarily.

Relying on an external agent to perform eviction by calling the pool manager is an acceptable solution, as long as the eviction occurs sufficiently often (but not too often).

For some of these triggers, the objects to be evicted are easily determined—they are directly associated with the trigger. In other cases, the evictor must search for candidates by examining each servant's eviction policy.

Eviction Policies

Every servant object that is registered with a pool manager has an eviction policy associated with it, specified when the object is registered. This allows the pool manager to perform eviction in a manner appropriate to each object.

Persistent objects are relatively straightforward to manage. By definition, their state is stored in some persistent mechanism. Therefore, these objects can be safely deactivated at any time. If a subsequent request is received for them, they are simply reactivated to service the request. An important consideration for persistent objects, however, is the cost of deactivation and reactivation. Persistent objects may have to write their state as part of deactivation, and must read their state as part of activation. Depending on the amount and location of the state, this can be a costly operation. If the persistent objects maintain their state only in the underlying storage (and not in memory as part of the servant objects), then they can be very efficiently activated and deactivated. These types of objects are good candidates for frequent eviction.

Transient objects can be more complex. By their nature, their state is only stored in memory. When these objects are deactivated, their state is destroyed forever. For this reason, eviction of transient objects must be performed more conservatively than for persistent objects.

If a persistent object is incorrectly deactivated, the only effect is an impact on the performance of an invocation. If a transient object is incorrectly deactivated, the client no longer has access to state that it needs.

Common Eviction Policies.   Eviction policies are only applicable to some of the eviction triggers explained previously. The explicit call and connection closure triggers apply to a single object and an easily identifiable set of objects, respectively. As such, there is no policy that must be applied to find matching candidates. Those eviction triggers are aimed at the first goal of memory management, eliminating resource leaks.

The remaining eviction triggers are aimed at the second memory management goal, reducing server resource usage. These are the triggers that need a policy to find candidate objects for deactivation.

The most common eviction policies include:

- Least-recently used object
- Object lease
- Oldest object

Least-recently used policy. A timestamp is associated with each servant object. Every time an invocation is made on an object, its timestamp is updated. When an eviction occurs, the pool manager finds those objects with the oldest timestamps. These are the objects that were used least recently, and are candidates for deactivation.

Object lease eviction policy. A timeout is associated with each servant object. The timeout specifies how long this object is leased to the client and is guaranteed to remain active. Any time after the lease has expired, the object can be deactivated. When the pool manager performs an eviction, it traverses the pool, looking for objects whose lease has expired. These objects are deactivated. Leases may be renewed; one reasonable approach to this is to extend the lease whenever an invocation is made on the object.

Oldest object policy. A timestamp is associated with each servant object. This timestamp is set when the servant object is created, and is never updated afterwards. Therefore, finding the oldest object is simply a matter of finding the oldest timestamp.

Note that the data structures used by a pool manager should clearly be optimized for the type of eviction policies used. For instance, a least-recently used policy could store its objects in a doubly linked list, ordered by their usage timestamp. Each time an object is used, it could be spliced to the beginning of the list (this is a constant time operation). When an eviction occurs, the pool manager can find the least-recently used objects by starting at the tail of the list, and traversing backwards. In this case, accessing the tail of the list is also a constant time operation. Other eviction policies would be more efficiently implemented by other data structures.

Selecting Eviction Policies.

Selecting eviction policies to use in a server can be a difficult task, since these policies are used to achieve both goals of memory management. The benefits of evicting orphaned transient objects are obvious, and any of these policies will accomplish the goal. The key aspect of evicting transient objects is to ensure that they are not evicted until we are reasonably sure that the client has finished using them. Evicting orphaned persistent objects is also straightforward. As long as we are reasonably sure that a client has finished using an object, it can be safely evicted.

Deciding whether to evict active persistent objects is a more difficult decision, since this leads us towards the softer memory management goal of reducing server resource usage. Deactivating idle persistent objects reduces the memory footprint of our server, at the expense of performing the deactivation and later reactivation. Writing and reading state from a persistent store can be an expensive operation. The benefit of server resource usage must be weighed against the performance impact of such a solution. Such an approach is often best applied only with large numbers of infrequently used active objects.

Using the lease policy with automatic renewal at each method invocation is generally the safest eviction policy. This ensures that we evict only objects that have been idle for the lease period. If the lease timeout is longer than our expected access patterns predict, the object is probably orphaned. This approach applies an absolute measurement to our objects. If they are unused for a specific period of time, then we assume that they are orphaned. Note that different objects may be assigned different lease periods, for instance, based on the CORBA interface they implement.

The least-recently-used eviction policy applies a relative measurement to our objects. We evict the objects that have not been used in the longest amount of time, relative to the other objects. If all the objects are actively being used, we run the risk of evicting objects that are not idle.

The oldest object eviction policy is simply based on activation time. It assumes that the longer an object has been active, the more likely it is to be inactive. This may or may not be true, depending on how business objects are utilized.

Case Study: Stock Price Iterator

Let's explore some of these issues with a brief case study. Recall the `StockWatchIterator` introduced in Chapter 4, "Performance." The IDL fragment for this is shown below.

```
// IDL fragment : Stock Price Iterator
interface StockWatch {
    StockPriceIterator queryPrices (
                              in QueryExpression aQuery);

    // Other operations not shown
};


interface StockPriceIterator {
    void getNextChunk (out StockPriceSeq nextChunk,
                       out boolean hasMore);
};
```

Iterators are good examples of transient objects with state, and are also an interesting pattern. Iterators are commonly applied in situations where an IDL operation can return a potentially large amount of data. Rather than immediately returning the full set of data to the client, an iterator object is returned. By making invocations on this object, the client can control when and how much data it receives. Iterators are typically used to provide faster response times for operations. Rather than waiting for the full result set, a user can begin examining the partial results sooner. They can obtain more of the results by clicking on a "more" button. Alternatively, the application could retrieve further chunks of data in the background, in a separate thread.

However, like most other transient CORBA objects, iterators must be deactivated eventually. If the client application exhausts the result set by invoking the getNextChunk() method enough times, then the iterator's useful lifetime is complete, and it may safely be deactivated. There is no more data to be returned, and any further methods invoked on the object will either return an empty set, or raise an exception. Note that in this case, the retrieval of the final chunk of data acts as a trigger, explicitly identifying this iterator object for deactivation.

However, consider what happens if the client never reaches the end of the iterator's result set. With the IDL shown above, our server application won't ever be explicitly told that it is safe to deactivate this object. In this case, one of the other eviction triggers and eviction policies must be applied. A periodic eviction trigger combined with an object timeout can provide us with a regular mechanism for deactivating these orphaned objects.

Now, let's examine an iterator that supports backward as well as forward iteration. Sample IDL is shown below:

```
// IDL
interface StockPriceIterator {
    void getNextChunk (out StockPriceSeq nextChunk,
                       out boolean hasMore);
    void getPrevChunk (out StockPriceSeq prevChunk,
                       out boolean hasMore);
};
```

This type of iterator would be useful for a GUI that can only display a fixed set of results at a time. This type of approach is commonly used in Web browsers, for instance, when examining search results.

This iterator provides no indication to our server of when the client application has finished using this object. In this case, we must rely on eviction triggers and policies such as those mentioned before. One alternative is to add an explicit method to the IDL, which the client can invoke to inform the server that it is done with the object. By adding a method such as `doneWithIterator()`, our server can deactivate this CORBA object as soon as the client is finished. As always, though, we cannot rely on client applications (or network connections) to operate correctly, so a backup eviction mechanism is essential for all our servant objects.

Distributed Memory Management

Distributed memory management is the act of tracking references to a data element across processes. In a CORBA system, this implies maintaining a distributed reference count on objects. Rather than just keeping track of references to objects from within a single process (which is what CORBA mandates), distributed reference counting would track all references to objects in all processes. Such an approach tends to be expensive and error-prone, which is why CORBA avoids it. For example, an erroneously written client could fail to decrement an object's reference properly, leaving orphaned objects in memory. Or, a transient network failure could cause the server to mistakenly delete an object before a client is finished using it.

By not implementing a general-purpose distributed reference counting mechanism, CORBA provides us as system designers with the ability to solve specific, simplified problems in our environment. There is no need for the additional development complexity and runtime overhead of a generic solution. The memory management topics that we have discussed here essentially implement small pieces of a distributed reference counting system. For many of our objects we can rely on their specific usage in our environment, and target a solution appropriate to them. For instance, a persistent CORBA object can be evicted from memory at any time, independent of the number of clients that currently hold references to it. An iterator can be evicted after all of its data has been retrieved, or (as a backup mechanism) after several minutes of inactivity.

Summary

Managing memory in a server is an interesting topic. We introduced the two goals of server memory management—eliminating leaks and reducing memory usage. We introduced the servant pool pattern as a framework for accomplishing these goals, and explored some of the most common eviction triggers and policies.

In order to best apply this pattern to a server application, carefully examine the different CORBA objects in the system and how they are used. Many systems benefit by having clients explicitly inform the server when they have finished using a particular object. Client connection closure or object leases are effective backup strategies. Together, this will ensure that no servant objects are leaked.

Deciding whether or not to deactivate idle persistent objects is more complex. Carefully consider the performance cost of doing so, before applying such a policy.

These policies are best viewed as a collection of potential solutions. It is up to you, as the system designer and implementor, to weave these solutions into your system so that they balance and support the rest of the system.

Connection Management

As pure object-oriented programmers, we would like to avoid thinking about or dealing with issues as mundane as the connections between our components. We'd like to be able to simply concentrate on how our objects behave, and how our business logic works. As system designers, however, we care immensely about the connections between our components. If we are going to build scalable CORBA systems, we need to ensure that as our systems grow we can avoid running into any limits.

Our CORBA components use the IIOP protocol to communicate with one another, and IIOP in turn uses TCP/IP connections to send and receive its messages. With most commercial ORBs, there is by default one TCP/IP connection open between each client process and its corresponding server process, no matter how many servant objects a client uses. This is illustrated in Figure 14.1.

Process P_1 (which is a pure client) contains proxies for three CORBA objects; two from process P_2 and one from process P_3. It has a TCP/IP connection open to each of these processes. P_3

Figure 14.1 Basic connections

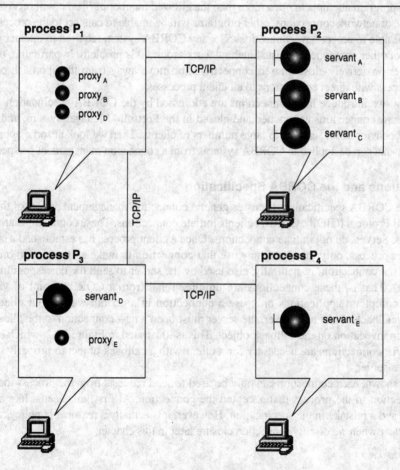

also acts as a client, containing a proxy for an object in process P_4, so it has a connection open to that process. Processes P_2 and P_3 do not interact with one another, so there is no TCP/IP connection between them.

We must concern ourselves with the number of connections that each process may have open, since each connection uses up a resource, and processes generally have limited resources. In particular, each open TCP/IP connection uses a *file descriptor*, which is an operating system handle that uniquely describes this connection within this process. A process is typically limited to a fixed maximum number of open connections. This limit may be imposed by the operating system, by the ORB, or by the data structure used to store the file descriptors. Operating system and ORB vendors are moving to raise or eliminate this limit, but commercially available systems today generally restrict a process from having more than 1024 open file descriptors. In addition to TCP connections, file descriptors are also used as handles for any data files opened by the application, as well as standard input, output and error streams in C++. In general, applications will have approximately 1000 file descriptors available to them; this is the figure we use for the remainder of this section.

If a program attempts to open more than the allowed number of files, it will receive an error. In the case of network connections, other programs will be unable to connect to the process, since it will not be able to accept new connections. So, any CORBA system required to interact with large numbers of other components must somehow work around this problem. In particular, the system must either proactively close unused connections, or move away from the approach of a single server process with direct connections to all client processes.

Now, we introduce how connections are addressed by the CORBA specification. Then, we examine how connections are opened and closed in the Portfolio Manager system, and we'll see why this behavior is not scalable to large numbers of clients. Then we look at some approaches to scalability that can be applied to CORBA systems from a connection management perspective.

Connections and the CORBA Specification

The CORBA specification discusses general connection management as part of the General Inter-ORB Protocol (GIOP). CORBA clients initiate connections. These connections are accepted by servers. Servers do not initiate connections. Once a client process has established a connection to a server process, only the client may use that connection to make an invocation on a remote object. (That connection, is, naturally, also used by the server to send the corresponding reply to the client). That is, these connections are unidirectional from a CORBA point of view, since CORBA-compliant applications only use a connection in a certain way. If our client process exports a callback object to a server, the server must open a new connection to the client in order to make an invocation on the callback object. This is illustrated in Figure 14.2, which shows that two TCP/IP connections are necessary for a client with a callback object to properly communicate with a server.

As shown, each connection can only be used to send requests from the process that initiated the connection to the process that accepted the connection. At first, this seems like a waste of resource, and a mistake in the specification. However, it is actually a reasonable policy, which will become clear when we discuss connection closure later in this chapter.

Figure 14.2 CORBA connections

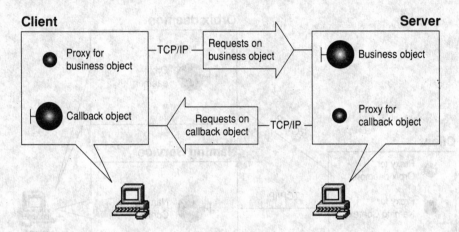

Connections in the Portfolio Manager Example

Let's examine how connections are established and used in our familiar Portfolio Manager example. This example uses IONA's Orbix, but other ORB implementations will behave similarly. In particular, we use this example to illustrate three general classifications of connections.

Figure 14.3 shows the connections and operations of the system. Our client process is running on host *basil*, while our servers are running on *garlic*. The client application's first step is to contact the naming service, to obtain a reference to a `PortfolioManager` object. In order to do this, the client's ORB runtime first establishes a connection to the activation component (the Orbix daemon) on host garlic.

The ORB runtime in the client invokes a method on the daemon, telling it that it is looking for the naming service. This invocation returns some forwarding information to the client, indicating the port number on which the naming service is running. Next, a connection to the naming service (OrbixNames) is established, and our client obtains a reference to the `PortfolioManager` object, in the server process on this host. (Note that it is *not* required that the naming service run on the same host as the Portfolio Manager server; we simply display it this way for simplicity. The naming service can store references to any object on any host.) When our client makes its first invocation on the `PortfolioManager` object, the ORB runtime establishes a connection to the server process containing the object.

Classifying Connections

These three connections illustrate the three basic classifications of connections. (ORBs other than Orbix may not establish their connections in precisely this manner, but they will likely exhibit each of these types of connections somewhere in the system).

The first connection, from the client to the Orbix daemon, is an example of an *implicit connection*. This type of connection is opened transparently to the application programmer, and is never directly used. That is, our application never explicitly makes invocations on the CORBA objects instantiated within the Orbix daemon process.

Figure 14.3   Connections in portfolio manager

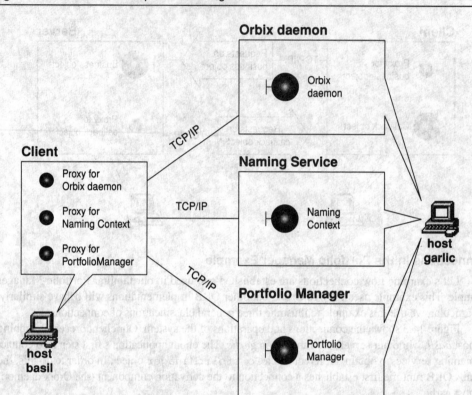

The second connection, to the naming service, is a good example of an *infrequently used connection*. This connection *is* explicitly used by our client application; in particular it makes invocations on the `NamingContext` object implemented by OrbixNames. The connection, however, is infrequently used. In our example, the application only uses the naming service when it initially starts, and never interacts with the naming service again (barring abnormal server termination and client recovery). Connections used only at process startup are the most common type of infrequently used connection, but not the only type; a component may make invocations on a server regularly but infrequently during its lifetime. Notice that *implicit connections* are also often *infrequently used* connections.

The final type of connection is *frequently used*. These are the connections to our normal application servers, which we use often during our client's lifetime. The connection to the Portfolio Manager is a frequently used connection.

The ORB makes no distinction between these three types of connections, even though they are used differently by the application. Specifically, the connection to the Portfolio Manager server is used extensively. Each invocation made on a business object is sent along this connection, as is the corresponding reply. Clearly, this connection is an important one, and is essential to our client. However, the connections to the Orbix daemon and the name server are not used at all, once the client has established its connection to the Portfolio Manager.

However, some ORBs will, by default, keep all of these connections open for the remainder of this client application's lifetime. This leads to some potential problems when we have large numbers of clients using a system.

Scalability Problems

If we have a large number of client applications concurrently using any CORBA system, then we must consider the potential problems, from a number of perspectives. Picture our Portfolio Manager running in a single server process, which must service 2000 workstations running the client application. If we simply configure all our clients to use this one process, then we must answer a number of questions:

- Will this single host have enough processing power to support all these clients? If our clients are frequently sending requests, the server will be unlikely to be able to service these requests acceptably fast.
- Our Portfolio Manager server (and its underlying host) is a single point of failure. How will our system handle a software or hardware fault?
- Our Portfolio Manager server process is limited to approximately 1000 connections. How will the remaining clients be able to connect to this process?

These first two points are discussed in depth later, in Chapter 15, "Load Balancing," and Chapter 16, "Fault Tolerance." Here, we focus on scalability from a connection management perspective. Ignoring for the moment the performance and reliability implications of such an approach, our single server process will simply be incapable of simultaneously communicating with all 2000 clients, over direct TCP/IP connections. As we mentioned previously, each server process is limited to approximately 1000 open connections at any one moment.

In fact, our Portfolio Manager application server is not the only limit—each client will also have a connection to the naming service, as well as possibly having one to the activation component. Clearly, if we are going to somehow support all 2000 clients, some alternative approaches will be necessary.

Approaches to Scalability

Generally, having a large number of clients directly connected to a single server process is not a good idea, and in some instances is simply not possible. Here, we discuss some concrete alternatives and actions that we can perform to avoid these problems. First, we discuss server replication, which is the preferred, general-purpose solution. Next, we discuss connection closure, which can be useful in large systems, even if our application servers are replicated. Finally, we discuss concentrators, a mechanism that allows us to have an arbitrary number of clients connected to a single server process.

Replicating Servers

The most obvious approach to scalability is to simply have multiple server processes running. By distributing our client connections across the server processes, we avoid the connection limitations.[2] From a performance perspective, these servers processes can be run on different hosts, allowing us deliver the required throughput from a group of relatively inexpensive machines, rather than from one very expensive machine. From a fault tolerance perspective, it also makes sense to service these clients on multiple hosts, in order to eliminate any single point of failure.

Keep in mind that server replication can be easy or difficult to implement, depending on whether we need to maintain server state across multiple server processes. These issues are explored in detail in the chapters on load balancing and fault tolerance, so we'll defer discussion of them until that time. In general, however, multiple server processes will permit us to scale up to any number of clients, and is the preferred solution to this problem. It eliminates the connection limitations faced at an application level, and again provides us with a system that runs more smoothly and is more resilient.

Closing Connections

Replicating application server processes eliminates some of the connection management limitations introduced earlier. However, there are still some instances where we do need to worry about exceeding a per-process connection limit, even with replicated server processes. In our StockWatch application each client has a connection not only to the Portfolio Manager server, but also to the naming service, and possibly to an activation component.

Even if our application servers are distributed across multiple hosts, all the clients will still have a connection to an instance of the naming service. If all the clients use the same name server, then we will once again run into a connection limitation problem. This is illustrated in Figure 14.4.

In particular, Figure 14.4 illustrates that, from a connection management perspective, the naming service is no different from any other CORBA server. In the case of a shared service such as this, we must be especially careful that all our clients can be serviced as needed, especially since we are often restricted from replicating these services. Fortunately, connections to these shared services tend to be infrequently used, which means that they can be safely closed once a client has finished using the service. Ideally, the naming service would close the connections to its idle clients. If this is not supported, then we must rely on the clients to close the connection.

Next, we discuss how the CORBA specification addresses connection closure, and then examine approaches to closing connections in our client and in our servers.

Connection Closure and the CORBA Specification

The CORBA specification states that connections can be legally closed by either the client or the server. A client can simply close a connection whenever it chooses. Typically, the client will only

---

[2] We avoid the connection limits for our server processes. However, with some ORBs, clients will open a connection to the activation component, before establishing a connection to the server. In this case, the activation component will encounter the connection limit. In order to scale, either the servers will have to be distributed across hosts, or the connection between the client and the activation component will have to be closed.

Figure 14.4   Naming Serving Connection Limitations

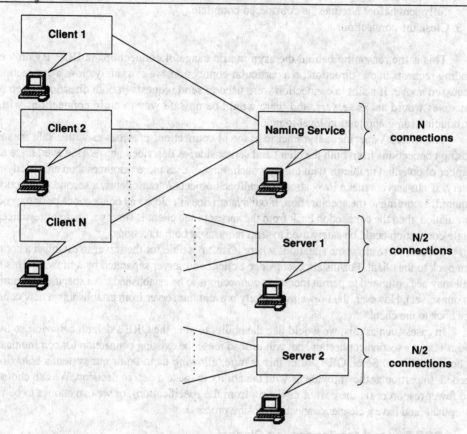

do so when it has no requests pending with the server, because doing so will naturally prevent the client from ever receiving the corresponding reply. Servers, however, cannot simply close a connection; the specification states that they must first send a GIOP CloseConnection message to the client. This message indicates to the client that the server is about to close this connection, and that the client should not send any further requests on it.

Servers behave in this manner due to a potential race condition. If servers simply closed connections at will, they could close a connection immediately after a client has sent a request. The client would have no indication of whether or not the request had been received and processed by the server. By following the rules outlined in the specification, the client can reliably determine whether or not its requests were received. In particular, a server is not permitted to close a connection if it has received any requests for which the corresponding reply has not been sent. A server can therefore only legally close its connections by performing the following steps, in this order:

1. Send a GIOP CloseConnection message (after this, the client will send no further requests on this connection).

2. Finish processing all client requests received on that connection. Replies must be successfully sent before a request is considered complete.
3. Close the connection.

This is the reasoning behind the asymmetric usage of connections in IIOP. By only ever sending requests in one direction on a particular connection, we can safely close a connection as discussed above. If a single connection were used to send requests in both directions, then both processes would act as servers, and there would be no safe way to close connections without introducing some application-level logic.

The CORBA-specified, asymmetric usage of connections provides us with a safe means of closing connections from both the client and server side, as described above. However, there are a number of potential problems with this approach. First, it uses more resources than are strictly necessary. If our servers make invocations on callback objects in our clients, a second connection is required, according to the specification. If our system doesn't close any connections prior to process termination, then the connection back from the server to the client is simply a waste of resources. A single connection could be safely used to send requests in both directions.

Second, there are some situations where it isn't possible for the server to establish a connection back to the client. For instance, consider a client and server separated by a firewall. This firewall may be configured to permit incoming connections to be established, on a specific port number (to our server). However, the firewall will likely prevent our server from establishing a new connection back to the client.

In cases such as this, we would like the ability to alter the ORB's default behavior, so that it doesn't open a second connection, but will instead reuse the existing connection for communication in both directions. Some ORBs offer this feature, allowing us to tailor our system's behavior as needed. In particular they provide us with the ability to make a design decision. We can choose to use fewer resources (at the cost of deviating from the specification), or we can choose to be fully compliant (and have a cleaner connection closure process).

ORB Support for Connection Closure

Currently, commercially available ORBs offer different levels of support for closing connections. Some ORBs provide hooks that permit applications to explicitly close connections at will, or to specify timeouts on unused connections. Other ORBs provide default policies, so that after a configurable number of connections is reached, the least-recently-used connection will be closed. In addition, many ORBS will transparently reopen connections that have been gracefully closed. Proxies will re-establish a connection to their associated server, and only throw an exception if the server terminated and cannot be found.

Closing Connections in Clients

As discussed, it often makes sense for our clients to close their infrequently used connections. The CORBA specification permits our clients to close these connections at any time, so we can do this in a place that is sensible for our particular application. In the Portfolio Manager example discussed above, we can close the connection to the naming service once we have used it to obtain the PortfolioManager object. For other infrequently used servers, we can close their connections whenever our application has finished using them, or at least finished using them for a relatively long period of time.

If our ORB supports explicit connection closure, then implementing this in clients is very straightforward. Our client application can simply instruct the ORB to close the connection associated with a specific proxy. (Keep in mind that multiple proxies in our client may be sharing a single connection to a server).

If our ORB does not support this, then we'll need to determine a way to configure the ORB so that it will close connections for us, as needed. For instance, if our ORB supports a configurable maximum number of connections, we could tell the ORB to only permit as many connections as we have to frequently used servers. This will automatically close connections to the infrequently-used servers (assuming a least-recently-used closure policy).

Closing Connections in Servers

In some instances, we may be able to safely close connections to clients within our server application. If this server is shared by a large number of clients, and is infrequently used by these clients, then these connections are good candidates for closure. Ideally, the clients would be responsible for closing these connections, but in some cases the server cannot rely on this being the case. For example, we may be developing a server that will be used by client applications developed by our customers. In this case, we can recommend that the clients close their connections to our server, but cannot rely on them doing so.

We can easily imagine different ways in which our server can manage its connections. It could keep track of the number (and usage) of connections, and when a predefined threshold is reached, it could close the least-recently-used connections. (Easily implemented by associating a timestamp with each connection, and updating the timestamp each time a request is received over the connection.) Or, we, as application designers, can specify a series of invocations on objects in this server as a logical unit of work. We would define this sequence of operations such that once a client has completed them, it is unlikely to use the server again for a long period of time. (For instance, if we were implementing a naming service, then a logical unit of work would be ended when a client resolves an object.) After each client has completed this logical unit of work, the server would close the connection to the client.

Keep in mind that server-side connection closure makes sense only for infrequently used connections. If we have many clients (more than our server can connect to at once) which all frequently use a service, then closing connections within the server is not a good idea. The server will end up closing connections that are actively used by clients, which will then waste considerable time re-opening connections to the server. In this case, alternatives such as replicating our server processes (discussed previously), or applying concentrators (discussed next) should be considered.

Implications of Closing Connections

If we choose to close connections to our application servers, then we must consider how this will impact our system. Recall the section on memory management where we discussed how client connection closure can be used as a catalyst for cleaning up server-side resources. Our server assumed that if a connection to a client closed, the client process had terminated and it was safe for the server to delete any resources that it had allocated on behalf of the client. If we are actively closing connections to our servers, then this assumption is wrong. Active closure of connections is incompatible with using connection closure to launch cleanup of resources. Our server will have to utilize some other approach to cleaning up client resources.

Another possibility is that clients will detect a connection closure, and react by assuming that the server process has terminated. If servers send a GIOP CloseConnection message before closing a connection, then clients will be able to distinguish between a temporary connection closure (to preserve resources) and a server process termination.

Figure 14.5 Concentrator

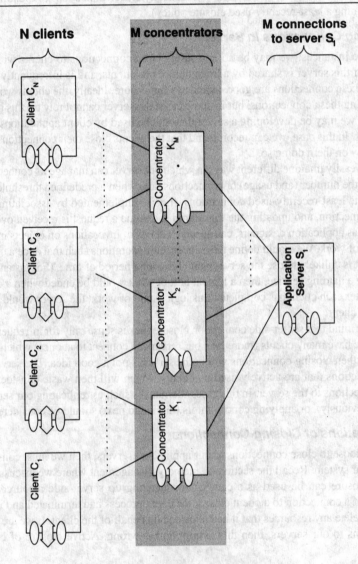

Concentrators

Using concentrators to avoid connection limits is quite interesting. At first, it seems to provide us with a solution to just this problem, but can also be a foundation for addressing fault tolerance and load balancing as well. The approach is explored in detail in Chapter 15, "Load Balancing," and will only be briefly introduced here.

The basic approach to a concentrator is quite simple, and is commonly used in transaction processing monitors, to permit them to scale. A *concentrator* (also known as a *funnel*) is a server process that sits between our clients and servers, as shown in Figure 14.5.

Our clients no longer have a direct connection to the server process. Instead, each client is connected to one of the concentrator processes. By inserting concentrators between our clients and servers, we can now service any number of clients with a single server process. If we add more clients, then we can just add more concentrator processes to service them. This permits a single server process to handle as many clients as necessary.

So, how do concentrators work? For every object that a client uses, the concentrator must, from the client's perspective, implement that object. Logically, the concentrator simply delegates the call to the *real* implementation of the business object, which is contained in our application server.

Figure 14.6 shows a logical view of a concentrator. How it may actually be implemented is discussed in Chapter 15, "Load Balancing."

Summary

In this section, we discussed connection management and scalability. The tools and techniques that we've introduced for improving the scalability of CORBA systems are quite useful, as long as they are applied in the proper manner. It's important to consider these problems in a holistic fashion, since often we are not just trying to overcome the per-process connection limit, but rather to build a robust large-scale system. In these cases, we must consider other goals, such as balancing the system load across multiple hosts, and surviving failure of a single process or host.

Figure 14.6 Logical view of a concentrator

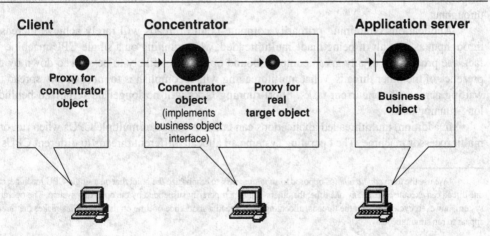

Specifically, by using concentrators, a single server process can scale up and service any number of clients concurrently. This is an important technical accomplishment, and can be utilized in our systems to great benefit. However, it is important to apply it only when it's sensible to do so. In particular, the performance impact can limit wide applicability of the concentrator pattern.

Thread Management

Adding multithreading to CORBA programs can be quite beneficial, depending on how the threads are used. Multithreaded clients can make multiple concurrent requests to servers, and multithreaded servers can service numerous client requests concurrently. In addition, multithreaded CORBA programs can avoid deadlock and better utilize multiprocessor hardware. All of this can help make our system more responsive, and have higher throughput, albeit at the price of increased complexity.

Multithreading—an Overview

Multithreading is a complex topic, and writing multithreaded programs is a challenging task. Our focus here is on effectively applying multithreading to our CORBA applications. We do not attempt to provide a rigorous introduction to threading. Instead, we have just a brief discussion of some terms and issues surrounding multithreaded application. Then, we examine in detail how multiple threads can be used in CORBA applications.

A thread is a lightweight path of execution within a given process. At any time, there can be many threads operating concurrently within any process.[3] By utilizing multiple threads, an application can improve its throughput, although the amount of gain is highly dependent on the type of work performed by a thread. If an application thread is working on purely in-memory variables (such performing some large and complex mathematical calculation), then it is said to be *compute-bound*. A thread which is primarily performing some sort of I/O, such as writing to a disk, or waiting for input from a network connection is said to be *I/O-bound*.

Applications containing primarily I/O-bound threads benefit the most from being made multithreaded. The operating system recognizes when a thread is waiting for an I/O call to complete, and switches to another thread that can perform useful work. When the I/O operation completes, the suspended thread is awakened and continues processing. This will increase the application's throughput.

Applications containing primarily compute-bound threads will rarely achieve increased throughput as a result of being made multithreaded, when running on a single-CPU machine. In fact, the processing of any given compute-bound operation is likely to be slowed down by the presence of the other threads. What multithreading will accomplish is to more evenly spread the waiting across all concurrent tasks. Short-running tasks will no longer be serialized behind a long-running task.

In addition, multithreaded applications can take advantage of multiple CPUs when run on a multiprocessor machine. The operating system can allocate different threads to different CPUs to

---

[3] We use the term *concurrent* (as opposed to *simultaneous*), to emphasize the point that on a single-CPU machine, only one thread can execute code at any one time; the others will be temporarily suspended by the operating system. The operating system, however, cycles through the threads, allocating each thread a short slice of time on the CPU. This makes the threads appear to run simultaneously.

achieve true parallelism. In such cases, even compute-bound programs can benefit from multi-threading.

Such benefits are particularly useful for our CORBA servers. A single-threaded server can, by definition, service only one client request at a time. Any subsequent requests received will be blocked, and will not be processed until the initial request has been completely serviced, and the reply sent to the caller. A multithreaded server can concurrently process more than one client request. If these threads perform blocking calls (such as database or disk access) the multithreaded server as a whole will be able to handle more requests in a given time period. We discuss multi-threading in CORBA clients and servers below, after a quick sidelight on some of the issues that must be addressed when developing multithreaded programs.

Complexities of Multithreaded Programming

The benefits of multithreading exact a price. Multithreaded applications are inherently more complex than single-threaded applications, and are considerably more difficult to develop and debug. Every data structure that can be concurrently accessed by multiple threads must be protected from this, through careful application of operating system primitives such as mutexes. If multiple threads do concurrently access unprotected shared data, then inconsistent results or process termination can easily occur.

Writing correct multithreaded programs is difficult, as is debugging them. Multithreaded programs can suffer from *race conditions*, which are situations that only occur when threads are scheduled by the operating system in a specific order, with detrimental effects. For example, if two threads concurrently update the same data structure, then part of one thread's changes could be mixed with part of another thread's changes, leaving our structure in an inconsistent state. The effects of this can range from catastrophic process termination (which is bad), to subtle errors in the results that the server produces (which is arguably worse, since the system appears to be operating normally).

Sometimes third-party libraries or internally developed applications or tools are not thread safe. This means that they cannot safely be accessed concurrently from multiple threads, and often limit the benefits of multithreading. All access to these resources will have to be serialized across threads.

Be careful when writing multithreaded code. It is difficult and complex to develop, and even more so to debug. Make sure that someone on the development team has had solid experience writing multithreaded code. Carefully consider whether multithreading is worth the effort, making sure to evaluate alternatives such as replicated server processes.

Multithreaded CORBA Clients

Multithreaded CORBA clients allows us to make remote invocations in one thread while using another thread for other application tasks. For instance, one thread can remain active to service a GUI while another concurrently executes a remote invocation. From an end user's perspective, this would improve the responsiveness of the application. Or, our application could make concurrent invocations on multiple CORBA objects. This would allow us to retrieve a set of results more quickly than if these calls were serialized.

Multithreaded CORBA Servers

CORBA servers can benefit from being made multithreaded. Multithreaded CORBA servers can exhibit improved throughput and avoid deadlock between CORBA processes. Servers are typically connected to multiple clients, and process requests as they're received. Since clients can submit requests at any time, our server can have multiple requests outstanding at any given moment.

If our server is single-threaded, these requests can only be processed serially, with predictable effects on the server's throughput. If instead we make our server multithreaded, our server can process multiple requests concurrently. As we mentioned previously, by letting the operating system take advantage of the times when a thread is blocked (for instance on an I/O operation), our server can perform more work in a given period of time. In addition, if our server is running on a multiprocessor machine, then our application threads may be run simultaneously on different CPUs for further performance benefit. Keep in mind, of course, that our server application will have to be made thread-safe, so that concurrent threads cannot interfere with one another by accessing unprotected shared memory.

Figure 14.7 Deadlock

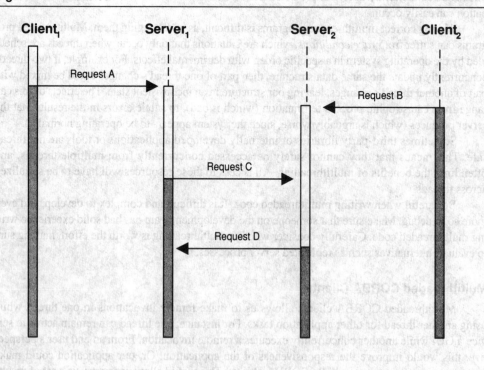

blocked

Multithreaded CORBA servers can also avoid deadlock in some circumstances. A CORBA server with a single application thread can only service one request at a time. While processing a request, any new requests received will be queued until the current request is completely serviced. If two single-threaded servers are both processing a client request, and the implementation of each of the requests requires an invocation on the other server, then both will deadlock. This is illustrated in Figure 14.7.

If our servers are multithreaded, however, then they will be able to handle this situation without any problems. When the request is received from the other server, it will be handled in a different thread from the original request. Everything will be processed, without deadlock.[4]

Next we discuss how to best take advantage of the multiple threads available to perform application work. We will not spend any time here discussing the mechanics of creating multiple threads in any operating system, or with any specific ORB, but will instead focus on general threading policies than can be implemented in a CORBA server. For a discussion of thread allocation during the lifecycle of a CORBA remote invocation, see Chapter 2, "CORBA Revisited."

Thread Policies

A key decision when writing multithreaded servers is the selection of a *thread policy*. A thread policy determines how many threads the server creates, when they are created, and how incoming client requests are delivered to particular threads. Each of the thread policies that we discuss has its own set of strengths and weaknesses, and is best applied in different situations. After we introduce the different policies, we discuss factors to be considered when selecting a policy.

Thread-per-Request.   The simplest threading policy is *thread-per-request*. Each time a new request is received from a client, a new application thread is spawned to handle this request. This thread completely processes this client request—the invocation on the servant object is made by this thread, and the results are sent back to the caller by this thread. After this, the thread exits. This is shown in Figure 14.8. This approach is very simple to implement (since there isn't any additional thread or queue management required) and provides the maximum concurrency (since each request has its own thread). Potential disadvantages of this approach include the overhead of creating and destroying a thread, and the lack of an upper bound on the number of threads that can exist at any one time.

Creating and destroying a thread takes time, of course. How long it takes is dependent on the operating system and thread package used, but it is typically small. Whether or not it's worth creating and destroying a thread to service a single request is dependent, of course, on the amount of time it takes to perform the requested operation. If, for instance, the client is retrieving a single attribute from an object, which is stored in a servant object data member, then the cost of thread creation and destruction will likely outweigh the cost of performing the work. If all our requests are this simple, then the thread-per-request policy would not make much sense, and we'd be better off using one of the alternatives outlined below. If, on the other hand, servicing the request involves complex work or I/O (such as database access and application of business rules), then the thread creation and

---

[4] Actually, recursive interprocess calls can cause deadlock in multithreaded servers, if the recursion is nested to enough depth to exhaust the available supply of threads (with a pool of threads), or to use up enough resources that the operating system is unable to create any more threads.

Figure 14.8   Thread-per-request

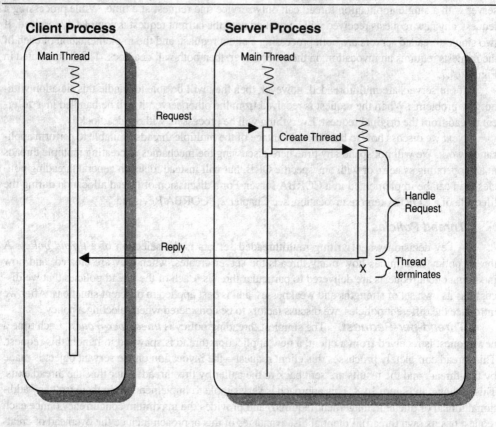

destination will be a small fraction of the total work performed by the thread. In this case, the thread-per-request policy can make sense. However, thread-per-request also suffers from another disadvantage, which is that there is no application limit on the number of threads that can be running at any one time.[5]

Consider a server, applying the thread-per-request policy, which in a flurry of activity receives N requests from clients, in a short period of time. The server will create N threads, and hand off a request to each thread. If N is very large, then our server process could end up spending more time switching between thread contexts than it does actually performing useful work. This condition is known as *thrashing*, and should be avoided. Thus, the thread-per-request policy is useful when the typical request requires some significant amount of server-side processing (to better mask the over-

---

[5] Operating systems will limit the number of threads that a process can create. This may be limited by the size of a data structure, a configuration parameter, or by sheer resource exhaustion. In any case, applications dynamically creating threads must check for failure, and gracefully handle it. CORBA servers can either reject the request (throwing an exception to the client) or process the request in the main application thread.

head of creating and destroying a thread), and when there are a relatively small number of clients (so that a large number of requests arriving concurrently is unlikely). Alternatively, our server can service a large number of clients, if they interact with the server infrequently.

The rest of the thread policies are slightly more complex, since they involve creating threads which are then suspended, waiting for incoming requests to be handed to them by the application. Typically, this is implemented by one or more queues. These queues store the incoming requests until they are picked up by an available thread. (For comparison, the thread-per-request policy never queues any requests; each is handed off to a newly created thread as soon as it is received). An excellent introduction to this approach with source code for an Orbix-based implementation is available from the IONA Technologies website, currently www.iona.com/support/cookbook/threading/eventqueue.html.

The remaining thread policies are distinguished by the number of threads they create, and by how requests are delivered to threads.

Thread Pool. One common and effective threading policy is a *thread pool*. The application prestarts a pool of threads, and incoming requests are delivered to waiting threads via a queue. If there are more requests pending than available threads, requests remain in the queue until a thread becomes available to service them. This approach is similar to thread-per-request, but it provides the safety of a fixed maximum number of threads—the overhead of dynamic thread creation and destruction is avoided.

This approach clearly has a number of advantages over the thread-per-request policy. Threads are only created at server startup, so even if the work performed by a request is quite simple, it can still be serviced efficiently (unlike with thread-per-request). Also, a fixed pool of threads can smoothly handle a large number of requests that arrive at once. The thread pool policy is shown in Figure 14.9.

Thread pools can be extended with some additional features, if necessary. For instance, rather than a simple fixed pool, we could use a flexible thread pool. This adjusts the number of threads in the pool based on the current queue size, and fluctuates between configured minimum and maximum sizes. This provides some of the flexibility of the thread-per-request policy, but with a ceiling on the number of threads.

Thread per Client (Thread per Connection). Another policy involves having one thread (and one event queue) dedicated to each client process connected to the server. (Typically, each client has only one connection to a server, so in that case this policy is the same as thread-per-connection. Some ORBS, however, do permit a client to have multiple connections to a server, which provides a subtle difference between the two policies.) Since each client has its own thread, all of a client's requests will be handled by that one thread. If a multithreaded client submits multiple, concurrent requests (or if a single-threaded client makes multiple oneway invocations in rapid succession), then the additional requests will be queued up while the thread processes the requests serially. Such a policy is illustrated in Figure 14.10.

This approach is useful if the server maintains some per-client state or resource that requires serialized access (for instance, a per-client audit log). When this approach is used by single-threaded clients making synchronous invocations, each request is handled immediately by its dedicated thread. This is a similar benefit to thread-per-request, but without the overhead of creating a thread each time. This policy also prevents one client from hogging the server. Even if a multithreaded

Figure 14.9 Thread pool

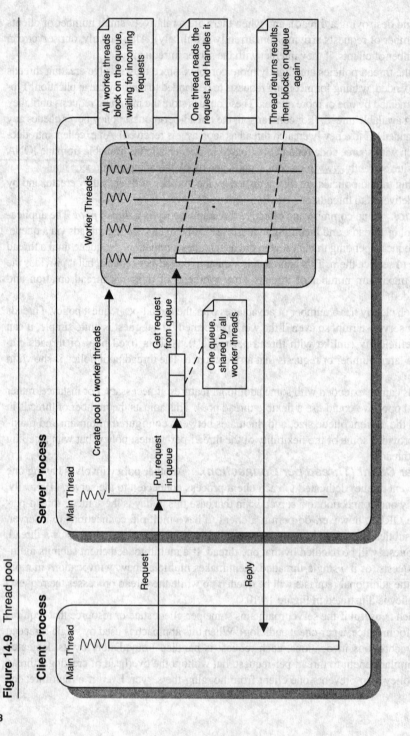

Client Process

Main Thread

Request

Reply

Server Process

Main Thread

Create pool of worker threads

Put request in queue

Get request from queue

One queue, shared by all worker threads

Worker Threads

All worker threads block on the queue, waiting for incoming requests

One thread reads the request, and handles it

Thread returns results, then blocks on queue again

Figure 14.10 Thread-per-client

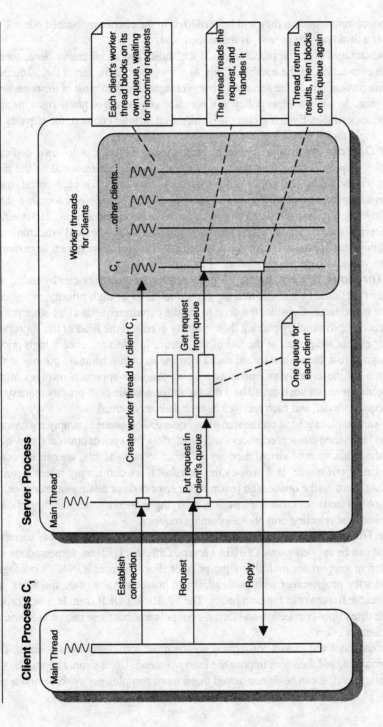

Client Process C_1

Main Thread

Server Process

Main Thread

Establish connection

Request

Reply

Create worker thread for client C_1

Put request in client's queue

Get request from queue

One queue for each client

Worker threads for Clients

C_1

....other clients....

Each client's worker thread blocks on its own queue, waiting for incoming requests

The thread reads the request, and handles it

Thread returns results, then blocks on its queue again

249

client sends many concurrent requests, they will be serialized in the client's associated queue (This may be considered as a disadvantage as well, as mentioned next).

Potential disadvantages of this approach include scalability and serialization. Since there is one thread per client connection, as the number of clients grows so does the server thread count. If our clients are making invocations on the server relatively infrequently, then most of the threads will be idle most of the time. In addition, this policy will serialize concurrent requests from the same client, which may be undesirable. Even if a client is invoking on different objects, the requests will be serialized by the single thread for each client.

Thread-per-Object.   With this approach, each servant object has its own dedicated thread. Each incoming request is placed on the target object's queue, and removed by the target object's thread when it is available. This policy is illustrated in Figure 14.11. This approach is useful if our server contains a relatively small number of servant objects, and these objects contain a shared resource that must have their access serialized (for instance, a database connection). However, the same goal can be accomplished by simply protecting these resources with standard synchronization mechanisms. In addition, this approach is also not very scalable, because if we have a large number of servant objects, we will also have a large number of threads.

Additional Thread Policy Features.   We can extend our thread policies by adding support for some further functionality, such as treating certain requests as high-priority, or rejecting requests if our queue is too large. Consider the need to handle certain requests at a higher priority than others. We can accomplish this by placing these priority events at the head of the appropriate queue, while regular events are placed at the tail of the queue. In addition, once a high-priority request has been assigned to a thread, that thread could increase its own scheduling priority, if such a feature is supported by the underlying operating system. Another approach involves mixing threading models; normal requests are handled by a pool of threads, while high-priority requests utilize the thread-per-request model, and each receives its own dedicated thread.

We may also want to place a limit on the size of our queue. The queue is simply a data structure, and if it gets too large, then our server process will bloat, slow the system down and may eventually crash due to the exhaustion of virtual memory. In order to prevent this, we can impose an upper limit on the size of our queue. If it crosses this threshold, we can simply reject incoming requests by not placing them on the queue, and returning an error code or raising an exception. We can be even more sophisticated about this, for instance, by trying to identify the offending client or operation being invoked, and rejecting only those incoming requests.

Selecting a Thread Policy.   The policies outlined above demonstrate the variety of threading models that can be applied to our CORBA servers. Different ORB implementations will, of course, offer different support for multithreading policies. For instance, IONA Technologies' Orbix product provides the programmer with the flexibility to implement any of the threading policies discussed, and sample frameworks for each policy. The VisiBroker ORB from Inprise Corporation supports only the thread-per-connection and thread-pool policies, but these can be used without any additional programmer effort.

In practice, thread-pool and thread-per-request are the most commonly used policies. They are the simplest approaches, and therefore impose the least overhead. Use a simple approach (such as the thread pool policy) until it can be demonstrated that a more complex policy will provide concrete benefits.

Figure 14.11 Thread-per-object

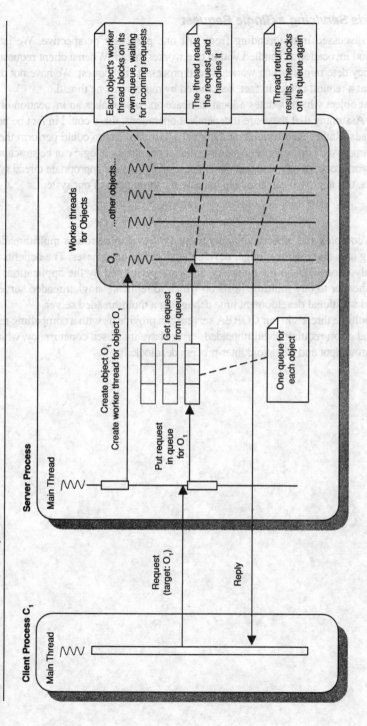

Client Process C₁

Main Thread /\/\/\

Request (target: O₁)

Reply

Server Process

Main Thread /\/\/\

Create object O₁
Create worker thread for object O₁

Put request in queue for O₁

Get request from queue

One queue for each object

Worker threads for Objects

O₁ /\/\/\

...other objects...

Each object's worker thread blocks on its own queue, waiting for incoming requests

The thread reads the request, and handles it

Thread returns results, then blocks on its queue again

Multiple Threads Servicing a Single Request

So far, we have discussed multithreading from just one particular perspective. We have assumed that each method invocation is handled within one worker thread. When a client request is received, our thread policy determines which worker thread processes the request. We have not discussed the possibility that a request could, in fact, be handled by more than one thread.

Consider a servant object which updates a local database and also makes an invocation on a remote CORBA object. Assuming that these are independent operations, these could in fact be performed in different threads. Rather than serializing these calls, our application could perform them concurrently and obtain improved performance. Assuming that our application logic can be structured to perform some of the work concurrently, and that our application utilizes the appropriate thread synchronization mechanisms, this approach can also help improve the throughput of our system.

Summary

Multithreading is complex and difficult to apply properly. Developing robust multithreaded software is a challenging task that requires longer development and testing phases. The benefits of multithreading are highly dependent on the nature of the work performed by the application. In many cases, it will be cheaper to buy multiple hosts on which to replicate singlethreaded servers than it would be to spend additional development time debugging a multithreaded server.

However, using multiple threads in our CORBA servers can provide us with a compelling reason to exert the additional effort required. Multithreaded servers have increased concurrency, which can provide increased throughput and can avoid inter-process deadlock.

Load Balancing

$\mathbf{L}$oad balancing is a complex problem to describe, and is even more difficult to solve. The problem domain is not well contained, for it is inextricably linked with its close counterpart, fault tolerance, as well as issues such as caching and replication. Balancing a system's load requires careful selection from an array of tools and techniques, for there is no single silver bullet that can be applied to all application systems to make them more scalable or provide them with better performance.

In the CORBA world, load balancing refers mainly to the distribution of client requests over a group of servant objects that typically live in different server processes and run on different hosts. Load balancing will not apply to every scenario. Applications that have a very high ratio of clients to servers, or servers whose methods take an uncharacteristically long time to complete will be more likely to benefit from a load-balanced solution.

In this section we identify a number of problems and factors that affect scalability and present a range of strategies that can be used to design load-balanced CORBA applications.

The Need for Load Balancing

Some of the more compelling motivations for load balanced applications are based on management and end user expectations of system performance, reliability, and availability. In essence, applications that perform core business functions are expected to have good performance even across a WAN, are expected to work in a thoroughly predictable manner, and are expected to be available on a $52 \times 7 \times 24$ basis. To satisfy the runtime expectations of each end user, the system developer needs to understand these requirements when designing the application. If this information is not available or not used until after most of the implementation work is complete, the finished application will almost certainly fail to meet the requirements. In order to develop a successful system, application designers need to initially consider ways to:

• **Improve scalability.** Distribute the application load over many executables and many hosts, using a combination of replication and partitioning.

- **Overcome resource limits.** Modify design to account for processor, memory, TCP connection, and thread limits. To conserve processing resources, ensure they are either freed or reused regularly.
- **Limit the damage caused by a failure.** Employ distribution, component partitioning, and component replication to limit the damage that would be caused by a failure in a single server.

However, there is a cost associated with implementing each of these objectives, as described in more detail later in the section on "Measuring the Cost of Load Balancing."

Aspects of Load Balancing

Factors that might influence a decision to load balance an application are:

- **Workload.** Does the server workload vary? That is, do servers receive a varying number of requests at different times of the year, month, or day? Alternatively, does the type of request vary according to some pattern? For example, an update-intensive period may typically follow a query-intensive period in a workflow driven application.
- **Access pattern.** Does the number of clients vary at different times of the day? Are there clearly defined peaks and periods of relative inactivity?

Figure 15.1 Factors that affect load balancing

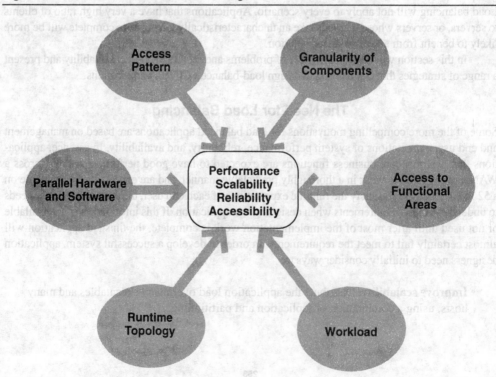

- **Access to functional areas.** Can the application logic be partitioned according to its usage patterns? For example, is it possible to separate client requests that are query (read-only) from those that update data and require transaction support?
- **Granularity of components.** Is the application logic large grained (monolithic) or fine grained (supporting well-encapsulated components)? If it does support fine-grained components, how much interaction is there between these components? For instance, is the interaction between them "chatty," "very occasional," or none at all? In the case of fine-grained application components, do these components support parallelism? That is, can a multi-threaded server handle a client request in parallel threads?
- **Runtime topology.** What is the geographical concentration of access to the application? For example, is the application to be accessed from locations around the globe or around a central office? In the former case, does the international network meet requirements for speed, reliability, and bandwidth? What is the topology of the deployed application?
- **Parallel hardware and software.** To what degree does the hardware and software support parallelism and concurrency? For example, some database systems have extensive support for parallel queries and replicated servers. Likewise, operating systems generally support multithreading and multiprocessor machines.

Application Partitioning

Application partitioning splits an application into a number of independent service components that provide a specific subset of the overall applications functionality. The sum functionality of all the partitions will equal that of the entire application. Application functionality may be allocated to a partition either horizontally or vertically. A horizontal approach splits a system functionally. Each server only provides a subset of the system's functionality. A vertical approach splits a system it based on data. Each server provides the full functionality of the system, but only has access to a subset of the data. We explore these approaches next.

Horizontal Application Partitioning

In horizontal partitioning, objects are assigned to one and only one dedicated partition (server) and should not be implemented in more than one partition. That is, the particular service should only be available from one server. Horizontal partitioning is often referred to as "service" or "interface" partitioning, as the separate servers normally provide the implementation of a disjoint subset of the application's interfaces. The overall application load should be evenly distributed across all the partitioned servers. An example is shown in Figure 15.2.

The client is responsible for locating the correct server to service the request. In most cases, a partition key, usually implemented as a well-known name, is used to identify the service. For example, we may use the key words "query" and "transaction" to identify the type of service we wish to use. The naming service would resolve the name "query" to an object in the query server and the name "transaction" to an object in the transactional server. In this context, a transactional server is one which services update as well as read-only requests. Alternatively, in a banking example, where each branch has its own dedicated server, the branch code maybe used as a partition key to locate the correct server. Although the CORBA naming service is ideally suited to the task of resolving a

Figure 15.2   Load balancing strategies—horizontal partitioning

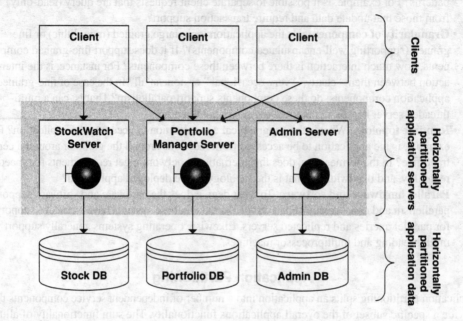

well-known name to an object reference, it is not a prerequisite for using partitioned servers—other, ORB-specific mechanisms can be used.

Vertical Application Partitioning

In contrast to horizontal partitioning, vertical partitioning partitions the data instead of the services; that is, one server will provide all the services for one particular group of objects while another will provide exactly the same set of services for another group. This type of partitioning is easily applied to database systems.

For example, one database may provide information for stocks starting with letters A through M while another services stocks starting with letters N through Z. Such an approach is illustrated in Figure 15.3. In this case, the client would normally provide a piece of key information, such as a stock symbol, to act as the discriminator. In a multi-tier CORBA application, it is important to minimize the so called "cross-partition" queries, as this might result in many conversations between various CORBA servers. In Chapter 7 we discuss the channel federation model, where separate event channels are created for each of the stocks a client might be interested in. We extend this example here to include the vertical partitioning pattern—in effect, each component exposes a StockWatch service, along with N event channels, each representing a service for a particular Stock object.

Figure 15.3 Load balancing strategies—vertical partitioning

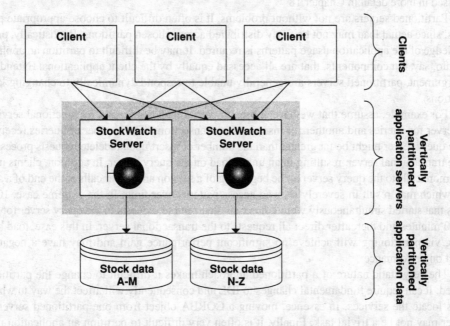

Partitioning Strategies

In the partitioned approach, the client can connect to the correct server using a well-known name (often resolved through the CORBA naming service) as a key. Once the partition key has been resolved to the object in the sever, all further remote invocations are made directly to that server; neither the CORBA activation agent nor the naming service are directly involved in further requests. Since entries in the naming service are usually sufficient as a means of locating services, the amount of context-switching between various servers is reduced. With either horizontal or vertical partitioning, the chance of an object (instance) being cached in more than one server is greatly reduced. With vertical partitioning, this is indeed a clear design objective. This reduces the need for complex cache-synchronization policies to ensure that objects cached in more than one server express the same state at any given point in time.

Many applications will require only a single instance of each of the partitioned servers to be present to service client requests; for example, we need a single StockWatch server to furnish requests for stocks starting with the letters A through M and another single StockWatch server for requests for stocks starting with letters N through Z. This model simplifies the object location process—in most cases, entries in the naming service will be sufficient. However, this pattern does not preclude using multiple instances of each to offset increasing load.

Horizontally partitioned servers support a more component-oriented approach; they can be built by different development teams in relative isolation, using different implementation languages to run on different operating systems. Specialist knowledge within the development community can be assigned to clearly defined problem boundaries. The notion of component-based development is discussed in more detail in Chapter 18.

Partitioned servers are not without problems. It is often difficult to choose appropriate partitions, since actual load may not be fairly distributed across chosen partitions. Realistically, prior knowledge of the application usage patterns is required. It may be difficult to partition an application into, say, ten components, that are all accessed equally by the client applications. Extending this argument, partitioned servers are generally unable to respond dynamically to changing load conditions.

For example, assume that we have chosen to partition an application by functional service: one server for queries and another for insert/update transactions. The number of queries received by the query server might be far greater than the number of insert/update/delete requests processed by the transactional server, resulting in an unfair load on the query server. In addition, clients may make more calls to the query server at the beginning of a session and fewer calls at the end of a session, which may result in severely skewed access patterns over time. In the extreme case, 1000 clients that started simultaneously would direct all their remote requests to the query server for the first 10 minutes and thereafter direct all requests to the transactional server. In this case, load balancing via partitioning will achieve no significant performance gain and may have a negative impact on performance.

The very static nature of a partitioned approach makes it difficult to change the partitions selected: It can require fundamental changes to IDL and consequently will affect the way in which clients locate the services. In essence, moving a CORBA object from one partitioned server to another may not be a trivial task. Finally, it is often very difficult to partition an application into many components that are completely independent from one another. Almost invariably, an object in one server will have to make requests on an object in another server. In the extreme case, the overall performance of the application may actually be poorer with this type of load balancing than without, because of *chatty* servers. In this context, "chattiness" refers to a group of servers that have a significant number of inter-process calls as part of their normal processing. Even if the partitioned servers were physically located on the same machine, a remote call (using IIOP) would be required for objects within these servers to communicate with one another.

As a general design guideline for the partitioned systems, we should strive to make the partitioning as transparent as possible to the clients. Client code should not have to be aware of the partitioning. Use the naming service to expose a few well-known entry points. Use factory or manager objects as key entry points to access underlying data objects residing in an RDBMS. Ensure that the IDL specified supports amendments and extensions without requiring wholesale changes to existing components.

Replication

Replication of a service means that there are multiple instances of the same server, each of which provides the same functionality and access to the same set of data objects. Since the replicas all provide the same service, a client request can be directed towards any of the servers currently available. As the name *replica* suggests, a single object might exist simultaneously in more than one server. Synchronization can be required to ensure that the contents of one server mirror those of all the others in the replicated group. In general, synchronization is expensive, so there is a tradeoff between the cost of synchronizing the contents of replicated servers and the performance gain expected from having multiple servers handling an application's clients.

The server that a client makes its invocations against is chosen in accordance with a *migration policy* which determines how often this selection is made. For example, each new remote invocation from a client could be directed towards a different (but not necessarily newly launched) server. Alternatively, the client might address all remote invocations to the same server instance for the duration of their client session.

Replication allows an application to support a certain quality-of-service in terms of performance and throughput. As more clients start using the application, additional replicants can be added to share the load. Previously, we discussed how server throughput can also be increased by using multiple threads in the server. However, multithreaded servers represent a single point of failure and are therefore not naturally as fault-tolerant as a pool of replicated servers.

Replication Aspects

In this section we will consider a number of aspects which influence the server to which a client will connect, namely *location* and *migration policies* and state management. A location policy determines the answer to the question "How does the system select a target server?" A migration policy determines the answer to the question "When does the system select a target server?" State management policies determine the answer to the question "How does the system manage state across replicated servers?" Each of these is discussed below.

Location Policies

Location policies attempt to answer the question "How does the system select a server?" The location policy is used to select a server from a set of replicants that all provide the same service. The most commonly used policies are:

- **Random.** A server is chosen on a random basis. Although this approach incurs very little processing overhead when selecting a server to connect to, it does not take into consideration the actual load on each server in the system. In addition, the policy does not consider whether the server is actually running and contactable. If the client is unable to connect to the server, it would have to make another request to whatever mechanism implements the server location policy.
- **Round robin.** A server is chosen using a round-robin strategy. This policy suffers from the same deficiencies as the random policy does. It is worth noting that with both of these policies, not all the servers registered in the server pool need to be launched and running when the request is received. If the server is not currently running, the activation agent may be able to launch it automatically.
- **Load based.** The load-based policy is the only one that takes into consideration the actual load on currently launched servers. Using this information, it will select the least-loaded server. However, there is a problem: How do we measure which server currently carries the least load? In general, this problem can be solved using instrumentation software to monitor the health of the running servers. The collection of instrumentation data can be done using specific process management tools such as SNMP-based managers or through

custom code in the locator that holds (and updates) information about all the servers that are registered with it. Additionally, the information can be collected actively or passively. If the server emits management information at regular intervals, in a fashion analogous to the push mode for events, the server is said to be actively providing information. Conversely, if the management tool has to ask a server for information about its state of health, we refer to this mode as passive, or, in the context of events, pull driven. It is important to ensure that the anticipated benefits to be gained from feedback-driven selection algorithms are greater than the cost of instrumentation.

Migration Policies

Migration policies attempt to address the question "When does the system select a server?" The migration policy controls the granularity at which application load balancing will occur. The most common policies include:

- **Per operation.** At the beginning of each remote operation, a client may be directed to a new server. This allows server load to be tuned at a very fine level of granularity although it does suffer from some drawbacks. In particular, if the server has cached state on behalf of a previous invocation, there is no guarantee that the client will be assigned to the same server and will therefore not be able to benefit from the caching. In addition, the redirection of clients to other servers will incur the additional cost of establishing new connections to many different servers.
- **Per transaction.** The completion of an ACID transaction, potentially involving multiple transactional remote method invocations, could be selected as the level of granularity for load balancing. The feasibility of this approach would depend largely on the comparative cost of load balancing with respect to the average duration of a transaction.
- **Per unit of work.** Logical work units to be executed by the system could be identified and used to drive the load-balancing mechanism. A unit of work might not be related to an ACID transaction. For example, a CORBA client that contacts a query manager to create and execute a query to a relational database and be returned an iterator (managed by the server) might constitute a logical unit of work. When a client calls next() on an iterator object, we really do want that remote call to execute the code on the server in which the query was run.
- **Per session.** A client is assigned to a server for the duration of their client session. This migration policy really decomposes to a "no migration" policy as far as the clients are concerned. Once they have been assigned to a server, all further remote invocations will be directed to that server.

State Management

When stateless servers are used in conjunction with a replication pattern, the issue of state management is straightforward: All servers are guaranteed to provide exactly the same service and there is no need to replicate cached state information between servers. In many cases, this type of server really just acts as a "cap" that sits on top of a database—its main purpose is to delegate client calls to manage stateful objects that live in the database server.

With stateful servers the story is very different. Stateful servers imply caching. Caching state within replicated servers means that the same data elements may be simultaneously represented in more than one (replicated) server. To ensure that all clients have a consistent view of the object's state, the cached state of objects within the replicated servers needs to be synchronized. Cache synchronization in the middle tier is viewed as being one of the most technically demanding objectives a developer will face. Furthermore, all the replicated servers may not be querying and updating data from the same database server; instead, each replicated server may be bound to its own database server, which means that synchronization may also occur at the database level rather than at the application level.

Replication Mechanisms

In the previous section we discussed three major aspects of load balancing, namely object location, migration and state management. We now describe a number of mechanisms that are available to implement each of these aspects. To locate a servant object, we describe the multiproxy, object group, and selector patterns. Migration from one server to another may be controlled by the client, by the server, or by a concentrator. Finally, we investigate a number of mechanisms that may be used to manage state, namely cache synchronization and database replication.

Location Mechanisms

The object group, multiproxy, and selector patterns provide a variety of mechanisms for finding objects in a replicated server community. The object group pattern extends the basic notion of mapping a well-known name to a single object reference to map the name to multiple object references. In contrast, the multiproxy implements a mechanism that re-directs a client to a different server implementation by caching a number of valid server object references in each client. Finally, the selector pattern is a standalone server that is responsible for assigning new clients to the least loaded server. Each of these techniques may be used in conjunction with one of the migration policies described above, although certain combinations will achieve better scalability.

Multiproxy Pattern

When an IOR is used to construct a proxy in the client's address space, the proxy object refers to one and only one remote implementation object. The proxy acts as a reference to that single object for its entire lifetime. The immediate consequence of this model is that the client programmer needs to manage aspects of fault tolerance (failover) and load balancing (object location), unless this functionality has been specifically built into the server(s). The concept of a multiproxy extends this model to allow the same proxy object to refer to different implementation objects at various times within its lifecycle; in effect, encapsulating the failover and object location functionality that would otherwise have to be built into the client code.

The multiproxy is implemented as a client-side wrapper class, which delegates its method invocations to the remote object's proxy. The application programmer interacts with the multiproxy rather than the normal proxy. The multiproxy wrapper class is responsible for implementing fault-tolerance and load-balancing policies. This mechanism provides a reasonable level of transparency for the application programmer and some relief from error handling or writing load-balancing code repetitively. The multiproxy is just a normal C++ wrapper class. It would not normally have an interface defined in IDL. In addition, unlike the custom proxy mechanism frequently used for caching state in a client, the multiproxy is not a specialization of an object's normal proxy. However, the implementation of the multiproxy will need to faithfully expose all the methods defined on the real object's IDL interface as public methods and would probably hold as private member data one or more proxies to the real objects.

Applying the architecture described above to load-balancing the StockWatch application (as illustrated in Figure 15.4), the object selection process is as follows. First, each StockWatch server binds its `StockWatch` objects to the naming service [1]. Then, as each client starts, it makes an initial connection to the naming service and resolves well known names for each of the `StockWatch` objects [2]. These IORs are cached in a list in a multiproxy object to be used later for load-balancing. This initial communication and resolution of names to objects need only happen once; after the multiproxy has cached the IORs, it won't contact the naming service unless a failure is detected.

Figure 15.4 Load balancing using a multiproxy

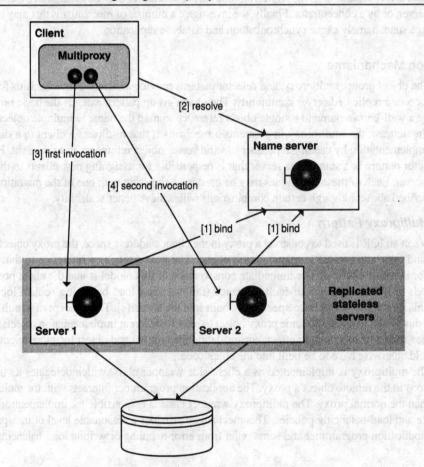

Next, the multiproxy implementation in the client selects the target object for the first request, by applying the pre-determined location policy [**3**]. When the client makes a second invocation on the StockWatch object, the multiproxy implementation will intervene and select (possibly) a different target server for the remote invocation [**4**].

Like most load balancing solutions, the effectiveness of a multiproxy-based solution depends to a great extent on the access pattern used. If servers are replicated and objects in those servers hold state, then using a client-controlled location/selection policy might return inconsistent results, unless the servers in the replicated pool constantly "chat" with one another to synchronize their cached objects. However, if the servers are stateless, then the multiproxy can provide a very fast and effective load-balancing solution.

For example, each invocation through a multiproxy might select a different implementation object based on, say, a round-robin location policy, resulting in a statistically even distribution pattern for the servers. Unlike other load balancing solutions (discussed later), which can introduce an additional level of indirection when making a remote call, the multiproxy ensures direct client-server communication.

Consider a "pull" driven stock price service, where thousands of clients intermittently request the latest price for a certain stock, based upon some key piece of identity information, such as the stock symbol. The server environment might consist of 20 or so replicated StockWatch servers, each of which can provide the latest price for any stock. In a simple load-balancing solution, the system administrator may preconfigure the number of servers to be started, each using a different name. Each of these persistently launched servers would register its (static) StockWatch object in the naming service under a different name. Upon startup, each client would bind to the naming service and retrieve the IORs for all the StockWatch objects currently registered. This list would be used by the multiproxy to select the server object to address the request to, using either a random or round-robin location policy. Each subsequent request would re-apply the location policy to select a different server. In effect, the multiproxy would implement a per-operation migration policy.

Different classes of client might implement variations of this basic load-balancing algorithm, although a well-balanced server community can only be achieved if all clients use the same location policy consistently. The major detraction from using load balancing policies controlled by the client is the problem of object state.

When objects are created by factory or manager objects in the server, they often cache state loaded from some persistent storage. If a multiproxy redirects a client to a different server on each invocation, there is no guarantee that the target object will exist in that server, and also no guarantee that even if it exists, its state will be as expected by the client. Servers might try to synchronize the objects they cache, which is generally regarded as expensive and error prone, or the client might change the location policy to per-session, so that the same remote object implementation would be used for the duration of the client's session. Alternatively, if each of the servers access the same shared database resource and the servers themselves avoid caching state information from the database, then it should not matter to which server a client redirects its request. In effect, each server is guaranteed to behave exactly the same as any other server, facilitating direct substitution. This concept is expanded in Chapter 16, "Fault Tolerance."

Object Group Pattern

The CORBA naming service is often used by clients to locate servant objects. Each entry in the repository of names contains a well-known name and an object reference. The relationship is strictly one-to-one; that is, a name can only be bound to a single object reference and names within a naming context must be unique. The notion of an *object group* extends this model by allowing a one-to-many relationship between names and object references; in essence, it allows many servant objects to be registered with the same name in the naming service.

Resolution of the name to an object reference is mediated with the aid of location policies, such as round-robin and random, although a general mechanism might allow the developer to specify their own location policy. Extended implementations of the CORBA naming service,[1] such as IONA's OrbixNames, have advanced features that support the object group pattern for load balancing out-of-the-box. OrbixNames employs the concept of a name group, which essentially allows a single name to be bound to multiple objects. When a client asks the naming service to resolve the name, the naming service chooses an object from the object group according to a preset location policy.

The objects that are registered into a name group will probably reside in different replicas of the same server, which may be persistently or automatically activated (by an ORB activation agent) on the same or different host machines. The client decides how long it will use the object reference returned by the naming service. For example, it may continue to use the same factory object until a failure occurs, at which point it may ask the naming service to resolve the name again to retrieve a (hopefully) different server object. In this way, the client can control the usage pattern and migration policy for various server objects.

The concept of an object group is illustrated in Figure 15.5. In the CORBA-compliant naming service, a name can be bound to one and only one object reference (IOR) within a single naming context. However, OrbixNames relaxes this constraint, allowing multiple IORs to be added to an object group which is then bound to the single name. In effect, a single name identifies a set of objects rather than a single one. When a client of the naming service attempts to resolve a name which happens to be bound to an object group, OrbixNames will return one of the IORs, depending on the load balancing algorithm that had been selected. Currently, OrbixNames supports two selection algorithms, round-robin and random. From the client's perspective, nothing changes. They are unaware that any load balancing is taking place.

Figure 15.6 illustrates the principle of client-controlled load balancing using the extended naming service. In this example, servers preregister the IORs of their respective entry point objects with the naming service [1]. Instead of binding each object under a different name, the objects are bound into an object group. The client connects to the naming service as usual and simply resolves the well-known name [2]. The naming service returns one of the entries in the object group.

While the object groups feature of OrbixNames does provide a first step at default built-in load balancing, it does not fully address some of the issues surrounding scalability and fault tolerance. For instance, the naming service is implemented in a single process, and therefore represents a single point of failure in the system. For this reason, additional fault tolerant measures (such as fed-

---

[1] The concept of "name groups" used by IONA Technologies in version 1.1 of their OrbixNames product is not currently part of the basic COS Naming specification. It is a proprietary extension built specifically for the purpose of providing some form of default load balancing.

Figure 15.5   Object groups in OrbixNames

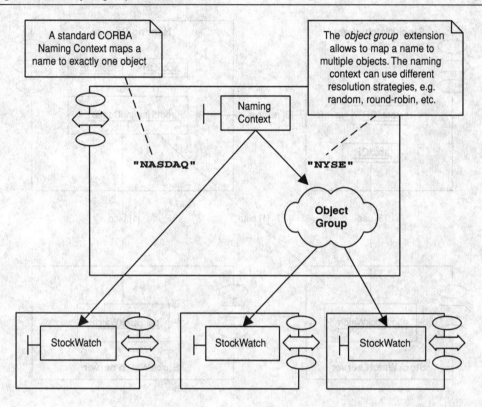

erating naming services together at an application level) are often used in combination with the object group model of load balancing.

As a second example, we summarize the load-balancing solution for the StockWatch system that was already described in Chapter 4. The migration policy is per-session. Each component consists of a StockWatch server and an event service server, and serves a number of clients. Load is randomly distributed over the components. During a session, a user would only interact with one component instance. This means that the objects in the selected component return only object references to objects that reside in the same component. A client session starts by getting a StockWatch object from the load-balancing enabled naming service, implicitly associating the client with the component instance in which the selected StockWatch implementation resides.

In conclusion, for the object groups load-balancing pattern to work well, there must be some cooperation between clients and servers. Specifically, clients must follow a certain pattern for accessing objects that was predefined by the developers of the servers. Switching from one instance of a stateless object to another is not a problem. However, when objects are associated with state, switching context is more complex.

Figure 15.6   Load balancing using object groups

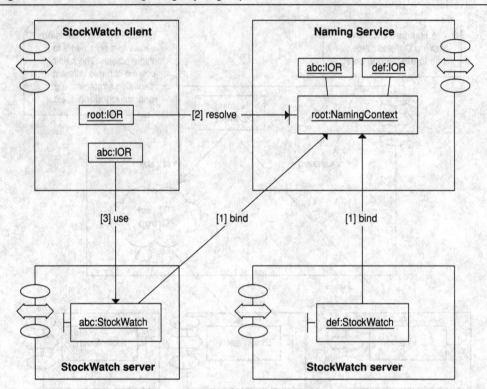

Selector Pattern

The selector pattern implements a load-based location policy using the abstract concept of a *selector*. The selector collects load information from replicated servers under its jurisdiction. It uses this information as input to a selection algorithm that is typically load-based. For example, it may select the server that has the fewest number of client connections. When a client wishes to access a remote object using selector-driven load balancing, it will make an initial call to the selector server to locate an implementation object. The selector will then return either the name or the IOR of an object in one of the real servers. Thereafter, clients access the server objects in the normal fashion, by making direct remote invocations, as illustrated in Figure 15.7. This approach has a number of advantages:

- The selection algorithm is well-encapsulated. It is not mixed with application interfaces. In our example, the selector server doesn't need to implement the Portfolio interface.
- New server instances can easily be added at runtime. They simply register themselves with the selector. Alternatively, the selector can take responsibility for launching application servers persistently as the client load increases.

- The selector can easily monitor the load on the servers registered with it.
- Although every selection requires a remote call, a client may only have to make a single call to the selector within a single session. For example, if the migration policy is per-session, the client continues to use the same server for the duration of the session. If the client detects a communication failure, it re-contacts the selector to request a new server to use for future invocations.

Figure 15.7 shows an example of the selector pattern. The steps involved are referenced below.

Clients are prebuilt and deployed with stub code for the selector interface, as well as stubs required by normal application interfaces, such as StockWatch.

The selector server registers an instance of the Selector interface under a well-known name in the naming service (not shown). In our example, the selector prestarts a number of application servers (**1**). In some instances, it may instead defer launching servers until clients specifically ask for them.

When these servers start up, they make an invocation on the selector, passing an entry point object reference (**2**). It is this object that clients will later obtain from the selector. These servers may also pass a load-monitoring object to the selector, if it performs active load monitoring. (By periodi-

Figure 15.7 Load balancing—selector pattern

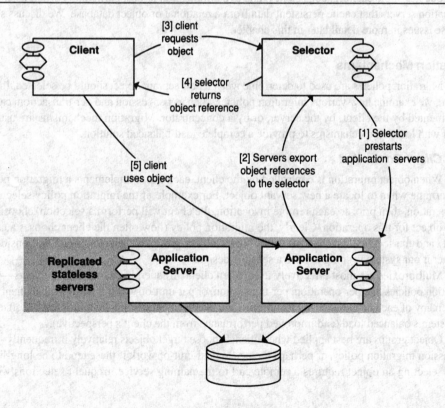

cally querying the load on each server, the selector can direct clients to the least-loaded server). In this example, our clients select a server only once per session, so our "server load" is based on a simple count of the number of client connections each server has open.

Later, a client application starts and connects to the naming service to resolve the well-known name of the `Selector` object (not shown). Then, the client makes an invocation on the selector, to obtain a `StockWatch` object (3). The selector determines which of the servers has the smallest number of open connections to clients, and returns a reference to a `StockWatch` object in that server (4). It also increments the connection count for that server. If our selector were more sophisticated, it would base the selection on actual server load, rather than just a client connection count. The client then (5) makes invocations on the `StockWatch` object.

In order for the selector to properly keep track of client connections to server, it also needs to know when clients close their connections to the application servers. This can be implemented by having clients explicitly notify the selector when they are finished (and are about to exit). Alternatively, the servers could notify the selector when client connections close. The latter approach is safest, since it is resilient enough to handle ill-behaved clients that exit without notifying the selector first.

The selector method is most applicable when we want to control the number of server instances dynamically or when the migration policy is per-client, per-session, or per-transaction (that is, the client does not change target servers very often, if at all). As before, this load-balancing technique has some caching, consistency, and synchronization issues, particularly when used with application servers that cache persistent data from a relational or object database. We discuss some of these issues in more detail later in this chapter.

Migration Mechanisms

Migration policies are used to determine *when* a new servant object should be selected. In this section, we examine how various migration policies, such as per-session and per-transaction, can be implemented by the client, by the server, or by a concentrator. Migration mechanisms are usually mixed with location mechanisms to provide a complete load-balanced solution.

Client-Controlled

When object migration is controlled by the client, each client implements a migration policy to determine when to locate a new servant object. For example, if the migration policy selected is per-operation, then prior to each remote invocation, the client will perform a selection, choosing a target object for this operation. Clearly, the migration policy (how often the client chooses a target object) and the location mechanism (multiproxy, object group, or selector) must be considered together if our system is going to have a sensible design.

Multiproxies are most effectively used when clients frequently choose target objects—with migration policies like per-operation, per-transaction, or per-unit-of-work. Since a typical client performs many of each of these during its lifetime, the overhead of creating the multiproxy is offset by the system's balanced load (and improved performance from the client's perspective).

Object groups are best applied when clients choose target objects relatively infrequently—the per-session migration policy, or perhaps the per-logical-unit-of-work if these tend to be long-lived. Since selecting an object requires a remote call to the naming service, frequent selections would incur a large performance penalty, and are best avoided. (Transactions should generally be short-lived, so making an invocation on the naming service for each transaction is likely to be too inefficient to consider.)

The selector mechanism, like object groups, imposes the cost of a remote invocation each time a selection is performed. In fact, the selector may even poll servers for their current load in response to a selection request, further increasing its cost. Clearly, this mechanism is also best applied with infrequent selections, per-session or for long logical units of work.

A good example of a client-controlled approach is the combination of the multiproxy for object location coupled with a per-transaction migration policy. The multiproxies essentially cache a list of references to various server objects. Shortly before a new transaction commences, the client selects the server in which the transaction is to be run. Each remote call made through a multiproxy on behalf of the current transaction uses the same server. When the transaction has completed (and the next one is about to begin), the client can choose another target server. An interesting sidelight is that, since the migration mechanism is based in each client, different classes of clients can implement different migration policies against the *same* group of replicated servers.

One potential downside of client-controlled object migration is that additional logic needs to be built into the client. If the client programs are being developed by a different group (or a different company) than the servers, it may not be possible to ensure that clients implement a particular mechanism. In such cases, server-controlled approaches should be considered.

Server-Controlled

In Chapter 2, we introduced the LOCATION_FORWARD mechanism, defined as part of the CORBA specification. Recall that with a POA-based ORB, this allows a server to redirect a client's invocation to a different servant object. This mechanism can be used very effectively by a server to balance its load. If the server decides that it is too heavily loaded, it may choose to delegate the call to some other server.

Instead of processing the request and returning a normal reply to the client, the server will throw a ForwardRequest exception, passing an object reference for the servant object to which the request is to be redirected. When the client ORB receives the reply, it will transparently resend the request to the new servant. Naturally, when a client's ORB receives this exception it will have to update its proxy object to reflect the new location of the target.

This pattern alleviates the need for a separate selector object to perform the load-balancing logic; instead, the (replicated) servers cooperate to manage the overall application load. However, as the objective is to reply with a ForwardRequest exception that contains the IOR of the *least* loaded server, each server needs to know the load state of each of its peers (replicants) in order to make this assessment.

Servers may implement management-style interfaces that allow other servers to probe various aspects, such as their responsiveness, throughput and current connection count, enabling them to build and maintain a profile of all other servers in the peer group. Alternatively, they may ask an independent monitor for this information.

The monitor is an independent process responsible for collecting load and performance information of each application server in the peer group. This particular approach to load balancing is very flexible and it is relatively easy to make changes to fine-tune the migration algorithm. It is particularly useful for per-transaction or per-unit-of-work migration policies and can be very effectively used in conjunction with the object transaction service (OTS).

In summary, the ForwardRequest API is a flexible redirection mechanism that can be used by a system to implement either local or remote selection approaches. With a local approach, the migration/selection logic is embedded within each of the servers that comprise the replicated group. Each server is responsible for collecting and maintaining load information for all the other servers in the group, and will forward clients directly to a more lightly loaded server.

Alternatively, servers within the replicated group may choose to delegate their load-balancing decisions to a remote selector process that is responsible for the collection and maintenance of load and performance statistics for all the servers in the group. Servers redirect clients to the selector process, which in turn redirects clients to the least-loaded server.

Unfortunately, this approach is only supported in POA-based ORBs. Users of BOA-based ORBs will have to use some other mechanism. One additional point of concern about the selector approach is that the selector process itself represents a single point of failure to the system as a whole.

Delegation with Concentrators

The concentrator approach, which was briefly introduced in Chapter 14, "Managing Server Resources," can be easily applied to object migration. Since the concentrator is responsible for delegating each call to an application server, it can implement any of the migration policies by simply changing the target server at the appropriate time. We fully discuss concentrators later in this chapter, in the "Replication Frameworks" section.

State Management

In previous sections we have examined aspects of location and migration and how different load balancing policies can affect performance and access patterns. We have not yet considered any of the problems that replicated or partitioned servers might introduce. In the simple case where the servers contain only static, stateless objects, it makes no difference which server a client connects to. Each invocation of the same operation executes the same (stateless) code, so all servers can be regarded as identical. However, this is rarely the case. Typically servers contain state, in the form of both transient and persistent objects, as well as the data stored in them.

This is an important distinction, and leads us to two problems, one of which is easy to solve, and one of which is difficult. The first aspect of server state is the set of CORBA objects active in a server. Client requests must be delivered to a server in which the target object is active, or can be activated. Obviously, if clients have an object reference directly to the target object, then this issue is moot; all client requests will by definition be sent to the proper object. If, however, services redirect clients to other servers, or a concentrator is imposed between client and server, we must be careful to direct the request to the proper application server. Note that by using stateless servants in conjunction with late binding, we can send a client request to any application server, which will be able to activate the target object. Basically, a migration policy has to be chosen so that it does not conflict with server state management. This is a relatively easy problem to solve. The more difficult problem relates to the data stored within servant objects.

Servers frequently instantiate persistent CORBA objects that represent constructs from a relational or object-oriented database. If the server is stateless, it will not store any of this object's state in memory; instead, it will simply offer a pass-through interface with calls like getName() and setName() that directly query or update the persistent state attribute in the database. Each call to retrieve or modify an attribute value will therefore result in a query to the database.

In contrast, stateful servers will hold copies of the persistent state of these objects in memory. In effect, the values of some of the persistent attributes are cached in the application server. When a client invokes a method to retrieve an object attribute, the server will be able to return a value cached locally in the middle tier, alleviating the need to query the database again. This model works quite well with a single application server, but can cause problems when scaled to multiple servers.

When multiple replicated servers are employed to balance application load, an object from the database may be cached in more than one application server. When a client updates the value of a persistent attribute, the change will be propagated to the database and also to the cache of that particular application server, but not to any other replicated servers. The values cached in one server are now different from those cached by the other servers. This is typically undesirable, since different clients will see different data, even though they are invoking on the same logical object. So, if our replicated servers cache state, we must consider some complex server synchronization issues.

Cache Synchronization

Synchronizing state between servers is a difficult problem to solve. First, we discuss the approach where no data is cached in servers, avoiding the problem entirely. Then we explore different ways in which server caches can be designed, and the effects of these designs.

No Caching.   The simplest solution to the problem of cache synchronization is to simply not cache any state at all. The objects in our servers are thin wrappers for the underlying database objects. When a client retrieves a persistent attribute from an object, the object delegates this call to the database, by reading the appropriate data. When a client updates a persistent attribute in the object, the object in turn updates the data item in the database. The data value is never actually cached in a member variable by an object in the application server.[2] With this approach, synchronization of concurrent access to objects' data is really delegated to the underlying database.

One possible disadvantage of this technique is that it can expose the underlying data directly to the client in a fine-grained fashion. For example, if a client holds a proxy to an object that has 25 persistent attributes, then a succession of calls to update each of the attributes would require 25 distinct database updates, with no guarantee that there were not interleaved reads or writes by another user. In addition, this simple action would require at least 25 separate remote invocations. It is often preferable reduce the granularity at which the objects are exposed to the client, for instance by defining and using IDL data structures.

Although this model may not be able to deliver the outright performance of a design that uses server caching for primarily read-only access, it has some significant benefits in an update-intensive application. Namely, the difficult issues of cache consistency are completely avoided.

Maintaining Server Cache.   In some cases, however, our systems do require cached information in the middle-tier server. Such systems can improve performance in cases where most access is read-only rather than update. However, maintaining state in multiple server processes can

---

[2] Actually, it may be cached in a variable in the application server, but only temporarily, while it holds the appropriate database locks.

be very difficult, expensive, and error-prone. Next, we outline the possible approaches, and their associated complexities.

There are two primary approaches to state management, coordination and validation. With a coordinated approach, our systems attempts to ensure that any data item that exists in multiple server caches will have a consistent value. With the validation approach, the servers rely on the database as the ultimate trustee of the data, and verify their cache before permitting a client to read or write the data.

Coordinating Cache.   Coordinating state among multiple servers is a very complex topic, which we can only begin to address here. There are two ways to coordinate state, synchronously and asynchronously.

With synchronous coordination, all cached copies of the data item, as well as the entry in the underlying database are all updated in one atomic operation. All the items must be properly locked prior to the update, and the all the updates must uniformly succeed or fail. In effect, this is a transaction. Clearly, this approach imposes a great deal of overhead—both administratively (since all servers must know about all cached instances of each data item), as well as in runtime performance. As a result, this is generally not recommended.

Asynchronous coordination introduces a delay between the local update of a data item, and the propagation of the change to the other servers. (We can easily imagine using mechanisms such as the CORBA event service, or a multicast messaging product to accomplish this). This is a much more lightweight solution, since an update can be performed without coordinating multiple application servers. However, this approach does introduce a window of inconsistency, between the time a data item is updated in server A and the update is propagated to server B. If a client reads the data item from server B during this time, the value returned will be out of date. This problem is even worse if multiple servers can perform updates. In this case, we also run the risk of one client overwriting another's changes. If two clients concurrently update the same data item different servers, then one client's changes will overwrite the other's.

How can these problems be solved? The window of inconsistency is inherent in asynchronous coordination, and cannot be avoided. In some cases, however, such a window may be acceptable. For example, if our server is updating Web pages, then there may be no real harm in a client reading an out-of-date page. The problem of clients overwriting one another's updates is more serious. In order to avoid this, we need to assign write permission to a single server. All other servers will only have read access to the data. In this way, one client will not be able to overwrite any changes made by another, since all updates are directed to a single server. However, the downside of this approach is that clients are exposed to some of the server-side implementation details, and are required to have connections to multiple servers for the same interface.

There are many other complex and difficult aspects of state coordination that must be considered. For instance, we also have to decide on the granularity of the data items that are coordinated. Should updates be propagated about database fields or rows, or perhaps about a business object that spans multiple rows in multiple tables? Also, should the new value be propagated, or only the fact that the value has changed?

In general, coordinating state is an extremely difficult problem to solve. Either avoid it entirely, or make some simplifying assumptions about your requirements, such as accepting the window of inconsistency.

Validating Cache. Cache validation is a simpler solution to this problem. With this approach, there is no attempt to coordinate state among different servers. Instead, the CORBA servers (which are database clients) depend on the shared underlying database to coordinate access to the state.

In most cases, the first thing an application server will do when it receives a request to access a cached object is to ask the underlying database if the requested data item has changed since it was cached. If it has, the server will re-read the values from the database. If not, it will simply returned the cached value.

One common model for cache validation with RDBMSs augments each database table with a "number-of-times-modified" (NTM) counter. This counter is incremented every time a value in the row is changed. The application server caches the NTM when it loads the object's state from the database. Before a server returns the cached value of an object to a client, it will make a call to the database to check whether the cached NTM is less than the NTM in the database. If it is, then the cached values are stale and the server will initiate a full refresh of that object in the cache. If the NTM's are equal, then the server can immediately return the cached values to the client. (A similar approach was discussed previously in Chapter 13, "User Sessions.")

Unfortunately, this simple model has a number of drawbacks. First, the server needs to make a call to the database to establish whether it needs to refresh the cache. Ideally, the query size and data passed would be very small, making this call more efficient than retrieving the entire state of the object. However, if the cache is stale, then the server needs to make yet another database call to retrieve the entire object's state. For this reason, this style of cache/database interaction is most suited to data that changes infrequently. Secondly, the database schema will be polluted with data that pertains to the management of the application rather than to the application itself. Also, if a cached object is refreshed from the database, should other related objects also be refreshed to maintain a consistent view of the data? The granularity of cache refresh should therefore be taken into consideration when using this approach.

Recommendations. This is a complex topic, which could be source of many Ph.D. theses. However, our recommendations are straightforward. For applications that require frequent updates, avoid caching in the middle tier if at all possible. Use middle-tier caching for query-centric applications, where the changes to the persistent data are infrequent. Accept a small window of inconsistency between server replicas, and consider designating a single server for updates, to avoid overwriting changes to the data.

Database Replication

The approaches to load balancing discussed this far have concentrated on the CORBA-centric issues of object location and migration. In this section we will discuss how database replication can be a part of a complete load-balanced distributed application.

The following discussion assumes that we have stateless CORBA servers. Trying to mix levels, where we coordinate state between servers *and* across databases is not feasible. Note that this discussion parallels our previous one on server cache synchronization. This is because both of these solutions are attempting to solve the same problem, just at different levels.

Many commercial databases support replication. Replication is the process of coordinating state between database instances. Currently available tools support replication between databases from the same vendor, as well as between databases from different vendors.

There are two primary approaches to replication, synchronous and asynchronous. With synchronous replication, updates to all replicated databases are performed within the context of a single transaction. This ensures complete and robust consistency across replicas, at the cost of a distributed transaction.

With asynchronous replication, updates are performed in the local database, and are queued for later delivery to the replicas. Like asynchronous application cache updates, this introduces a window of inconsistency, as well as the possibility for conflicts. Database replication tools can be configured to handle these conflicts, for instance by permitting the last update to overwrite the first, or by storing information about the conflict in an administrator's error log. In many cases, neither of these solutions will be acceptable. In such cases, designating one database as write-only and the others as read-only can help solve the problem, although the window of inconsistency remains.

Database replication can be very effectively used to help make a system fault tolerant. This is explored further in Chapter 16, "Fault Tolerance."

Replication Frameworks

In the previous sections we have identified three key aspects that affect load balancing solutions, namely location, migration, and state management. We also discussed a number of mechanisms that implemented various policies for each, and stressed that a combination of location, migration, and state management mechanisms is usually required to implement a complete load-balancing solution. When developing real-world systems, we need to put all the pieces of the puzzle together to form a cohesive solution. In this section, we discuss component replication and concentrator patterns that do just this.

Component Replication

We have discussed a number of techniques that leverage server replication to achieve load balancing. For example, the object group and selector patterns provide a service that we can use to register objects from multiple replicated server instances. Clients use this service to locate objects in one of the replicas.

Similarly, we have also discussed how federated event services and channel federation can be used to improve the scalability of event-driven (push) applications.

We now demonstrate the concept of component replication. An example is shown in Figure 15.8. We have defined the StockWatch component to include a singe StockWatch server and two event servers. Each component contains two event servers because these programs tend to be more heavily loaded than the StockWatch program. The event servers continually push updates to clients, while the StockWatch server is relatively infrequently used. Both of the event servers use the same intermediate event server to receive the stock price updates.

The important point is that the component becomes the unit of replication, rather than the individual servers themselves. Although the StockWatch server and each of the event servers are separate executables, and may in fact run on different hosts, the StockWatch component logically includes all of these servers.

We have chosen to use a selector server for object location. Clients contact the selector once per session, to obtain an initial object reference. The selector implements the random-choice policy and returns an object in the one of the StockWatch servers.

Figure 15.8 Component replication

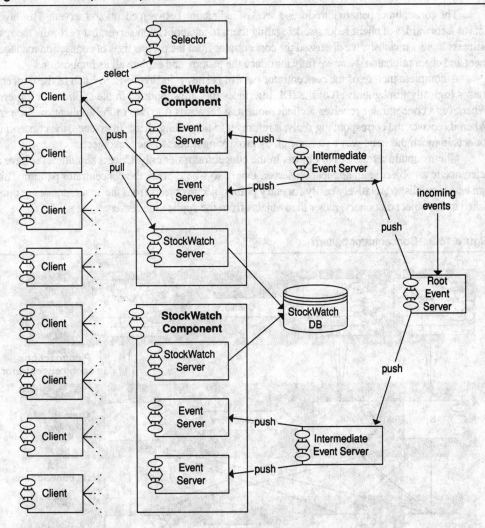

This object acts as a factory. Clients use this object to obtain any other object references. This allows our application logic to ensure each client uses only servers contained in a single component. Recall that a client obtains a reference to an event channel by invoking the getFeed() method on a Stock object. The application returns a reference to an event channel within this component only. (In this example, the application alternates between the two event servers within this component to balance the load). If the client were to instead contact an external program (like the selector) to obtain an event channel, it could be given a reference to one in a different component. This breaks the component model and must be avoided. Rather than having the selector coordinate components, event servers, and clients, it is far easier to rely on the factory method instead.

Concentrator Pattern

The concentrator pattern introduces a level of indirection between clients and servers. This layer acts as a forwarder of client requests, delegating them to an application server that performs the real business logic. Previously, we discussed the concentrator from the perspectives of connection management and client migration. Now we fully introduce the pattern, and explore all its implications.

A complete picture of the concentrator pattern is shown in Figure 15.9. Each of the concentrators logically implements all of the IDL interfaces that are supported in the application servers. Whenever a concentrator receives a client request, it forwards it to one of the application servers. When it receives the corresponding reply, it returns it to the calling client. In essence, the concentrator acts in much the same way as a firewall, by proxifying access to the real objects.

Clients obtain references to objects in the concentrator tier only. Clients should never have a reference to an object in an application server. Doing so would break the concentrator pattern. This can be accomplished relatively easily for entry point objects; objects from the concentrator are published to the object dictionary, rather than objects from the application servers.

Figure 15.9   Concentrator pattern

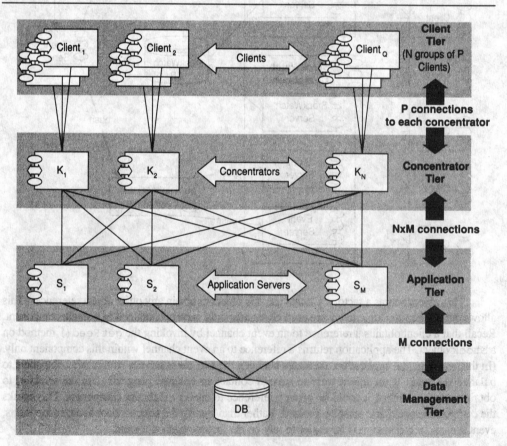

Concentrators and Load Balancing

The concentrator encapsulates all the load balancing logic of the system. It chooses target servers based on location and migration policies chosen by the programmer. The client application is completely unaware of any load balancing performed by the concentrator. In addition, it is easy for the concentrator to launch additional application servers as the load increases, enhancing scalability.

Different migration policies can affect the concentrator in different ways. For example, a concentrator can very easily implement a per-operation migration policy. Whenever a request is received, the concentrator can choose a target server based on some location policy such as round-robin or load-based. There is no additional effort required for this. However, a per-transaction or per-unit-of-work migration policy requires that the concentrator be aware of some additional information about the request. A per-transaction policy, for instance, means that the concentrator must be able to determine which transaction a given request is part of, and when transactions begin and end. Likewise for the per-unit-of-work approach; the concentrator must be able to determine when a unit of work begins and ends. These requirements have implications when choosing how to implement a concentrator (we discuss this later). Finally, a concentrator can also implement the per-session migration policy. This static approach does not provide much benefit from a load-balancing perspective, but can be useful for overcoming connection limitations, or with stateful application servers.

Potential Problems with Concentrators

However, there are also a number of potential problems that arise with concentrators. First, the concentrator itself must be multithreaded, otherwise it will become a bottleneck as additional clients try to connect. Second, there is a performance overhead induced by the additional remote call from the concentrator to an object in the real server. In order to reduce the network latency of the second call (and its corresponding reply), concentrators should be deployed close to the application servers. Third, the concentrator represents a potential single point of failure in the system. To improve the fault tolerant capability of this approach, multiple concentrators are often launched, as shown in Figure 15.9.

The biggest problem with concentrators, however, occurs when factory objects are used. Recall that a factory is simply an object that returns a reference to another object. Consider what happens when a factory returns an object reference to the caller, in the reply to a method invocation. This is illustrated in Figure 15.10, which uses the Portfolio Manager server as an example.

First, our client obtains a reference to the `PortfolioManager` object in our concentrator. It invokes a factory method (in this case, `login()`), which is delegated to the real object in our application server. This method verifies the login id and password, creates a servant `Portfolio` object, initializes it with the specified portfolio's state, and returns an object reference to the caller (in this case, the concentrator). Our concentrator simply returns this object reference to the client. This is a mistake! This object reference will direct the client to the application server. The first time our client makes an invocation on this Portfolio object, a new connection will be established directly to the application server, bypassing the concentrator. This breaks the concentrator pattern, eliminating all its benefits.

Clearly, something must be done differently when object references are returned from a server. Specifically, the outbound object reference must be modified, so that it directs the client to the concentrator, and not to the application server. How easy or difficult this is to accomplish depends on the way in which the concentrator is implemented.

Figure 15.10 Factory creation: the problem

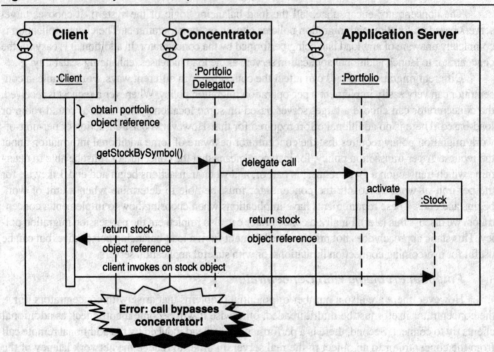

In fact, this problem gets worse with further thought. Outbound object references may be returned in any legal IDL format or structure. For instance, instead being returned as a simple `Portfolio` object, the application server may return an object reference contained in a structure, a sequence, or even in an `any`. Either the concentrator will have to examine the outbound data, or the application server will have to modify the object reference as it is being marshaled, to properly point the client to the concentrator being used. Furthermore, it is not sufficient for the concentrator to blindly modify all outbound object references; the server may be returning references to objects in foreign server, to which the client *should* have a direct connection. In this case, it would be incorrect for the concentrator to modify the object reference. And, as icing on this cake of complexity, all these issues must also be considered for any callback objects passed from the client to the server.

Approaches To Implementing Concentrators

There are three ways in which concentrators can be implemented—static ORB interface, dynamic ORB interface, and IIOP Sniffers. The first approach is a general solution, which is implemented at the application level. Thus, it is applicable to any ORB. The latter two approaches require lower-level access to the request data, and may or may not be supported in all ORBS.

In all cases, the issues to be addressed are the modification of outbound object references, and the difficulty and performance of a particular implementation. Ideally, the ORB itself will support the modification of outbound object references in the application server. That is, when the object reference is being marshaled in the application server, it will be modified to direct the client to the concentrator process through which this request arrived. This relieves the concentrators of the need to modify any outbound data, and greatly simplifies their implementation. If such a feature is not supported in the ORB, then the concentrator is responsible for modifying the object references.

Static ORB Interfaces. The most general approach to implementing a concentrator can be done at an application level, by using the static ORB interfaces generated by the IDL compiler. The concentrator is simply a CORBA server, which implements all the IDL interfaces supported in the application servers. These interfaces are implemented as delegators. Whenever a method is invoked on a concentrator object, it simply acts as a CORBA client to the application server, making the corresponding invocation on the corresponding object in an application server.

This approach to implementing a concentrator is well-suited to code generation, since the concentrators can be mechanically derived from the application IDL. However, this approach can suffer from poor performance. Each request is fully marshaled and unmarshaled twice. This overhead is in addition to the cost of the second remote call inherent in concentrators.

How does this approach handle outbound object references? Since the concentrator implements the server IDL, it has access to the outbound data in a structured way. It is a relatively simple manner for the concentrator to instantiate new, local delegator objects, and return these instead of the business objects returned from the application server. Likewise, this type of concentrator can easily examine the request's arguments to determine when a transaction or unit of work begins and ends. Thus, static ORB interfaces can be readily used for the more fine-grained migration policies.

Naturally, this approach is also highly dependent on the IDL. If the application IDL changes, then the concentrator to be rebuilt. If a code-generation tool is used to create the concentrators, this step becomes trivial.

Dynamic ORB Interfaces. This approach relies on ORB support for the dynamic skeleton interface and dynamic invocation interface. recall that these permit CORBA applications to receive and make invocations on objects without any IDL-generated code. Like the static approach, a DSI/DII concentrator will simply delegate any incoming requests to the corresponding target object in an application server.

Depending on the ORB implementation, this approach may permit the concentrator to forward the request and reply without fully unmarshalling the message body. If so, it can provide better performance than with the static approach. However, modifying outbound object references is typically not possible without unmarshalling. Likewise, access to additional request data (other than the target object and method name) may be difficult. This prevents this approach from easily being used with the per-transaction or per-unit-of-work migration policies.

IIOP Sniffer. The final approach relies on an even lower level of support from an ORB: access to the raw IIOP message. With this approach, the concentrator will parse the header of each IIOP message and create a new message directed to the target object in an application server. The message body can be copied without any unmarshalling. The same steps are taken for replies from the server.

This approach can result in the highest performance concentrator. However, without an understanding of the structure of the message body (which is dependent on the application IDL), modifying outbound or inbound object references will not be possible. Likewise, unless this information can be determined by the target object and method name, this concentrator will not be able to determine when transactions or units of work begin or end.

This approach can be used successfully if the application server modifies outbound object references before they are returned. In this case, the message body needs no modification, and can simply be returned to the client.

Concentrator Summary

As we can see, there are a number of complex issues associated with concentrators, some of which have no easy answer. Implementing a general-purpose concentrator that can be used in any environment is clearly a difficult task, since inbound and outbound object references must be modified. Despite all the potential problems, however, concentrators can be effectively used, particularly when code-generation tools are used to ease their creation.

This is one area where solving a problem with CORBA is actually more difficult than with a non object-oriented approach such as Remote Procedure Calls. We leave this as a challenge to ORB vendors, to produce tools that make it easier to develop concentrators with CORBA.

BOA Activation Modes

The activation modes supported by BOA-based ORB activation agents are specifically designed to offer some basic out-of-the-box load-balancing capability. The CORBA specification defines a number of activation modes, which control when and how the activation agent launches new server processes. For example, should it start a new server process for each new client? Should each object have its own dedicated process? Or should the agent start a new server process for each new request?

These activation modes really only provide a primitive form of static load balancing. They are only applicable to BOA-based ORBs, and do not support any of the advanced load-balancing features discussed previously. The POA specification focuses on objects, not processes, and is silent on the issue of server process activation modes.

Measuring the cost of load balancing

Unfortunately, the implementation of a load balancing strategy isn't free. System designers should be careful to assess the cost of each load balancing technique in an effort to ensure that the performance and scalability benefits of load balancing are not offset by the additional cost. Additional costs include:

- **Cost of arbitration.** When selectors, concentrators, or switches are used, at least one additional level of indirection is introduced. In some cases, an additional server needs to be contacted prior to making the intended request to the real server.
- **Cost of switching context.** Switching context from one server to another will require at least one additional TCP/ IIOP connection to be established.
- **Cost of additional remote calls.** A useful guideline to keep in mind when partitioning application functionality across multiple servers is to try to introduce as few interdependencies between the servers as possible. Give them an identity of their own. In practice, this goal is often difficult to attain. Consequently, servers will frequently make calls to objects located in other servers, switching application context as they do so, and incurring

an additional remote call. One way to minimize the cumulative latency is to use one-way calls where possible, particularly with servers whose purpose is related to monitoring or logging rather than to processing core application logic.

- **Cost of resolving contention for scarce shared resources.** Machine memory is not inexhaustible, nor are TCP or database connections. As many clients vie for these limited resources, the application may simply see a graceful degradation in performance or may fail catastrophically. In the latter case, additional code needs to be incorporated in both client and server to ensure that this category of exception is correctly handled.
- **Cost of resolving contention for access to data.** In most applications, we strive to retain ACID properties for transactions involving persistent data. To maximize throughput for many concurrent users, mechanisms such as caching, locking, and the careful selection of what constitutes a logical unit of transactional work need to be considered. However, as transactions increase in complexity (and duration), the contention for data resources will increase, blocking other users for longer periods of time. By default, most CORBA servers will simply block until they eventually gain access to the data, adversely affecting server speed. Servers may wish to incorporate additional logic to manage slow data access.
- **Cost of delays introduced by the synchronization of data.** When multiple instances of a server cache state data retrieved from a relational or object database, it is possible for the contents of each of the server caches to be different, especially if objects are loaded into the cache lazily. Changes made to one cache (and possibly propagated to the underlying database) are not automatically propagated to the caches of other sibling servers, resulting in data inconsistency. Complex messaging or event-driven code (normally asynchronous in nature) is needed to ensure that the contents of each of the server caches are kept in sync. For most applications, the additional cost of ensuring cache synchronicity is prohibitive; the benefit is simply less than the cost. However, many products can use simple application add-ins to ensure that all the clients (each of whom may cache a small amount of state) of an application server are notified of changes to the state cached in the server. For instance, this can be done through the use of custom proxies or via the CORBA event service.
- **Cost of launching additional servers.** Most servers will have a base memory consumption when they are launched, which will then creep up as additional transient objects are instantiated on demand. Multiple lightly loaded servers will therefore consume significantly more memory than a single heavily loaded one would. In addition, as each new server instance is not launched instantaneously, the first remote call a new user makes might be slow due to a new server instance being launched.
- **Cost of writing and testing load-balancing code.** There is no single pattern or strategy that will fit all applications. Consequently, most load-balancing code is customized from a design pattern and requires some hand-crafted code.
- **Cost of monitoring the production application environment.** Although an application might have been designed with load balancing in mind, fine-tuning the runtime environment will almost certainly be required. Monitoring, logging, and auditing functionality can help measure load and identify potential bottle necks.

- **Cost of additional hardware and software.** Load-balancing solutions may demand additional hardware and software resources to permit replication of data servers or multiple instances of application servers to be supported.
- **Cost of application deployment.** The more complex the application, the more complex the deployment. Migration from development to test to production environments might require additional steps to guarantee integrity.
- **Cost of dynamic load balancing.** By its very nature, dynamic load balancing allows parameters that affect the load-balancing engine to be changed while the system is running. Not only do these parameters need to be exposed through an API to the person (or process) responsible for changing the load-balancing characteristics, the underlying server code has to be written to allow dynamic management.

Many large-scale system have to address the issue of load balancing, since no single host is likely to be able to provide the necessary throughput. It is important to carefully consider the environment, and ensure that whatever approaches to load balancing are chosen, their benefits outweigh their costs.

Summary

If ever there was a case for refuting the "one size fits all" idiom, then load balancing would certainly be it. Although many well-established patterns exist, the selection of an appropriate mechanism will depend on the access and usage patterns of the client applications. In short, we have to choose among load balancing controlled by the client or by the server, a plethora of location and migration policies, replication and/ or partitioning or, of course, a combination of all of the above. There is no limit to the number of variations available. However, mechanisms such as selectors and concentrators rely heavily on multi-threaded code, which is typically difficult to write and maintain. Often, simpler approaches will yield better results. From a standards perspective, CORBA does not currently address either load balancing or fault tolerance, although it has released RFP's for each. It will be some time before these ideas are formalized in a specification or in products. In the interim, application developers will have to select the load-balancing model that is most appropriate to their particular application.

Fault Tolerance

Allcomputer systems are subject to failure. Taken to its logical conclusion, there is no completely failsafe solution that can absolutely guarantee availability and performance *ad infinitum*. System designers must accept that there is always a reasonable chance of a failure occurring. It is up to us to define what is "reasonable," in terms of performance, availability, reliability, and recoverability. The field of fault tolerance is enormous, ranging all the way from power supply and hardware technology to operating systems and application-specific aspects. We do not attempt to address all of these areas in this text, but instead concentrate on a number of approaches that can be integrated into a distributed CORBA application.

In CORBA-based applications, which naturally include components distributed across a network, developers are more acutely aware of potential failure points. In a monolithic system, the whole application was either working or had failed, and corrective action could be taken at that level. In contrast, the topology and structure of a distributed application means that partial failures will be common. To be more precise, CORBA systems are made up of a number of elements, typically distributed across processes and hosts. Any one of these elements can fail at any time. The focus of this chapter is on handling these failures at the CORBA system level. Given that any element in our CORBA system can fail at any time, we discuss some realistic approaches that we can take so that the system as a whole will not fail when this happens.

What Is Fault Tolerance?

In formal terms, fault tolerance is a measure of an application's resistance to failures caused by factors as diverse as:

- Loss of processing resources—hardware and software or O/S failures
- Loss of logical and physical communication paths—network and connectivity failures or severe disruptions to service
- Both transient and permanent failures in the application itself—faulty logic, incomplete exception handling, mismatched client and server versions, and deadlocks, to name a few.

One primary measure of fault tolerance is based upon the amount of time an application is available to clients. Availability is calculated using the mean-time-between-failures (MTBF) and the mean-time-to-repair (MTTR). Formally,

```
Availability = MTBF/(MTBF + MTTR)
```

where the MTBF is the average time between failures occurring and the MTTR is defined as the total time taken to (a) identify the fault, (b) recover the servers, and (c) complete any synchronization required to restore consistent state. To improve overall availability, we strive to increase the mean-time-between-failures and reduce the mean-time-to-repair. Apart from the ORB-or application-specific approaches to fault tolerance, we must consider approaches that aim to improve the reliability and availability of the basic hardware and software components on which distributed application are based. At the most basic level, a power disruption can crash an entire application system. Simple remedies, such as the installation of an Uninterruptible Power Supply (UPS) can significantly improve the availability of the hardware platform. Similarly, as application servers are dependent upon operating systems and other system software, it is important to plan upgrades to these components carefully. An application should not be assigned a production status before it has been fully tested on the target software and operating system versions.

An exhaustive discussion of hardware and software related measures that address fault tolerance is not within the scope of this text. Instead, we concentrate on CORBA and application-specific techniques aimed at reducing or eliminating single-points-of-failure and improving overall availability. For a good introduction to fault tolerance, see Gray and Reuter, 1993 or Bernstein and Newcomer, 1997.

A Pragmatic Approach to Fault Tolerance Is Required

It's easy to get carried away with elaborate architectures that aim to improve an application's resilience to failure and improve its availability. Here, we propose a pragmatic approach, based loosely on the following observations.

- **Prevention is better than cure.** By writing more robust applications in the first place, the probability of failure is dramatically reduced and likewise the need for fault-tolerant measures. However, no matter how hard we try, no application is going to be perfect.
- **Accept the fact that processes don't stay up for ever.** Experience tells us that the longer a process remains active, the more likely it is that a programming error will surface, and the program will fail.
- **Complex heterogeneous applications are combined from many tool components.** For example, a distributed transactional CORBA application might include a variety of middleware and technology components, including:
  - C++, a programming language with powerful features but not trivial to use correctly
  - Multithreaded code, again, another non-trivial technology
  - Database management systems—either relational or object-oriented
  - Multithreaded CORBA ORB

- ORB-integrated object transaction service (OTS)
- Component deployment and management services
- XA interface between resource managers and the transaction manager
- Other tools and libraries such as C++ Standard Template Library (STL), Persistence, RogueWave DBTools.h++

Combining and using tools and libraries from many vendors greatly increases the chances of an application programming error, a bug in one of the off-the-shelf libraries, or an incompatibility with compiler versions, compiler options, or runtime library versions.

- **Simple fault tolerance measures tend to work best.** Complex fault tolerance architectures, although appealing to technical purists, might not be resilient to failure themselves, compounding the original fault rather than solving it.
- **Immediate recovery and seamless availability is not always needed.** Sometimes, an application client is prepared to accept a certain amount of latency in the recovery process, essentially increasing the acceptable MTTR. In general, as recovery latency approaches zero (immediate recovery or transparent failover to a working server), the marginal return gained from lowering the MTTR latency can be offset by the additional resources or code required to support and maintain the fault-tolerant environment. Due to scarce resources, it may not always be viable to have standby "hot swapping" servers or hosts launched and ready on an ongoing basis.
- **Fault tolerance is rarely the most important item on the project plan.** We've seem this time and time again. An application system is modeled, designed, and implemented without giving much thought to the issue of fault tolerance. It comes as something of a surprise that the first production version doesn't meet availability expectations. At this point, limited technical resources are hurriedly re-directed to retrofit fault-tolerant behavior to the application. As a result, fault-tolerant proposals should be lightweight, practical and easy to integrate with existing application code—another good reason to "keep it simple"!

In general, fault-tolerant systems aim to provide a certain "level of service" when confronted by a failure. The expected level of service should be stated as part of the system architecture. Failures themselves are not black and white. In many cases, the system will experience a partial failure that may manifest as slower performance rather than causing a complete system stoppage. We will now examine a range of factors that can cause a failure to occur.

Types of Failure

Failures can be roughly classified into two groups: catastrophic and performance-related. A catastrophic failure is the complete failure of an element in the system. The most common such failure is the unexpected termination of an application process when an error in the software surfaces, and the application references invalid memory. Alternatively, such failures may be due to some unrecoverable logic failure, resulting in an internal inconsistency.

Other catastrophic failures can be caused by external events that are unrelated to the application, including power failure, host crash, network failure, or system overload.

In contrast to catastrophic failures, which generally stop the failed element from working at all, performance-related failures might simply be a slow response due to server or network overload. Common failures in CORBA distributed applications include:

- A process has terminated unexpectedly, due to a programming fault.
- It is not possible to establish a TCP connection (or an IIOP) connection between the client and server because there are no sockets available on the server.
- The underlying database is unavailable; the server cannot therefore complete the transactional request.
- The server is overloaded and is unable to respond to a particular client request.

We do not focus on programming errors here, although many of the approaches that we cover are relevant for them as well. For example, consider a client using an object. If the server mistakenly deletes this object, the client will receive a CORBA exception the next time it makes an invocation on the object. This is not a "fault" at the system level, since the server process is running and processing requests just fine. This is just an error, from which the client may or may not be able to recover.

We now discuss a number of techniques that can be used to detect failures in servers, and to notify other elements of the system. After all, detecting failure is of limited value unless a component capable of taking corrective action receives timely notification.

Detecting Failure

It may seem like a fairly obvious statement, but in order to recover from a failure, we need to have detected the failure in the first place. Failures can be detected in the client, in the application server, by an independent monitor, by the operating system or by one of the elements in the transport layer.

In some systems, a failure may be detected by an operator or user who is able to take immediate action to recover the application, or who can notify the system administrator or some other responsible party, such as a help desk. In other systems, the end user may never be aware of a failure in one of the underlying application components.

Since elements of a distributed system can be scattered across many machines, networks and even geographic boundaries, we cannot rely on a system administrator to manually monitor and repair systems. In fact, we should also avoid relying on end users to detect that something has failed. Instead, we need to consider fault tolerant systems that are both capable of monitoring their own health and of initiating remedial action.

Detecting Failures in the Transport Layer

By their very nature, components of a distributed system are deployed on nodes that are connected by some form of network. The network itself is composed of a number of hardware and software components, which may exhibit fault tolerant characteristics in their own right. For example, the TCP protocol, configured over IP and running on Ethernet cable, supports "guaranteed delivery," where the packet of data is guaranteed to reach the destination it is being sent to (assuming, of course, that it can establish a TCP connection between the initiator and the target host). A CORBA application which uses IIOP as its transport mechanism can therefore detect failures at the transport level.

In particular, some commercial ORB products can be configured to notify the application each time a connection to another CORBA program is opened or closed. For example, in Chapter 14, "Managing Server Resources," we discuss how a server may use this connection closure information to clean up resources allocated on behalf of the client. From a fault-tolerance perspective, a client may, for instance, react to this notification by selecting another server to address remote calls to.

Each application can choose how to react to this notification, for instance by terminating itself, propagating an error message to the end user, or attempting to continue processing. Some ORBs offer client-side support for transparently and automatically re-establishing a TCP connection when the next remote call is made. If the server in which the target object lives has crashed, the ORB may even ask the activation agent to restart the failed server, in which case a new connection would be established and the remote call will proceed, albeit with a short delay.[1]

It is worth examining what happens when a client crashes catastrophically, due to a machine failure or external intervention. When a connection terminates, the TCP layer sends a message to notify the other side of the connection about the closure. This could be a client terminating by crashing, or by a normal shutdown. In any case, when a process terminates, a TCP message is sent to the other end of the connection, to notify it that the connection is closing. However, if the client machine fails catastrophically, or is switched off before it has a chance to gracefully close the connection, TCP does not have the chance to send the "end of connection" message from the client machine to the remote host(s).

In this case, the remote machine will eventually notice that the TCP connection has been broken, as TCP makes use of "keep alive" messages if there is no transmission of data on a connection for a certain period of time. It is possible to configure (a) the timeout period that is used before these "keep alive" messages are sent and, (b) how long these "keep alive" probes will be sent before the lack of a response will terminate the connection. The default for the timeout period (a) is about 2 hours and "keep alive" (b) probes will be sent for about 8 minutes before a lack of a response assumes that the connection is broken. Therefore, if your server was to wait around for this two hours and eight minutes, the lack of a "keep alive" message would notify the server side that the connection had been closed. For this reason, TCP cannot always be relied upon to provide timely notification of client failures (although the keep alive timeouts can be modified). Note that this only occurs when the remote host or network fails. If the remote process fails (but the host and operating system continue working), the server will receive a timely notification of connection closure.

Using Monitor Processes to Detect Failure

Although servers may be started automatically by a CORBA activation agent, the agents in general do not perform any flexible or accessible type of monitoring of the ongoing health of auto-started servers.

Instead, the task of monitoring the health of servers is generally left to application components. Consider the selector pattern. It is the job of the selector to start and stop servers in accordance with the required load balancing strategy. In this case, the selector will monitor the health of

---

[1] Assuming that the newly launched server process contains or is able to activate the target object.

various application servers under its control. For example, if a selector determines that an application server has crashed, it might start a new one and re-assign all the clients of the failed server to the newly started one.

This behavior by the selector is an example of a very useful pattern in fault tolerant systems: a monitor process. A monitor is responsible for monitoring the health of a set of server processes. If the monitored processes fail, the monitor must be able to handle this in the appropriate manner.

Mechanisms used for monitoring the health of processes can be as simple as periodically invoking a simple "ping" method call on a prescribed interface implemented by the application server. If the monitor receives no reply after a few attempts, it can assume that the application server has either crashed or become unresponsive.

Another approach is to have the servers periodically emit "heartbeat" invocations on the monitor server. If the monitor detects no heartbeats in a given period of time, it can assume that the server is hung, or has terminated. If our ORB supports the connection closure callback mechanism, we can rely on this to provide us with nearly instant notification of server process termination. However, this approach will not help us when the server's host (or the network) fails as noted above. It also won't help determine when a server has hung, so systems typically do rely on periodic ping or heartbeat messages, in addition to connection closure detection.

Detecting whether or not a server has hung is a tricky area. If a server fails to respond to heartbeat messages, or fails to emit pings, the monitor must eventually assume that the server is hung, and take steps to recover. However, this is only a statistical guess, since the server may simply be temporarily busy with work, or the network may be temporarily down. When the server catches up with its load, or when the network rights itself, things will be back to normal. To avoid this problem (and to eliminate the hung process, in the case where it truly is hung), the monitor may terminate the server as part of its repair logic. If the server is not hung, but only busy, then we run the risk of mistakenly killing a viable server. There are no simple solutions to this problem.

Who Watches the Watchmen?

Whatever approaches to fault tolerance we use, we must be careful that we haven't simply pushed the problem somewhere else. We may very well succeed in eliminating our application servers as a single point of failure. For instance, we may have multiple application servers, watched over by a monitor program. If any of the servers fail, the monitor detects this and initiates recovery.

However, what happens if there is a failure in the monitor? Do we need a monitor for the monitor? What happens if *that* monitor fails? Starting down this path can too easily lead us to very complex solutions. One solution to this dilemma is to mix fault tolerance approaches, and couple this with some simplifying assumptions, such as assuming that multiple failures won't occur simultaneously.

Consider the case where the monitor process fails. By assuming that only one element will fail at a time, we can concentrate on recovery of the monitor, without worrying about the health of the application servers. For example, we could rely on the ORB's activation agent to restart the monitor, or we could use a pair of monitor processes. These topics are discussed in detail below, in "Application Server Strategies."

Notification of Failure

Although failure detection is an important consideration when building a fault-tolerant distributed application, it alone cannot provide the recoverability component that is crucial to fault-tolerant applications. Not all failures should be handled at the point the failure was originally detected. Sometimes we want to delegate responsibility for taking corrective action to some other process.

In particular, we want to be certain that we notify the appropriate element when a failure is detected. For instance, consider a selector that does not monitor the servers. This system relies on the clients to detect the failure of a server. When a client detects this, it contacts the selector, sending a message notifying it that a particular server has failed, and that it wants a replacement object.

Consider another case, with primary and backup servers. The clients would detect this failure, and automatically switch over to the backup server. The backup server would also notice this failure, and promote itself to primary. It may also notify an operator or an administrator of the failure, so that corrective action could be taken.

It is worth noting that the standard CORBA exception handling mechanism has not been discussed under failure detection or failure notification. For the most part, user exceptions are regarded as part of the application logic rather than as part of a fault-tolerant infrastructure. However, the propagation of an exception back to a client could be considered a fault notification mechanism, as the normal request lifecycle is interrupted.

Logging Services

Logging services are used to provide a passive notification of faults and failures. Simple cout and printf commands are usually embedded within the code to provide application-level information. In addition, catch clauses will often stream textual information to an output device of choice. This form of notification is passive because the creation of a log message does not nominate any target object and does not expect any reply.

Log files are often used to determine what went wrong after a failure has occurred, but are themselves unable to initiate corrective action at the time of failure. Although they are a useful debugging aid during the development process, they are generally not robust or structured enough to provide recoverability. (Certain transactional systems do use highly structured log files for this, however. They record the state of incomplete transactions, and when a failure is detected, the contents of the log file can be used to replay the transactional events).

For large application systems, a dedicated logging server can be created for the sole purpose of recording and collating various events that have occurred in the various application servers. The logging server will normally expose a *LogMessage* interface that comprises a number of oneway method calls. The oneway signature ensures that the client (which from the perspective of the logging server, is any of the real application servers) making a log entry will not be blocked, which would otherwise detrimentally impact performance.

In the scenario where a logging server is already employed, fault tolerant capabilities may be built on top of this by defining a fault monitor process that reads the log file and initiates corrective action when necessary. Assuming that the log file is in a structured, parsable format, this architecture would allow existing non-fault tolerant applications to be extended to support some level of fault tolerance in a simple non-invasive way.

Fault Tolerance and Clients

CORBA clients play an important role in fault-tolerant solutions. Many times, they are the element that is first exposed to a failure. As such, they can be in the best position to start the recovery process. For example, if a system is using the selector pattern, clients would typically contact the selector in the event of a server failure. The selector would be responsible for redirecting the client to another server, which could service it. The behavior expected from a client depends on the fault tolerance approach taken. When we discuss solutions below, we also cover the client's role in each case.

Current CORBA Support for Fault Tolerance

CORBA does not inherently support reliability; that is, CORBA-enabled applications will not behave in a predictable manner when partial failures occur. The CORBA specification does provide a partial solution by relying on the detection and recovery features of the transport layer (most commonly IIOP) and through support for activation transparency using basic ORB services such as BOA and POA.

Most commercial ORB vendors also implement a higher-level of location transparency and recovery, although these are typically not sufficient for building enterprise applications. In this section, we examine the current support for fault tolerant behavior in commercially available ORBs. At the end of this chapter, we discuss forthcoming support for fault tolerance with CORBA.

ORB Support

Commercially available ORBs provide their degree of fault tolerance through information stored in object references, and also provide some level of recoverability of the activation agent.

Location Transparency

Object references obtained by clients typically direct them not to the application server, but to the ORB activation agent on the server's host. This has two advantages. First, the server does not have to be running all the time—the activation agent can launch the server process only when a client needs it. The client first contacts the activation agent, which launches the server and redirects the client to the application server. Second, in the case of server process termination, the client ORB runtime can fall back on the original information in the object reference, and contact the activation agent (which can relaunch the server). This provides some level of fault tolerance, and is generally implemented so that it is transparent to the client application. That is, some level of fault tolerant behavior is achieved with no additional coding effort on behalf of the client.

However, this approach does have its limits. First, it is inherently limited to a single host. If that host were to fail, the client would not be able to recover. Also, it does not address the recoverability of any server state. Simply relaunching the server will not solve the problem if the client's reference is to a transient object—the client application will still receive a CORBA system exception. Also, it may not be appropriate for the activation agent to launch servers, particularly if specialized load balancing solutions with concentrators or selectors are used.

Recoverability of the Activation Agent

Some commercial ORBs have built-in support for recoverability of the activation agent itself. As the activation agent generally represents a single point of failure and as there is usually only one per host, it is important for the agent to be able to recover from a crash or other serious failure. Some activation agents can be configured to persistently log their state, so that in the event of a failure, the state can be recovered. But what detects that the activation agent has crashed? Furthermore, what is responsible for restarting the agent? On some operating systems, it is possible to embed the agent's launch command within a "fault tolerant" script—should the agent fail and the process exit for any reason, the script would simply restart it immediately. Alternatively, it would be possible to write a monitor that was responsible for checking the health of the agent. In the event of a failure or slow access, the monitor can take corrective action.

Ideally, we would be able to configure our system such that we don't rely on the activation agent for any dynamic information. For instance, we may be able to configure our servers to always listen on predefined port numbers for incoming client connections. This will allow our system to run even if the activation agent were to fail, since clients will be able to open connections directly to the servers.

Fault Tolerance and Replication

Because there is currently limited support in the CORBA specification for building fault-tolerant applications, the task of providing these services falls upon the application programmer. There is no standardized mechanism by which applications can convey their reliability requirements to the ORB. Since much of a system's fault-tolerant behavior is inherent in its design, an application's fault-tolerant requirements must be considered when it is designed.

Application State: Replication of Servers and Databases

The key to fault tolerance is the replication of the application state. If this can be accomplished, then the system will be fault tolerant. The application state may be stored in one or more application server processes, in one more databases, or in both. Therefore, in order to make our systems fault tolerant, we must replicate our servers, our databases, or both.

Note that these replicas do not necessarily have to be simultaneously active or synchronized. For example, we may choose to replicate our servers over time. Rather than having two server processes run simultaneously, we can have one process running that persistently logs its state. If this process fails, a new server process can be started that recovers the state from the log. Likewise, replicating state across databases does not necessarily imply synchronous updates to the databases; database replication mechanisms can introduce a lag between updates. The remainder of this chapter discusses such approaches to fault tolerance in CORBA systems, which vary in their speed, effectiveness, and difficulty of implementation. However, they all attempt to accomplish the same goal.

Application Server Strategies

We generally classify the approaches to fault tolerance into three types, termed *cold*, *warm*, and *hot*. These terms refer not to temperature, but to the degree of readiness of the backup component. (We admit that these terms make much more sense when applied to machinery rather than software). In a cold approach, the backup component is only launched when failure of the original component is detected. Thus, there is a perhaps significant delay before the component is available—MTTR can be relatively long. This is like the spare tire in Jason's car—it's kept in the trunk until one of the regular tires gets a flat. Then he stops the car, and spend 20 minutes changing the tire. After that, he can continue driving.

With a hot approach, the replicated components run alongside one another, all servers handling all client requests. This naturally requires synchronization of any state. Failure of one server is nearly invisible to clients, since their requests are handled by all servers concurrently. With this approach, a client can switch to another server without any latency—the MTTR is essentially zero. This approach is like the parallel pairs of tires on Dirk's tractor-trailer. Even if one tire fails, he can keep driving without stopping.

The warm approach lies in between these two. A backup server runs alongside the primary server, ready to take over if it detects a failure in the primary. The backup server should have its state synchronized with that of the primary server, so that in the event of a failure there is no loss of state. (This also serves to reduce the MTTR). Note that with the warm approach, the client communitcates only with the primary server until a failure occurs.[2] This is like the set of training wheels on Perry's bicycle, which are always there, but normally not used. Only if the main wheels fail to hold him upright will the training wheels be used, albeit with a slight wobble before they hold him up. (Okay, we admit that Perry does not have training wheels on his bicycle, but it's a good analogy.)

The diagrams below illustrate the three approaches to replication. The diagrams for the cold and warm approaches show a component named the *Fault Tolerance Agent* (FT Agent). Although a logically separate entity, this may actually be part of the client, part of the server, or part of some other system element such as the activation agent, or a selector. We'll give concrete examples of FT Agents when we discuss scenarios, below.

Cold Backup

The cold backup approach is shown in Figure 16.1. As discussed above, this model waits until a failure is detected before launching a new server. The new server must be started, and then recover the application's state, before it can begin processing requests from clients. That is, the MTTR consists of the time it takes to notice that a failure has occurred, plus the cost of launching a new process, plus the amount of time it takes the server to recover its state. This approach is the most costly, in terms of performance, of the three fault tolerance solutions. The benefit of this approach is its relative simplicity.

With stateless servers, this approach can be implemented "out of the box" with most ORBs. In this case, the FT Agent role is performed by the ORB's activation agent. When a client program detects a failure in a server, it will contact the activation agent, which will automatically launch a new instance of the server, essentially returning a new object reference to the client. The client application then uses this new object. With most ORBs, this can be accomplished transparently to the client application. If the server relies on late binding, then in fact there is no distinct step of recover-

---

[2] The warm approach is frequently used with server pairs, hence our use of the terms *primary* and *backup*. Actually, this approach can be used with any number of servers.

Figure 16.1 Cold replication model

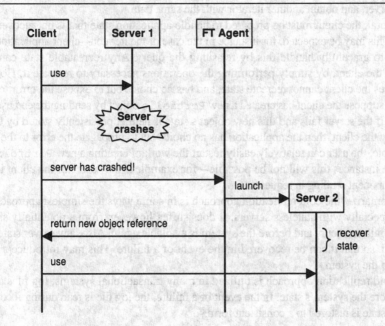

ing state: the server's state consists only of the set of target objects active, and these can be dynamically activated on demand.

If, however, the server is stateful, then it must recover its state. This is typically done via a checkpointing approach. While the original server is running, it writes its state to some persistent storage (termed a "checkpoint file," although it is likely to actually be implemented with a database). This file must be structured in a way so that if the server were to fail, a later server would be able to read this file and recover the server's state. This checkpoint file may or may not contain the server's complete state, due to a time lag or a design decision, as discussed below. When the second server is started by the FT Agent, it reads this checkpoint file and recovers the state of the original server at the time of the failure. After this, it is ready to begin processing client requests. This recovery period may be significant, which is one of the potential downsides of this approach.

Another potential problem is that the primary server, in addition to performing work on behalf of clients, also has to continually update this checkpoint file. This will naturally impose a performance penalty on the server.

The checkpoint file, in fact, may not contain the original server's complete state. For instance, the server may have crashed before it was able to persistently store its latest state. Or, we as system designers may have decided not to store certain types of information in the checkpoint file. For instance, we may not want to store any information about transient iterator objects that the clients use to query the database, for two reasons. First, these objects may have considerable state associated with them, which would take a lot of time to write to and read from the checkpoint file. Second, these objects are easily re-creatable. The client application could simply reissue the same query in the new server, and obtain another iterator with the same data.

In general, the client must be prepared to handle application state that is not recovered in the new server. This may be expected, for instance in the case of the iterator—client applications should be prepared to gracefully handle this by reissuing the query. Any recreatable state can handled smoothly by the client, by simply performing the operations necessary to recreate it. However, in some instances the client cannot recreate state, and has no choice but to expose the error to the user. For instance, suppose the client has created a new `Portfolio` object by sending the end user's name and address. If the server fails and this new object's state is neither persistently stored by the server nor cached by the client, then the application has no choice but to propagate the error to the end user. In this example, the user can relatively easily restart the work of creating a new `Portfolio`. However, in some instances this will not be possible—for example if the "user" of the client is another CORBA component sending in requests.

To summarize, the cold replication approach is in some ways the simplest approach to fault tolerance, especially with stateless servers. It does suffer, however, from a potentially significant delay after a failure occurs and before the system is available again. Also, any server state must be checkpointed, so that it can be recovered in the event of a failure. This may introduce significant complexity in the system.

The cold replication approach is utilized in many transactional systems; log files are maintained that store the system's state. In the event of a failure, the log file is read during recovery, and the system's state is restored to a consistent form.

Recovering from a Failure

With the cold start approach, we are essentially implementing recoverable servers, which can restore their state upon restart. The difficulty lies in ensuring that there is no loss of state due to a failure. This is an extremely difficult problem to solve. In general, servers that require bulletproof behavior should be made stateless and transactional.

Applicability

The cold start approach is applicable in many situations. Even the simplest CORBA client-server architecture can be made fault tolerant by using the built-in relaunch features available in ORBs. As long as the application is stateless, or can restore its state through a combination of checkpointing and recreation, then this solution can usefully be applied. This is also applicable for more complex architectures, such as the selector and concentrators patterns. With a selector, the client still notices that the server has terminated, but contacts the selector rather than the ORB activation agent. That is, the selector is the FT Agent. With the concentrator approach, it is the concentrator (not the client) that notices that a failure has occurred, and that causes the replacement server to be launched.

Warm Standby

The warm standby model is illustrated in Figure 16.2. With this approach, a backup server is always running alongside the main (primary) server.[3] The main server processes all client requests,

---

[3] There may actually be more than one backup server running, but for simplicity we discus a single backup server. This is the classic "'process pair" approach to fault tolerance.

Figure 16.2 Warm standby model

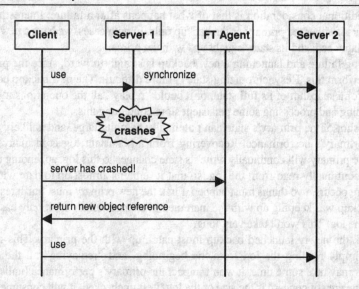

and is also responsible for synchronizing its state with the backup server. In the event of a failure in the primary, the backup server is promoted to the primary, and begins processing client requests. It typically also starts another process to act as the new backup, in the event that this primary process fails in the future.

This approach has the benefit of a relatively small MTTR. Since the backup server is always running, and its state is synchronized with the primary, the only delays encountered are the detection of the failure, and the overhead involved in the redirection by the FT Agent. Unlike the cold approach, clients do not have to wait for a new server process to start up and recover its state. The backup process is always running, and the cost of state synchronization is paid in small bits over the lifetime of the system, rather than in one large chunk when a failure occurs.

As expected, this approach is straightforward to accomplish with stateless servers. Since there is no state to synchronize, the only potential difficulty is the redirection of the client to the new primary server. With state, naturally, this approach is more interesting.

The primary server has to somehow synchronize its state with the backup server. This may be done synchronously, with blocking CORBA invocations, or asynchronously, with oneway calls. Another particularly useful approach is to use a persistent storage mechanism (such as a persistent queue) to transfer the state. This approach is especially helpful when recovering from a failure, explained below.

The primary may fully synchronize its state with the backup, or it may synchronize only part of its state. For instance, easily recreatable elements (such as iterators) may not be synchronized; the system will instead rely on client applications to reissue the operation to create the iterator. There may also be a lag before server state is replicated in the backup, which may cause a delay (or a loss of state) in the event of a failure. As usual, clients must be defensively programmed to handle this gracefully.

Recovering from a Failure

One additional consideration is that of what happens after a failure. Interestingly, the same problem occurs if either the primary or the backup fails. In both cases, we have a new backup server that must be launched, and its state "caught up" with the primary.

Detecting failure and launching a new backup is straightforward, since the primary and FT Agent can perform this. Resynchronizing state is more difficult. The new backup could either ask the primary for a snapshot of its full state, or it could "replay" all the operations made on the primary, by reading and processing some persistent store containing this.

A snapshot of the primary's state can potentially be quite large, and is likely to temporarily impact the primary's performance. Recovering from a persistent log is in many ways a better approach. The primary will continually write its state changes to this log, appending to the end. The backup will continually read from the log, so that it remains almost up to date with the primary. When a failure occurs, two things must happen. First, the new primary must finish restoring its state. Since the backup was keeping up with the incremental changes all along, it only has to process the very end of the log. This won't take very long.

Second, the newly launched backup must catch up with the primary. This can be accomplished by simply reading the log from the beginning, and "replaying" all the state changes. Although this may take some time, it won't impact the primary's performance (unlike the snapshot approach). One area of concern is the size of the log. Left unchecked, it will consume large amounts of storage and cause excessively long playback times during recovery. Therefore, it must be purged periodically, in a manner appropriate to the environment and data contained in it. For instance, the log may be purged daily at midnight, when the whole system is shutdown and restarted. Or, when the log file crosses a size threshold, the primary could write a snapshot of its state to a new log, and begin appending any further changes to that one. The backup would likewise switch to reading from the end of the new log, and the old log could be deleted. In the event of a failure, the server recovering state would begin by reading the snapshot, then applying the changes appended after that. This approach will prevent arbitrarily large logs, at the cost of having the primary occasionally write a snapshot of its state to the new log.

Applicability

The warm replication approach is useful when clients need to rapidly switch to a backup server in the event of a failure. It can be used with the selector or concentrator patterns, as well as with a client-side multiproxy. Since primary and backup are application-level concepts, the ORB activation agent is not involved in this approach.

The primary and backup are in constant communication (to synchronize state). The key issues are, of course, the synchronization of application state, and the subsequent recovery (in the new backup process) after a failure. If these can be solved in an efficient manner, this approach can be effectively applied.

Hot Standby

The hot standby approach consists of two or more redundant servers that each receive and process every client request. In effect, we have created an "object group" in which multiple objects concurrently process each request. Each server will keep its own state updated, which means that the order in which requests arrive and are processed by the servers must be preserved. When a failure occurs in one of the servers, the remaining replicas continue to operate without the failed replica. Thus, the MTTR is negligible as the other running replicas simply continue to process the request. This approach is illustrated in Figure 16.3.

Notice that there is no explicit FT Agent in Figure 16.3. Because all client requests are delegated to all servers, there is no need for an agent, since the client never switches servers—it is always using all available servers. Server state is implicitly synchronized between all servers, since they all begin with the same state, and all process the same requests. These servers will often interact with distinct databases, since having multiple servers perform the same updates on a single database is likely to lead to incorrect results. (Multiple read-only operations on a single database will not lead to inconsistent results.)

There are two important considerations with the hot standby approach—request ordering and replies. It is essential that all servers perform the requests in exactly the same order. Failure to do so could lead to inconsistent state between servers. For example, consider a bank account with $500 in it. Two requests arrive (from two different clients) withdrawing money from the account, one asking for $100, the other asking for $450. Clearly, only one of these two operations will be successful; the other will return to the caller indicating insufficient funds. However, if two servers process these requests in different orders, one server can end up with an account that has a $400 balance, while another server's account has $50. Ensuring consistent ordering naturally imposes some serialization on the server, which can degrade performance.

The other issue is the reply from the request. Since multiple servers process each request, multiple replies will be returned. Depending on the system's design, either the client must be able to handle multiple results from a single request, or an intermediate process (such as a concentrator) must filter all replies but one.

Now, we illustrate the hot standby model in two brief examples, one that uses the standard IIOP communication protocol, and another which utilizes a multicast protocol.

Figure 16.3 Hot standby model

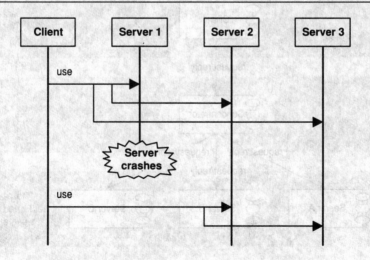

An Object Group Using a Concentrator

The hot standby approach can be used to provide an object group, via the concentrator pattern. This is illustrated in Figure 16.4. We discussed the concentrator earlier, in Chapter 15, "Load Balancing," where it was described as a request-forwarder. It received a request from the client and forwarded the request to one of the servers, ideally the least-loaded one.

In contrast, the concentrator acting as an object group server forwards the request to *all* members of the object group. The behavior of the object group is transparent to the client. From the client's perspective, it simply makes a normal blocking call to a server from which its expects a reply.

The concentrator can perform the important tasks of request ordering and reply filtering. Since all requests go through the concentrator, it can ensure that all servers receive all requests in the same order—for instance, by serializing the requests. The concentrator also receives all the replies in response to each replicated request, so it can simply return the first one received to the client, and discard the rest.

Object groups combine all the benefits of the concentrator model for load balancing with additional reliability and automatic failover capability. Note that the concentrator itself still represents a single point of failure, and so multiple concentrators may actually be instantiated to further enhance fault tolerance.

Multicast Solutions

The hot standby approach can be implemented using a multicast approach, in which a client sends requests directly to multiple servers. There is no need for an intermediate concentrator to fan out the request—a multicast-based approach is clearly more efficient in this regard. Such an architecture is illustrated in Figure 16.5. Like the object group approach, each of these servers indepen-

Figure 16.4   Object group model

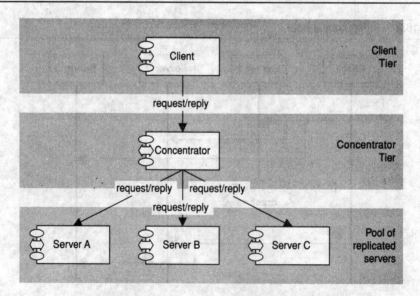

Figure 16.5 Hot Replication with multicast

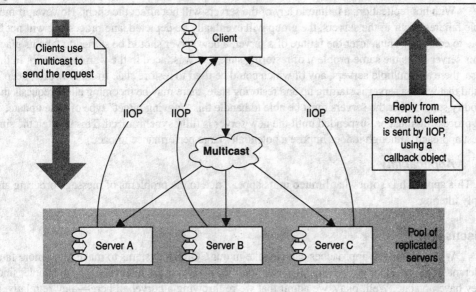

dently processes each request. In effect, we have created multiple parallel processing channels where each channel performs the same task.

The same difficult issues of request ordering and replies are present with this approach as well. Because clients communicate directly with servers, there is no central mechanism such as the concentrator that could serialize requests. If all the servers are on a single subnet, they will all receive the requests in the same order, at the network card level. However, there are a number of software layers between the card and the application, such as the network stack, the operating system, and the ORB. Any of these elements could be multithreaded, and could cause near-simultaneous multicast messages to be delivered to different servers applications in different orders. If the servers are deployed over multiple subnets, then the problem is compounded, since the multicast message must be forwarded by a router, which introduces a further delay and increases the chance of inconsistent message processing between servers.

Clients will typically want to receive a reply to their requests. How can this be done? Multicast could be used, in which case all nodes on the network would receive the reply. The system would have to be designed so that applications other than the originating client would ignore the results. This could be accomplished, for instance, by embedding a client ID in each of the replies. Another approach, which is shown in Figure 16.5, uses an IIOP connection between each server and client. Clients pass in references to callback objects, which are used by the servers to send the reply, when the operation has completed. The client will need to set up an event loop to poll for incoming replies and must also be able to handle multiple replies to the same request. In practice, the combination of a multicast request and a unicast reply works well for applications whose client communication model is "Someone, anyone, please answer my request!" Of course, in a system with many clients, this approach can cause servers to have too many TCP/IP connections open.

Recovering from a Failure

With hot replication, a failure in any of the servers will not affect the client. However, if multiple failures occur in the servers, the group will eventually be depleted, and processing will not be able to continue. Thus, after the failure of a server, a new server should be started to take its place. This server faces the same problem of restoring state that was faced in the warm approach. In this case, there are multiple servers, any of which could be used to restore state from. However, keep in mind that while a server is starting up and restoring state, there may be incoming client requests that modify state. Either the servers must be able to handle this "moving target" type of state update, or all processing must be suspended until the new server is fully synchronized. This is often the simplest approach, although it does impose a potentially large performance impact.

Applicability

This approach is somewhat limited in its appeal, due to the problems of message ordering and reply filtering.

Discussion

What reasonable approaches can we take in our CORBA systems to make them more fault tolerant? First, consider the servers. Stateless application servers are relatively easy to handle, since they have no state. Well, okay, we admit that we're throwing a curveball here—they're relatively easy to handle at the application level, since we have pushed all the complexity associated with state down to the database level.

One approach with stateless servers is to simply assume a completely reliable database. In some cases, it may be acceptable for the application to be down when the database is down. In others, it will not be, and some form of database replication will have to be applied.

Servers with state are more interesting. Their state must be replicated across processes, over time. That is, if a server process fails, a client *must* be able to contact another server process that contains the same state. If it cannot, then our system is not fault tolerant. The process that our client switches over to may have been running in parallel with the original server process, or it may only be launched after the original failure is detected. The approaches discussed previously differ in whether more than one application server is running, and how quickly the server can restore the application state, but they all accomplish the same goal.

Databases are the other area of focus. We should do all we can to ensure that our database remains operational, by purchasing the appropriate hardware and software. If we need to continue processing even if a database failure occurs, we must replicate the database. Approaches to this are described in the case study, next.

Case Study—A High-Availability CORBA System

Throughout this chapter we have focused on the factors that affect the availability and performance of a distributed application system and on some of the techniques that can be used to meet these requirements. Implicitly, we strive to maximize the MTBF (Mean Time Between Failures) and at the same time minimize the MTTR (Mean Time To Recovery).

High availability (HA) systems, often referred to as *24 × 7* systems, are so critical to an organization that a complete break in service cannot be tolerated. In general, HA systems require a special combination of hardware, network and software to realize this requirement. In this section, we describe how aspects of load balancing, object location, fault tolerance, and OTS can be combined to provide an HA capability. We explore such a system using the warm standby approach to fault tolerance.

Introduction

Consider the scenario depicted in Figure 16.6. A number of clients require this system's services.[4] With the warm replication model, all requests are sent to the primary server, although a warm backup is on hand. In fact, all clients store object references to both the primary and the backup servers. The backup replica receives continual state updates from the primary via CORBA invocations. Every time the primary replica changes its state, it propagates that state to the backup. The backup also monitors the primary—if it has not received any updates from the primary in a while (say 5 seconds), it begins pinging the primary by making regular method invocations on it. This permits the backup to monitor the primary efficiently in both busy and idle environments. If the backup detects that the primary has failed (terminated) it will promote itself to be the new primary. If it determines that the primary has become unresponsive, it will terminate the primary process and promote itself. (This is discussed further in the section entitled "Have We Achieved High Availability?")

Figure 16.6   High availability using warm standby

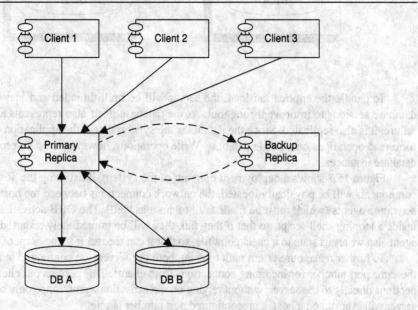

---

[4] Note that the clients depicted here might actually represent an intermediate set of cooperating servers that have been created to manage the overall load.

Figure 16.7   Deployment diagram

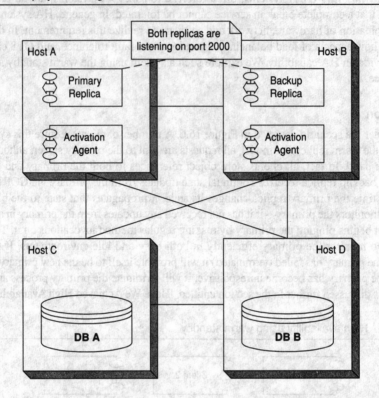

To handle the application load, the server will be multithreaded and may establish many database sessions to improve throughput. As the database itself also represents a single point of failure, it is also replicated. Since the databases are synchronized, the application can simply perform read operations on a single database. Write operations, however, must be propagated to both database instances.

Figure 16.7 shows a deployment diagram of the system, illustrating the hosts on which the components will be physically located, the network connections between the hosts, and the ORB activation agents (which must be made fault tolerant as well). The ORB activation agents are run inside a looping shell script, so that if they fail, they will be immediately restarted. The activation agent also writes its state to a checkpoint file, so that it can recover it in the event of a failure.

To further make our system fault tolerant, both our servers are configured to always listen on the same port number for incoming connections from clients. This permits our clients to open connections directly to the server, without relying on the activation agent. Since only one instance of a server will ever run on a host, a preconfigured port number is safe.

Database Replication

Figure 16.8 shows two different ways by which updates can be propagated between databases. Method (a) updates both databases within the context of a single transaction, coordinated by a 2-phase commit mechanism (possibly using OTS). If one of the databases fails to commit the transaction, the work will be rolled back in the other database as well. The application will have to fall back into single-database mode, and redo the work on the remaining database. All subsequent updates will only be performed on the operational database.

With method (b), the application normally interacts only with the main database, and relies on a database replication mechanism to propagate any updates. This is the simplest approach from an application perspective, since the server is only ever interacting with a single database. However, recall our discussion of database replication in Chapter 15, "Load Balancing." This replication may either be synchronous (in which the cost of a distributed 2PC is incurred), or asynchronous, which introduces a delay between updates in DB A and the corresponding update in DB B. This is explored further below, when we discuss handling database failures.

Have We Achieved High Availability?

Is the basic design outlined here robust enough to satisfy the requirements of a true 24×7 HA system? To answer this question, we consider the set of conditions that could cause the application to fail either completely or partially.

Figure 16.8 Database replication models

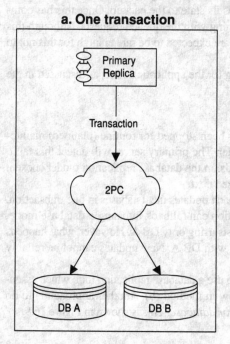
a. One transaction

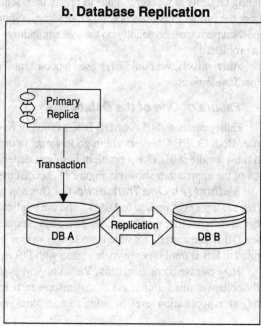
b. Database Replication

Failure of the Primary CORBA Server: Process Termination

The primary server has a fault, and has crashed. Both underlying databases are in good working order. The backup server will detect the failure of the primary, and promote itself to primary. All the clients already have object references to the backup, so they can quickly switch over to it. The backup had its state synchronized by the primary, so it is also ready to process requests. In short, the system can almost immediately begin processing client requests. Note that the new backup has to synchronize its state somehow, which may delay the new primary from servicing client requests. This is discussed below.

Failure of the Primary CORBA Server: Process Freeze

If the primary server has frozen, the backup will detect this. It must terminate the primary, promote itself to be the new primary, and launch a new backup on the other server's host. The activation agent has a role to play in this case. The backup will contact the activation agent, and tell it to terminate the frozen process. Then, it will tell it to re-launch the server process, which will automatically come up as a backup.

Recover from Failure of the Primary CORBA Server / Failure of the Backup CORBA Server

Both these cases are the same—a new backup server is launched by the primary (this may be the original primary, or the recently promoted primary). This new backup must somehow synchronize its state from the primary. In this example, we choose to suspend the processing of any new client requests while the state transfer completes. That is, the backup contacts the primary, and asks for a snapshot of its state. The primary queues up any new incoming client requests, waits for all pending requests in worker threads to finish, then sends its state to the backup. Once this has completed, the primary resumes normal processing, beginning with the queued requests. Although this imposes a performance penalty on the system, failures are expected to be rare enough for this not to be a problem.

Alternatively, we could have used a persistent log for the application state, as discussed in the *Warm Standby* section.

Failure of One of the Databases

Either database DB A or DB B has failed or has been stopped for routine (planned) maintenance. Both CORBA servers are in good working order. The primary server will detect this fault, and must handle it. How this problem is solved depends on the database replication model chosen. Each of the approaches shown in Figure 16.8 is discussed next.

Method (a): One Transaction. This approach updates the databases in one transaction. If (for example) the update to DB B fails, the application can fallback into single-database mode, notify an administrator, and continue processing requests using only DB A. However, what happens when DB B is restored? Its state is no longer in synch with DB A. New updates cannot be reliably applied to DB B until it is re-synchronized with DB A.

How can we accomplish this? Well, one way is to use a database replication tool, which essentially collapses this failure case to that discussed below in method (b). Another approach is to do things at an application level, by using an additional *error database*. This is shown in Figure 16.9.

Figure 16.9   Database replication with error databases

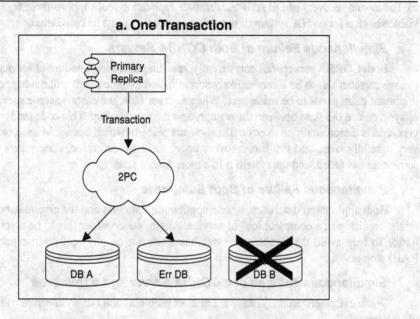

a. One Transaction

When DB B is down, the primary writes all the changes to DB A and to the error database. Often, the Error database is not a full production database; rather than performing the actual updates on it, the primary instead stores information *about the updates being performed*. This permits a later "playback" of these updates against DB B when it is restored. Once the playback has completed, DB B has caught up with DB A, and the primary can then begin directing new updates to DB B, rather than the Error DB. The advantage of synchronizing DB B from the Error DB rather than DB A is that it will typically be more efficient to simply replay a sequence of update operations than it will be to resynchronize an entire production database from DB A to DB B.

Method (b): Database Replication.   The viability of this solution is highly dependent on the capabilities of the underlying database replication mechanism, as well as the replication model chosen. Consider the case where database DB B fails. The primary server must be able to continue operating normally, since DB A is still functioning. However, synchronous database replication typically propagates updates to both databases within a single transaction. If DB B is down, this will cause the update on DB A to also fail. This is unacceptable in our environment. We like synchronous database replication since the replicas are kept in tight synchronization, but we must be able to fall back to a single-database mode in the event of a failure in DB B. When DB B is eventually restored, it must of course be able to "catch up" with DB A.

If database DB A fails, our application must be able to detect this, and smoothly switch over and use DB B in single-database mode. Ideally, the replication mechanism will permit all these things to occur. For instance, it should support synchronous replication, but permit an application to operate in single-database mode in the event of a failure. It must support asynchronous "catch-up" when a failed database has restarted, with a switch to synchronous replication when that has completed. And, it must be able to switch between replicating from DB A to DB B, to the reverse after the failure and recovery of DB A. If our database replication tool supports these features, it will be a viable solution for an HA system. If not, other approaches must be considered.

Simultaneous Failure of Both CORBA Servers

Both CORBA servers fail concurrently, resulting in a complete loss of service. In this example, we consider this to be a very unlikely scenario, and assume that it will not happen. However, an important point needs to be made here. When a server fails, we exercise some special-case code to re-synchronize the state between the primary and the new backup. This code tends to be very complex, and is therefore prone to error. This is worst place in which our application can fail! We must very carefully write and test this recovery code, since by definition, it only gets executed when something has failed, and the system is in a more fragile state.

Simultaneous Failure of Both Databases

Both application databases, or one application database and the error database fail concurrently, resulting in a complete loss of service. Again, we consider this to be a very unlikely scenario. To help avoid this problem the databases are run on physically separate machines, with RAID storage.

Simultaneous Failures of a CORBA Server and a Database

While extremely unlikely, these are distinct problems and our architecture will be able to handle this gracefully.

Catastrophic Network Failure

The network connecting clients to servers or servers to databases has failed in such a way that no interprocess communication is possible, resulting in a complete system failure. We utilize appropriate hardware and software to eliminate this as a concern. Our servers are run on machines contained in a physically isolated computer room with restricted access. If we wish, we could use redundant network connections between hosts (using multi-homed hosts, or a Virtual LAN utilizing multiple pathways between hosts), to further reduce the chance of this type of failure.

Process Degradation

Our servers were written by a team of three programmers, and use a number of home-grown and third party tools, including ORB, OTS, database access library, threading package, object-oriented database access wrapper, and STL. This is not an unusual combination for a complex server. Our developers are not perfect, nor are the developers at the software vendors from whom we purchased tools. This is why we're building this architecture in the first place. However, failure can manifest itself in different ways. Besides catastrophic failures (which we can handle) our servers are also likely to have resource leaks. As our servers run, their process size will increase, as memory is leaked. Allowing this to continue unabated is a poor plan—the server will increase in size, causing it (and other processes on the same host) to run more slowly. Eventually, it is likely to fail catastrophically, due to resource exhaustion.

We adopt a more defensive approach, and plan to gracefully recycle our servers at particular times. For example, we may choose to have the entire system shut itself down and restart at midnight every night, assuming it is idle at that point. Alternatively we may choose to have the primary server shut itself down regularly (say every 90 minutes), gracefully transferring control to the backup. This ensures that no server process will run for more than 3 hours, reducing the potential for resource leaks to have an adverse impact.

Future CORBA Support for Fault Tolerance

At the time of this writing, the OMG had received four initial submissions in response to its Fault Tolerance Request For Proposal. The submissions vary considerably in their approach and depth of coverage. In this section we look at some of the key elements of each submission and how they might apply to the patterns described in this chapter.

The submission from Ericsson, IONA Technologies, and Nortel Networks places considerable emphasis on making small changes to the IIOP specification that would improve its fault tolerant capability: "the submission proposes changes to IIOP that will provide clients with transparency to processor and network failures in an entity group."[5] The key change proposed to IIOP is the extension of the support for multiple IIOP profiles to include direct support for a TAG_ALTERNATE_IIOP_ADDRESS as an integral part of a tagged profile. Instead of repeating the entire profile for each IOR in the IIOP address, the use of tagged alternate IIOP addresses allows the key IP Address and port number components to be changed without duplicating all the other (unchanged) pieces.

With this approach, configuration of the groups of replicas is done at the POA level. That is, the POA is configured with a POA policy that tells the ORB the other host addresses that might be able to respond to this request. This proposal does not extend CORBA to include database interaction, recoverability or notification.

In contrast, the submission from Oracle Corporation proposes the use of object groups, coupled with the LOCATION_FORWARD protocol of IIOP. It does not use the hot standby model because of the substantial computing resources required to implement multiple parallel processing streams. Similarly, it does not address the issue of *servant transparency*, whereby a replicated object's implementation is aware of the replication and is able to synchronize with the other replicas. In effect, the Oracle proposal is more closely aligned with the warm standby model discussed in previous sections. However, the submission does formalize the notion of a *replication coordinator* and a *logger* to manage group creation, membership, group activation and deactivation, as well as interoperability between replicas supplied by different vendors.

One of the more complete submissions from Inprise Corporation, TIBCO Inc., and Lucent Technologies (among others) proposes a set of IDL interfaces for managing replicas, notifying a client of a change in servant IOR, and coordinating recovery after a failure has occurred. This proposal also includes extensions to IIOP consistent with those of the Ericsson proposal and describes how the notion of object groups can be implemented by the CORBA naming service to provide client-controlled failover (switching from a failed server to a functioning one).

Let's examine the Ericsson proposal in more detail. This proposal recommends extending the IIOP protocol to support fault tolerance. If an IOR can contain more than one IP address/ hostname combination, then a client ORB that detects a failure using one of these pairs can transparently swap

---

[5] Ericsson, IONA Technologies, Nortel Networks, *Fault Tolerant CORBA Initial Submissions,* October 1998, Object Management Group, orbos/98-10-10, pp. 2–10.

across to the other without any further intervention from either the client application or any other part of the system. Note the similarity between this approach and the multiproxy, which essentially accomplishes the same thing at an application level.

Figure 16.10 illustrates how such a mechanism might work. There are two replica servers, each of which has an instance of a particular servant object. When the servers register their respective objects with the CORBA naming service (which the client will use to locate the objects later), they will use a POA policy to instruct the ORB to create a "tagged internet IOR"; the IOR that is associated with a name in the naming service will contain two tagged IIOP profiles, instead of the usual one. When the client resolves a name and creates a proxy, the IOR embedded within the proxy will contain both IOR components. Normal invocations are sent to the object identified by the TAG_INTERNET_IOP profile. If an error is detected, the client-side ORB will automatically reissue the remote call to the object identified by the first of the TAG_ALTERNATE_IIOP_ADDRESS. In this context, failure consists of:

- The destination address is unreachable
- There is no process listening for requests at that address
- No object with the corresponding key exists at that address

Figure 16.10   Multiple profiles in IIOP

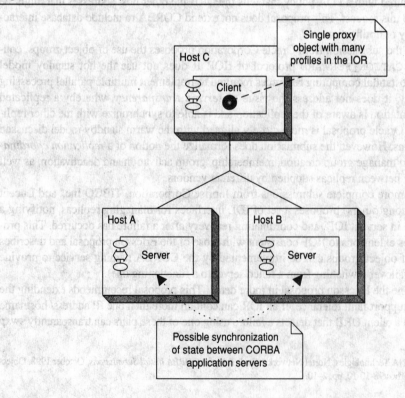

Although this mechanism allows clients to automatically and transparently failover to use a "backup" object, it does not provide a means for the server community to recover. Unless a monitor process, or heartbeat, is used, the administrator of the servers may never be notified of the failure. However, assuming the failure is detected and a restart initiated, the server would, as part of its startup procedure, re-register its entry-point objects with the naming service, thus refreshing the IOR for this profile in the naming service. New clients would simply start using the newly restarted server when they resolved the name to an IOR.

This technique attempts to provide fault tolerant behavior without making huge changes to the basic IIOP specification. In fact, most of the pieces of the architecture, including multiple IOR profiles, are already available in IIOP. An IOR is essentially composed of an object type and a number of IOR profiles. Each IOR profile contains an id and a profile body. In turn, each IIOP profile body contains attributes like IIOP version, host, port and object key. In theory, at least, it would be possible to store more than one IP Address/ hostname in an IOR. The interoperability specification states that "Unless otherwise specified in the definition of a particular profile, multiple profiles with the same profile tag may be included in an IOR." So, if we simply replaced the normal IIOP profile with a "tagged" profile, the problem would be solved without making any changes to the existing IIOP specification.

Unfortunately, the specification neglects to say what the client-side ORB should do with such a complex IOR. Not all commercial ORB's will process multiple profiles in the same way. The submission from Ericsson, IONA Technologies, and Nortel Networks proposes a small change to the IIOP specification which will provide support for tagged components without the need to duplicate the entire profile. In addition, it clearly states how a client-ORB should interpret the tagged components to facilitate failover. Finally, the submission discusses a number of ways in which the object groups can be configured and managed.

Summary

It is clear from topics discussed in this chapter that the design of fault-tolerant systems is not trivial. This is the case whether we are using CORBA or not. However, as CORBA currently has no standards-based support for developing fault tolerant systems, the onus falls upon the application developer to combine various technology components into a robust and scalable solution. As always, we should try to minimize single points of failure, to the extent that even the recovery mechanism itself should be fault tolerant. However, there is a tradeoff between performance and fault tolerance—although we may be tempted to over-engineer a system to address the .01% failure chance, we should ensure that the fault tolerant mechanisms do not adversely affect the performance of the application for the 99.99% case. The success of such mechanisms depends on their design, as well as on solid testing and tuning during development, as default out-of-the-box solutions are unlikely to meet the fault tolerance or performance requirements of the application.

System Management and Maintenance

Managing and maintaining complex distributed systems is an extremely challenging task, including the management of computers, networks, applications, and data. In this chapter, we look at system management and maintenance of distributed systems in general, and we also explore management and maintenance of large-scale CORBA systems in particular.

System management is a necessary cost in any system but adds no direct value to the business. Management solutions must minimize the *cost of ownership* of the system and lower the knowledge required by the customer to manage the system.

System Management

Traditionally, the area of system management includes functions such as hardware and software inventory management, installation and updates of software, network management, problem diagnostics and solution, data management, user setup, and security administration.

If we talk about system management in the context of CORBA, what are the systems that we usually have to manage? A common CORBA system comprises of a set of clients, for instance, Visual Basic or Java clients, a set of CORBA application servers, and usually some persistence mechanism like a DBMS or a queue manager.

In this section, we look at the relationship between management of CORBA-based systems and traditional network management systems. Based on this discussion, we define the requirements for management of CORBA-based systems, which forms the basis for the reminder of the chapter.

Network Management

Management of large data and telephony networks is an extremely complex task. Network management systems must deal with a large variety and number of communication resources and network components. A network management domain may span thousands of miles, different support organizations, and many machines and databases. Especially in the telecommunications industry, enormous resources have been invested in defining, building, and applying network management systems.

In fact, for many people with a network management background, network management is not simply a subset of system management, but is really the heart of the management infrastructure, which can be expanded to include system management, forming in integrated management framework for all resources in a distributed system.

We take an approach in this chapter which is different from this network-management-centric viewpoint. We focus more on the application side of system management, taking into account the specifics of CORBA-based applications. However, before we motivate this approach, we give a brief overview of network management.

The most common network management framework is the OSI Management Framework, which defines the so-called FCAPS model. The FCAPS model decomposes the management tasks into the classes Fault Management, Configuration Management, Accounting, Performance Management, and Security Management. However, most existing network management implementations do not cover all of these areas.

Most network management architectures are based on similar concepts, including the concepts of managed object, agent, and manager. The managed object represents the resource that is subject to management. A managed object usually has a set of properties and management operations, and can also trigger notifications. Agents make managed objects available to managers, for instance managers can access objects only through agents. The management space is usually structured in a Management Information Base (MIB). Figure 17.1 gives an overview of a typical management architecture.

Network management protocols define the message formats for the interaction between agents and managers. Common network management protocols include SNMP (Simple Network Management Protocol) and CMIP (Common Management Information Protocol). SNMP is a relatively simple, TCP/IP-based protocol for the management of data networks, initially designed to manage network elements like routers, bridges and repeaters. CMIP has its roots in the world of telecommunication; it is a very complex protocol, designed for the management of complex telephony networks. CMIP was originally designed to run over the OSI communication stack, but is nowadays more widely used over TCP/IP.

In the large networks of the telecommunications industry, there is often a clean separation of the managed network and the management network. For example, CMIP may be run in a TCP/IP based management network to manage a telephony network that includes elements like switches or cross connectors.

The idea of an integrated management framework for all resources in a distributed system seems compelling. The basic management architecture elements of managed object, agent, and manager could be mapped to the CORBA world. Especially in the context of TMN (Telecommunications Management Network) and JIDM (Joint Inter Domain Management working group), we see a lot of activity on mapping SNMP and CMIP to CORBA. In fact, doing research on CORBA and system management leads directly in this direction, due to the large amount of work that has already been done in this area.

If a telecommunications company has already made a huge investment in CMIP, it is often essential to integrate these existing technologies into new CORBA systems. For industries outside the telecommunications industry, a CORBA/CMIP bridge will usually not be of much interest.

Figure 17.1 Typical management architecture

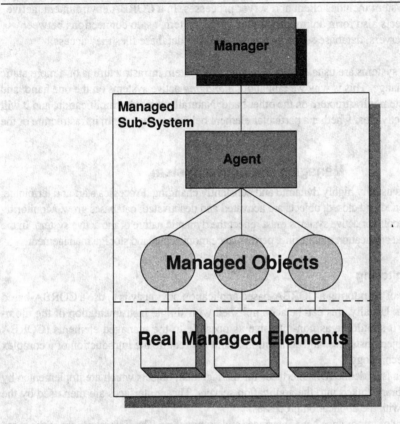

Active System and System Infrastructure

As compelling as the idea of an integrated management framework for all resources in a distributed system is, currently there is no single supplier capable of delivering a total end-to-end solution that really integrates the management of all aspects of a system, including inventory management and software distribution, network management, application monitoring, database administration and user management, all in a distributed, heterogeneous environment.

As we can see, system management is an extremely complex topic, and it is difficult to find a simple structure for discussion in a single chapter. We loosely divide the topic into two general parts: system infrastructure maintenance, and management of active systems.

• **System infrastructure.** By system infrastructure we mean the infrastructure that is required to run the actual system. This includes hardware like desktop PCs and server computers, and network infrastructure like routers and bridges. Also, software is an important part of the system infrastructure: operating system, TCP/IP stack, CORBA middleware, DBMS, application executables. Many of these software components also require configuration files.

• **Active system.** The active system is the system that runs on the system infrastructure. The active system includes client and server processes. In a CORBA environment, active CORBA objects also form an important part of the system, as do connections between clients and servers, database server processes, and the database files they access.

While active systems are usually very dynamic, the system infrastructure is of a more static nature, slower to change. This is why we talk about *managing* active systems on the one hand, and *maintaining* the system infrastructure on the other hand. Naturally, this is a simplification, and it will not always be perfectly clear whether a particular element belongs to the system infrastructure or the active system.

Managing the Active System

The active system is usually highly dynamic and constantly changing. Processes start and terminate, connections are opened and closed, objects are activated and deactivated, databases grow. Monitoring and administration tools for active systems must reflect the dynamic nature of the active system. In the following, we look at application monitoring, performance monitoring, and storage management.

Application Monitoring

The best way of monitoring a CORBA-based application obviously is to use a CORBA-based application monitor. Usually, this can be accomplished with simple instrumentation of the monitored applications. It should be as non-intrusive as possible to the managed elements (CORBA servers, CORBA object instances, and connections), and not require the introduction of a complex new management technology.

The basic idea is to define IDL interfaces for management objects which are implemented by the management library linked into the application servers. These interfaces are then used by the monitor to interact with the application processes.

Two things are of importance here, interfaces and architecture. The IDL interfaces of the management objects define the monitoring functionality. The architecture defines how the management component interacts with the management objects. For example, a monitor could follow the common network management architecture, which we discussed above. This means we would have managed objects, agents, and managers. But other architectures are also possible, for instance, using only a manager and managed objects, using the basic ORB functionality to replace the agent. Figure 17.2 shows three sample architectures for monitors in a CORBA environment. The first example is analogous to the network management architectures we described in the section "Network Management." The second example leaves out the agent, which is not always required in a CORBA environment, since objects can be directly invoked upon. The last example shows how to combine the functionality of a concentrator and an application monitor.

A monitor for CORBA applications could gather the following information on a per-server, per-object, per-interface, or even per-method basis:

• Number of requests sent/received
• Number of bytes sent/received

Figure17.2 CORBA-based application monitors: three different ones

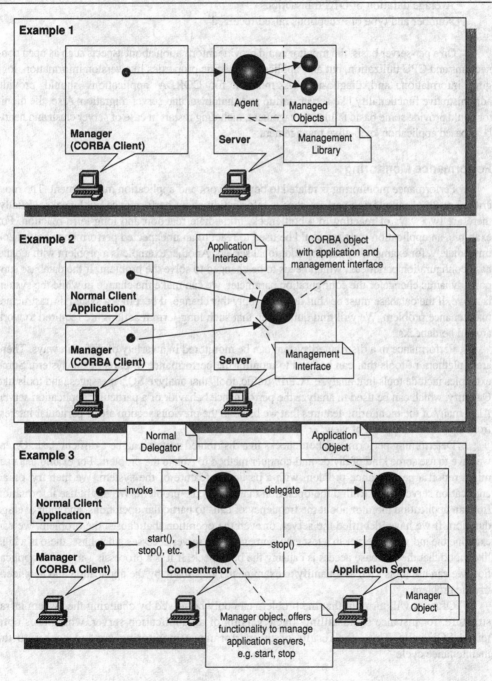

- Average duration of requests
- Average duration of OTS transactions
- Number and type of exceptions raised/received

On a per-server basis, the monitor could provide information about aspects such as open connections and CPU utilization, but also application-specific properties like version information, logging information, and diagnostics. A monitor for CORBA applications should provide administrative functionality like server startup and shutdown, and server migration. Also, the monitor could provide some basic failure management, including restart in case of server crash and heartbeat-based application keep-alive management.

Performance Monitoring

Performance monitoring is related to both network and application management. The most critical result of monitoring performance is information about performance bottlenecks. Usually, there are two ways of reacting to a bottleneck, immediate reaction and long-term reaction. For example, an application monitor could be used to react to an unexpected performance bottleneck immediately, for example, by starting additional servers. Another example is a problem with a database configuration parameter, which needs to be changed to solve the problem. If the database supports dynamic change of the configuration parameter, we can make the change in while the system is active. If the database must be shut down to apply this change, it becomes a system infrastructure maintenance problem. We will find quite often that such long-term reactions are required to work around bottlenecks.

Performance in a distributed system can be monitored in a variety of different ways. There are a plethora of tools that can be used to monitor the performance of parts of the system. Some examples include tools that analyze TCP/IP traffic, tools that analyze SQL messages, and tools like Quantify, which can be used to analyze the performance behavior of a particular application server. Also, many of the monitoring features that we listed in the previous section are of particular interest from a performance point of view.

Determining performance bottlenecks in a distributed system can be a difficult task. Often, we have to use some kind of divide-and-conquer method to isolate the problem. For example, a user might report a performance problem with a particular feature of the system. We then try, on an application server level, to find the operation that causes the problem. We might use information from an application monitor about the frequency of calls to particular operations, and their average duration. If we have identified the server, or even the operation that causes the problem, we can examine the individual server in a test environment. If the server accesses a database, there is a high likelihood that the database access is causing the bottleneck. If it is a processing-intensive application, we can use tools such as Quantify to examine the calls made by the application and help identify the problem.

Often, it will turn out that the problem can only be solved by changing the system infrastructure, for instance by installing a new version of an application server, which uses optimized SQL calls. Thus, the results of the performance monitoring are fed back into the maintenance cycle.

Storage Management

Managing persistent storage in an active system can be a quite difficult task. How difficult it will be depends often on how much support the DBMS provides. Storage management in an active system usually includes:

- **Backup and recovery.** Production data must be backed up continually to prevent the loss of data in case of a catastrophic failure. Some modern DBMSs support backup while the database is active. If the DBMS must be shut down for backups, this can become a major problem in systems that must provide 24×7 availability. In case of a catastrophic failure, we must be able to recover from a backup. How much data we lose in the case of a catastrophic failure depends on the frequency of backups.
- **Managing historical data.** The amount of data in an active system usually grows continually, and often a lot of the older data is only accessed extremely infrequently. Therefore, it makes sense to migrate this historical data from expensive, fast-access media to less expensive backup storage. Obviously, we also need to provide a solution to make the data available again on demand.

System Infrastructure Maintenance

In general, system infrastructure is of a more static nature. Changes like hardware and software upgrades are usually not done very often, and they must be carefully planned. Many application developers simply take the system infrastructure for granted, underestimating the complexity of ensuring that the system and the infrastructure integrate seamlessly.

An important part of system infrastructure management is inventory management. In a network of thousands of computers, it is vital to have a detailed inventory of the different hardware and software components. This information is absolutely essential for any upgrades that are made to the system. For example, if we want to upgrade a particular application, we must make sure that all machines have the right operating system version installed. Automated software distribution systems that are used to manage software updates in large networks usually provide an integrated inventory mechanism.

Deploying CORBA Systems

Deployment is a complex issue, and we focus here on the deployment of CORBA applications. If our system is component-based, we can reduce deployment complexity by deploying on a per-component basis. However, an important challenge is ensuring that the different components interact seamlessly with each other. We address this problem in the next section, "Administration."

Installing a CORBA component on one or more machines usually requires a careful check of the following:

- **Operating system compatibility.** Check that the production environment's operating system has exactly the same version as the test or development environment. This not only includes the operating system version, but also the configuration and minor versions of libraries and patches. This point can't be stressed enough, since it is very often over-looked that a minor difference in the basic setup of the production and the test environment can have fatal consequences.

- **TCP/IP.** When using IIOP, check that the right TCP/IP stack version is installed, and also make sure that the TCP/IP stack is correctly configured. This can be a non-trivial activity. Wrong configuration of the TCP/IP stack can lead directly to communication errors, or extremely long waiting times followed by timeouts.
- **ORB installation.** Installation of the ORB can be another difficult task. Only a few ORB vendors provide a clean separation between development environment and runtime environment. Therefore, it can be quite time-consuming to find the runtime components required for running ORB-based applications. Also, most ORBs require an activation agent on the server side. Distribution and maintenance of configuration files required by the ORB can be difficult as well.
- **ORB library versions.** Be careful about the different library versions required by ORB-based applications. Often, you will have cases where different CORBA-based applications using different ORB versions are installed on a single machine. For example, you might have a naming service server and an event service server running on the same machine, and both require different versions of ORB libraries, or even ORB libraries from different ORB vendors.

Setting up CORBA Services

Many CORBA systems make use of higher-level CORBA services, like the event service, the security service, the naming service, and the trading service. Each of these services usually requires a certain amount of configuration and administration.

For example, a system might use a complex naming schema to make several different components available through entry point objects. Setting up such a naming schema can be a quite complex task. Similarly, when using the trading service, we have to set up the service offer space before the trader can be used. Having done this, we usually also have to export component entry point objects to the naming services and trading services as part of the deployment, so that when the system is activated, clients can find the components they want to interact with.

Another example of a service that needs a lot of thought before it can be successfully deployed includes the event service (and, similarly, the notification service). We need to think about configuration of event channels, and possibly the federation of event channels.

Finally, deploying CORBA-based security services involves a lot of work, and should be carefully planned, in particular if interaction with third-party products is required, such as X.509 certification services. Setting up a secure environment can be quite complex.

Managing Change

Managing change in the system infrastructure is often one of the most expensive and time-consuming activities in maintaining a system.

In our discussion on active systems, we said that their management tools must take into account the dynamic nature of active systems. For example, application monitors are specifically designed to deal with highly dynamic system elements. On the other hand, the nature of the system infrastructure is more static, since changes occur much less frequently. However, if changes do occur, the consequences can be quite drastic.

There are several factors that have an influence on changes to the system infrastructure. One such factor is to what degree the system has to keep running while the changes to the infrastructure are made. If we are lucky, the entire system can be shut down for the duration of the maintenance period. However, many 24×7 systems can't be shut down at all, or only for a very short time, for example for 2 minutes every 6 months. This is an extremely difficult problem to deal with. If we can't shut down the entire system, we might at least be able to shut down parts of the system for short times. If not, we will have to think about more sophisticated solutions, including service migration.

Another question is whether updates can be applied to all deployed components at once. Often we have situations where changes can only be applied to parts of the system, which means that we have to handle multiple versions of components running concurrently in the same system. Especially in cases where we have many distributed CORBA applications (for example clients on thousands of PCs), and in cases where we can't shut down the system we will have to face the problem of dealing with multiple versions in one system. In the following, we discuss some ways of dealing with these different problems.

Administration of CORBA Services

Changes in the system infrastructure often need to be reflected by administering CORBA services. For example, we might have to change the naming service hierarchy, or add a new service offer type to the trading service. Or, the results of our performance monitoring may show that the current structure of our event service federation is the bottleneck, so we have to rearrange the structure of our federated event channels.

Fortunately, more and more CORBA service implementations have GUI-based administration tools, which allow us to administer our CORBA systems relatively easily. How easy it will be again depends on many factors.

For example, adding a new service offer to our trader's service offer space is relatively trivial, since it doesn't affect current clients of the trader. However, changing the hierarchy of our naming service's name space has drastic consequences for all the clients that use the current naming schema. If they are programmed in a dynamic manner, they might be able to cope with it, but this is unlikely. This means that we have to do something with our clients as well. If they read logical names from configuration files, we will have to change these configuration files. If they have names hard-coded in their implementation, we will have to change the implementation of the clients, and then redistribute these changes to all client installations.

Another good example is our system of federated event channels. If we have to change the federation hierarchy without affecting the active system, we have to be very careful.

In the section "Migration Strategies for Multi-Version Systems," we look at how CORBA services can be used to deal with multiple versions of CORBA components in one system.

Versioning in a CORBA Environment

In this section, we look at two cases of versioning in a CORBA environment. In the first case, the component IDL is not changed, but only the component implementation. In the second case, we actually have to deal with changes on the IDL level.

Component Substitution

Since CORBA encapsulates our distributed components, it is well-suited to support us in managing changes in our component implementations. There are many good reasons to change component implementations, most prominently including bug fixes, performance enhancements, and database schema modifications. However, these changes usually have no effect on the component IDL. Notice that we have to be careful about changes in the behavior of the component, including performance enhancements.

If the system can be shut down for a short period of time, it is trivial to make the changes by simply replacing the old component installation with the new one. In cases where we can't simply shut down the entire system, we must use some kind of migration mechanism.

A good solution to this is to use an object location service like the naming or the trading service. Assuming we have a component entry point for the particular component registered with an object location service, we can simply replace the entry to the new component. Hopefully over time all clients will resolve the name or service in questions again, so that we migrate them from the old component implementation to the new one.

IDL Versioning Granularity

Often, we face the need to make changes to our IDL. In cases where we can simply replace the system as a whole, this is no problem, and does not require a lot of thought about version management. Unfortunately, when dealing with large distributed systems, we can rarely afford the luxury of this *big bang* migration. In cases where we have to support an *incremental* migration of all components to the new version, we have to solve the problem of versioning in IDL. In this section, we discuss the levels of granularity on which we can address IDL versioning.

Versioning Individual IDL Elements.   The CORBA IDL specification permits versioning of individual IDL elements; that is exceptions, type definitions, operations, interfaces, and so forth. This versioning mechanism is based on the #pragma version statement, which is used to associate a name in an IDL file with a major and a minor version number. This version information is then represented in the repository ID for the specific IDL name.

At first glance, this sounds like a reasonable approach to IDL versioning. However, it is questionable how practical this approach is in reality. This feature can potentially lead to more trouble than benefit. If not used carefully, this feature can lead to a very fine-grained version model, especially if multiple names with multiple versions are combined in a single system. Instead of using this fine-grained approach, we recommend versioning on a per-module basis.

Versioning Modules.   The simple idea of module based-versioning is to use module names to express version numbers. For example, we could have a module StockWatchSystem_1_0, and then a new minor revision StockWatchSystem_1_1. This way, all elements included in the new version of the module have the same version, and it is easy to separate them.

There are obviously some drawbacks to this solutions as well; for instance, when using modules that include other modules, things can become a little bit more difficult. Nevertheless, it seem like versioning modules is the cleanest way of managing the version problem.

Migration Strategies for Multi-version Systems

In this section we want to discuss strategies for managing multiple versions of IDL in the same system. From an implementation point of view, the easiest way to provide implementations of components with a new IDL is to implement them as new applications. Combining multiple versions of a component in one application can be tricky, due to subtle differences in IDL structure or semantics. In the following we discuss how CORBA services can be used to manage multiple versions of CORBA component implementations.

Location Service. Using a location service for managing different versions of component implementations is relatively straightforward. With the naming service, we can simply embed each component's version into the logical name used to identify the component entry point object. That is, the version information is exposed as part of the naming hierarchy. With the trading service, the version of the component would become a property of the service.

Concentrator. A concentrator could be used to manage component version information. Each time a new target is chosen, the delegator would, based on the client's version, direct the client to a server with a compatible version.

Client Redirection. The location forward feature allows a server to transparently redirect clients to another server. This feature could easily be used to direct clients to the server that implements the requested interface version. Either each server knows about all the other servers, and can make the decision itself, or a dedicated server is provided that acts as the version manager. If a server doesn't provide the requested version, the client is redirected to the version manager, which in turn redirects the client to the correct server.

Summary

In this chapter, we have given an overview of the different aspect of managing distributed systems, with an emphasis on managing CORBA based systems. An important differentiation that we made is that of active system management versus system infrastructure maintenance.

Managing highly dynamic active systems includes application monitoring, performance monitoring, and storage maintenance. An application monitor can help to monitor connections, requests, exceptions, and provide administrative functionality, for instance to start and stop servers. Performance monitoring is important to help overcome immediate problems by using administrative tools, as well as for long-term improvements to the system (for instance by changing the implementation.) Storage maintenance includes backup and recovery.

System monitoring has a close relationship to many of the topics covered in the chapters on Load Balancing and Fault Tolerance, including concentrators, server pool management, and failure detection.

Maintaining the more static system infrastructure includes deployment and administration, but also the important issue of change management. A central role for change management in a CORBA environment is played by the IDL interfaces. IDL encapsulates all changes in implementations, which makes it relatively easy to manage implementation changes in a CORBA environment.

More complex are changes to IDL, since these changes affect the system as a whole. IDL versioning can be dealt with on different levels of granularity, but usually the IDL module level is appropriate. Different versions of server implementations can be managed by combining a versioning schema with a naming schema (CORBA Naming Service), or by exporting version information as a property of the service description (CORBA Trading Service).

Engineering CORBA Systems

In this last part of the book we look back at what we have covered so far, and apply the results to the process of engineering CORBA systems. An interesting question is how the engineering of CORBA systems differs from other software engineering processes. We know that CORBA combines object-oriented concepts with client/server computing. How is engineering CORBA systems related to the classical object-oriented software engineering process?

Also, at this point we provide a more formal description of the component model we used throughout the book. We give a more precise description of our understanding of CORBA components, and how they can be modeled with UML.

We also explore the automotion of the CORBA-based software engineering process, looking at CASE tools in general. An important role in the automation process is played by code generation. In relationship to CORBA, we also explore the possibility of IDL-based code generation. But code generation cannot be the answer to everything in our attempt to automate CORBA-based software engineering. We also look at how the process itself can be automated, for example through the use of process wizards.

In the conclusion of this book, we summarize the complexity that we have to manage in the context of enterprise CORBA systems. Finally, we provide an outlook on how recent and future developments in the CORBA world could help make the development of enterprise CORBA systems a mainstream task.

CHAPTER 18

Consequences for the Engineering Process

So far, we have focused on the technical issues, restrictions, and problems associated with designing and implementing distributed object systems. In this chapter, we examine the consequences that development of such systems have for the software engineering process. We look at existing software engineering techniques, and examine how they can be adapted to reflect the distribution aspects of a CORBA environment. Closely related to this discussion, we examine how to adapt the Unified Modeling Language to reflect the specifics of distributed object computing.

CORBA and the Software Engineering Process

You might be surprised to find a chapter on software engineering at the end of this book. You could argue that software engineering is something that you should take into consideration in the very early stages of a software project, and therefore you would expect a book on building enterprise CORBA systems to cover this topic right at the beginning. However, we felt that it makes more sense to have a discussion of all the specifics of CORBA and distributed object computing, and then use the results of this discussion to determine what the consequences from a software engineering perspective are.

Recall our discussion on IDL and performance in Part 1; there are fundamental differences between traditional, non-distributed object-oriented programming and designing IDL interfaces for distributed objects. CORBA is not only an extension to the traditional object paradigm, but represents the combination of client/server computing and object orientation. This fact must be reflected in the CORBA-based software engineering process. In Chapter 10, "Database Integration," we discussed making enterprise data accessible as CORBA business objects. Thus, CORBA allows us to provide object-orientation at the enterprise level.

Finally, CORBA provides not only an object-oriented RPC mechanism, but also adds a set of higher-level services such as object location, messaging, and security, which were discussed in Part 2 of the book. Another complex area is the integration of CORBA with databases and transactions, as covered in Part 3 of the book. Finally, we have seen that there are many other scalability issues related to building CORBA systems, as discussed in Part 4 of the book.

From a software engineering point of view, this means that we must deal with not only simple modeling of objects and classes, but also with complex software architectures. These architectures are somewhat encapsulated by the CORBA service interfaces, but this does not mean that we can ignore them in the process of modeling and designing our systems.

Object Management Group

The OMG has recognized the need to address the issues related to CORBA and the software engineering process. On the modeling front, OMG has formally adopted a version of the Unified Modeling Language as the standard object modeling language. Based on this, the OMG is now in the process of defining a variant of UML called Component Definition Language (CDL). In addition, the OMG is defining an extension to CORBA called Business Object Component Architecture (BOCA). Both of these modeling specifications are designed to work with the new Meta-Object Facility (MOF), which will allow tools and IDEs to store and retrieve model information through a common interface.

The basic idea is that analysis and design work is done in UML. The UML models are then mapped to CDL, where additional information for business object configuration and deployment can be added. All this information is stored in a MOF-based repository. From this repository, IDL interfaces can be generated.

Related to all this is the currently emerging CORBA Component Model (CCM) specification, which will focus on a common packaging model for CORBA components, similar to the Java Beans model.

Unfortunately, the OMG Component Definition Language and the Business Object Component Architecture were not available at the time of writing. However, we hope that our discussion in the following is not contradictory to the work currently done by the OMG. While the OMG approach seems to be simply to say one should *use* UML to model distributed CORBA systems, before components are defined with CDL, we want to look at exactly *how* UML can be used to do so. From our point of view, this includes two things: first, a discussion of how the object-oriented software development process should be adapted to reflect distribution aspects and, second, how UML artifacts can be used to reflect elements of CORBA systems.

The Traditional Software Engineering Process

Traditionally, the object-oriented software development process contains phases like analysis, system design, object design, and implementation. Although a thorough analysis of each methodology is not relevant at this point, we will assume that there are several common artifacts: problem statement, analysis model, system architecture, object model, and system. These elements are produced as output from the various phases mentioned above. There might be additional artifacts and phases, and phases may be ordered differently, ranging from basic waterfall models to cyclic and advanced spiral models. In most cases, precious little attention is reserved for aspects of distribution in general, or even object distribution in particular. It is our intention to show how these traditional software development processes can be adapted to reflect the complexity of distributed object computing.

Adapting the Software Engineering Process to Reflect Distribution Aspects

When building a CORBA application, one of the first implementation tasks we undertake is to define the application interface in IDL. From a systems engineering perspective, where does this task fit into the software engineering process? It seems too early to start defining IDL in the analysis phase, as we really want to focus on identifying and modeling the business processes, and defining classes that reflect the business domain. Ideally, the analysis model should focus on business objects that are understandable for everybody, even non-technical people. Some aspects of distribution may be considered at this point, but this should definitely be an IDL-free zone.

In the system design phase, we need to create both a system architecture as well as a component model, both of which address the distribution aspects of the system. This is because we usually refine the analysis and design artifacts to eventually describe the system's implementation details. For a distributed object system, it is crucial that the distributed object interfaces be an integral part of the object model. This means that we have to combine our traditional analysis model that describes business functionality with the component model that describes distribution.

These models will let us derive a consolidated object model that includes IDL interfaces. Note that by assigning an IDL interface to a class, we are implying that it will participate in distribution; that is, other processes will make remote invocations on this class. Therefore, before we start defining CORBA interfaces, we need a more thorough understanding of the distribution aspects of the system. This relies on a system architecture that describes these distribution aspects. This is where components fit in. Defining a component model helps to clarify the distributed nature of the system.

In some cases, the IDL interfaces may simply be a refinement (specialization) of the classes defined in the analysis phase. However, a strict refinement relationship between class and IDL interface should not be enforced. Instead, it should be possible to derive appropriate IDL interfaces from one or more classes by considering the distribution criteria inherent in the design. We will address the refinement versus derivation argument in more detail later.

By overlaying the traditional OO design process with these additional steps, it is possible to propose an extended development process as illustrated in Figure 18.1.

It is worth noting the importance of clearly separating the analysis process from the design process. In many projects, where no clear separation is defined, the models are simply allowed to evolve, reflecting finer and finer detail with each successive iteration. The big picture and business model are often victims of this style. In addition, nobody feels responsible for maintaining the repository of diagrams and models, which means that there is usually only one working version, which naturally becomes more implementation-centric with the advance of the project. If the modified approach described above is to succeed, it is essential to make a clean separation between the analysis model and the design models.

Figure 18.1   Extending the traditional OO software development process

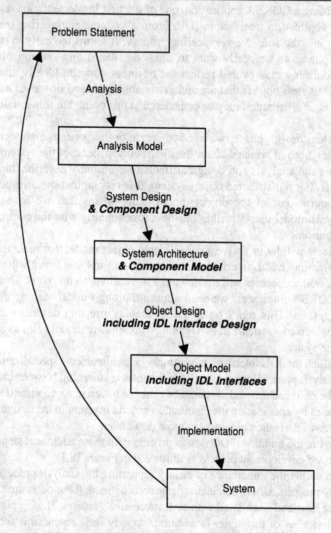

CORBA Component Model

In this section we review the role components play in helping us model a distributed system and reintroduce a number of extensions to the standard UML that allow us to describe the relationship between classes, interfaces and components.

The Unified Modeling Language

The Unified Modeling Language is a widely accepted standard for describing object-oriented systems. The OMG recently adopted the UML as a standard modeling language. UML defines a graphical modeling language that is used to describe models of complex systems in a graphical manner. However, UML is not a methodology. Instead, it is a suite of graphical tools that can be used to support many development methodologies. At this point, we will examine how UML can be used to support a methodology used to develop CORBA systems.

In the previous section, we defined two basic requirements for such a methodology, namely the creation of a component model and the inclusion of IDL interfaces into the object model. The basic UML provides similar concepts named, appropriately, interface and component. In UML, an interface describes the externally visible behavior of classes, packages, or components. A component describes the physical structure of software components. It represents an executable unit of code that provides encapsulation for related services. The services exposed by a component can only be accessed through an interface. Components can be connected to other components by means of a dependency relationship. Executable components can have instances, which are represented in deployment diagrams.

Figure 18.2 shows an example of the various modeling elements in UML. The class "figure" exports the interface "drawable." The class in turn is part of the component "DrawTool," which is an application running on the node "Kingston."

Components in UML

In the UML, a component is defined as an executable software module with an identity and a well-defined interface. Components provide a mechanism for encapsulating fragments of functionality in such a way that the component becomes a unit of access and also a unit of deployment. Components are service-oriented. They expose their functionality through "service" style interfaces, offering a more complete service than a single object or a group of individual objects would. Component models are used to model components. Specifically:

Figure 18.2   UML notation example, including interfaces and components

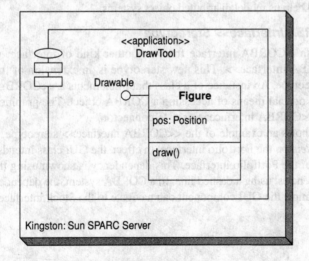

• A component is a reusable software building block that encapsulates application code to provide a logical grouping of objects. Components can be combined to create larger components (a process known as component assembly).

• The services of a component can be accessed only through a published interface. Every component must therefore export at least one interface, although it is free to expose more than one.

• Components provide encapsulation that is often difficult to attain with fine-grained objects. In addition, as the services of a component must be exposed through interfaces, the contents of the component don't need to be objects at all, which allows us to effectively wrap legacy or non-OO code in a component interface.

Adapting UML to Reflect Distribution Aspects

Clearly, we need a standard way in which to model the distribution aspects of a CORBA system. The obvious choice is to base any new model on UML, which contains concepts very similar to those in a CORBA system. The UML concepts of component and interface, in fact, are the foundation on which we have based certain modeling extensions, described in this section. Unfortunately, neither the basic component nor interface defined in the UML provides sufficient semantic detail for describing components and interfaces that participate in a distributed application. Fortunately, UML provides a mechanism that makes it easy to extend the semantics of existing UML modeling elements, stereotypes.

UML Stereotypes

A stereotype allows us to take an existing UML modeling element and extend its semantics. Stereotypes can either be expressed in textual form or graphically. The textual representation uses two angle brackets ("guillemets") before and after the stereotype name, for example, <<application>> (the <<application>> stereotype is actually pre-defined in UML). Optionally, a graphical icon can be associated with a stereotype. In the following section, we describe some additional stereotypes that will help us model distributed object systems.

The <<CORBA interface>> Stereotype

To distinguish a CORBA interface from any other kind of interface, we introduce the stereotype <<CORBA interface>>. This new stereotype is an extension of the standard UML <<interface>> stereotype. An instance of a class that implements a <<CORBA interface>> can be accessed by the normal means of accessing a CORBA object. The graphical symbol that is associated with a <<CORBA interface>> is a "T-connector."

Figure 18.3 shows an example of the <<CORBA interface>> stereotype. The GUI class is shown to be *dependent* on the Portfolio interface. In effect, the GUI class intends to make calls on interface methods of the Portfolio interface. This dependency is shown using the standard UML notation for dependencies, using a dashed line. In a CORBA system, the dependency implies *navigability*; in this example the GUI component can navigate to the Stock interface via the Portfolio interface.

Figure 18.3   View of the <<CORBA interface>> construct

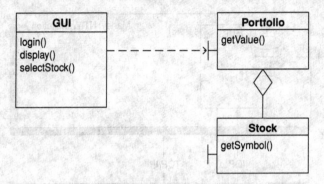

This diagram shows the *external* view of the <<CORBA interface>> construct. There is no explicit linkage between the IDL interface and any programming language class that may implement the interface. Instead, the interface name (`Portfolio`) is simply shown where UML notation places the class name. This style of representation is more useful during the early modeling phase as it makes no assumptions about the implementation class that will eventually export this IDL interface. (There is a corresponding *internal* view, which is introduced later.)

The <<CORBA component>> Stereotype

The introduction of the <<CORBA component>> stereotype allows us to make a clear distinction between a component whose intended use is in a CORBA application versus one created to provide a convenient container of non-CORBA objects. The key semantic difference with a CORBA component is that it exports or imports services that can only be accessed via CORBA IDL interfaces. The iconic symbol associated with a <<CORBA component>> stereotype is a stylized version of the CORBA architecture icon; an ellipse above and below a horizontal arrow. These icons can appear on either the left or right side of a component, and are illustrated in Figure 18.4. This notation is used for both server components (which implement interfaces) and client components (which use these interfaces).

This diagram shows an example of the use of the <<CORBA component>> stereotype. Notice that the example describes the type of interaction on two different levels: component and node level. Between two components, we can choose whether we want to indicate the communication mechanism at a very low level (for instance, TCP/IP) or at a higher level (IIOP). In this example, communication between nodes is shown as a *connection* with the label "TCP/IP." In contrast, communication between the GUI and Portfolio Manager components is shown using a connector (of stereotype <<communication>>) with the label "IIOP."

Note that this diagram explicitly shows the nodes in this system (`Kingston` and `Marley`). These are very useful for illustrating the physical distribution of components. This example shows multiple CORBA components contained within the node `Kingston`. CORBA components may also span multiple nodes. The relationships between the components also show how the components are related, and in this example illustrates their communication mechanisms.

Figure 18.4   CORBA component notation

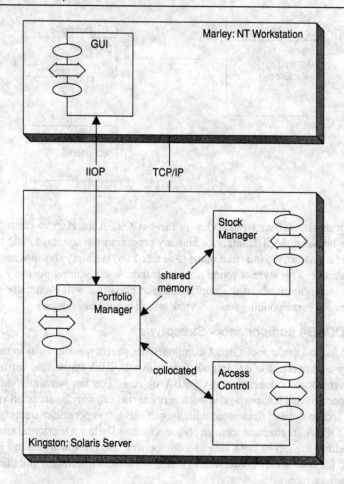

Definition of a <<CORBA component >>

A <<CORBA component>> exports services by implementing CORBA objects. These CORBA objects export IDL interfaces, which can be accessed from outside the component via the normal CORBA means of accessing a CORBA object. A <<CORBA component>> can also access services of another <<CORBA component>>.

A <<CORBA component>> can be provided as a library, a single server executable, or a set of different server executables. An instance of a <<CORBA component>> consists of one of more running executables.

Interaction between CORBA components is orchestrated by CORBA invocations. The standard CORBA access protocol is GIOP. At a lower level, CORBA objects may be accessed via a variety of different transport mechanisms, such as TCP/IP, shared memory, or even collocated access (client and object reside in same process). From the perspective of distribution, the interaction between various components and the mapping to physical entities such as executable processes is important, as it defines those messages or method calls that are interprocess (that is, remote). It is important to capture this information in the component model as dependency relationships between various components.

The <<entry point>> Stereotype

A CORBA component offers a service that is provided by a set of objects, implementing a variety of interfaces. How does an actor (that is, a CORBA client) access the services of a component? The actor must locate an initial object, a starting point, from which it can then obtain references to other objects contained in the component. In most cases, a CORBA component will have a distinguished object that acts as an *entry point* to the service provided by the component. To represent the concept of an entry point, we have defined an additional stereotype called <<entry point>>. An <<entry point>> is a global singleton, provided by a <<CORBA component>> to make the component's services accessible. For example, Figure 18.5 shows how a CORBA naming service usually has a dedicated "root" object, which acts as the entry point to the naming service component.

Figure 18.5 Defining component entry points

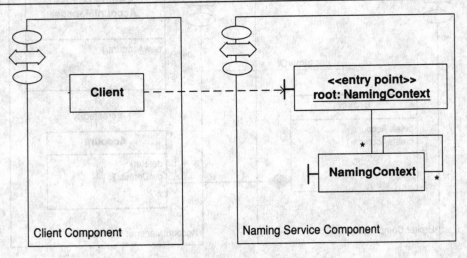

Modeling CORBA Components

To describe the functionality and interaction between a group of CORBA components, we define a "CORBA component diagram" which includes both <<CORBA component>> and <<CORBA interface>> stereotypes. That is, this diagram contains only those elements that are specific to CORBA. Diagrams that show details of the underlying class structure or the binding between interfaces and classes should be separate. The intention of a CORBA component diagram is to show only those details of the classes that are visible through the CORBA interfaces they expose. In particular, the only relationships that should appear on the diagram are those which can be navigated through CORBA interfaces. An underlying class can a have much more complex definition, with a myriad of additional relationships. However, if these relationships are not exposed on a CORBA interface, then the details should not be exposed on the CORBA component diagram.

Figure 18.6 shows an example of a CORBA component diagram, with two components: Broker and AccountManager. The Broker class is dependent on the AccountManager class, which is used as the entry point of the AccountManager component. The exposure of a class through an IDL interface makes the class relationships accessible. In this example, we have defined a composition relationship between the Broker and Account classes. In effect, the Account objects belong to the Broker object, which implies that an action to delete the Broker object will propagate the action to each Account object it currently owns.

In this model, a Broker object will make initial contact with the AccountManager interface, acting as both an entry point and manager interface for Account objects. The Broker class does not necessarily have an explicit association to the AccountManager class. Instead, it is simply a con-

Figure 18.6 Component model semantics

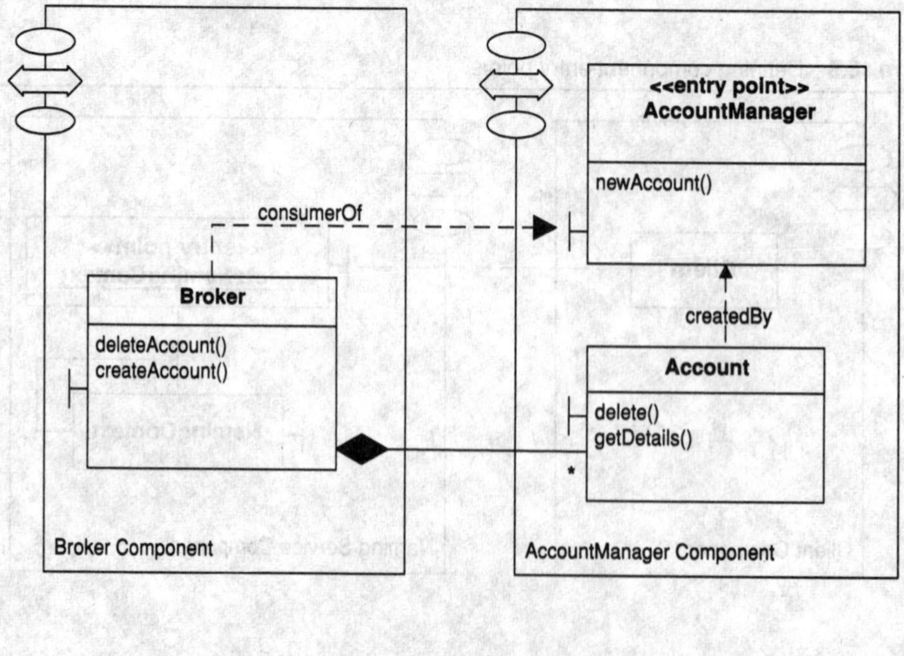

sumer of the methods on the IDL interface exposed by this class. The Broker will use AccountManager to create new Account objects, each of which will be bound to a single Broker object, as represented by the composition association.

It is worth noting that the models we have introduced here say very little about the semantic content of the interfaces. Other UML artifacts, such as use case, sequence, and state diagrams will be needed to help define the semantic behavior of the methods.

Component Characteristics

Components have a number of characteristics that should become a part of our vocabulary for discussing components.

Component Identity

Because components do not exist as distinguished CORBA objects, the component itself cannot publish an IOR. However, if each component has exactly one <<entry point>>, the IOR of the entry point object effectively becomes the component's identity.

Component Instances

The question "do components have instances?" has implicitly been answered—like classes and objects, we must differentiate between component implementations and component runtime instances. A component runtime instance will at least contain an instance of the component's entry point object, for components that implement objects. However, there is no notion of a distinguished "component" object—launching the involved server processes is logically equivalent to instantiating a component.

Publishing Components

Components must expose their services to the CORBA world. The entry points of a component are likely to be published to an object directory, such as the CORBA naming or trader services. Thus, higher-level location services can be used to locate components, represented by their entry point objects. In many cases, the only objects that are statically instantiated as singletons when a component (CORBA server) starts are factories and managers. These objects have previously been published and are prepared to accept invocations from remote clients. Publication was discussed in Chapter 6, "Locating Objects."

Internal Versus External View

Our earlier discussion of the <<CORBA interface>> introduced the notation associated with this stereotype. There are actually two views that this notation can be used with, an *external* view of a component, and an *internal* view. The external view is similar to a UML use-case diagram, where the concept of an actor (as a user of another piece of the system) is used to describe interactions with the system from an external point of view. No internal (implementation) aspects should be visible. This external view was illustrated previously, in Figure 18.3. In contrast, the internal view *is* used to illustrate the implementation details. Internal helper classes and non-CORBA classes should be shown in these diagrams. An example of an internal view is shown in Figure 18.7.

Figure 18.7   Internal <<CORBA interface>> diagram

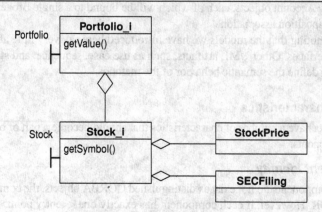

Notice how the diagram in Figure 18.7 differs from the external view. The IDL interface name (Portfolio) has been moved outside the class above the T-connector. This is consistent with the position that UML uses for interfaces. The programming language class that implements the interface (Portfolio_i) is shown inside the class, occupying the class name position. This diagram also shows two non-CORBA classes, StockPrice and SECFiling. These are internal classes, used by Stock_i to do its work.

Component Interaction

Component diagrams describe components, their contents and their interactions. As part of the extended system design phase of the development process, the designer will propose a set of CORBA components and a complementary set of IDL interfaces that will be exposed by classes contained by those components. To accomplish this, the external view of CORBA components should be used. This is similar to the external specification expressed through UML use-case diagrams. Unfortunately, neither of these types of diagrams provide any way of expressing detailed semantics. This leaves us with the dilemma of how to provide an external specification of the component that contains sufficient semantic detail to direct the implementation logic.

Generally, we do not want to resort to a pseudo-specification language to accomplish this. In the UML, interaction (sequence), state and activity diagrams all contribute towards the specification of semantic behavior of an application. However, it is not possible to describe persistence logic or mapping, security, or other quality-of-service (QoS) indicators such as performance, reliability, accessibility, or recoverability with such diagrams. These aspects are normally addressed by designers in separate "technical architecture" or "system requirements" documents that are not linked to the component design in any way. Given the current limitations of the notational language, component designers should view the various UML artifacts as a basic draft rather than as the complete specification of a distributed system.

Component Substitutability

The ability to substitute one component with another one that provides the same functionality has often been heralded as one of the key objectives of object-orientation and, in particular, componentization. To a certain extent, CORBA has achieved this goal. It is possible to replace a CORBA server with another one that exposes exactly the same IDL interfaces (external contract). However, there is currently no way to guarantee that the components are semantically equivalent. For example, even though two components expose exactly the same IDL interface, a method call to getStockPrice() on one component might have completely different semantics from the same call in the other component.

Interface substitutability is relatively easy to judge, since this is explicitly determined by the IDL. However, determining semantic substitutability is much more difficult, since it is typically only described in documentation or in peoples' minds, and therefore requires careful, detailed coordination between human beings.

Example

Now we utilize our new notation to illustrate a reasonably complex system. The model in Figure 18.8 shows the StockWatch system that was introduced in Chapter 15, "Load Balancing." The StockWatch system as a whole is made up of as many as 10,000 StockWatch clients, a maximum of 20 replicated StockWatch components, and a single event backbone component. In turn, each Stock-

Figure 18.8 StockWatch component diagram

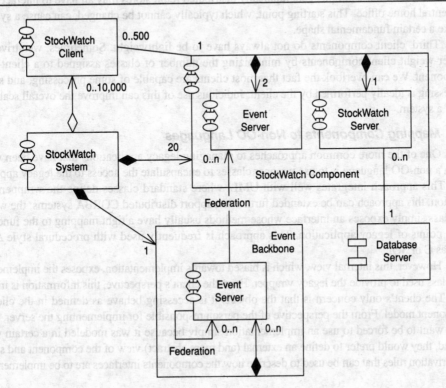

Watch component is made up of a single StockWatch server and two event servers—principally because event servers are likely to be more heavily loaded than the basic StockWatch server.

The StockWatch component is the unit of replication, even though each of its constituent parts maps to separate physical processes—it is not a physical entity in its own right. The StockWatch servers all access data in a single central database, shown as a normal UML component.

Finally, the event backbone component is made up of a configurable number of intermediate event servers, each of which forwards events to event servers embedded within various replicated StockWatch components. This follows the event service federation pattern discussed in Chapter 7, "Messaging."

General Guidelines for Modeling Components

When modeling CORBA components, there are a number of factors to keep in mind. First, consider the frequency and size of messages passed between classes. Use the knowledge that messages sent between processes are much more expensive than messages sent between collocated objects. Take this into account when assigning classes to components, since these messages will map to remote method invocations between components. These topics are discussed in depth in Chapter 5, "Performance Considerations."

Second, understand the logical and business distribution aspects before addressing component distribution. In many cases, the physical distribution of components is strongly affected by an existing environment. For example, geographically distributed retail stores may all have to interact with the central home office. This starting point, which typically cannot be changed, can cause a system to take a certain fundamental shape.

Third, client components do not always have to be lightweight. Sometimes, we strive for lighter-weight client components by minimizing the number of classes assigned to a client-side component. We can overlook the fact that most clients are capable of some processing, and some processing is ideally performed by the client. Judicious use of this can improve the overall scalability of a system.

Mapping Components to Non-OO Languages

One of the more common approaches to managing legacy applications that have been written in a non-OO language is to use wrapper classes to encapsulate the access to the legacy application. This approach integrates well with UML, where standard classes define the wrappers. In addition, this approach can be extended further to support distributed CORBA systems; the wrapper class simply exposes an interface whose methods usually have a tight mapping to the function entry points of legacy application. This approach is frequently used with procedural style APIs such as C or SQL.

However, this internal view, which is biased towards implementation, exposes the implementation class used to provide the legacy wrapper. From the client's perspective, this information is irrelevant. The client's only concern is that the objects it is accessing behave as defined in the client's component model. From the perspective of the person responsible for implementing the server, they don't want to be forced to use an implementation simply because it was modeled in a certain way. Instead, they would prefer to define an external (and more abstract) view of the component and specify derivation rules that can be used to describe how the components interfaces are to be implemented.

For example, a single IDL interface may be implemented by a plethora of small C++ wrapper classes, each of which wraps up a single C function call. Leaving the implementation out of the model allows a developer with the relevant expertise to choose the most appropriate implementation vehicle.

Designing for Reuse

Code reuse within an application component has been with us for many years—we naturally use existing software libraries and foundation classes without a second thought. Although we know that the finished component is not as portable as one written from scratch, the time we save in not having to reinvent the wheel is significant.

CORBA provides a sound basis for component-level reuse, since it is not tied to a single platform or implementation language—CORBA components are specified in a language-neutral way using IDL. CORBA components written in different languages for different operating systems will still be able to communicate with each other—that's all part of the standard. What we focus on here is not how this is achieved technically, but rather aspects of component design that ultimately promote reuse.

Consider the problem of designing a component for maximum reuse where its future usage pattern is unknown. There are two basic approaches to solving this problem, which we discuss next.

The Kitchen Sink and the Amorphous Blob.   We could strive to make the component's interface as flexible as possible, so that the component will be usable by all current and future clients. However, this tends to turn our components into one of two undesirable forms. The first is the "kitchen sink" component, which supports all the interfaces and functions that any client could ever need. These components tend to be unnecessarily complex (internally and externally), and tend to get even worse over time, since it can be very difficult to remove functionality if there are existing clients using it.

The second form is the "amorphous blob" component, which exposes an interface so generic that it can conceivably be used by any client to perform any task. These components tend to be difficult for client programmers to use, sacrifice type safety, and often require extensive external documentation explaining how they work.

Small, Focused Components.   The better approach is to write small, tightly focused components. The IDL will be specific enough to provide type-safety and will be reasonably descriptive, so that they are easy for client programmers to use. They should also be written with particular usage patterns in mind. This will allow them to perform their intended task in the intended manner, in a superior fashion. (Contrast this with a more generic component, which, while it can perform many tasks, is very likely to perform them all poorly.) Because these components are small, it is also possible to quickly develop new ones when new usage patterns become apparent.

Another benefit is that with small components, client programmers will be able to combine them in interesting ways.

The Impedance Mismatch—Again

We have discussed the phenomenon of the *impedance mismatch* already, especially in the context of database integration. An excellent example is the object-to-relational impedance mismatch as described in Chapter 9, "Object Persistence." However, a similar mismatch can also exist between the world of modeling and that of implementation.

As suggested by Figure 18.9, we use refinement to construct an object model from an analysis model, and an object-oriented implementation from the object model.

Refinement is a central theme of the object-oriented development process; the output from each successive phase is a refinement of the input to that phase. For example, the object model is a refinement of the analysis model, and the implementation itself is a refinement of the object model. On the one hand, this is one of the strengths of the object-oriented approach, since it provides views of an application system at various levels of abstraction and enables us to easily switch between these different levels. However, this approach is sometimes naïve—our nemesis, the impedance mismatch, makes it difficult to move from one level of abstraction to another using refinement alone. Common examples of this mismatch include C++ classes that use features like the "friend" mechanism, calls to external functions implemented in assembler or C, programs that access relational data using embedded SQL or a SQL wrapper mechanism, systems that integrate with transactional environments or components that integrate with legacy systems. All of these are examples of an impedance mismatch between the pure object model and the implementation, which is often less object-oriented than the model.

On the CORBA level, we can often observe a similar phenomenon, since CORBA is not as purely object oriented as, for example, Smalltalk—it provides non-object oriented features such as data structures. There are sound justifications for these, as we have discussed in the previous chapters, especially from a performance perspective. However, this often means that integrating CORBA

Figure 18.9   Refinement in the traditional OO development process

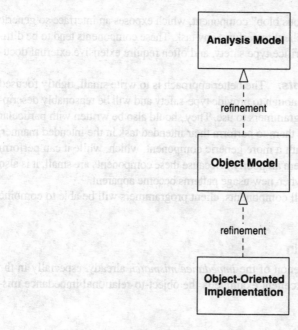

IDL into the object model can introduce an impedance mismatch between the analysis model (which in our approach focuses on business functionality, and does not include IDL) and the object model (which in our approach includes IDL design).

CASE tools like Rational Rose from Rational Software Corporation support the idea of refinement by providing functions to generate implementation code from the object model on one hand while providing re-engineering functionality to generate an object model from implementation code on the other. This allows the developer to add the required refinements (code) to the generated code. The most common form of generation is of implementation classes. Some tools also support the generation of database access code (SQL), and CORBA IDL interfaces. The generated SQL can be very useful for simple read and write access to objects and data, but many seasoned developers will agree that such a tool is often of limited use in medium- or large-scale projects, where performance and scalability requirements will almost certainly require extensions or changes to be made.

Managers and designers often believe in the power of code generation from a CASE tool, and consequently overestimate its ability to deliver realistic large-scale solutions. In contrast, developers and technical staff often believe in the power of hand-coded implementations and often underestimate the usefulness of CASE and code generation tools. The truth seems to lie somewhere in the middle.

The generation of IDL interfaces from modeling artifacts also suffers a similar dilemma. CASE tools that support the generation of IDL often take a very naïve approach; for example, they might only support a one-to-one mapping between a class in the model and an IDL interface. Realistically, developers need fine-grained control of the mapping, to allow, for example, classes to be generated as complex data structures rather than interfaces. Without this control (accompanied by proper analysis of the distribution aspects of an application), the IDL generated by such tools can fail to meet performance expectations.

Deriving vs. Refining

As a result of the preceding discussion on the impedance mismatch, we can conclude that using "refinement" as a technique for getting from an analysis to a design to an implementation model is not always appropriate. What can we use instead? We propose using "derivation" in preference to "refinement"; that is, we will derive an object model that contains certain CORBA elements from the analysis model. Derivation differs from refinement in two ways: First, refinement implies a more direct relationship between the source and the target. Second, for class diagrams, refinement means specialization. The is_a relationship is quite restrictive, as it states that an instance of the specialized class can be treated as though it was an instance of its base classes. Derivation, on the other hand, implies that the two model are related to one another, but that there is not necessarily a simple is_a relationship between them. Figure 18.10 illustrates a derivation.

We start with an analysis model that depicts Stock, StockPrice and SECFiling classes. During the analysis phase, it seemed reasonable to define a class called StockPrice to hold price/date combinations, and an SECFiling class to contain published financial data for the company. The composition relationship between Stock and StockPrice is one of composition; that is, a Stock object is composed of one or more instances of StockPrice objects. Likewise with the SECFiling class.

Although this model seems perfectly valid at the analysis level, a naïve one-to-one mapping to IDL interfaces would yield inefficient IDL definitions. Instead, at the design level, we elect to

Figure 18.10 Derivation of an object model from an analysis model

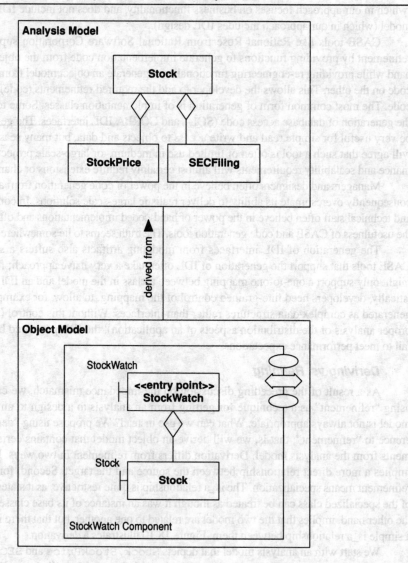

derive IDL structures from the StockPrice and SECFiling classes. In essence, each stock price or SEC report is represented as an IDL structure rather than as a fully fledged object. We have also introduced an additional class (with attendant IDL interface) called StockWatch, the purpose of which is to provide an initial starting point to access stock information. In effect, the StockWatch interface is acting as a factory or manager of stock objects.

Mapping Modeling Artifacts to Implementations

In the previous sections, we have proposed a number of modeling extensions to the UML that allow us to model CORBA applications. In particular, we have defined a component model for CORBA that defines the basic architecture of a component by specifying the structure of its interfaces and the mechanisms through which it interacts with other components. We refer to the process employed to distill a component model from various analysis and design artifacts as *componentization*.

It is now time to look at how we can make the transition from *model* to *implementation*. In effect, we want to map each of the elements that comprise a component model to representative implementation constructs. For example, we have defined a modeling element called *IDL interface* (as a stereotype of interface). Instances of the IDL interface element belong to component diagrams and live in design repositories—they're not executable code, or even IDL interface definitions in a text file. The diagram in Figure 18.11 maps each modeling construct to an implementation construct.

Figure 18.11 Meta-model for component implementation

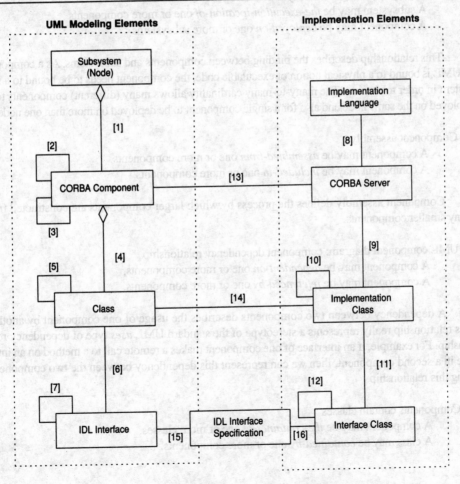

The diagram shows three distinct element groups, namely:

- **UML modeling elements**, such as CORBA components, IDL interfaces, classes and nodes, which constitute the bulk of element types use to compose class, component, and sub-system diagrams.
- **IDL interface specifications**, which help bridge the gap between model and implementation. Normally expressed in textual form in a file with the extension IDL.
- **Implementation elements**, such as interface classes, implementation classes, and executables (CORBA servers in this context).

The following list explains each of the relationships from Figure 18.11 in detail.

UML Modeling Elements

[1] UML deployment diagram: subsystem—component

A subsystem may be *the-execution-location-of* one or more components

A component may be *deployed-on* one or more subsystems

This relationship describes the binding between components and subsystems. As a component in UML is bound to a physical notion of executable code, the component needs to be bound to a subsystem in order to execute. The many-to-many cardinality allows many (different) components to be deployed on the same node and also for a single component to be deployed on more than one node.

[2] Component assembly

A component may be *assembled-from* one or more components.

A component may be *included-in* one or more components.

Component assembly defines the process by which larger components are constructed from many smaller components.

[3] UML component diagram: component dependency relationship

A component may be *dependent-on* one or more components.

A component may be *referenced-by* one or more components.

A dependency between two components describes the usage of one component by another. This relationship really represents a stereotype of the standard UML *uses* type of dependency relationship. For example, if an interface of one component makes a remote call to a method on an interface in a second component, then we can represent this dependency between the two components using this relationship.

[4] Components contain classes

A component may be *the-container-of* one or more classes.

A class may be *contained-by* one or more components.

The aggregation (part-of) relationship between components and classes describes the inclusion of a class within a component.

[5] UML class diagram: class inheritance relationship
    A class may be *a-specialization-of* one or more classes.
    A class may be *the-generalization-of* one or more classes.

Classes have standard generalization/specialization relationships with other classes, as defined in UML.

[6] Exposure of an IDL interface by a class
    A class may be *exposer-of* one or more interfaces.
    An interface may be *exposed-by* one or more classes.

The exposure relationship is a refinement of the relationship between the interface (as a stereotype of class) and class element types, which states that a class may expose one or more interfaces and, conversely, that an interface must be bound to one or more classes. The cardinality of the association provides support for a class exposing multiple interfaces and an Interface being exposed by more than one class.

[7] Interface inheritance
    An IDL interface may be *specialized-from* one or more IDL interfaces.
    An IDL interface may be *generalized-from* one or more IDL interfaces.

The inheritance relationship between interfaces is really a refinement of relationship [5] which describes a generalization/specialization interface between classes. As IDL interface is defined as a stereotype of interface (not shown on the model) which in turn is a stereotype of class; the inheritance relationship is available for refinement at this level. Multiple inheritance of interface is supported in CORBA IDL.

Implementation Elements

[8] Implementation language
    A CORBA server must be *implemented-in* one or more implementation languages.
    An implementation language may be *used-to-implement* one or more CORBA servers

Every CORBA server must be implemented in one of the languages for which there exists a CORBA mapping. For example, C++, Java, Smalltalk, ADA, C, and COBOL. A single server can actually be implemented in more than one language, via "callouts" to functionality implemented in other languages (frequently used for wrapping legacy systems).

[9] Linking an implementation into a server executable
    A CORBA server may be *the-container-for* one or more implementation classes.
    An implementation class may be *linked-into* one or more CORBA servers.

This relationship describes the process by which implementation is bound into a server executable. In languages like C++, this relationship would be represented by linking object files to create an executable program.

[10] Implementation class inheritance

> An implementation class may be *a-subclass-of* one or more implementation classes.
> An implementation class may be *a-superclass-for* one or more implementation classes.

Most implementation languages support inheritance of implementation, although not all will support multiple inheritance.

[11] Implementation of an interface

> An implementation class may be *providing-methods-for* one or more interface classes.
> An interface class may *have-method-code-in* one or more implementation classes.

This relationship describes the binding between the interface class (typically generated by the IDL compiler) and the implementation class that provides the real method code for those interface methods. In effect, it allows the developer to reuse existing implementation code to satisfy an interface contract.

[12] Interface class inheritance

> An interface class may be *a-subclass-of* one or more interface classes.
> An interface class may be *a-superclass-for* one or more interface classes.

Interface inheritance in the abstract specification (IDL) is mapped to interface class inheritance in the implementation. Although IDL supports multiple inheritance of interface, some implementation languages do not support multiple inheritance of implementation (for example, Java).

Model and Implementation

[13] Component imaging

> A component may be *imaged-in* one or more CORBA servers.
> A CORBA server may be *an-image-of* one or more components.

Components in the design space have a fairly direct mapping to executable pieces of an application. In the case of CORBA, a CORBA component will be mapped directly to a CORBA server, which is an executable process. The fact that a design component can be implemented in multiple languages or in many different ways is reflected by the cardinality of this relationship.

[14] Implementation of class methods (not exposed on an Interface)

> A class may be *the-basis-for* one or more implementation classes.
> An implementation class may be *an-implementation-of* one or more classes.

When using an "internal" view of the modeling space, classes marked on the model are directly mapped to equivalent implementation classes.

[15] Interface (model) to interface (specification)

>An IDL Interface may be *used-as-the-basis-for* one or more IDL specifications.

>An IDL specification may be *derived-from* one or more IDL iInterfaces.

This relationship specifies how an IDL specification (as statements in a file with an .idl extension) is derived from IDL interfaces defined in the modeling phase.

[16] Interface (specification) to interface class (IDL compiler)

>An interface may be *used-to-generate* one and only one interface class.

>An interface class must be *generated-from* one and only one interface.

The notation does not allow us to express on the model how we connect interface class and implementation class on the implementation level (for example, using the TIE, BOA, or POA approach). However, this is information that is rarely required at the modeling level. Often, this decision is made on a per-component basis, and we don't want to show it explicitly for each class.

Summary

In this chapter we briefly introduced the work in progress at the OMG related to components and business objects. The OMG's approach addresses a number of important higher-level processes and techniques, which will be standardized in the future. As we have throughout this book, we focus instead on tools and approaches that can be applied today, with existing technology.

We discussed CORBA from an object-oriented analysis and design perspective, focusing on process, architecture, and notation. We augmented the development process by including *CORBA component design* and *IDL interface design* to complement existing *system design* and *object design* tasks, respectively.

From a modeling perspective, we exploited the concept of a stereotype to extend the standard UML modeling constructs to allow us to model CORBA interfaces and CORBA components. Finally, after identifying issues with a pure refinement model, which tended to produce naïve implementations suitable for prototyping purposes only, we continued to describe how an implementation architecture could be derived from the various modeling artifacts.

Our overall objective was to define a small number of extensions to both the process and the notation that together will add significant value to the system engineering process. We're certainly not promoting a wholesale change to either process or notation; it would be irresponsible to propose yet another new approach to modeling distributed applications when so much work has already been put into unifying existing OO modeling approaches. However, the ability to attach semantic detail to an interface or component is important from a reuse and substitutability perspective. Component assembly on a grander scale will not flourish unless we are able to express and model more of the business logic. The introduction of the notion of an external view of the component allows us to model component semantics without necessarily implying a certain implementation. By adopting a more rigorous approach to component specification, we can define precisely the behavior of the component while saying nothing about the implementation.

Automating the Engineering Process

Very often, CORBA is seen as rocket science, which can only be mastered by witchdoctors, voodoo priests, and computer gurus. The truth is that building distributed systems is a difficult task. CORBA provides a lot of help, but doesn't necessarily make it trivial to build such systems. In this chapter, we look at how the complexity of building distributed systems can be reduced by automating the software development process, helping to increase the development productivity.

CASE

The obvious approach to automating the software development process is to use software tools. CASE—Computer Aided Software Engineering—can loosely be defined as the idea of using software tools to build new software. So, what kind of software tools do we usually use when building new software?

- Basic tools like text editors, compilers, make tools.
- Integrated development environments (IDE) like Microsoft Developer Studio, Borland C++Builder, and Symantec Café.
- 4GL tools such as PowerBuilder and Oracle Designer 2000.
- Tools that help to deal with access to relational data, for instance, ERWin for Entity-Relationship based modeling and code generation, and Persistence Software's PowerTier for object/relational code generation.
- Testing tools like Purify, Pure Coverage, or Quantify.
- Rational Rose and Select: originally simple modeling tools, which have added a lot of functionality over time, providing code-generation mechanisms to map UML models to OO languages like C++ and Java, but also to SQL and IDL.
- Tools like Forte and Dynasty, which enable developers to build multi-tier applications in a single development environment. These tools are usually able to integrate client tools like Visual Basic, and can generate complete applications, including SQL-based database access.

In the context of our discussion in this chapter, we assume that a tool has to meet the following criteria to qualify as a CASE tool. Most of the above tools would not qualify as CASE tools according to these criteria:

- Support for a particular software development process. An OO CASE tool would therefore have to support an OO software development process.
- Support for code generation. The tool would have to be able to map a more abstract model to a concrete implementation. This implementation does not need to be complete, but could require some adaptation by hand.

In the following we look at code generation first, before we discuss how the CORBA-based software development process itself could be automated. Looking at code generation from a CORBA perspective, it seems that IDL-based code generation is particularly promising.

Code Generation

As we identified above, code generation can significantly help automate the software development process. Examples of code generation include:

- **C compiler.** A C compiler generates assembler code from C program code. This type of code generator allows us to use advanced programming concepts like structured programming, typed variables and function calls.
- **C++ compiler.** A C++ compiler allows us to use object-oriented programming concepts like classes, inheritance, and polymorphism. The first implementations of C++ compilers, called C-Fronts, used two compilation passes. In the first pass, a C++ compiler generated a set of C code files. In a second pass, this C code was translated to assembler code. Today most C++ compilers directly generate assembler code.
- **GUI designer.** A GUI designer usually allows us to graphically define the layout of GUI components, and then generates a skeleton implementation for our GUI. Usually, we have to modify the generated code to add the logic for handling GUI events, such as the GUI's business logic.
- **Parser generator.** A parser generator like "yacc" takes the definition of a grammar as an input argument, and generates code (for instance, C code) that implements a parser for the given grammar.
- **Persistence.** Many tools that deal with persistence in some form use code generation. We discussed tools like PowerTier and CocoBase for object/relational mapping that generate C++ or Java code. Other examples are tools like ERWin, which generate SQL access functions for simple DDL and data access operations. Even most ODBMSs use some form of code generation, generating logical schema descriptions and programming code to access and manage these schemas.
- **IDL compiler.** An IDL compiler takes an IDL file as input and generates code that can marshal and unmarshal the IDL data types that are defined in the IDL file, that is, transform a complex in-memory data structure into a flat message buffer, and vice versa.

As we can see, there are many different instances of code generators; we have only mentioned a few of them. It seems that code generation is a very popular technique. Why is code generation so popular? We believe that there are two main reasons:

- **Knowledge reuse.** A code generator allows us to reuse existing knowledge and techniques, for instance, programming concepts like function calls and typed variables; object-oriented concepts like classes, inheritance and polymorphism; strategies for data access, like object/relational mapping; marshalling techniques; and many other techniques and patterns. This seems to be a very important point, since a code generator allows us to capture this knowledge and make it accessible to others, without requiring them to fully understand the underlying technology (for example, how exactly a virtual function call is used to implement polymorphism).
- **Avoiding repetitive tasks.** Code generation allows us to define the exact structure of a repetitive task once, and from then on have the code generator do the work for us. This means that we are relieved not only of a lot of coding, but also testing and debugging.

Usually, a code generator has built-in some kind of pattern (for instance, a grammar, a translation logic, a mapping). To use the code generator, we have to provide it with some problem-specific information, such as an IDL file or an object model. The code generator will then apply the pattern to the problem, and generate a solution. This solution is provided in form of a static coding. Usually, we need to further process this static coding of information and rules to get a dynamic behavior (run an executable on a CPU, have a Java virtual machine execute some bytecode). Often, it requires many code generation and transformation steps before we can actually dynamically process the static coding.

IDL-Based Code Generation

IDL-based code generation is, if you like, a type of extension of the IDL compiler. Indeed the IDL compiler is probably misnamed and should be called the "IDL Stub and Skeleton Code Generator" but that doesn't roll off the tongue quite as well. The output of the IDL compiler for the IDL definitions is a set of logical statements in the form of source code. This generated source code facilitates the marshalling of the specified IDL types as per the CORBA standard. It would be possible of course to hand write this code as required, but this would be very monotonous, time-consuming, and error-prone, so we use the IDL compiler to generate it.

The question is whether stub and skeleton implementations really are the only interesting things that we could derive from an IDL interface using a code generator. Very often, we will find that there are many other tasks related to specific IDL interfaces which are repetitive and could be simplified using code generation. A more generic IDL-based code generator could be used to generate code for the following purposes:

- **Client/server templates.** The basic form of client and server implementations is often very similar. An IDL-based code generator could generate templates for clients and servers, which would then require only the modifications to add the business logic. The generated code could even include examples of the correct usage of the different data types, including correct memory management.

- **Persistent storage of IDL data types.** As we discussed in the Chapter 10, "Database Integration," it is often difficult to store IDL data types in persistent storage, since data stores usually don't support IDL data types directly. A code generator could be used to generate code that transforms IDL data types into data types that are supported by the persistent store, and vice versa. For example, a code generator could generate methods that allow mapping of IDL data types to a format that allows storing them in relational tables. This seems to be an approach that is particularly promising in the context of the newly emerging persistent state service.
- **Gateways.** Generate a gateway implementation that can be used to bridge between CORBA and other worlds, including non-OO worlds like DCE. There might be some advantages using an interface-specific gateway over a DII/DSI based gateway.
- **Concentrators.** As we discussed in Chapter 15, "Load Balancing," a concentrator would be an ideal candidate for IDL based code generation.
- **Client-side caching.** Many ORBs provide a mechanism to use customized proxies, which can be used as substitutes for standard CORBA proxies. Such a customized proxy can be used, for example, to implement a client-side cache. The simplest form would cache only read-only values; a more sophisticated version could even add some kind of synchronization mechanism for attributes that are write-accessed by concurrent clients.
- **Client-side load balancing and fault tolerance.** Generate customized proxies similar to the example above, which implement the multiproxy pattern.
- **Testing.** Generate client implementations which can be used to stress-test server components. Test clients could randomly invoke methods on object in a real server implementation, passing arbitrary arguments. Similarly, dummy server implementations could be generated to allow testing of clients.
- **Separate client and server development.** Similar to the examples in the item above, dummy clients and servers can be generated to separate the development of client and server components; client developers use generated dummy servers to do sporadic test runs while developing client components. The same applies for server developers. Once the real clients and server implementations are finished, it is simply an administrative task to replace the dummy clients and servers with the real implementations.

In small systems, these examples are easy to write by hand and provide huge benefits. Unfortunately, in large systems they become almost as monotonous to implement as marshaling/socket code. Things get worse when there's a slight change halfway through the project as to the auditing procedure and all the code must be systematically changed, and changed again when some new CORBA services become available which make this or that redundant and so on. The thought of handwriting IDL-stubs seemed absurd when it was mentioned, yet many large projects hand-write the types of code listed above. What they need is their own version of the IDL compiler, which generates part of their application code instead of CORBA stub and skeleton code. Lets call such a beast an IDL code generator.

Earlier, we defined a code generator as having some kind of pattern built in. In our case, this would be the grammar of CORBA IDL. The input of our IDL code generator would be twofold: first, we would need something that is actually close to a built in pattern, which describes in a generic way what to do with the second input argument, the IDL file. Let's call this first input argument a template. The template describes, for example, how to generate a client or server implementation for a given IDL.

The problem is, how can we support templates in the most generic and flexible way? Providing them as a static configuration file wouldn't be very helpful, since most likely our patterns would have to deal with things such as string manipulation. Therefore, it would be helpful if the code generator could treat our templates like a piece of program. Templates would be associated with rules of the IDL grammar—for instance, specific templates could be called when the code generator parses an interface, and operation, or an argument. Obviously, the template should get a description of the element that was just parsed—for instance, the interface name and base interfaces, operation name, and argument passing mode, type, and name.

It seems like it would make most sense to provide our templates as normal program fragments, which would be integrated into the IDL code generator, so that the code generator logic could call them in the parsing process. Scripting language like Tcl and Perl seem to be ideal for building such an IDL code generator, since they are interpreted don't require a recompilation in case of changing a template, and are also well-suited to string manipulation.

Thus, an IDL code generator could be implemented as a Tcl or Perl script, which enables us to add or modify procedures, which provide the template descriptions, independently of the target language. To generate code, we could run the modified script, and provide the IDL as input.

The whole area of IDL code generation seems to be increasingly important from an ease-of-use point of view, and we look forward to forthcoming tools from the ORB vendors.

Model-Based Code Generation

An important class of code generation tools actually takes a model as input and generates concrete implementations. There are many different types of models, like entity-relationship models, or object models. Most model-based code generators provide some kind of GUI to allow the user to define a concrete model. Some also provide a re-engineering functionality that supports generating the model from an existing implementation.

One example is ERWin, which supports the definition of entity-relationship models, which are then mapped to SQL data definition and manipulation statements.

Another example of a model-based code generator is Persistence's PowerTier. Using the provided GUI, the user defines an object model, consisting of classes with attributes and relationships between classes. Another important part of the model is mapping information that is used by the code generator to map the object model to C++ classes, which in turn are mapped to relational tables. Therefore, the model elements must be associated with mapping information, mapping class names to table names and attribute names to column names.

A final example of a model-based code generation tool is Rational Rose. Rational Rose allows definition of UML-based object models, and can then be used to generate implementation classes from the models. Each implementation class provides methods that support navigating the classes relationships to other classes. In addition, Rational Rose can be used to generate "persistent classes,"

classes with method implementations that access data via SQL. Also, Rational Rose can map classes to IDL interfaces.

Discussion of the Different Approaches

All these different approaches to code generation that we discussed have their benefits and limitations. For example, tools like PowerTier really make it easy to access relational data from an OO language like C++. However, due to the object/relational impedance mismatch, these tools are often only usable for simple create/read/update/delete applications. More sophisticated and performance-critical functionality must often still be implemented by hand.

IDL code generation tools often lack meta information—information that describes the semantics of the IDL. For example, let's say we want to generate smart proxies that keep read-only attributes in a cache. This means that we get the value from the remote object the first time the attribute is queried, and then store it locally, so that we can directly return it the next time. However, since attributes can't throw user-defined exceptions, the IDL designers decide to use simple get() operations to make these attributes accessible. How can we express that these get() operations should be treated differently from other operations by the IDL code generator?

Tools like Rational Rose that generate IDL interfaces often lack fine-grained control, which would allow us, for example, to map classes from the object model to IDL data structures rather than IDL interfaces. Take, for example, a CORBA service—CORBA services are defined using IDL interfaces, but they are seldom defined with a UML object model. How can we use a model-based code generation tool to model a CORBA service, and ensure that the IDL generated by the model exactly matches the CORBA service IDL? This shows how fine-grained control over the mapping between model and IDL can be required, since we really need IDL that precisely matches the service specification in order to provide a CORBA-compliant service implementation.

Another question is where IDL-based code generators fit into the picture. Is there a relationship between model based code generators and IDL code generators? The former generates IDL, the latter takes IDL as an input. So it seems there is no need to have a tight integration between the two; we could use them independently of each other.

However, there are many cases where a tight integration would make sense. Take, for example, a model that contains a class with public and private methods. The public methods are exposed via IDL, the private methods are used to implement the CORBA object's functionality. If we use the model-based generator to generate a C++ skeleton implementation, it is unlikely that the public methods will have a signature that matches exactly the IDL-to-C++ mapping, since the model based code generator doesn't know anything about IDL-to-C++ mappings. If we simply use the model-based code generator to generate IDL, and then use the IDL code generator to generate the skeleton implementation, we would lose the information about the private methods that are part of the object model.

Another example is navigation. An object model contains information about relationships between classes, and many model-based code generators use this information to generate navigation methods. Our model-based code generator might even be able to use the model's class relationship information to generate IDL that implied a certain navigation pattern. Let's take our Stock example: Stocks aggregate StockPrices. The fine-grained mapping control mechanism allows mapping class Stock to an IDL interface and class StockPrice to a data structure. The tool could be intelligent enough to make the aggregation hierarchy navigable by adding operations to the Stock interface which support getting and setting sequences of StockPrices. Now we want to use this IDL as an input for the IDL code generator to generate a skeleton implementation. Unfortunately, our IDL code generator will have a hard time finding out that there is an aggregation relationship between Stocks and StockPrices—a pair of get/set operations is not really sufficient to support such a conclusion. Therefore, the IDL code generator would have difficulty providing a skeleton implementation that reflects the aggregation relationship, for instance, by having the Stock's remove() operation remove all related stock prices from the database.

In general, it will be difficult for an IDL code generator to get context information that describes the IDL in more detail. Comments in IDL are not really sufficient. Therefore, it would be ideal if we would have an integrated, model-based code generation tool, which also supports more sophisticated, IDL-based code generation.

Meta-Object Facility

It will be interesting to see what kind of features the upcoming CORBA component definition language and the CORBA meta-object facility have to provide. These new CORBA standards will ideally address exactly those problems that we discussed above, that is, by providing additional semantics for IDL interfaces, which can be used as input for code generation tools.

Rapid Prototyping using Code Generation

Finally, we briefly want to discuss how code generation tools can be used to support rapid prototyping. A good example is object/relational code generation. As we discussed in Chapter 9, "Object Persistence," we rarely get results from an object/relational code generator that are completely satisfactory. Often, we will have to replace large amount of generated code with optimized, hand-written code. Sometimes we might even have to replace the generated tool itself, for instance, switching to an OO SQL wrapper tool. So what is the benefit of starting with an object/relational generation tool, if it is likely that we have to write handcrafted code afterwards anyhow?

The most important point is that such a rapid prototype allows us to develop our system in an iterative manner. Rarely will we have a case where we do not have to change parts of the system over and over again. Rapid prototyping gives us the chance to learn more about our system using a working version to play around with.

Using rapid prototyping in combination with code generation allows us to easily change our object model and database schema, until we have it right. If we feel that the object model and database schema are relatively stable, we can start looking for the real performance bottlenecks in the system, instead of having to guess what they would be in advance. Having identified the bottlenecks, we can now start to handcraft optimized solutions, without being in great danger that the business model will change soon after again.

Process Wizards

To automate the software development process, code generation alone is not sufficient. A real CASE tool should also support a well-defined development process. Tools like Select from Select Software Tools go a step further than simple UML modeling and code generation tools. They actively support an object-oriented methodology. This can be done, for example, in a kind of "wizard" style. The tools asks the right questions at the right time in the process, using the wizard functionality to guide the developer through the development process. This can be extremely helpful for less experienced developers, but it also helps more advanced developers to work in a structured way.

The ideal CASE tool for building large-scale CORBA systems would not only provide a sophisticated code generation mechanism with real support for IDL, but would also help the less experienced developer to navigate the minefield of distributed system development. For example, a CASE tool could store knowledge like that provided in this book, and make it available to users on demand.

This could start with general process guidelines. Recall our discussion on CORBA and the software engineering process. If a user selects *"new project,"* the tool would ask the user to define a UML-based analysis model, followed by a component architecture that reflects the system's distribution aspects. After the user is finished with this, the tool would guide the user through the process of transforming the analysis model to an object model (including IDL interfaces) under consideration of the distribution aspects defined in the component architecture. Most likely this would involve some hand-coding of IDL, or at least IDL fragments like operation signatures. A sophisticated tool could analyze the IDL, and give some design guidelines. For example, if the user defines an operation that returns a sequence of objects, the tool could pop up a warning that tells the user about possible performance implications when transferring large numbers of object references.

Summary

In this chapter we have examined the possibility of automating the CORBA-based software development process. We looked at existing solutions and also examined possible tools that could be built in the future.

An important aspect of automating the engineering process is code generation. In a CORBA context, this could be IDL-based code generation. We discussed examples of how IDL-based code generators could be used, including data conversion routines for persistence support, gateways, concentrators, and automated testing.

We also discussed model-based code generation, and discussed the different approaches. We said that the emerging CORBA meta-object facility seems to be very promising from a code generation perspective, since it allows the addition of semantic information to IDL interfaces, which could be used as input for code generators.

Finally, we discussed how a process wizard could support aspects that are specific to the CORBA-based software development process.

Conclusion

As we have seen throughout this book, the development of enterprise-class CORBA systems requires a lot of background knowledge. There are many issues to consider, from IDL design, access patterns, and software reuse to memory management, multithreading, database integration, and transaction processing. We have hopefully provided an interesting and educational discussion of these topics. Although these are complex problems, in many cases they can be more easily solved by making simplifying assumptions in the design, and by using the proper tools to guide parts of the software development effort.

The Complexity Remains, ...

Currently, no tool can automate 100% of the development process, and it is doubtful that future tools will do so. For example, accessing a relational database will most likely always require some handwritten optimizations in addition to the generated create/read/update/delete functionality. However, it is likely that we will be able to generate more and more pieces of applications, with the increased sophistication of our tools. A good analogy is C++: initially, many people doubted that C++ could compete with C or assembler from a performance point of view. C++ can be used to link in C code, or even directly call into assembler using the asm keyword. However, as computers and compilers advanced, these low-level hooks became less necessary—when have you last used the asm keyword? Nevertheless, it is important that tools provide enough flexibility to combine generated code with hand-written code, and support transparent regeneration and re-engineering mechanisms, to avoid problems while the system evolves.

One problem with all-encompassing tools/development environments is that they lock the user into a proprietary technology, and a single vendor. CORBA solves this problem by reducing this dependency to the component level: components can be accessed via IIOP, independently of the technology used to implement the component. This allows us to select and combine the technologies for each component independently.

... But There Is Hope On The Horizon

Our belief is that it doesn't require a Ph.D. in rocket science to develop CORBA systems for the enterprise. The concepts of distributed systems in general, and those of CORBA systems in particular are well understood. Hopefully, books like this one help to make these concepts understandable to a larger audience. Although there is still a long way to go, CASE tools are getting better and better. They continue to provide more sophisticated development process guidance and support for code generation, enabling automated development of large parts of the application, including persistence and distribution aspects. CORBA, which helps to encapsulate system complexity within components with well-defined, technology-independent interfaces, is a powerful ally of CASE tools in the enterprise.

Currently, it looks like most CORBA vendors are focusing on tools that make it easier to use the technology. This includes integrated product suites as well as ease-of-development GUI tools. For example, a recent trend is the move towards object transaction monitors. BEA's M3, based on TUXEDO, and IONA's OTM, based on Encina, both address the need for TP monitor-style development environments for building large-scale TP Systems. Another interesting development is the focus on GUI-based development tools. Borland became Inprise, and acquired VisiBroker. We can surely expect many GUI-based development tools from this GUI powerhouse. IONA Technologies' acquisition of EBOF-based server development technology from Electronic Data Systems (EDS) is another indication of how seriously the CORBA vendors are taking the demand for development tools to help CORBA become more and more a mainstream technology.

Third-party vendors are also supporting the idea of providing tools for developing CORBA systems. A good example is Persistence Software's Distributed Object Connection Kit (DOCK) tool, which can be used to automatically generate CORBA IDL servers for accessing data in relational databases.

And of course, the OMG is very active in supporting the whole idea of automating the CORBA-based software development process. Interesting developments are the definitions of the component definition language and the business object component architecture, in combination with the meta-object facility, which will enable providers of integrated development environments (IDEs) to better support CORBA with their tools.

Finally, the OMG work on the CORBA component model promises to introduce a simple packaging mechanism for CORBA components, similar to the idea of Java Beans.

We look forward to the acceptance of these standard, and the products based on them.

REFERENCES

Allen, P. (1998). *A practical framework for applying UML*, SELECT Software Tools.

Bernstein, P. A., & Newcomer, E. (1997). *Principles of transaction processing*. San Francisco: Morgan Kaufman Publishers, Inc.

Ericsson, IONA Technologies, Nortel Networks (October, 1998). *Fault tolerant CORBA initial submissions*. Object Management Group, orbos/98-10-10

Gray, J., & Reuter, A. (1992). *Transaction processing: Concepts and techniques*. San Francisco: Morgan Kaufman Publishers, Inc.

IONA Technologies (1997). *Orbix programmer's reference* (release 2.3). Cambridge, MA: IONA Technologies.

IONA Technologies (1997). *Orbix programmer's guide* (release 2.3). Cambridge, MA: IONA Technologies.

Lewis, B., & Berg, D. J. (1995). *Threads primer: A guide to solaris multithreaded programming*. Upper Saddle River, NJ: Prentice Hall.

Kleiman, S., & Shah, D. (1995). *Programming with threads*. Upper Saddle River, NJ: Prentice Hall.

Loosley, C., & Douglas, F. (1997). *High performance client/server*. New York: John Wiley & Sons.

Object Management Group (August, 1997). *The common object request broker: Architecture and specification*, Revision 2.1, Object Management Group. OMG and CORBA are copyrights or property of the Object Management Group.

The Open Group (February, 1996). *X/Open distributed transaction processing reference model*, Version 3, The Open Group. www.opengroup.org

Persistence Software (1998). *PowerTier development kit—CORBA server programming guide*, Persistence Software Inc.

Plasil, F., Kleindienst, J., & Tuma, P. (October, 1996). "Lessons Learned from Implementing the CORBA Persistent Object Service," Proceedings from OOPSLA '96, ACM.